PUBLICATIONS OF THE
ARMY RECORDS SOCIETY
VOL. 27

MONTGOMERY AND
THE BATTLE OF NORMANDY

Montgomery and the Supreme Commander, General Eisenhower, confer at meeting of senior OVERLORD commanders in London on 1 February 194 Seated next to Eisenhower is Air Chief Marshal Tedder; standing, left to righ are Lieutenant-General Bradley, Admiral Ramsay, Air Chief Marshal Leigl Mallory and Lieutenant-General Bedell Smith. *(Reproduced by kind permission the Imperial War Museum, London.)*

MONTGOMERY AND THE BATTLE OF NORMANDY

A Selection from the Diaries, Correspondence and other Papers of Field Marshal The Viscount Montgomery of Alamein, January to August, 1944

Edited by
STEPHEN BROOKS

Published by

THE HISTORY PRESS
for the
ARMY RECORDS SOCIETY
2008

Dedicated to the memory of my father,
Walter Alfred Brooks (1912–96), who served
as a sergeant in the 5th Battalion of the Dorset
Regiment throughout the Battle of Normandy

First published in the United Kingdom in 2008 by
The History Press · The Mill · Brimscombe Port · Stroud ·
Gloucestershire · GL5 2QG

British Library Cataloguing in Publication Data
A catalogue record for this book is available from the British Library.

ISBN 978-0-7509-5123-4

Typeset in Ehrhardt.
Typesetting and origination by
The History Press.
Printed and bound in England.

The Army Records Society was founded in 1984 in order to publish original records describing the development, organisation, administration and activities of the British Army from early times.

Any person wishing to become a Member of the Society is requested to apply to the Hon. Secretary, c/o the National Army Museum, Royal Hospital Road, London, SW3 4HT. The annual subscription entitles the member to receive a copy of each volume issued by the Society in that year, and to purchase back volumes at reduced prices. Current subscription details, whether for individuals living within the British Isles, for individuals living overseas, or for institutions, will be furnished on request.

The Council of the Army Records Society wish it to be clearly understood that they are not answerable for opinions or observations that may appear in the Society's publications. For these the responsibility rests entirely with the Editors of the several works.

The Society's website can be found at
www.armyrecordssociety.org.uk

Contents

Preface and Acknowledgements

It was in 1991 that the Army Records Society published my first volume based on the Montgomery Papers, *Montgomery and the Eighth Army*. In 1994 the Society invited me to edit a follow-up volume on Montgomery's period as Commander-in-Chief, 21st Army Group, 1944–5. When I was working on the Eighth Army volume I considered that the 1942–3 period was the richest in terms of source material, because Montgomery had kept a personal diary throughout. I believed that he had stopped writing it just before D-Day. In the Introduction to *Montgomery and the Eighth Army*, this is what I told my readers. My first duty in this volume is to 'untell them'.[*] The revelation that Montgomery *did* keep a personal diary throughout the campaign in North-West Europe meant that I was pleased to accept the invitation from the Army Records Society, in the knowledge that Montgomery's records are every bit as rich for this volume as for the earlier one.

Pressures of work and family life meant that it was ten years before I was able to tackle the project. By 2004 Lord Montgomery had deposited at the Imperial War Museum all the additional papers, including the North-West Europe diary, he had found at Isington Mill after his father's death. Thanks to a generous grant from the Porter Foundation, I was able to spend six months sorting and cataloguing this second tranche of Montgomery's papers, an essential preliminary to producing this volume.

I am grateful to the Army Records Society for patiently waiting for ten years for work on this volume to begin, and also for agreeing that it should take the story only up to the end of August 1944. With the additional material made available by Lord Montgomery, it was clear that there was far more material for the 21st Army Group period up to the German surrender in May 1945 than could be accommodated in one volume. Montgomery's diary from June 1944 to May 1945 alone added a further 50,000 words to the pot. The preparatory period from January to May 1944 was too important to be omitted, so the only solution was to end this volume with the Allied victory in Normandy.

* See pp. 6–8. When, in 1948, Montgomery protested to Attlee that he had already told Crocker he was to be the next CIGS, the Prime Minister famously replied, 'Well, untell him.' Slim got the job.

In acknowledging the help I have received in editing this volume, I should first like to thank the present Viscount Montgomery of Alamein for his support and for giving permission as copyright holder of all his father's writings. I am grateful to all the other copyright holders who were kind enough to agree to the publication of documents, including Brigadier-General John S.D. Eisenhower, whose father's letters and messages to Montgomery form an important part of this volume. I also owe a continuing debt to the late Sir Denis Hamilton and his son, Nigel, for their work in identifying source material relating to Montgomery's career, and for acquiring important papers for the Montgomery Collections at the Imperial War Museum.

It would not have been possible to produce this volume without the support and encouragement of the Imperial War Museum. I should once again like to express my very warm thanks to the Keeper of the Department of Documents, Rod Suddaby, who arranged for me to catalogue the Montgomery Papers Part II and then helped in many ways with the production of this volume. My thanks are also due to the staffs of the National Archives, the Liddell Hart Centre for Military Archives, Churchill Archives Centre and Petersfield Library, for the friendly and efficient service I have received from all of them.

Stephen Brooks
Hampshire
April 2008

Notes on Editorial Method

Much the same approach has been adopted in this volume as in *Montgomery and the Eighth Army*. The aim has been to bring together the most important Montgomery documents for the period 1 January to 20 August 1944, reproduce each of the chosen documents in full and arrange them in a straightforward chronological order.

This volume naturally draws most heavily on the Montgomery Papers at the Imperial War Museum. The introductory notes on 'Montgomery and his Papers' explain how a second tranche of Montgomery's papers came to be deposited at the Imperial War Museum by the present Lord Montgomery. The Montgomery Papers Part II contain a great deal of significant material relating to the Normandy campaign, including Montgomery's personal diary notes for that period. Other archives have also been consulted and a selection has been made that reflects the extent and variety of Montgomery's written output.

In order to reduce the enormous field from which to select documents, those reproduced in full in Montgomery's *Memoirs* have been omitted, including his notes for a speech at the Mansion House on 24 March 1944 and for his talks to senior officers before D-Day. Also omitted are the four Personal Messages Montgomery issued during this period – on 5 June, 10 June, 11 July and 11 August – which were published in *Forward to Victory* (Hutchinson, 1946).

The most significant letters and messages received by Montgomery have also been included, in particular letters from Brooke and those written by Eisenhower relating to Allied strategy in June and July 1944. The majority of Eisenhower's letters had been reproduced in Chandler (ed.), *The Papers of Dwight David Eisenhower: The War Years*, but Montgomery's replies are only summarised in the footnotes, so it seemed a valuable exercise to set out both side of the correspondence in full in this volume.

As in *Montgomery and the Eighth Army*, it was possible to include only a selection from Montgomery's diary notes, but where a daily entry is included then that is the complete entry for the day. It was decided to put the daily entries separately in their chronological sequence with letters, messages and so on, placing the diary notes as the last document for the particular date. However, this should not be taken as implying that Montgomery always wrote his diary on a daily basis.

The documents are in chronological order and have been numbered in one sequence from 1 to 211. To prevent the numbering becoming too unwieldy, the accompanying notes have been numbered separately for each of the eight months, January to August (and placed together at the end). D-Day is a natural dividing line in the story, but it did not seem to be necessary to make any special division in the book to reflect this fact.

In the documents, grammar and spelling have not been changed and irregularities in these areas have been noted in the traditional manner: [*sic*]. However, minor discrepancies in the spelling of French place names, e.g. 'Cherburg' for Cherbourg, 'Arramanches' for Arromanches, have not been noted as the intended location is invariably clear. In the case of letters and messages, the 'top' and 'tail' have generally been omitted. Closing familiarities are included where something has been added after the signature, so that the postscript can be seen in its context. The title accorded an individual in the heading is that applicable at the time of writing. In all cases where the heading begins 'letter' or 'message' *to*, it is to be understood that the communication is from Montgomery.

Also given in the heading is Montgomery's own reference number for a particular document. Soon after D-Day Montgomery began to give most of his official letters, messages and operational directives a reference number, prefixed by the letter 'M'. M1 is a situation report (sitrep) from Montgomery to his chief-of-staff, Major-General de Guingand, dated 7 June 1944. Two days later Montgomery opened a second series beginning at M500 for what he regarded as particularly significant documents. M500 is a letter dated 9 June 1944, again to Major-General de Guingand.

Montgomery's 'M' references should not be confused with the IWM catalogue reference given at the end of a document: BLM for Montgomery Papers Part I and LMD for Montgomery Papers Part II. Because there is a good deal of duplication between Parts I and II, the following has guided the choice of whether the catalogue reference is given from Part I or II: in the case of letters received by Montgomery the number is that of the original letter, rather than typescript copies made by Montgomery (this particularly applies to Eisenhower's letters); where there was a copy of a document in both Part I and Part II, the reference from Part I is given; the exception to this is Montgomery's diary from January to June 1944 (copies are in Parts I and II) – all diary references are to Part II which holds the complete diary January to August 1944.

In the case of items from the Montgomery Papers, their format is described as 'holograph', 'typescript' or 'cyclostyle'. It was decided not to use 'carbon copy', because this might be assumed to mean that it was a carbon copy of the actual letter sent out. However, Montgomery had letters typed and retyped for filing and distribution purposes and a carbon copy is just as likely to be a carbon from a copy of a copy of the original. As the term 'carbon copy' then has no particular significance, it was thought better simply to use 'typescript'.

Abbreviations

AA	anti-aircraft
A Branch	Adjutant-General's staff dealing with personnel and discipline
ACIGS	Assistant Chief of the Imperial General Staff
ACIGS (Ops)	Assistant Chief of the Imperial General Staff (Operations)
ACK	acknowledge
ACM	Air Chief Marshal
ADC	Aide-de-Camp
AEAF	Allied Expeditionary Air Force
AGRA	Army Group Royal Artillery
ANCXF	Allied Naval Commander-in-Chief Expeditionary Force
A/Q	administration/supply
Armd	armoured
Arty	artillery
AS	air-to-surface
A/Tk	anti-tank
AVRE	Armoured Vehicle Royal Engineers (a special conversion of the Churchill tank, armed with a 29 mm mortar and capable of mounting devices for bridge-laying, mine-clearing, etc.)
Bde	brigade
BGS	Brigadier General Staff
Bn	battalion
Br	British
BUCO	Build-Up Control Organisation
CAS	Chief of Air Staff
Cdn	Canadian
CG	Commanding General
CGS	Chief of the General Staff/Chief of Staff
CIGS	Chief of the Imperial General Staff
C-in-C	Commander-in-Chief
CNS	Chief of the Naval Staff
CO	commanding officer

Comd	Commander
COS	Chief/Chiefs of Staff
COSSAC	Chief of Staff to the Supreme Allied Commander
Coy	company
CRA	Commander Royal Artillery
DACOS	Deputy Assistant Chief of Staff
DCIGS	Deputy Chief of the Imperial General Staff
DD tank	duplex drive tank (amphibious Sherman tank)
Div	division
Divis	division
DMO	Director of Military Operations
DMT	Director of Military Training
DSD	Director of Staff Duties
DUKW	amphibious lorry (pronounced 'duck')
DZ	drop zone
ETOUSA	European Theatre of Operations United States Army
Ex	example
Excl	excluding
FMC	Field Maintenance Centre
G Branch	General Staff dealing with operations, planning, staff duties and Intelligence.
G1 (L)	Staff Officer Grade 1 (Liaison)
G2	Staff Officer Grade 2
GAF	German Air Force
Gds	Guards
Govt	government
GS	General Staff
GSO1	General Staff Officer Grade 1
H	Hussars
HQ	Headquarters
I	Intelligence
Incl	including
Inf	Infantry
Int	Intelligence
J	network of battlefield reporting centres established to relay information gathered from wireless traffic to headquarters.
K	killed
LCA (HR)	Landing Craft Assault (Hedgerow)
LCI	Landing Craft Infantry
LCI(L)	Landing Craft Infantry (large)
LCG	Landing Craft Gun

LCT	Landing Craft Tank
LCT(A)	Landing Craft Tank (armoured)
LCT(R)	Landing Craft Tank (rocket)
LCT(SP)	Landing Craft Tank (self-propelled [gun])
LO	Liaison Officer
L of C	lines of communication
LSI	Landing Ship Infantry
LST	Landing Ship Tank
M	missing
MA	Military Assistant
MG	machine gun
MGA	Major-General Administration
MO1	Section 1, Directorate of Military Operations (War Office)
Mov	Movement
MOVCO	Movement Control
MS	Military Secretary
MT	motor transport
NCO	Non-commissioned Officer
O	operations
OC	Officer Commanding
Ops	operations
PG	Panzer Grenadier
Pt	Point
Pz	Panzer
QBranch	Quartermaster-General's staff, dealing with supplies, etc.
QMG	Quartermaster-General
RAC	Royal Armoured Corps
RE	Royal Engineers
Recce	Reconnaissance
RHA	Royal Horse Artillery
RMC	Royal Military College
SAS	Special Air Service
SASO	Senior Air Staff Officer
SHAEF	Supreme Headquarters Allied Expeditionary Force
Sitrep	situation report
S of S	Secretary of State
SP	self-propelled
Sqn	Squadron
SS	Special Service
SS	Schutzstaffel (Protection Detachment)
TA	Territorial Army

Tac HQ	Tactical Headquarters
TAF	Tactical Air Force
Tn	transportation
Tps	troops
V1 and V2	*Vergeltungswaffe* (reprisal weapons) 1 and 2.
VCIGS	Vice-Chief of the Imperial General Staff
Vehs	vehicles
W	wounded
WE	War Establishment
W/T	wireless telegraphy
Y	monitoring of enemy wireless traffic

Glossary of Christian names and nicknames

Alex	Field Marshal Earl Alexander
Archie	Lieutenant-General Sir Archibald Nye
Arthur	Marshal of the RAF Baron Tedder
Beedle/Beetle	General Walter Bedell Smith
Bill	Brigadier E.T. Williams (Montgomery's Chief Intelligence Officer)
Bimbo	General Sir Miles Dempsey
Brad	General of the Army Omar N. Bradley
Freddie	Major-General Sir Francis de Guingand (Montgomery's Chief of Staff)
Ike	General of the Army Dwight D. Eisenhower
Johnnie	Captain J.R. Henderson (Montgomery's ADC)
Kit	Lieutenant-Colonel C.P. Dawnay (Montgomery's Military Assistant)
L-M	Air Chief Marshal Sir Trafford Leigh-Mallory
Mary (Maori)	Air Marshal Sir Arthur Coningham
Miles	Major-General Sir Miles Graham (Head of Administration, 21st Army Group)
Simbo	General Sir Frank Simpson

Introduction

This volume takes up the story where *Montgomery and the Eighth Army*, published by the Army Records Society in 1991, breaks off. In the early hours of Christmas Eve 1943 Montgomery received a telegram from General Sir Alan Brooke[1] telling him that he was to relinquish his command of the Eighth Army in Italy and return to England to become Commander-in-Chief, 21st Army Group – the British and Canadian forces assembled for the invasion of North-West Europe. When Montgomery arrived in Algiers on 27 December, he was informed by General Eisenhower, the Supreme Commander for Operation OVERLORD, that he was to take overall charge of the land forces, including the American contingent. It was Montgomery's experience and reputation that had clinched his selection for this role. When Churchill informed President Roosevelt on 18 December that the War Cabinet favoured Montgomery, he added, 'I feel the Cabinet are right, as Montgomery is a public hero and will give confidence among our people, not unshared by yours'.[2] On 28 December Montgomery wrote to Brooke: 'It is a big job and I will do my best to prove worthy of your selection.'[3]

This book covers the period from January 1944 to Allied victory in the battle of Normandy towards the end of August. The amount of material available, once it was known that Montgomery had continued to write a personal diary throughout the campaign in North-West Europe, made this cut-off date a practical necessity. There is also logic to it. From January to August 1944 Montgomery had, at Eisenhower's behest, the role of an *Allied* commander. On 1 September 1944 Eisenhower took over the role of commander of land forces, with Montgomery as Commander-in-Chief, 21st Army Group. Montgomery's prolonged attempt thereafter to persuade Eisenhower to modify the command structure and the strategy for the advance into Germany, foreshadowed in the closing documents in this volume,[4] is another story.

The first fifty-three documents in this selection cover the build up to D-Day in the months January to May 1944. Although Montgomery was fortunate not to share with Admiral Jellicoe the position of being 'the only man on either side who could lose the war in an afternoon',

1

had the military planning and preparation for D-Day gone wrong, the Allied progress towards ultimate victory over Nazi Germany would have received an incalculable setback. In an essay entitled 'D Day Fails', Stephen Ambrose speculates that 'Stalin might have overrun Germany, then France, and the war in Europe would have ended with the Communists in control of the continent'.[5] Montgomery may have been at his happiest when fighting battles against the enemy, but this period shows how effective he could be when battling with his own side for what he believed to be necessary to ensure the success of D-Day. Returning to England on 2 January, Montgomery's determination and clarity of mind ensured that a revised plan for the Allied landings was accepted. While his experienced staff undertook the detailed planning, Montgomery made it his priority to tour the invasion forces to convince them to have faith in him – and themselves – in the coming battle. And he also took on the task of addressing factory workers and other civilian groups in an effort to dispel the mood of uncertainty about OVERLORD that had gripped the nation as a whole. A few remained sceptical, but the documents show Montgomery as a brilliant communicator. The notes for two of the key lectures he delivered at this time have been included in full: those for his addresses at Exercise THUNDERCLAP on 7 April and at the final Presentation of Plans at St Paul's School on 15 May.[6]

There is a testimonial to the impact Montgomery made at this time from his own brother-in-law, Major-General Sir Percy Hobart. Hobart was summoned to see Montgomery on 8 January. Expecting to be retired, Hobart was gratified to learn that he was being kept on as commander of the 79th Armoured Division. On 18 January Hobart paid this tribute in a letter to his friend, Captain Liddell Hart:

> Monty has grown in stature and grasp: and has
> matured. He always had complete self-confidence: but
> it was apt to be shrill. He now inspires confidence in
> all under him and, I should say, in most of his peers
> and superiors. He is fit, hard, ruthless and decisive. A
> real 'professional' soldier in the best German sense.
> Whether he is more than that –? … But it is a relief
> and a comfort to serve under someone who knows his
> job and his mind: and can express himself clearly. We
> cannot expect a genius, anyway. And it does not seem
> as if that would be essential to victory.[7]

Although the term 'professionalism' tends to be rather overworked in relation to Montgomery, it was this quality of 'knowing his job', and the self-belief that went with it, that made his contribution to the build up to D-Day and his role as Allied ground forces commander in Normandy perhaps the most outstanding achievements of his military career.

There are some 150 documents in this volume covering D-Day itself and the subsequent battle of Normandy up till 20 August when Montgomery wrote in his diary that the battle was over and had been 'decisively won'.[8] Notwithstanding this great victory, Montgomery's generalship and the performance of the Allied forces under his command were controversial as the battle unfolded, they were a matter of controversy in the post-war writings of the participants and they have been much debated by historians over the pasty sixty years. Comments on the historiography of the principal issues are made in the notes to the documents,[9] but this volume provides an opportunity to look afresh at the campaign through Montgomery's writings at the time. This approach commended itself to Chester Wilmot as early as 1952 when he wrote in his book *The Struggle for Europe*,

> Was it ever intended, as Eisenhower states in his
> Report, that the British should 'break out towards the
> Seine'? Did Dempsey fail at Caen? Was Montgomery
> forced to change his plan? The answer must be sought,
> not in post-war dispatches and reflections, but in the
> orders issued and statements made by Montgomery
> before D-Day and during the first few weeks ashore.[10]

Particular attention has therefore been paid in this volume to including the documents that could be regarded as essential to an understanding of Montgomery's direction of Allied strategy. For example, the nine directives that Montgomery issued to his army commanders during the battle of Normandy have been reproduced in full. However, it is noteworthy that Montgomery did not issue the first of these written directives until D+12, 18 June 1944. In his talks before D-Day and during the campaign, Montgomery stressed that he wished everyone to follow his example of keeping paperwork to a minimum and commanding by verbal orders.[11] Thus the formal 'paper trail' for decision-making could never be as full as historians might wish. Having said this, writing actually played an immensely important part in Montgomery's life, if not in his method of command, and he did commit an enormous amount to paper. So there is much to be found in the combination of his diary notes, letters, memoranda and messages in this volume that sheds light on the controversial aspects of the Normandy campaign. What is more, it is to be hoped that, as Field Marshal Lord Carver wrote of *Montgomery and the Eighth Army*, the combination of the formal and the informal will ensure that Montgomery is 'revealed, both as a person and as a professional soldier, in a way that no other method has done'.[12]

Montgomery and his Papers

In the summer of 1962, when Field Marshal Montgomery was in hospital recovering from a stroke, he sent for his friend and literary adviser, Denis Hamilton, to put a proposal to him about the future of his diaries and military papers. He asked Denis Hamilton (then editor of *The Sunday Times* and editorial director of Thomson Newspapers) whether he would be prepared to arrange for Thomson Newspapers to purchase his papers and then to direct the preparation of a biography based on them after his death.

When the Field Marshal came out of hospital he repeated the proposal about his papers in a letter to Denis Hamilton dated 8 September 1962, in which he wrote, 'I offer them to you in complete confidence that all will be well. I would have to have absolute right of veto on anything published in my lifetime. After that, you could do as you liked.'[1] An agreement for the sale of the papers was signed on 6 December 1962. Montgomery began to go through all the papers stored at his home in Hampshire, Isington Mill. In due course he despatched his extensive diaries and files, relating to a military career that stretched from 1908 to 1958, to Denis Hamilton.

Montgomery insisted that the arrangement with Thomson Newspapers was not made public during his lifetime, though he never made any secret of the fact that he had kept diaries and papers relating to his long military service. In his *Memoirs* Montgomery wrote that he had kept a 'very precise diary' throughout the Second World War, but enquiries were simply met with the response that his papers were not available for inspection. When Lord Chalfont embarked upon a biography of the Field Marshal in the late 1960s, he pressed him to reconsider. Montgomery's reply, wrote Chalfont, 'was typical and unequivocal. "Certainly not," he said. "If those papers ever came to light they would cause a Third World War, I have given instructions in my will that when I die, they are to be burned."'[2]

After Montgomery's death Sir Denis Hamilton made a statement that was reported in *The Times* on 5 November 1976, revealing that the Field Marshal had sold his papers to Thomson Newspapers some fourteen years earlier, when he was 'anxious to make various contributions to charities when he was alive'. Sir Denis announced that a biographer would shortly be chosen and that the papers would ultimately be given to the nation. The papers were duly presented to the Imperial War Museum by Sir Denis Hamilton on behalf of the International Thomson Organisation (ITO) on 7 July 1982; and Nigel Hamilton's three-volume biography was published between 1981 and 1986.

However, this proved to be far from the end of the story. In the late 1980s Montgomery's son decided to move from Isington Mill, and started to clear the house. Lord Montgomery began to find more papers relating to his father's military career. This is referred to briefly in the introduction to *Montgomery and the Eighth Army*, but at that stage it was not apparent how extensive and important these papers were going to be. Eventually they constituted a second substantial collection of Montgomery's papers, filling more than fifty archive boxes. Lord Montgomery deposited these additional files on loan in the Imperial War Museum. The original (ITO) gift to the museum has been re-designated the Montgomery Papers Part I, and Lord Montgomery's deposit is referred to as the Montgomery Papers Part II. Owing to the different terms of deposit, Parts I and II remain separate at the time of writing (2007). Part II was catalogued at the Imperial War Museum in 2005–6 with the aid of a grant from the Porter Foundation. Documents in Part II were given the letters LMD (Lord Montgomery Deposit) as part of their cataloguing reference, to distinguish them from those bearing the BLM reference used for the original ITO material.

Although there is a considerable duplication between the two parts of the Montgomery Papers, a great deal of significant new material was found amongst the papers Montgomery had retained at Isington Mill. This applied particularly to the period 1944–5, where it transpired that Montgomery had withheld his personal diary notes relating to the campaign in North-West Europe from the files sent to Thomson Newspapers.

Montgomery began to keep a diary in mid-1940 when the momentous events following the German invasion in the west prompted him to keep a daily record of the Dunkirk campaign, spanning the period 10 May to 3 June 1940.[3] But it was with his appointment to command the Eighth Army in North Africa in August 1942 that Montgomery began to keep a diary in earnest. This is extensively quoted in *Montgomery and the Eighth Army*. From the outset Montgomery's diary notes are typed on foolscap sheets. Montgomery presumably dictated the text or more likely produced handwritten drafts, although no manuscript material is known to have survived. The diaries are divided into sections, with copies of important documents added at the end of each instalment as appendices.

Montgomery continued to write up his diary notes in this way when he returned to England in January 1944. The preparations for D-Day were covered in two instalments, covering January to March and then April to 3 June. After D-Day Montgomery asked his Military Assistant, Lieutenant-Colonel Kit Dawnay, to compile a narrative of the campaign for him. Dawnay had frequent conferences with Montgomery, and then wrote up summaries of events based on what he had been told. This document was called 'the Log'.[4] A section was written looking back at the preparations for D-Day so that eventually the Log covered the period from January 1944 to May 1945. Copies of the Log were sent to a number of VIPs during the war, including King George VI.

When the Montgomery Papers Part I were catalogued in the mid-1980s the evidence supported the idea that Montgomery's 'personal' diary ended on 3 June 1944, apart from four typescript pages in which he wrote his own daily notes on the end of the campaign in Europe. In 1983 Richard Lamb wrote in the foreword to his book *Montgomery in Europe 1943–45* that Kit Dawnay had told him that he had been commissioned to write up the Log because 'his general was too busy to write a daily diary'.[5] Furthermore, although Montgomery included lengthy quotations, which he describes as being passages from his diary, in the North-West Europe chapters of his *Memoirs*, these were, in fact, extracts from letters. The account of the conference at Maastricht on 7 December 1944 is taken from a letter Montgomery wrote to Brooke later in the day; and the description of his meeting with Eisenhower at Zonhoven on 14 February 1945 is part of a letter to the VCIGS, General Nye. Finally, when in the 1960s Montgomery sent the Log to Thomson Newspapers as part of the sale of his papers, he attached a handwritten note to the first volume (BLM 74) that read: 'From "D Day" onwards my diary was written up by my Personal staff.'

This statement was misleading. Amongst the files Montgomery had retained at Isington Mill were found two sets of diary notes that he had written up himself, covering the period 4 June 1944 to 14 May 1945. These 'personal' diary notes run to 140 typed foolscap pages, amounting to some 50,000 words. They are divided into ten section (three of these cover the battle of Normandy) and each section has a collection of original documents filed with it – letters, messages, memoranda and so on. Why Montgomery decided not to forward a set of his personal diary of the North-West Europe campaign to Thomson Newspapers, and indeed to disguise the fact that it existed, is something of a mystery. Perhaps he was anxious that there might be 'a leak' and that during his lifetime the diary could used to rekindle the controversies over the campaign in North-West Europe. He must have assumed that upon his death it would be found at Isington Mill. As it was, the time delay before its discovery meant that it was not available to Nigel Hamilton in the 1980s when he was writing the authorised biography.

This must have had Montgomery turning in his grave. His personal diary of the Normandy campaign was written very much with future historians in mind. It was not an Alanbrooke-style way of privately letting off steam, and it contains no revelations that Montgomery was plagued by inner doubts about his ability to prove himself worthy of this 'big job' for which he had been selected. Montgomery included far more pungent comments about events and personalities in his letters, and these were probably more of a safety valve than his diary writing. (Further thoughts on Montgomery the letter writer can be found in the Introduction to *Montgomery and the Eighth Army*.) In his diary Montgomery focused on setting out, day by day, what mattered above all else to him in the summer of 1944: how the Allied armies under his command went about the task of defeating their enemies. The diary was quite possibly not written every night, but the entries have a degree of detail and immediacy that precludes their being written up much later with the benefit of hindsight. Having the diary gives a sense of completeness to Montgomery's documentary record of the battle of Normandy in this volume. To set alongside his letters, memoranda and messages directed to Eisenhower, Churchill, Brooke and many others, we have in the diary Montgomery's sitrep for posterity.

Chronology of main events and Montgomery's movements January–August 1944

	message to Combined Chiefs of Staff saying that it is impossible to mount Operations ANVIL and OVERLORD simultaneously.
21–22	Montgomery undertakes tour No. 6 to Portsmouth dockyard and Nuffield factories in Birmingham and Coventry.
24	Montgomery launches Salute the Soldier campaign at Mansion House.

April

7–8	Montgomery holds Exercise THUNDERCLAP at 21st Army Group HQ.
11–16	Montgomery visits Canadian exercise at Slapton Sands, Royal Navy at Plymouth and US troops at Exeter and Oxford.
17–19	Montgomery observes Force G exercise at Studland.
20–23	Montgomery visits Glasgow; he addresses factory workers, inspects SAS Brigade and attends England v. Scotland football match.
26–27	Montgomery attends exercises at Studland and Slapton Sands.
27	Montgomery joins Tac HQ, which has moved to Southwick House.

May

2–5	Montgomery attends Exercise FABIUS.
5–9	Montgomery visits the Home Fleet at Scapa Flow in Scotland.
9–13	Montgomery on leave in Scotland.
15	Final Presentation of Plans held at St Paul's School.
22	The King has lunch with Montgomery.
23	Montgomery commences his final tours of the invasion forces, addressing senior officers.

June

6	D-Day
	Montgomery leaves Portsmouth in HMS *Faulknor* at 2230 hours.
7	Montgomery spends the day off the beaches in HMS *Faulknor*.
8	Montgomery lands in Normandy at 0700 hours. Tac HQ moves from Ste-Croix-sur-Mer to the grounds of the Château de Creullet.
	US First Army and British Second Army link up near Port-en-Bessin.
12	Prime Minister and CIGS visit Normandy.
	Omaha and Utah beachheads link up.

13	British 7th Armoured Division checked at Villers Bocage.
	First V1 flying bomb strikes England.
14	General de Gaulle visits Normandy.
16	The King visits Normandy.
18	Montgomery issues Directive M502.
	Sir James Grigg visits Normandy.
	US VII Corps reaches west coast of Cherbourg peninsula at Barneville.
19	Montgomery issues Directive M504.
19–22	Great storm in the Channel.
23	Tac HQ moves from Château de Creullet to Blay.
25	Second Army offensive – Operation EPSOM.
26	Americans capture Cherbourg.
30	Montgomery issues Directive M505.

July

2	Orders issued in London for invasion of southern France to be launched on 15 August (Operation ANVIL/DRAGOON).
3	American advance southward makes slow progress due to weather and the *bocage*.
4	Canadian attack on Carpiquet.
8–10	British mount Operation CHARNWOOD against Caen.
10	Montgomery issues Directive M510.
11	Pt 112 north-east of Evrecy captured.
17	Rommel is wounded in an air attack.
18–21	Operation GOODWOOD to the east of Caen.
18	Americans take St Lô.
20	Hitler wounded in Bomb Plot.
21	Montgomery issues Directive M512.
23	HQ of First Canadian Army becomes operational.
25	Bradley launches Operation COBRA.
	Canadians launch Operation SPRING.
27	Montgomery issues Directive M515.
30	British launch Operation BLUECOAT south-east of Caumont.
	Americans take Avranches.

August

1	US 12th Army Group activated under Bradley. Patton's Third Army becomes operational.
3	Tac HQ moves from Blay to Cerisy-le-Forêt.
	Bucknall and Erskine removed from command of 30 Corps and

11

	7th Armoured Division.
4	Montgomery issues Directive M516.
6	Montgomery issues Directive M517.
7	Germans launch Mortain counter-attack.
7/8	Canadians attack towards Falaise in Operation TOTALIZE.
8	Patton's Third Army takes Le Mans.
11	Montgomery issues Directive M518.
12	US XV Corps takes Alençon.
14	Canadians attack towards Falaise in Operation TRACTABLE. Tac HQ moves from Cerisy-le-Forêt to near Le Bény-Bocage.
15	Allied landings in the south of France.
16	Falaise is captured.
19	First Canadian Army and First US Army link up at Chambois.
21	Eastern end of the Falaise pocket 'closed in strength'.
25	Liberation of Paris.

September

1	Eisenhower takes direct control of the land battle in the west. Montgomery is promoted to Field Marshal.

Documents
January to August 1944

January

Extract from Montgomery's diary notes headed 'My return to England from the Eighth Army to take command of 21 Army Group', 31 December 1943–2 January 1944

[Typescript]

3. I flew on 31 December to MARRAKECH to stay for 24 hours with Winston CHURCHILL.

When I arrived at 1800 hours the Prime Minister was in bed reading a copy of OVERLORD;[1] he was recovering from his recent illness and did not look very fit.

He said I was to read OVERLORD and give him my opinion about it. I replied I was not his military adviser. He then said he was very anxious to have my first impressions of OVERLORD, which I had never seen. So I said I would read it through and would give him my 'first impressions' in the morning. These are attached at Appendix 'A'.[2]

4. That night was New Years Eve, and we had a very amusing evening with the P.M. and Mrs. CHURCHILL, and their staff. Lord BEAVERBROOK was present; he is commonly supposed to be an unpleasant person, but he seemed to me to be a very pleasant person and all out to win the war.[3]

On 1st January we all went for a picnic in the country.

I drove with the P.M. in his car and I impressed on him the need to get experienced fighting commanders 'in' on any future operational plans early; if left too late it might not always be possible to change the lay-out of the operation; in every operation in which I have been brought into in this war, changes in plan have been necessary and there has been all too little time, e.g. HUSKY[4] in May, 1943, and now OVERLORD did not look too good.

5. The P.M. and EISENHOWER both refused to let me fly to

England in my own aeroplane, which had only two engines. So I transferred to the routine C/54, a four-engine ship, and reached PRESTWICH at 0900 hours on 2 January.

My own C/47 followed, full of oranges!!

I flew on to London, which I reached at 1300 hours.

IWM, Montgomery Papers Part II, LMD 54/1

2
Memorandum by Montgomery headed 'First Impressions of Operation "OVERLORD" made at the request of the Prime Minister by General Montgomery'

[Typescript]

1. The following must be clearly understood:

(a) Today, 1 January, 1944, is the first time I have seen the Appreciation and proposed plan or considered the problem in any way.[5]

(b) I am not as yet in touch with Admiral RAMSAY[6] and have not been able to consult any Naval expert.

(c) I have not been able to consult the Air C-in-C,[7] or any experienced air officer.

(d) Therefore these initial comments can have little value. They are merely my first impressions after a brief study of COS (43)416(o).[8]

2. The initial landing is on too narrow a front and is confined to too small an area.

By D+12 a total of 16 Divisions have been landed on the same beaches as were used for the initial landings. This would lead to the most appalling confusion on the beaches, and the smooth development of the land battle would be extremely difficult – if not impossible.

Further Divisions come pouring in, all over the same beaches. By D+24 a total of 24 Divisions have been landed, all over the same beaches; control of the beaches and so on would be very difficult; the confusion, instead of getting better, would get worse.

My first impression is that the present plan is impracticable.

3. From a purely Army point of view the following points are essential:

(a) The initial landings must be made on the widest possible front.

(b) Corps must be able to develop their operations from their own beaches, and other Corps must NOT land through those beaches.

(c) British and American areas of landing must be kept separate. The provisions of (a) above must apply in each case.

(d) After the initial landings, the operation must be developed in such a way that a good port is secured quickly for the British and for American forces. Each should have its own port or group of ports.

4. The type of plan required is on the following lines:

(a) One British Army to land on a front of two, or possibly three, Corps. One American Army similarly.

(b) Follow-up Divisions to come in to the Corps already on shore.

(c) The available assault craft to be used for the leading troops. Successive flights to follow rapidly in any type of unarmoured craft, and to be poured in.

(d) The air battle must be won before the operation is launched. We must then aim at success in the land battle by the speed and violence of our operations.

5. It is hardly possible to discuss the broad plan without Naval and Air discussion. But if such a thing were possible there would be many advantages in putting armies on shore in such a way that:

(a) The British effort was directed to securing the CAEN–CHERBOURG area, with CHERBOURG as the main British port initially.

(b) The American effort was directed to securing the area ST. MALO–ST NAZAIRE–BREST, with the main American ports in the BREST peninsula.

6. I am disturbed at the limitations of transport aircraft referred to in para 17 of the Digest.

There are four Airborne Divisions, and four U.S. Parachute Regts available. All of these will be needed for the initial effort. We must surely take steps to ensure that we can lift at one time at least the equivalent of four Airborne Divisions.

Marrakech,

1st January, 1944.

IWM, Montgomery Papers Part I, BLM 72/1

3
Montgomery's diary notes, 3–12 January 1944[9]

[Typescript]

3 January.

6. I became involved immediately in a series of conferences[10] on OVERLORD.

The more one examined it the more it became clear that the original plan was thoroughly bad.

The front of the assault was too narrow; only one Corps HQ was being used to control the whole front; no landing was being made on the East side of the CHERBURG peninsula though the early capture of the port of CHERBURG was vital; the area of landing would be very congested.

7. After several meetings I evolved a new plan for the assault; this was agreed to by the Naval and Air Cs-in-C provided the necessary resources were made available.

From a Naval point of view this involved:

> More assault craft,
> more minesweepers,
> more war-ships for coast bombardment,
> more escort craft.

The Chiefs of Staff were informed that to get quick and good success the revised plan was essential; that it was recommended that operation ANVIL[11] be reduced to a threat and the craft thereby saved be transferred to OVERLORD; and that a very early decision was desirable.

8. For some days discussion went on in the various service departments, and in Government circles, as to the wisdom of scaling down ANVIL.

I sent a cable to EISENHOWER who was in WASHINGTON;[12] I attach as Appendix 'B' my cable[13] and his reply.[14]

12 January.

9. The three Cs-in-C under EISENHOWER were:

Navy	RAMSAY.
Army	MONTGOMERY
Air	LEIGH-MALLORY.

We decided we must begin to plan, working on the assumption we could get what we wanted.

I had already told my Army Commanders my outline plan,[15] and on this day (12th January) we had a big conference[16] at my HQ when the Army Commanders gave their outline plans.

This was sufficient to allow our staffs to carry on with the work.

IWM, Montgomery Papers Part II, LMD 54/1.

4
'Notes taken at a meeting of Army Commanders and their Chiefs of Staff, at HQ 21 Army Group, 7 Jan. 1944'

[Typescript]

1. Commander-in-Chief explained the present arrangements for the chain of command for the invasion of EUROPE:

General EISENHOWER has been appointed Supreme Commander of all the forces to be employed.

Air Chief Marshal TEDDER has been appointed as his Deputy.

Under General EISENHOWER there are three Commanders-in-Chief, viz:

Commander-in-Chief, Allied Naval Expeditionary Force – Admiral RAMSAY.

Commander-in-Chief of the land forces – General MONTGOMERY.

Commander-in-Chief, Allied Expeditionary Air Force – Air Marshal LEIGH-MALLORY.

There exists at present:

First (U.S.) Army Group.

21 Army Group.

General MONTGOMERY has been appointed to command all Allied forces to be engaged in the land battle,[17] and has been instructed by General EISENHOWER to form an Allied Army Group Headquarters.

C-in-C pointed out that the British, having reached their limit of man-power, cannot form another Army Group HQ. The question is, therefore, whether the Americans can contribute the necessary staff to be incorporated in HQ 21 Army Group which would then become HQ Allied Army Group, and also fill the vacancies caused in HQ First (U.S.) Army Group by the transfer of those officers.

It was decided that the Americans would send whoever is required to HQ Allied Army Group and fill up the vacancies in HQ First (U.S.) Army Group.

2. C-in-C pointed out that experience had shown that successful invasion operations required that Armies and Corps must go in initially on their fighting fronts and not be passed in subsequently through a front developed by another formation. Therefore the areas originally selected for the landings must be extended. This means that two Armies will be committed in the assault, each in charge of their own sector. The extended area for the assault is now from VARREVILLE (East side COTENTIN Peninsula) to CABOURG (West of R. ORNE). The American Army will be on the right and the British Army on the left.

The inter-Army boundary has yet to be defined, but it was decided that the town of BAYAUX will be incl to the American Army.

3. Task of the American Army will be the clearing of the CHERBOURG peninsula and the capture of the port of CHERBOURG. They will subsequently develop their operations to the South and West.

Task of the British Army will be to operate to the South to prevent any interference with the American Army from the East.

It is hoped eventually to get a firm lodgement from CAEN to NANTES with the British Army being built up through the CHERBOURG peninsula and the American Army through BRITTANY.

4. C-in-C said that owing to the limitations imposed by the necessary minesweeping, naval support and craft, it has been decided that only eight brigade groups can be landed initially. The initial allotment of these brigades between the British and American Armies cannot yet be decided. Owing to the limitation in beaches in the American Army sector and in view of the fact that the Navy are averse to landing to the West of the CANAL DE PORT DE CARETAN on D day, the American Army can

probably only employ three brigade landing groups, whereas the British Army might well employ five brigade landing groups.

Commander First (U.S.) Army[18] was instructed to come to the conference on Wednesday, 12 Jan, with his outline plan, taking the extended area into consideration.

C-in-C stressed that it was preferable to land everywhere at once, rather than spread the assault over two days.

C-in-C also stressed that the British effort must be strong in the initial phase if it was to succeed in preventing interference with First (U.S.) Army from the East. For this reason Second (British) Army would land on a two-Corps front, employing 30 Corps and 1 Corps. Owing to the present positioning of these Corps in England, and to avoid the crossing of convoys in the Channel, 30 Corps must be on the right and 1 Corps on the left. 1 Corps will be placed under command Second Army forthwith.

C-in-C explained on the map the area protected by the HAVRE coast defence guns which set a limit to the assault on the East. He considered the marshy area in conjunction with the River ORNE would assist to protect the left flank of Second Army. The town of CAEN is an important road centre and must be secured. The object of Second Army is therefore to seize CAEN and the airfield area to the S.E., subsequently exploiting to the South to cover more effectively the flank of First (U.S.) Army.

In view of the urgency of securing the airfields and ensuring protection of the First (U.S.) Army, C-in-C considered that it would entail five British brigade landing groups, thus giving First (U.S.) Army only three brigade landing groups. Commander First (U.S.) Army stressed that it would be difficult to explain away to the American public the seemingly small initial American effort.[19] The decision on the number of landing groups was therefore left open until the meeting on 12 Jan.

5. The C-in-C pointed out that Second Army would consist of:

1 Corps
8 Corps
12 Corps
30 Corps

and stressed that the grouping within the Army was a matter for decision by the Army Commander.

It might well be that each Corps to land might want one Armd Div. Sufficient Armd Divs were under command of Second Army to make this possible. Commander Second Army[20] was instructed to give his views on the necessary re-grouping at the meeting on Wednesday 12 Jan. If it was found that more Armd Bdes were required, they could be made available.

6. C-in-C pointed out that the initial planning had best be carried out in LONDON at HQ of COSSAC, where a planning room for each Army had been reserved from 8 to 12 January.

After the meeting on 12 Jan, planning would continue at HQ 21 Army Group until the outline plan was firm, when detailed planning would be handed over to the Armies. Detailed planning would probably start at HQ 21 Army Group on or about 20 Jan.

C-in-C said that he would set up at HQ 21 Army Group a small planning staff of experts, with experience from the Mediterranean theatre of war. This select planning staff would co-ordinate the plans of the Allied Army Group and would be available to give advice in the detailed plans of the two Armies.

7. C-in-C pointed out that as he had been appointed Commander of the land battle, he must control the administration of both Armies involved. C-in-C further pointed out that the administrative set-up was difficult to determine until it was known whether, when the development of operations necessitated an American Army Group HQ controlling two American Armies operating from the BRITTANY peninsula, General EISENHOWER would assume command of the two Army Groups. As General EISENHOWER'S views on this could not be obtained until his arrival, Commander First (U.S.) Army said that he agreed in principle to the administrative control of the American Army being under the C-in-C. This will be confirmed at the meeting on 12 Jan.

8. C.G.S.[21] said that the Navy had undertaken to effect eight landings, i.e. two brigade landing groups from four divisions. He further said that it might be possible to increase the number of divisions to five, i.e. three Divs on a two-Brigade front and two

Divs on a one-Brigade front. If this would materially assist the Army plans they were to submit it at the meeting on 12 Jan.

HQ 21 Army Group,	[Signed] H Mainwaring
10 Jan. 1944.	Lt.-Col.,
	M.A. to Commander-in-Chief.

IWM, Montgomery Papers Part I, BLM 122/1

5
Message to General Dwight D. Eisenhower

[Typescript]

10 January 1944

MOST SECRET (.) personal and private for General EISENHOWER'S EYES ONLY from General MONTGOMERY (.) have made a close examination of the whole OVERLORD problem in consultation with RAMSAY and LEIGH-MALLORY (.) in my opinion it is highly desirable that the extent of the initial assault area should be widened and that five divisions should be put on shore on the first tide and a good build-up be possible (.) this can be done only if ANVIL is reduced to a threat and the assault craft thus released are made available for OVERLORD (.) this has been put up to the Chiefs of Staff (.) it seems quite clear that no final decision on this matter will be given until you yourself give your opinion and wishes (.) the really important point is to get a decision now at once (.) provided we can get what I recommend then I consider OVERLORD has every chance of being a quick success so far as can be seen at present (.) if we do NOT repeat NOT get the ANVIL craft then I consider the chances of quick success are not good (.) I suggest it is essential to make a really good lodgement in Northern FRANCE and that this must be given the necessary resources to ensure success (.) time is very short (.) will you hurl yourself into the contest and get us what we want

IWM, Montgomery Papers Part I, BLM 108/1

6
Message from General Dwight D. Eisenhower to Montgomery

[Typescript]

13 January 1944

To: Theatre Commander for his eyes only for MONTGOMERY from EISENHOWER. I will go into the matters brought up by your W-9418 10 Jan[22] on my arrival which will be very soon. I have been discussing them intensively with the staff here. The following considerations appear pertinent. The desirability of strengthening OVERLORD is universally accepted. However we must not lose sight of the advantages to OVERLORD which ANVIL brings. The fact that ANVIL presents the only opportunity for use of the large land forces in the MEDITERRANEAN to aid OVERLORD directly is important. This consideration is particularly applicable in the period from 10 to 15 days after launching the attack. Furthermore there are certain strong considerations not purely military which have been brought to my attention here and which must be weighed.[23] My own conviction is that OVERLORD should be strengthened to the maximum possible but the abandonment of ANVIL should be accepted only as a last resort.

IWM, Montgomery Papers Part II, LMD 54/3

7
Montgomery's notes for 'Talk to Generals – 13 Jan. 44'[24]

[Holograph; with typescript sections (indicated by italics)]

1. Reason for assembling the senior commanders and their staffs.[25]

    Big things lie ahead.

    Explain the set-up:

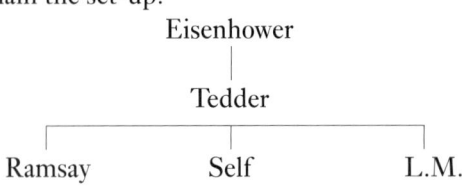

Command of the land armies; all under me – great honour to command USA Army. Allied Army Group.

We do not know each other well; much to be done; vital you should know my views on war, the fighting of battles, training and so on.

Time is short and there is much to be done; I have got to prepare the weapon.

We must stop experimenting and prepare for battle.

I will lay down the general form; everyone must accept it and act on it; all bellyaching[26] will cease. You must give me your confidence. American doctrine their own affair & General Bradley will act as he thinks most suitable.

The British and Canadian Armies will do as I say.

No criticism of Allies.

2. <u>My system of working</u>.

On my level I must keep clear of detail; I have great responsibilities.

Have a chief of staff. Explain the C.O.S. system; he gives decisions on all matters and is <u>NOT</u> merely a coordinator.

I exercise "personal" command; give verbal orders to my subordinate generals.

Within the general limits of framework of my instructions or plan – subordinates do as they like.

Essential to establish confidence; accept responsibility and get on with the job. Armies, Corps and Divis. run their own show getting the general form from me.

I work by "Personal" command; I issue no written orders; I read no paper; I expect everyone to act on my verbal orders, in battle or out of it.

Big events lie ahead; I have got to prepare the weapon. Time has come to stop experimenting and prepare for battle. When my decision is given everyone is to act on it; no bellyaching about it; all must accept it as a general guide.

3. I like Army Commanders to ring me up on the telephone <u>direct</u>, or come to see me and discuss their problems, whenever they like.

Don't let us make mistakes.

Have personal command and touch <u>backwards</u>, as well as <u>forwards</u>.

Deal with Chief of Staff also.

When in doubt, ask verbally; do not write; previous discussion saves mistakes. Must cut down all the mass of paper.

4. <u>The Staff</u>

Adopt the Chief of Staff system; use this nomenclature. Great liaison and friendship between staffs i.e. Army & corps, Corps & DIVS. Be a proper C.O.S. Know his stuff and give decisions; great powers; no delay.

Importance of the "I" staff; co-ordination of O, I, A.S. Control, and the Air. Best system at an Army or Corps HQ; group the Ops, Int, A.S. Control, J, all under one head; want two BGS's one of whom is C.O.S., or one BGS & one Colonel. This set-up hand-in-glove with RAF; air recce (G2 Air) works under "I".

<u>NOTES ON ADMIN</u> Staff.

1. The closest and friendliest liaison between G & A/Q. A/Q must be in on future plans from the beginning.

2. There must be no over insurance by Q, the Commander must be given the longest rein possible. In order to avoid over insurance G must stick to their contract. They must not beat the pistol or wangle up additional troops. In short must not cheat. If they do Q also begin to cheat and Q are usually better cheaters than G.

3. <u>Demands from front to rear.</u>

Whatever is asked for during operations must be sent up if physically possible without belly-aching. If demands afterwards turn out to have been excessive or unnecessary then the hammer can be applied.

4. <u>F.M.C. system.</u>[27]

This has been tried out not only in the desert but in enclosed country in Europe. It is the modern method of administration and must be followed.

5. The importance of an efficient traffic control system in modern warfare cannot be over emphasised.

6. Army the active master.

7. Army always prepared to relieve Corps of R.E. and Traffic Control responsibility; quite apart from the normal admin boundary.

4.[*sic*][28] <u>Basic principles of war.</u>

Start by giving my views on the general matter of making war.

<u>First</u>

The things that matter i.e. the basic fundamental principles on which everything is based.

The 7 principles of war:

Win the Air Battle (or aim at doing so).

Administration.

Co-operation.

Surprise.

Concentration.

Simplicity.

Fighting spirit and morale.

Every commander to be quite clear as to what are the things that matter on his own level.

Different things matter on different levels.

Difference between

Fighting

and

Frigging about (light forces)

5. <u>The stage-management of the Battle.</u>

The rules for winning battles:–

(a) Surprise.

(b) Foresee your battle and make enemy dance to your tune (Ex: Mareth).[29]

(c) Balance and poise.

(d) Initiative. "Drive" required right down.

(e) Plan communicated right down below.

(f) Confidence established e.g. no failures.

(g) Troops made wild with enthusiasm.

6. The technique of "grouping".

Cannot group till the problem has emerged.

Then group Divisions, and armour, in the best way to fit the problem. Similarly within Corps and Divisions. No fixed organization for a Corps. Divisions the only fixed organization.

7. <u>The Conduct of the Battle.</u>

(a) The initial blow; carefully prepared; resources built up; great fire power; enemy hit a colossal crack.

Generally best to "break in" at one or two carefully selected points; then to bring up fresh troops, pass through the gap, and attack remaining enemy positions from the flank and rear. The "schwerpunkt" and "aufrollen".[30]

(b) As battle becomes more mobile, essential to thrust deep with armoured formations and seize important ground; <u>armoured pivots well ahead</u>; staggered dispositions and layout.

Need to swing the battle about, and make it difficult for the enemy to by-pass your pivots.

All orders to be verbal.

(c) Divisional thrusts on main axes. Armour well forward.

(d) The doctrine of the "firm base".

(e) Keep the business on a Brigadier level in the planning stage; ensures full use of the experience of senior officers; keeps them in on it and well in the picture should higher control become necessary.

(f) <u>Gapping minefields – set piece attack.</u>

Three 8-yd gaps per Bn. Front.

Later – one 40 yd gap.

When using flails or scorpions,[31] you require 4, properly staggered and aligned to cover the ground:

The 4th one follows, and adjusts the direction by W/T.

8. *THE EMPLOYMENT OF THE ARMOUR – BASIC PRINCIPLES.*[32]

1) ORGANISATION:

(a) <u>Type of tank.</u> We want only two types of tank in the army:–
a capital tank
a light tank

A heavy tank specially designed for supporting inf only is not required. It is the gun that counts, and not armour. The gun will always defeat the latter.

(b) <u>Formations.</u> All armd bdes should and must be the same. There are at present, a number of tk bdes in this Army Group. This

we hope to adjust as opportunity offers. All armd bdes must be able to work in an armd div or with inf. There are not sufficient motor bns available to allot one to each bde. This is not a serious disadvantage. The personnel of an inf bn riding on the tanks or in M.T. if available, is satisfactory. The signal layout must be adjusted.

2) *GROUPING OF THE ARMOUR:*

(a) <u>Armd Divs.</u> All Corps Comds must be prepared to handle armd divs. It may be found necessary, during the early stages of an operation, to group all or most of the armd divs into one or more Corps. During the later stages it may be advantageous to have mixed Corps consisting of armd and inf divs. All Comds must be prepared for either contingency.

(b) <u>Independent Armd Bdes.</u> Besides the armd bdes in armd divs there are a number of independent armd bdes organised the same as the bdes included in the armd divs. All armd bdes must be interchangeable.

A Comd must be able to pull out the armour from an Armd Div when he thinks it necessary for reasons of armoured or personnel casualties, and replace it with a fresh bde, in order to maintain the momentum of the advance.

For instance, 8 Armd Bde operated with 7 Armd Div as far as TRIPOLI – its place was then taken by 22 Armd Bde. After resting, 8 Armd Bde took up the inf role in support of the N.Z. Div.

In the same way, an armd fmn supporting inf in the attack must be prepared to act in an independent role, and "lead the chase" should a break through occur. Time is not available to wait for other armd fmns to do so, even if they should be present in sufficient numbers. Whenever this occurs, an arty SP regt must be allotted to support it.

(c) <u>Scale.</u>

(i) From experience gained up to date Independent Armd Bdes should be available on the scale of:– one per Corps, and one in reserve under Army control. That is, with an Army of two corps, three Armd Bdes are required.

(ii) The number of armd divs required depends mainly on the type of country through which the land forces are directed. In ITALY there was no scope for an armd div. On the other hand, on the plains of the Ukraine or North France there is almost unlimited scope for their employment.

(d) *Armd Cars.* There was very little scope for the employment of Armd Cars in SICILY or ITALY. In AFRICA the cars were employed under div control, and rarely under the Corps Comd. They are now Corps tps, a policy I do not altogether agree with. There will undoubtedly be great scope for Armd Car work in Western Europe.

3) *COMMAND.*

(a) The control of an armd bde and its units when operating in support of inf has raised in the past, many problems.

As we see it, there are no difficulties, provided the following rules are followed:–

(i) The bde may be placed under comd of the inf div Comd for any particular operation.

(ii) Should the attack be carried out by one inf bde, and armour is required to co-operate, then the armd bde or regt will be placed *in support* of the inf bde, the tank Brigadier advising in exactly the same way as the C.R.A. of a div. Armour will, only under exceptional conditions, be placed *under comd* of inf Bdes or bns.

(iii) The Armd Bde brigadier will be called in to attend all planning conferences, and his opinion will always be given serious consideration. During the battle, he should locate his headquarters alongside the Comd controlling the attack.

(b) The question of comd within an armd div does not arise.

4) *ROLE OF THE ARMOUR.*

Whatever may be the task of an armd fmn in offensive operations, its first step towards achieving success will be to secure ground which dominates the battle area. The ground is required as a firm base from which to operate offensively, and upon which subsequently to reorganise.

When considering the use of armour, ground must always be given serious study. There are less natural obstacles to armour if the attack is directed along the grain of the ground than across it.

NOTE: If you agree, it is proposed to issue the Eighth Army Pamphlet "Notes on the employment of tanks in support of infantry in battle" to all fmns under your comd. It may be opportune to say so in your address.

5) <u>Important points when tanks work with infantry</u>:
Have a combined plan.
Ensure that tanks are drawn into sqn packets when the task is done, so as to facilitate maintenance; do not let them be used as pillboxes all over the place.
6) <u>Handling of Armd DIV</u>
Complete integration of armour, infantry, guns, etc.

9. <u>Artillery.</u>
(a) The evils of decentralisation.
(b) Great battle-winning factor if properly used, and applied in concentrated form. Keep on Brigadier level in the planning stage.
(c) DIV. concentrations.
(d) Control by the C.C.R.A. of the Corps.
(e) No commander can deal directly with more than one gunner. An artillery adviser is equally concerned with all types of artillery – field, medium, heavy, anti-tank, anti-aircraft, and when necessary coast defence.
All artillery brigadiers in the field army must understand thoroughly the training and employment of A.A. Artillery.
(f) Regiments must be thoroughly trained technically; this can be done efficiently only under a gunner Brigadier.
(g) Amm rates of expenditure – 25 pdr.
(h) Artillery versus mortars.
10. <u>DIV support Bns.</u>
Very unweildy [*sic*] at present.
The right answer is a MG Bn with one coy of mortars; the flak Btys to go to light A.A. Regts.
Use of mortars; we use artillery more than mortars.
11. <u>Adjustments within a Division to suit the conditions.</u> The W.E. and organization is there to suit general conditions. Modify as necessary to suit particular conditions.
Example of Inf. Bn.
Four weak coys or three strong ones.
Number of men in a platoon.
Will you keep 4 coys so long as each coy has two strong platoons?

31

Only the C.O. can decide, supervised by the Brigadier.

The only real test is – what will win the battle?

Example of DIV. Support Bn.

12. Training.

The first responsibility of a commander is to lay down a tactical doctrine and indicate clearly how the battle will be fought.

The organization of training to fit the conditions is then the task of DIV and lower commanders.

I issue no training instructions.

Army Comds train their armies.

Good troops who are well officered, well trained, mentally alert, and who are fit and active, will adapt themselves to any conditions.

Do not cramp initiative or break the chain of command, in the issue of training instructions.

Army group Monthly Training Letter to be discontinued; no more issued.

All orders in these letters saying that unit commanders will do this, or that, are cancelled; unit commanders will presumably do what their DIV Comds say.

Any views on training that I may want to send out will be given by me to Army Comds, and only one copy sent.

Comds to learn about the air.

USA doctrines their own affair; British Army to do what I lay down.

Reduced scales of transport; essential to reduce tpt that goes into battle with the unit.

Peace time habit of asking people what to do; must get "the form"; then get on with it within those limits. Ask verbally; no paper. Get realism and battle atmosphere and procedure. But a commander must lay down the general form, on broad lines on a level with his rank; keep criticism and instructions on a level with your rank.

13. Casualties

Comds must study their casualties as regards missing. If undue number of missing it means something is wrong.

Never let a DIV get so down that it takes a long time to come up; if it loses too much in leaders it will never recover quickly as all the teams.

14. Medical

Present standard of efficiency in Field Medical Services has been built up on the active fronts to a degree not previously considered possible or essential. As a result our sick and wounded soldiers have been spared much unnecessary suffering and many lives and limbs have been saved.

The soldiers all know that should they fall in battle they will have the best possible expectations of sound treatment and human consideration; this is a great factor in maintaining morale, and morale is the big thing in war.

Air evacuation.

Surgical teams.

Blood transfusion.

Nurses well forward.

Many bad cases have to be kept at Fd. Ambs for days; accommodation or tentage is necessary.

All comds must take a keen interest in their medical services, and ensure they have what they need in the way of transport, etc.

My own future movements.

IWM, Montgomery Papers Part I, BLM 90/3

8
Montgomery's diary notes, 14[–20] January 1944

[Typescript]

14 January.

12. I left London on a 5-day tour of the First American Army. I was anxious to visit the American troops at once, and to talk to them, and so gain an impression of the quality of the American Divisions. It was also essential that they should see me, and that personal touch should be established between us.

My immediate aim was to gain their confidence.

I therefore set off in my special train[33] to visit the following troops of the First Army:

5 Corps	29 Div.
7 Corps	1 Div
	9 Div
	2 Armd Div.
	3 Armd Div.
Airborne Div	82 Airborne Div.

I arranged that there would be about three parades of 3,000 to 4,000 each in each Div area, and I would address the officers and men using a loud speaker. I would see them and talk to them; they would see me; in this way I hoped that mutual confidence would be established.

I returned from the Tour on 20 January and there is no doubt it was a great success.[34]

IWM, Montgomery Papers Part II, LMD 54/1

9

Memorandum by Montgomery headed 'Notes for the Commander-in-Chief for SUPREME COMMANDER'S MEETING, Norfolk House, 1030 hrs 21 Jan. 1944'[35]

[Typescript]

<u>ORIGINAL OVERLORD PLAN.</u>
<u>1. Main weaknesses.</u>

(a) A three divisional sea-assault against the probable defences and the estimated enemy strength is hardly a sound operation of war.

(b) The assault is on a narrow front which means:–

    (i) the enemy's problem of containing our enforced shallow covering position should not prove a difficult one.

    (ii) It will be difficult for us to prevent our beaches from being within enemy arty fire.

    (iii) The area we can hope to seize and hold in the early stages will become very congested indeed.

(c) Limitations of craft, and of the roads leading inland from the beaches, suggest that our rate of build-up would be unable to compete with the enemy's theoretical rate of reinforcement. It is, however, difficult to assess the effect of air attack to prevent such reinforcement.

(d) The waterlogged areas in the British sector canalise the exits for vehicles through a number of small coastal villages. These may take some time to clear and capture.

(e) Owing to the inundations at the foot of the COTENTIN peninsula and the River VIRE, the enemy should be able to seal off the landing economically and so make the advance to and capture of CHERBOURG a lengthy operation.

(f) Without the early capture of CHERBOURG we should be dependent upon beach maintenance and the untried artificial ports.

REVISED OVERLORD PLAN.
2. The Plan.

(a) See attached diagrammatic maps showing enemy dispositions and outline plan – Appendix 'A'

(b) Further information on beaches, defences, etc. is contained at Appendices 'B' and 'C'.[36]

(c) <u>Main advantages over original plan.</u>
  (i) The enemy will not find it easy to destroy the larger forces landed with his immediate reserves.
  (ii) The wider frontage of the assault should confuse the enemy.
  (iii) The greater weight of the assault should permit a bolder policy, and a deeper covering position to be established.
  (iv) The greater the width of the assault the greater the chance of finding a weak spot.
  (v) The early capture of CHERBOURG becomes a probability.
  N.B. The Navy and Air will produce the disadvantages!

(d) <u>The Build-up.</u>
  (i) <u>The assault.</u>
      The initial lift (in LSTs and LCTs); assuming 50% ANVIL and the June date: = 20,000 vehicles
      At present it does not look as if 20,000 vehs will lift more than the following at minimum assault scales:–
      Five and two-thirds Divisions.
      Five Tank Brigades
      Necessary overheads.
      The proportion of the above lift that can be landed on D day will depend on
      Beach exits   (under examination)
      Craft beaching limitations   do. [ditto]
      It would be optimistic to count on landing more than the following on D day:–

Five divisions or equivalent.

Five tank brigades.

Necessary proportion of overheads.

The balance of the 20,000 vehicles would be landed on D+1 (i.e. third tide).

(ii) <u>The follow-up divisions.</u>

Anything further landed on D+1 would be carried in MT ships or MT coasters, and, not being tactically loaded,[37] must be regarded as non-effective before D+2.

The following table gives an estimate of build-up programme:–

Day.	Divs (incl assault divs) ready for action (i.e. 24 hrs after landing).	
	<u>British.</u>	<u>U.S.</u>
D+2	3 ⅔	2 ⅔
D+5	4 ⅔	3 ⅔
D+6	5 ⅓	4 ⅓
D+7	6	5
D+8	7	6
D+10	8 ⅓	7 ⅓

Unless a port has been captured, it might not be possible to maintain more than sixteen divisions over beaches and MULBERRIES.

Day.	Divs (incl assault divs) ready for action (i.e. 24 hrs after landing).	
	<u>British.</u>	<u>U.S.</u>
D+11	9	8
D+13	10	9
D+15	11 ⅓	10 ⅓
D+16	12	11

(iii) <u>Airborne Divisions.</u>

The above table does not include Airborne Divisions which might be dropped as under:

D day – One division.

D+1 – One division.

(e) <u>Maintenance</u>.

The above forecasts might have to be reduced if maintenance requirements cannot be met.

An examination is now proceeding to see what modifications in the strength of assault <u>or</u> the composition of the assaulting formations may be necessary in order to ensure a satisfactory administrative position.

BASIC WEAKNESSES IN EITHER PLAN.

3. The following basic weaknesses are apparent in either plan:

(a) The MULBERRY is relied upon to work.

(b) Peat and clay foundations may exist on some of the beaches. We are still not happy that we have a real solution to the problem.

(c) The theoretical rate of enemy reinforcement compares favourably with our own build-up.

(d) The uncertainty of the weather.

THE DATE.

4. To undertake the revised plan the June date would at present appear to be desirable.

(a) The ANVIL craft and ships are unlikely to arrive in time for the May date.

(b) The craft required include the May output.

(c) Most unlikely the new assault divs could be trained in time for the earlier date.

(d) Present forecasts suggest that we may not get the necessary equipment in time for the May date.

(e) The June date should give us four months of reasonably good campaigning weather. The June weather should be at least as good as May.

LOCATION OF H.Q.s.

5. (a) There appears to be complete divergence of views between the three Cs-in-C as to the set-up of HQs on D day.

(b) The Supreme Commander must decide whom he wants with him during the early stages of the operation.

He will no doubt wish to act as he did during HUSKY, i.e.

have the Naval Commander, land commander and an air commander with him. The airman could be TEDDER if LEIGH-MALLORY cannot move from his own HQ.

(c) As far as this HQ is concerned the following are the main points:–
   (i) As long as telephones are really good <u>you</u> need not be <u>at</u> your main HQ for that early period. You can take a very small staff with you to join the Supreme Commander.
   (ii) The alternatives open to main Army Group HQ appear to be:–
   Stay at St. Pauls.
   Move to PORTSMOUTH (mostly in the open)
   Move a large Tac HQ only to PORTSMOUTH.
   Move a Tac HQ to where the Supreme Commander is situated.
   WENTWORTH might be made use of.
   (iii) HQ Second Army should be at PORTSMOUTH.
(d) A lot will depend upon when you consider Army Groups should move over to the continent.

IWM, Montgomery Papers Part II, LMD 54/4

10
Letter to Lieutenant-General Sir Oliver Leese
[Holograph]
22 January 1944

Thank you for your letter of 8 January.[38] I am sorry to hear about the storms and bad weather you had just after I left. I arrived in England on 2 Jan, having spent 24 hours with the P.M. in Morocco en route. On arrival in London I was plunged straight in to the problems of the invasion of Europe – the so-called "second front"!! I considered that the plan was quite theoretical and un-practical, and was not in any way a sound operation of war. I said so in open court, and then gave my views on what form the plan should take. This led to great argument and discussion, during which I went round and saw the C.I.G.S., the First Sea Lord, the C.A.S.,[39] the Deputy Prime Minister,[40] and other "great ones" – and squared them and put my ideas to them. I then cabled[41] to Ike, who was in USA, and he rushed over here at once.

We had a meeting[42] of C's-in-C (Self, Ramsay, Leigh-Mallory) under the chairmanship of Ike, and my revised plan has now been accepted in all its details. This will have repercussions in other theatres of war, and so we have now got to get the Allied Chiefs of Staff to agree.

It is all very exhausting work. And it is curious how history repeats itself and we never seem to learn from our mistakes; it is "Husky" over again with all the frightful troubles in the planning stage.[43] But this time it is very serious as if Overlord were to fail, or to be only a partial success, it would put the war back months and months.

2. I have assembled all the general officers, British and American, in the field armies in England and have talked to them for a whole day[44] on how to make war and to win battles, given them my views on tactical doctrines, use of tanks and armour, and so on.

This has, I think, done good.

3. I then set out on tour in my train and visited every American Division in England, and talked to the troops on big parades.[45] This went down very well I gather.

4. I am busy trying to reduce my staff here. I have already made the following reductions:

Infantry Directorate (Utterson-Kelso's party)[46]	Abolished
C.W. Directorate	Abolished
Training "	Cut 50%
Intelligence "	Cut 50%
Operations "	Cut 25%

A very large number of major-generals and other senior officers who were in this party have gone to their homes to await other jobs; they were mostly quite useless. I have abolished the BGS Training & sent Pyman[47] as BGS 30 Corps.

No more time for more news.

IWM, Leese Papers

11
Montgomery's diary notes, 23 January 1944

[Typescript]

23 January.

14. I went to Chequers to lunch with the Prime Minister. He was

in very good form and seemed to have made a good recovery from his illness. It is terribly important that he should keep fit and well; we shall need his strong support and backing in the preparations for the second front, and during the initial days of fighting.

15. I explained to him the revised plan which I had recommended to EISENHOWER for the operation 'OVERLORD'. I also explained how I proposed to develop the operations after the initial landing, and my plan for securing quickly important road centres, for pushing armoured and mobile forces forward quickly,[48] and generally how I proposed to 'swing the battle about'.

He was delighted with the revised plan, and with the new aspect of the land battle on the Continent.

IWM, Montgomery Papers Part II, LMD 54/1

12
Prime Minister's Personal Minute M. 44/4 to Montgomery[49]
[Typescript]
27 January 1944

1. Herewith is an interim answer from the Minister of Production[50] about D.D. Tanks. It does not look too bad.

2. I shall have a further report presently about waterproofing material.[51] 200,000 vehicles seems a vast outfit to attach to an Army which, at 30 divisions of 20,000 men apiece, would only have 600,000 men, of which less than three-quarters would actually fight. As each vehicle takes at least a man and a half to drive and look after, here are 300,000 men already absorbed. One hopes there will be enough infantry with rifles and bayonets to protect this great mass of vehicles from falling into the hands of the enemy.[52]

IWM, Montgomery Papers Part II, LMD 54/14

February

13

Extract from Montgomery's 'Notes on Planning the Campaign in North Western Europe, January to June 1944'[1]
[Typescript]

<u>War Office Control of the Army in England</u>

8. On taking over command of 21 Army Group, General Montgomery found that the War Office exercised a very much closer control over the activities of the Army in England than over an Army on active service in the field. The Armies in 21 Army Group however were already in effect on active service and were preparing in the very near future to challenge the veteran German Army in the field after undertaking the largest combined operation of history. These armies lacking battle experience needed firm guidance and quick decisions, in order to ensure that this operation was properly launched in the very short time available. Under the system of close War Office control it was hard to get quick decisions and to counteract bad doctrine which had been taught in the past.

General Montgomery tackled this problem at once, and commenced to make certain changes without waiting for War Office approval. This quickly provoked considerable opposition, and the Secretary of State for War, Sir James Grigg, strongly disapproved of General Montgomery's apparent disregard for War Office authority.[2] General Montgomery therefore visited Sir James Grigg,[3] and explained to him how short a time there was and how much required to be done. He apologised if he had gone too fast, but he hoped Sir James Grigg would trust his judgement as to the operational necessity for what he had done.[4] This conversation greatly helped to clear the air, and Sir James Grigg and General Montgomery became firm friends. Thereafter the War Office never failed to support General Montgomery in preparing the Army for "OVERLORD". Just before D day, General Montgomery wrote to Sir James Grigg to thank him for the help and guidance which the War Office had unsparingly given, and to say how glad he was of the confidence and trust which had been built up between the War Office and 21 Army Group. A copy of this letter[5] is at Appendix 'A'.

The King and General Montgomery

9. Shortly after taking command of 21 Army Group, General Montgomery had an audience with The King.[6] He had privately heard that The King objected to his wearing a black Royal Armoured Corps beret. At this audience therefore General Montgomery spoke to the King about the value of high morale throughout the Army, and of how it could be achieved. As one of his methods in building up a high morale, he instanced his wearing of a black beret, by which all the soldiers now knew him. He claimed that the beret was worth at least an Army Corps, and that, while the war lasted, it was vital that he should continue to wear it. The King was interested to hear the reason for the black beret, which he had not realised before, and no further objections were raised to his wearing it.

IWM, Montgomery Papers Part I, BLM 74/1

14
Letter from Lieutenant-General Sir Ronald Weeks[7] to Montgomery

[Typescript]

2 February 1944

I enclose herewith, for your information, a schedule of the various vital items for 21 Army Group.[8] This schedule is the result of discussions between myself and the Ministry of Supply, and Herbert[9] knows all the details. You probably will not wish to wade through the schedule yourself, but I would just make the following points:–

(a) I understand from de Guingand that he is having a meeting almost immediately to go into the various bits of equipment which may be wanted for your special operation, with the idea of simplifying the demand as much as possible.

Naturally, as far as I am concerned, I would welcome any simplification which helps to reduce some of the bottleneck items.

(b) I have discussed the matter with the S. of S.,[10] and with Duncan Sandys, and we all think it would be an excellent idea if, in the course of your visits to your troops, you could, in isolated cases, go to some of the Works where the bottleneck items are being manufactured.

In anticipation of your willingness to do this, I have asked Duncan Sandys to prepare a list of a dozen places, so that you could fit some of them into your tours if you so wished.

I shall be very grateful to know whether you can do this; whether you would talk to the workpeople or the shop stewards is, of course, for you to say. Anyhow, the Ministry of Supply would lay on the arrangements for you. Publicity would be restricted, though it may be impossible to prevent the general statement that you had visited munition works in certain localities.

(c) You will be glad to see that we have been fairly successful as regards the D.D. Sherman, and I have every hope of achieving the target of 200 by the end of April. In this particular case a visit by you might just tip the scale.

IWM, Montgomery Papers Part I, BLM 120/36

15
Montgomery's diary notes, 11 February 1944

[Typescript]

11 February.

20. I assembled my three Army Commanders, and went through the operation with them (DEMPSEY, BRADLEY, PATTON).

I emphasised the need for simplicity.

The following notes give my ideas which I got across to the Army Commanders:

Notes.[11]

(1) Hold the balance between need to get ashore, and need to exploit quickly inland.

(2) Heavy air bombing before, and at, H hour.[12] Cancel all complicated fire-support methods. Go for <u>utmost simplicity</u> in all things.

Use largest possible number of craft to get infantry and supporting weapons on shore so as to develop the land battle quickly. Tank best initial supporting weapon.

Take initially the bare essentials in vehicles only.

(3) All five assaulting Divisions to be put on shore in the first tide.

(4) The following diagram gives my views on the general outline lay-out for the assault:

H hour = 1½ hours after Nautical twilight.

Intensive air bombing from dawn to after H hour

Forward Body to land all at the same time. Composition to be in accordance with the with the problem on the Bn front.	DD tanks	
	AVRE	Arks Flails (Menu as Ploughs necessary) Snakes
	Inf Bn (less two coys) S.P. arty	

Main Body and Overheads	Sherman Sqns Remainder Inf Bn
To follow closely	S.P. arty etc. etc.

<u>Fire Support</u>[14]	<u>Abolish</u>
LCG	LCT(a) with gutted
LCT(R)	tanks.
LCT(SP)	Also the LCA(HR).
Warships	Above extra lift is
Flak ships	needed so as to get
Air bombing	complete Bns on shore
	quickly.

<u>Notes:</u>

1. Fighting troops of all five Divisions to get on shore in the first tide.

2. Keynote of everything to be: <u>SIMPLICITY</u>.

IWM, Montgomery Papers Part II, LMD 54/1

16
Letter to General Dwight D. Eisenhower[15]

[Typescript]

19 February 1944

I am told by the Operations Directorate at the War Office that the Divisions in Italy have had a lot of casualties, are tired, and generally are not too well situated for getting on to ROME and beyond. They require re-grouping, resting and so on. Also the battle has to be continued so as to keep drawing GERMAN Divisions down that way – all of which is very good.

Under these circumstances I do not see how the withdrawal of Divisions from ITALY for ANVIL is possible.

If this is the case I hope that we shall get the full number of craft that we would really like for OVERLORD; there is no point in cutting ourselves down and accepting a compromise solution for OVERLORD, if ANVIL can never come off; it would be far better to have a really good OVERLORD, with a good choice of craft, a good reserve of craft, a good margin all round, and so on. I suggest that this aspect should be cleared up. Would it not be a good thing for the Chiefs of Staff to ask the Supreme Commander in the Mediterranean Theatre[16] to give his views <u>now</u> as to whether ANVIL is a practical possibility or not?

IWM, Montgomery Papers Part II, LMD 54/8

17
Montgomery's diary notes, 20 February 1944

[Typescript]

<u>20 February</u>.

26. I have now been in England for about six weeks and this seems a good point at which to set down my impressions.

27. I would say that the great mass of the people are getting war weary. Enthusiasm is lacking.

The miners, the factory workers, the dockers, the railwaymen, the housewives – all have been working at high pressure and the tempo has been great. They cannot get away for holidays; so holidays have to be spent at home. The blackout adds a dismal tone.

I consider it is very important to try and win the war in EUROPE early next year. I consider also that it could be done – provided we make no mistakes.

But to do so requires a great effort on the part of everyone, and the nation must be roused to make the effort. And above all, there must be great enthusiasm.

28. I also believe that if we make this great effort, and do not make any mistakes, we might well finish off the war in EUROPE early next year. The bombing of Germany will play a big part in rendering victory next year possible.

29. But the nation wants a leader who will rally it to the great effort. And he must do so personally, by showing himself and speaking to them. I am taking on this job for the land forces, and am visiting all the troops and addressing them.[17]

In my journeying round the country I am seen by the civil population; their re-action is immediate, and great enthusiasm results from my visits. I have been asked to address the railway-men, the dockers and stevedores, the workers in the big factories, and so on.

The Ministry of Transport, and the Ministry of Supply, make demands on me.

The Secretary of State for War is using me to make the big speech at the Mansion House in March to launch the 'Salute the Soldier' campaign.[18]

The result of all this is that the nation is beginning to look to me to lead them to victory. The whole of England know me as 'Monty', and I am recognised at once by every man, woman and child, in the land.

All this makes it difficult for me; I have to be careful what I say and do; I am bound to make enemies whatever I do.

I shall go on doing my duty, come what may. But I see dangers ahead, and politicians who now acclaim me will probably stamp on me when the war is won.

The public, and the Army, are firmly behind me and would support me to the end. But not so the Generals; my own Generals in the field armies are my firm supporters, but outside the field armies is much jealousy.

I shall want wisdom, understanding, and a sound judgment to see the thing through; also divine guidance.

IWM, Montgomery Papers Part II, LMD 54/1

18
Letter to General Dwight D. Eisenhower
[Typescript][19]

21 February 1944

I was asked out to Chequers yesterday (Sunday) to have lunch with the Prime Minister. He gave me a great deal of information about the Italian front which was news to me. It seems quite clear that we are now engaged in Italy in a major war; it is not just a battle for ROME. We are suffering heavy casualties; but so is the enemy, and all this will help OVERLORD far more than would a reduced ANVIL.

2. As a result of what he told me about the situation in Italy it is my definite opinion that all resources in the Mediterranean theatre should be put into the campaign in Italy. I further consider that we should now make a definite decision to cancel ANVIL; this will enable the commanders in the Mediterranean theatre to devote their whole attention to fighting the Germans in Italy – at present they have to keep ANVIL in their minds, and plan for it, and this must detract from the success of the present battle in Italy.

3. If para. 2 above is agreed, then all the craft now being kept for ANVIL can be released at once for OVERLORD. The effect of this on OVERLORD will be tremendous.

4. To sum up.

I recommend very strongly that we now throw the whole weight of our opinion into the scales against ANVIL. Let us have two really good major campaigns – one in Italy and one in OVERLORD.

IWM, Montgomery Papers Part II, LMD 54/19

19
Letter from General Dwight D. Eisenhower to Montgomery
[Typescript]

21 February 1944

I have thought over carefully your two messages of the 19th and 21st[20] regarding the prospects of ANVIL. I am bound to say that the events of the past week[21] have influenced my general conclusions very strongly along the lines you express.

However, there are aspects to the situation that make a simple answer most difficult to render. The first of these is that sooner or later the Allies must go into southern France, though it is possible that this may have to be deferred until a much later date and, in any event, cannot come about until after victory in the present battle. After that it still might be impossible to stage an ANVIL as now conceived for a very considerable time; on the other hand opportunity created by partisan action or withdrawal of German forces should be seized at a moment's notice. The partisans are particularly strong in South France, and the German defenses are less strong there than in the Northwest. I feel that unless the Mediterranean Theater has the responsibility for continuous planning in that specific direction we may lose a tremendous opportunity.

Another consideration that has influenced me is this. It is my understanding that our OVERLORD loadings on the first and second tides would be affected scarcely at all by additional landing-craft from the Mediterranean. (I mean those over and above those already agreed.) I feel therefore that adjustments in our own plans – particularly when such adjustments will be wholly on the advantageous side – in the third tide movements and subsequent build-up can be rather easily made. Consequently, I do not see the tremendous rush for making a decision adverse to ANVIL. If the Italian situation should quickly resolve itself in our favor, then, as always before, I would want a strong ANVIL.

Although agreeing to all you say about the need for all our troops in winning the present battle, let us suppose the battle receded to the North of Rome by early April. Then the German, by using delaying tactics, could impose a slow advance upon us, and keep us from using, effectively, more than 4 or 5 divisions at a time. Under such circumstances how could there be an opportunity for <u>all</u> our forces there to be used effectively if we do not leave them a strong lift in landing craft? OVERLORD would then have <u>no</u> real support from the Mediterranean. This bothers me. All these considerations make it seem wise to me to preserve flexibility in strategic plans as between the Mediterranean and the Channel for as long as we can without hurting our own planning.

I tried to get hold of you today to talk over these things but you are out of town.[22]

IWM, Montgomery Papers Part II, LMD 54/20

20
Montgomery's notes for 'Talk to Railway men: Euston', 22 February 1944

[Holograph]

1. Glad of chance to speak to the Railwaymen. Without your help we could achieve no results on any front; <u>you</u> handle the stuff <u>we</u> want; the better you do <u>your</u> work, the better we can do <u>our</u> work; if we do <u>our</u> work well it helps <u>you</u>.
2. The great principle of co-operation.

    The best co-operation is born of confidence.

    Cannot have confidence each in the other unless we know each other.

    Your co-operation is vital to me.
3. Would like to tell you something of the Army, and my methods. I want to interest you in what we are doing, and I will tell you how I fight my battles and what influences everything I do.
4. <u>The human factor</u>.

    The big thing in war. It is the man that matters and not the machine; the man in the tank and not the tank itself.

    It is the same in every profession, and in every concern.

    Study the human factor.

    The team – tank and crew.
5. <u>The German General</u>

    Apply this to the German commander.

    He is good so long as he is allowed to dictate the battle.

    Therefore he must be made to dance to your tune.

    How is this done? Decide how you will fight the battle before you start it, and force it to swing your way.

<u>Examples</u>

Alamein.

Mareth.

6. <u>No failures</u>.

How is this done.

Limit the scope to that which can be done successfully.

Tell the soldiers what you are going to do. Then do it.

Every man knows that when the army gets on the move it is going to win. Having won, he then has great confidence. And <u>that</u> is a pearl of very great price. The British soldier is a wonderful person – and never fails you.

7. <u>The sick and wounded</u>.

Sick always about 6 times the wounded.

Obvious importance of a healthy army.

The 4 things that save many lives:

Surgical teams.

Blood transfusion.

Air Evacuation.

Nursing sisters well forward.

8. <u>The German soldier</u>. His three main characteristics.

Technical ability.

Eye for country.

Obedience.

Very good soldier.

But well trained British soldier is better.

9. <u>The Italian soldier</u>.

Stories of:

5 divisions in my Army.

Rizzio wanting to command me.[23]

10. <u>The war.</u>

The black days of 1940, & after.

Change since 1942.

The future outlook.

11. <u>The Second front</u>.

Has begun.

12. The war has gone on long enough.

The women bear the real burden.

Let us all rally to the task and finish off this war; it can be done; and together, you and I, we will see this thing through – to the end.

IWM, Montgomery Papers Part I, BLM 90/5

21
Montgomery's diary notes, 22 February 1944

[Typescript]

<u>22 February.</u>

32. I addressed at Euston Station a big representative gathering of railwaymen drawn from all over England. The Secretaries of the Railway Trades Unions were present, all the men's leaders, and in fact a selection from every type of railway official. The meeting totalled 500.

I spoke for 1½ hours. I told them how I did my business and fought my battles; my chief point was that the big factor in war was the human factor, i.e. the man <u>in</u> the machine was what really mattered.

I said we had the war in a very good grip; the bad days of 1940 and 1941 were over; we must now all rally to the task and try and finish off this war; together, 'you the railwaymen and I the soldier', we will see this thing through to the end.

After I had finished speaking the Secretaries of all the Railway Unions pledged their full support. So it did good.

IWM, Montgomery Papers Part II, LMD 54/1

22
Letter to General Dwight D. Eisenhower

[Typescript]

23 February 1944

Reference your letter of 21 Feb 44.[24] I think the argument in favour of making a decision NOW adverse to ANVIL is as follows:

1. The present idea is to use the same number of craft as originally planned on the first and second tides. This means in effect that the recent reduction in LST and LCI(L) will be felt on the third tide, (a.m. D+1) where it will be offset by the use of personnel and MT ships. These take longer to unload, and vehicles have to be married up with their units after landing. The ultimate result will therefore be a slowing down in the operational availability of troops landed on D+1.

2. It is probably impossible to make use of any additional craft on the first and second tides owing to beach and loading limitations. If

additional craft are made available, they can best be used to replace personnel and MT ships on the third, fourth, and fifth tides (NB. There are NO craft at present for the fourth and fifth tides. The first "Turn-round" of craft does not start until the sixth tide).

This will result in a substantial acceleration in the effective rate of build-up during the first three days, when speed is most vital.

3. The accelerated build-up would have considerable repercussions not only on the tactical plan but also on the whole administrative arrangements. It is essential therefore that we should know without delay whether the additional craft are likely to be available. If the decision is postponed, it will be impossible to make the best use of the additional craft, and moreover the last moment alteration in the plan may lead to hasty and inadequate preparations with consequent risk of confusion.

IWM, Montgomery Papers Part II, LMD 54/21

23
Letter to Lord Louis Mountbatten

[Holograph]

24 February 1944

I have got your letter sent by Desmond Harrison,[25] and it has been duly burnt!!

They explained to me your ideas.

My immediate reaction was that everyone seems to be trying to have his own war, because he wants to do something.

The question I asked was: What is the Allied plan for making war on Japan?

The answer given me was: There is no plan.

That seems to me to be the trouble.

And as there is <u>no</u> plan everyone is making <u>his</u> plan, to suit him.

We shall do no good that way.

Why do not the Allies make a plan, and tell commanders what to do?

———————————

Here in England I found everything and everyone was just drifting along. Rather pathetic really.

The plan for OVERLORD was definitely quite unpractical and

could never have succeeded. It all had to be changed. I myself, of course, again became the bad man – just like HUSKY.[26]

However I don't mind; it is put on a sound basis now and everyone is cracking along on the revised plan.

Southampton University, Mountbatten Papers

24
Letter to Field Marshal Sir Alan Brooke

[Typescript]

26 February 1944

I would like to discuss with you some time the whole question of the teaching that is given in the schools, which are all now under the D.M.T.[27]

2. I have been disturbed to find that C.O's in experienced fighting Divisions that I sent home from overseas will not send their young officers and N.C.Os to these schools; they say the teaching is not in accordance with what goes on in battle.

I have not been to any of the schools myself so far, but from what I have been told I should say they are right.

3. The average young officer is at a very receptive age, and he takes in readily what he is taught at a school; if this early teaching is not right then great harm is done.

I find that C.Os. prefer to organize their own instruction within the unit, and thus ensure it is the proper stuff. All this is a great pity.

Furthermore, there are a great many Divisions in England in which there is little battle experience; in these Divisions the teaching of the schools is accepted without comment.

4. I suggest that the D.M.T., who is charged with the general supervision of the schools, should be an officer who has seen much fighting in this war and who is thus able to ensure that the teaching in the schools is closely related to the practical realities of the battlefield.

5. I feel that Whitaker is not able, as D.M.T., to get the instruction at schools on sound lines. I suggest he should be replaced by an experienced officer who has great practical experience in battle fighting. I could name you such an officer.[28]

6. You may decide it is inadvisable to have further changes at this moment, and this may well be so.

In this case would you allow me to assemble a meeting of the commandants of schools and the D.M.T., and to get across to them certain basic points on which I consider the tactical teaching should be based. Actually, of course, the D.M.T. would call the meeting and invite me to attend.

7. Para 6 is possibly the best solution as it would cause no loss of confidence. We would all lend a hand and try and get the thing right. The field armies would then accept the schools and everyone would "sing the same song".

IWM, Montgomery Papers Part I, BLM 115/2

25
Montgomery's diary notes, 26 February 1944

[Typescript]

26 February.

34. We had a conference of Commanders-in-Chief with EISENHOWER. I saw the P.M. and the C.I.G.S. before the conference.[29]

It has now been decided definitely that all resources in the MEDITERRANEAN theatre are to go into the Italian campaign. The ANVIL operation is to be planned only, and no resources in craft, shipping, troops, etc. are to be held in reserve for it. On 20 March a decision is to be taken as to whether ANVIL is possible; if it is found to be NOT possible, then all the craft wanted for OVERLORD are to be sent to England – so as to make a really good OVERLORD.

The President has agreed to this plan.

35. This is, at last, a firm statement. There has been a great deal of passing the ball backwards and forwards between London and Washington. EISENHOWER has had great pressure from WASHINGTON, where opinion is very much in favour of ANVIL. But the tactical picture in WASHINGTON as to what is going on in ITALY is not so clear as it is in LONDON, as the British Commanders in the MEDITERRANEAN communicate direct with the P.M. and the C.I.G.S. The British Chiefs of Staff in

London 'get at' EISENHOWER and he is accused by Washington of being influenced by the British.

So it is very necessary that we should all try and save EISENHOWER from reproaches from WASHINGTON, and save his face when he wants to come down hard on the side of what we want to do.

My own position is very difficult.

I serve under EISENHOWER. But I also have immense responsibilities to the C.I.G.S., which actually must over-ride all other considerations.

So I have to walk very delicately.

36. The Italian campaign has now become a major war. We have had 16,000 casualties in the bridgehead[30] since 22 January; any further offensive action on our part is not possible for the present; we will have to re-group and assemble fresh forces for an offensive later on. It is not good, and, in my opinion, ALEXANDER has failed to 'grip' the war in ITALY. See my comments in my diaries.[31]

IWM, Montgomery Papers Part II, LMD 54/1

March

26
Montgomery's diary notes, 3 March 1944

[Typescript]

<u>3 March.</u>

38. I went to the London Docks and spoke to some 16,000 dockers, stevedores, and lightermen. There were 5,000 around me in an open shed, and my talk was relayed to big audiences in other places.

I had already addressed the railwaymen on 22 Feb at Euston.[1]

My general theme was the same – there is a job to be done and together, you and I, we will do it. See para 32.[2]

39. In the afternoon I had a talk with EISENHOWER and Bedel [*sic*] SMITH. I said I was not happy on two matters:

(a) The closing of the South coast to visitors. I gave EISENHOWER my views in a D.O. letter. See Appendix 'K'.[3]

(b) The question of operation ANVIL.

We really could not go on any more in this indecisive way. We could not possibly do:

The ANZIO battle

The ANVIL operation.

The OVERLORD operation.

The first and the last were obviously essential. Therefore, ANVIL must be cancelled. It should be cancelled NOW; we could not wait till 20 March.

I obtained the complete agreement of EISENHOWER and Bedel SMITH on these two points.[4]

IWM, Montgomery Papers Part II, LMD 54/1

27
Montgomery's diary notes, 7 March 1944

[Typescript]

7 March.

40. I can see trouble ahead in AIR matters. HARRIS (Bomber Command) and SPAATZ (American Heavy Bombers) will not take orders from LEIGH-MALLORY. I am not surprised. L.M. is a very nice chap indeed and is easy to work with; but he is definitely above his ceiling in his present job and is not good enough for the job we are on.[5]

The only solution is for TEDDER to co-ordinate the air operations of HARRIS, SPAATZ and L.M.

41. Actually the air side has too many H.Q., now that CONNINGHAM [sic] has been brought in. He is in command of all the Tactical Air Forces, i.e. mediums, lights, fighters. L.M. is not really required – provided TEDDER is brought in to run the whole air side.

IWM, Montgomery Papers Part II, LMD 54/1

28
Letter to General K. Sosnkowski[6]

[Typescript]

14 March 1944

Thank you for your kind letter of 7th March; I was sorry you could not be present when I visited your troops, but I quite understand the reason.[7]

2. I cannot express adequately how very much I enjoyed my visit.[8] The men of the Armd Division, and of the companies of the Parachute Bde that I saw, are quite first class; it was a very great privilege to be able to meet them and to speak to them. I met quite a number of men that had fought against me in the Africa Corps under Rommel [sic]; I now know why the Africa Corps was so good!!

3. I shall want to use your Armd Div in the operations of the Second Front, and it is important that it should be brought up to full British War Establishments at a very early date; I would be very grateful if you will see that this is done.[9]

4. It is also important that the Division should carry out some

training with other formations; it cannot do this in Scotland and I am examining the possibility of moving it further south.

5. Having now met your Polish soldiers I am quite determined that I want them to fight with me in operations for the liberation of Europe.[10] And I will do all I can to further this aim.

IWM, Montgomery Papers Part I, BLM 120/18

29
Montgomery's diary notes, 17 March 1944

[Typescript]

<u>17 March.</u>

43. St. Patricks Day.

I had lunch with the Prime Minister and Mrs. Churchill.

I have been having trouble with the Poles who have been laying down conditions about the use by me of their Parachute Bde,[11] and who will not comply with my wishes about bringing their Armd Div up to strength.[12] I told the P.M. that we ought to be very firm with nations that have been under the heel of GERMANY; they should be made to do what they were told.

The P.M. asked me my views on Herbert LUMSDEN;[13] I said he had failed me in battle, and he was disloyal and was given to intrigue.

44. It has now been agreed by the P.M. that the coastal belt can be closed to outside people as from 1st April. See para 39(a)[14] and Appendix 'K'.[15]

45. I told the P.M. that there was far too much talk going on in the House of Commons, and elsewhere, about demobilization and work for soldiers after the war.

IWM, Montgomery Papers Part II, LMD 54/1

30
Montgomery's notes for a talk to 'HQ Second Army', 20 March 1944[16]

[Holograph]

1. We are going to be associated in great events. Must know each other. Very important you should know my views on things.

2. In the business of war, very clear thinking is required.

You have to sort out those things that <u>really</u> matter; certain other things will matter too, but not so much. The really vital points must be your beacon lights through all your soldiering.

We British have had many disasters in this war; they have been due to neglect to define clearly these matters, and to give clear guidance on them.

3. What are the things that <u>really</u> matter when you go fighting.

In my opinion there are 8 things; some of them are in no book.

The Air battle.

Administration.

The initiative.

Surprise

Concentration

Co-operation

Simplicity

Fighting spirit & morale

4. Many other points matter in a less degree. These sort themselves out in battle, and you get your sense of values.

You get a dividend in accordance with your training i.e. ability to teach your officers and N.C.O.'s, who are the leaders.

Battle cunning can be learnt only in battle.

5. Among these other points I suggest you have a good line of approach if you use the following questions:

(a) Can you launch your troops properly into battle i.e. can you tee-up the various types of battles that occur.

(b) Do you realise that, having done this, the issue then passes to the regimental officers and men. Their training is therefore vital.

(c) Do you understand that the human factor is the big thing in war.

(d) Do you understand the requirements of a good plan for command & control.

(e) Do you understand battle admin.

6. We have many troops as yet untried in battle. Vital to see they have a good show their first battle.

7. <u>The Human Factor</u>.

The man and not the machine.

Inspiration for the armies.

Carry the doctrine into everything.

Divisions are all different.

Generals are all different.

You want the right man in the right place at the right time. It is all a great study of human nature; you have certain human material at your disposal and what you can make of it will depend on yourself.

Battle a contest between two wills.

IWM, Montgomery Papers Part I, BLM 90/7

31
Memorandum by Montgomery headed 'Some Army Problems', 20 March 1944[17]

[Typescript]

Notes by C-in-C 21 Army Group.

1. I have made some notes for Army Commanders which I consider are important. These deal with Army problems, but they can be discussed with great advantage with naval commanders.

B.L.M.

SOME ARMY PROBLEMS.

1. We must get ashore.

Fire support from the sea and air will all be concentrated on the problem of getting the Army ashore.

In some places we may get ashore easily; in other places with difficulty.

Those who do get ashore must work outwards and help those who are in trouble.

Once ashore we must stop the counter-attack while we get sorted out, and generally build up. Best way to stop counter-attacks is to be offensive ourselves; must not let initiative pass to the enemy; we must crack about and force the battle to swing our way.

2. GERMAN is good at the small local counter-attack. We want little firm bases from which infantry and tanks can be offensive without difficulty and can therefore take great risks.

Best firm base is A/Tk guns and tanks; vital to get these ashore early. The A/Tk gun is a better A/Tk weapon than the tank.

3. The tank is initially the best supporting weapon. But the infantry must marry up with their own supporting weapons early, and release the tanks for offensive action.

4. Remember:
    (a) the need to mop up; value of tanks for mopping up.
    (b) use of armour working with infantry.
    (c) the value of high ground; a few tanks on the high ground with the infantry.

LAYOUT FOR ASSAULT.

5. Breaching parties, or forward bodies, consisting of:
    Flails,[18]
    A.V.R.E.
    Infantry,
    Div R.E.

The exact composition must vary with the problem. There may be a mass of under-water obstacles on the beach, above or below the waters edge, at any state of the tide.

Close touch must be kept with this and the menu for forward bodies varied accordingly.

It is definitely becoming clear that infantry, and Div R.E, will be wanted in forward bodies.

No obstacles are going to stop good infantry.

6. <u>Command and control for the assault.</u>

Each breaching party, or forward body, must have its own commander.

There must be a commander for the whole forward body on any Bn front.

The Bn Comd must be in close touch with the O.C. Forward Body; he must therefore be well forward and in front of his battalion so that <u>he can take charge of the battle on the</u> <u>beach at the earliest moment</u> and fight his battalion to the best advantage from the beginning.

The Bn Comd himself should be in a tank.

7. Generally, Bn Comds must be on shore in a tank very early, – close behind the forward bodies and ahead of their rifle coys.

8. Command and control is vital. A definite, and distinct, commander is essential for every echelon; and all must know who that is. That commander must have good communications, both within his command and back to his next superior.

PENETRATION INLAND.

9. As we penetrate inland we may expect to find important areas, such as high ground or centres of communication, held by static and immobile Divisions.

These may not counter-attack, but are likely to hold doggedly in defensive action and thus form pivots for mobile Divisions brought in from other areas.

They may well be supplied with food, ammunition, etc., so as to hold out for some days.

10. We must not let these areas hold up our rapid penetration inland. We have to gain the tactical advantage quickly, and to push ahead and seize our own pivots – using armoured and mobile forces.

11. The enemy static pivots must be by-passed, and dealt with by our reserves coming on behind.

AIRFIELDS.

12. As we secure airfields, and good areas for making airfields, so we get increased air support, and so everything becomes easier. It is very important that the area to the S.E. of CAEN should be secured as early as Second Army can manage.

DEPTH IN BRIDGEHEAD.

13. We are dependent on beaches for our administration, and then on artificial harbours. We have no proper commercial ports, and will have to establish Army dumps on shore and live like this for some time.

Therefore depth to our initial bridgehead is very necessary; we must have space in which we can develop our administrative lay-out.

IWM, Montgomery Papers Part II, LMD 54/25

32
Memorandum by Montgomery headed 'OVERLORD: Air Requirements as viewed by the Army', 20 March 1944[19]

[Typescript]

1. <u>Pre-D Day</u>.

Air efforts in order to:

(a) Destroy the enemy air forces.

(b) Destroy and disrupt communications so as to impose delay on enemy movement toward the lodgment [*sic*] area.

(c) Mislead the enemy as to the real point of attack.

(d) Attack certain targets such as coastal batteries, oil installations, etc.

2. <u>D Day.</u>

(a) The Army must be got on shore.

Therefore the first task must be such air action as will ensure this. Direct air assistance to the assault will be vital, <u>and must be laid on up to the extent</u> <u>required by the Navy and Army.</u>

(b) Protection of the ships against air attack – also vital.

(c) Action as in para 1 above.

IWM, Montgomery Papers Part II, LMD 54/26

33
Montgomery's diary notes, 20 March 1944

[Typescript]

<u>20 March.</u>

46. At the weekly meeting of Commanders-in-Chief it was agreed to send a cable to the Combined Chiefs of Staff in WASHINGTON that ANVIL was now clearly impossible, and asking for the increased lift for OVERLORD. See paras 34 and 39.[20] There were signs of wavering at the meeting as American opinion very definitely favours an ANVIL; but at long last they now see it is quite impossible; however much they would like it, the troops for it are not available.[21]

IWM, Montgomery Papers Part II, LMD 54/1

April

34

Montgomery's diary notes, 1[–2] April 1944

[Typescript]

<u>1 April.</u>

50. I went to HINDHEAD[1] to have a quiet two days.

<u>General Comments.</u>

(1) This seems a good time at which to close this section of the diary. I arrived in England from Italy on 2 January and it is now 2 April; the past three months have been hard work, and things have not been too easy.

(2) The original plan for 'OVERLORD' was wrong; there was little fighting experience in the Army in England; HQ 21 Army Group was very theoretical and many of the more senior staff officers were definitely not good enough for their jobs; many changes had to be made, and quickly.

All this has drawn a good deal of adverse comment, and much mud has been slung at me; I have always had enemies and now probably have many more.

But the job has been done; 'OVERLORD' is now properly 'teed-up['] and the plan is good; I have got my H.Q. well organised, and have brought in the experienced officers I required. If I assembled the heads of the various sections of my staff you would think you were back in the Eighth Army, since they all were part of my team there; they are now part of my team here and if I had not brought them in I do not think I could have done the job in time.

(3) Operation 'OVERLORD' is now in good shape. We have got ANVIL relegated to a back seat and got agreement that we must have what we want for 'OVERLORD'.

(4) I myself have doubtless made enemies as you cannot do quickly what I had to do unless you <u>do</u> make enemies. But I have got

beyond caring about that; once we have won the war I will gladly retire into obscurity. I am firm friends with all those necessary to do the task in front of us, i.e.

The Prime Minister.

The Secretary of State for War.

The C.I.G.S.

The C.A.S. and C.N.S.

General EISENHOWER.

Admiral RAMSAY.

Air Chief Marshals TEDDER and LEIGH-MALLORY

These are the people who have to do the job and whose goodwill is necessary. I think I have their trust and confidence. For my enemies I care little.

The public and the Army are firmly behind me, and my earnest prayer is that I may not let them down.

(5) I am very lucky in my Chief of Staff, and my M.G.A.[2] We are an Allied H.Q. and they work in very well with the Americans.[3]

IWM, Montgomery Papers Part II, LMD 54/1

35
Letter to Lieutenant-General Sir Ronald Weeks

[Typescript]

3 April 1944

Referring to your letter of 23 March 1944[4] re the G.S. Policy on Tanks, and the "Tortoise", and so on. You may also care to refer to Nye's letter of 7 October 1943 (CIGS/BM/20/7729), written in answer to my letter of 28 August 1943.[5]

1. I consider that we have not been very successful in our endeavours to produce a good tank. I have my own views as to why that is the case, but I do not want to enlarge on that point in this letter; the past is behind us. I think it was Meterlink[6] who said:–

> "the past is only of use to me as the eve of tomorrow;
> my soul wrestles with the future."

But maybe some other writer said it.

2. I often feel that one of the possible reasons for our comparative

lack of success in the tank line has been the lack of a clear conception as to what a tank is for. My own view is that a tank is merely an armoured vehicle in which you carry about weapons and ammunition, i.e. firepower. You want a vehicle which <u>can</u> get about; and you want to be able to develop the firepower properly from the vehicle; and you have got to balance up the conflicting claims of armour, speed, gunpower, crew-space, etc. etc.

3. I do not know if you accept para. 2. If you do, then it follows that to produce a really good tank you must have a really good knowledge of what goes on in battle. A very great many people – give off a very great many views about tanks – who have NOT a very great deal of knowledge about battles!! This last sentence seems to read somewhat curiously, but you will know what I mean. I have recently met civilians from the Ministry of Supply, including Duncan Sandys, who tell me what tank we ought to have!! How <u>can</u> they know?

4. I have been studying the paper you sent me entitled "General Staff Policy on Tanks, Sept 1943". I am unable to agree with certain things in it. I consider that the conception of what is wanted is faulty.

In my opinion we do not want a cruiser tank and an infantry tank.[7] I consider we want a capital tank and a light reconnaissance tank; I have always said this; I say so now; and I will continue to say so. See paras 7 to 9 of my letter to Nye dated 28 August 1943, written from SICILY. The capital tank must be of the 40 to 50-ton type, definitely not more.

5. So far as I know neither of the tanks that I advocate, now and for the future, are contemplated. That is of course not my business, and only the War Office can decide what is needed. But I am very anxious that you should be in no doubt as to my views.

6. With regard to the "Tortoise".

It will weigh over 80-tons, and is over 12 ft wide. These factors limit the use of such a tank. I doubt if it could be moved by rail; even if the width of any bridge would permit there are very few capable of taking the weight; the tank on a transporter would be a gigantic problem. It will I believe go through 18 ft of water, but much work would often be necessary on approaches to, and exits from, the river obstacle. It would be a major operation to assemble even a regiment of these tanks for an attack against a prepared position; in fact I doubt if you could do it in certain cases.

7. I consider we are wrong to go into production with a tank of this nature. We must keep our capital tank down to the 40/50-ton mark.

8. I suggest that before the requirement or design of any tank is even decided upon, and definitely before any wooden mock-up is built, the users should meet together under the Director R.A.C, at the War Office and consider the whole matter. If this procedure were adopted I am sure we would save a lot of time and avoid wasted effort. It must always be remembered that it is the firepower that matters; we must find the guns we want and then build tanks to take them about; see paras 10 to 14 of my letter to Nye dated 28 August 1943.

9. I suggest we should not write any more to each other on this problem. I would be quite delighted to discuss the whole subject with you verbally sometime; it is so much easier to explain what one means. To explain everything in one letter is very difficult; and so one does not do it; and then misconceptions creep in, and we start all over again.

So do come and have a good talk about the whole matter.

IWM, Montgomery Papers Part I, BLM 117/9

36
Montgomery's notes for 'Brief Summary of Operation "OVERLORD" as affecting the Army. Given as an address to all General officers of the four field armies in LONDON on 7 April, 1944'[8]

[Cyclostyle]

<u>Exercise THUNDERCLAP.</u>
<u>Address by C-in-C.</u>[9]

1. This Exercise is being held for the purpose of putting all General officers of the field armies in possession of the whole outline plan for OVERLORD, so as to ensure mutual understanding and confidence. Secrecy is vital; far too many people know far too much about things that do not concern them. The greatest care is necessary from now on. Especially must we all

beware of people who are trying to find out things and who resort to the "confidence" trick, and other similar methods.

Object of OVERLORD.

2. The object of OVERLORD is to secure a lodgement on the continent from which further offensive operations can be developed. It is not an isolated operation but is part of a larger strategic plan designed to bring about the total defeat of GERMANY by means of heavy and concerted assaults upon GERMAN occupied EUROPE from the U.K., the Mediterranean and RUSSIA.

The Allied Team.

3. This is an Allied operation, being carried out by BRITISH and AMERICAN forces with the forces of our other Allies cooperating. It is a great Allied team and none of us could do any good without the others. The Supreme Commander, or captain of the team, is GENERAL EISENHOWER. For the initial operations I am GENERAL EISENHOWER'S ground force-commander. ADMIRAL RAMSAY is the naval force-commander. AIR CHIEF MARSHAL LEIGH-MALLORY is the air force-commander. All General officers must understand that H.Q. 21 Army Group is an Allied H.Q. exercising operational command and control over the land forces of the Allies, under the Supreme Commander.

The Intention.

4. To assault simultaneously:
(a) immediately north of the CARENTAN estuary.
(b) between the CARENTAN estuary and the R. ORNE with the object of securing as a base for further operations a lodgement area which will include airfield sites and the port of CHERBOURG.

The Enemy Situation.

5. The present enemy situation in the WEST will be known to you. The present number of identified enemy Divisions is 55, of which 8 are Pz or PG.[10]

What the situation will be by D Day is not certain. We shall keep very close touch with the changing situation.

6. Since ROMMEL toured the "Atlantic Wall"[11] the enemy has been stiffening up his coastal crust, generally strengthening his defences, and re-distributing his armoured reserve.

The present general trend of movement of his mobile reserves is SOUTH i.e. away from the NEPTUNE area; this shows that our target is not yet known to the enemy.

7. ROMMEL is likely to hold his mobile Divisions back from the coast until he is certain where our main effort is being made.

He will then concentrate them quickly and strike a hard blow; his static Divisions will endeavour to hold on defensively to important ground and act as pivots to the counter-attacks.

8. By dusk on D−1 day the enemy will be certain that the NEPTUNE area is to be assaulted in strength. By the evening of D Day he will know the width of our frontage and the approximate number of our assaulting Divisions; it will be quite evident that ours is a major assault. The enemy is likely that night to summon his two nearest Panzer Divisions to assist.

9. By D+5 the enemy can have brought in 6 Panzer type Divisions. If he has decided to go the whole NEPTUNE hog, he will continue his efforts to push us into the sea. We ourselves will have 15 divisions on shore by then. After about D+8 I think the enemy will have to begin to consider a "roping off" policy i.e., trying to stop our expansion from the lodgement area.

10. The GERMANS seem to be trying to insulate the WEST from the mounting disasters on the EASTERN front. No enemy division has left the WEST for the EASTERN front since January; two Panzer Divs have actually arrived in FRANCE from RUSSIA since then.

But already the RUSSIANS have affected OVERLORD in two ways:

(a) the build-up in the WEST is no longer increasing to the extent hitherto; though nothing is going away, nothing much is coming in.

(b) the ultimate build-up from other fronts against OVERLORD during its first two months was estimated in January at 15 divisions; it is now estimated at 6.

11. I suggest we should plan in general on the enemy having a round total of 60 divisions, of which 10 will be Panzer or P.G.

12. Some of us here know ROMMEL well. He is a determined commander and likes to hurl his armour in to the battle. But according to what we know of the chain of command the armoured divisions are being kept directly under RUNSTEDT [*sic*], and delay may be caused before they are released to ROMMEL. This fact may help us, and quarrels may arise between the two of them.

13. When considering the estimated rate of enemy build-up against us, no regard is paid to the effect of air attack on enemy reserves – especially in movement. This cannot be disregarded. But the enemy build-up can become <u>considerable</u> from D+4 onwards; obviously therefore we must put all our energies into the fight and get such a good situation in the first few days that the enemy can do nothing against us.

<u>Preliminary Air Operations.</u>

14. Certain preliminary operations are to be carried out by air forces, and these will be explained by the Air C-in-C when he speaks to us.

As regards the Air, the main requirements from an Army point of view are as follows:

    (a) destruction of the enemy air forces.

    (b) destruction and disruption of communications so as to impose delay on enemy movement towards the lodgement area.

    (c) mislead the enemy as to the real point of attack.

    (d) destruction of certain specified targets such as coastal batteries, etc.

These air operations have already begun.

<u>Army Tasks.</u>

15. Four armies are taking part in the operations:

First U.S. Army Second British Army	} Assault armies.
First Canadian Army Third U.S. Army	} Follow-up armies.

The order of battle of these armies can be seen on the diagrams.[12]

16. The tasks given to the armies are as follows:

First U.S. Army.

(a) To assault astride the CARENTAN estuary.

(b) To capture CHERBOURG as quickly as possible.

(c) East of CARENTAN, to develop operations southwards towards ST LO in conformity with the advance of the Second British Army.

After the area CHERBOURG–GAUMONT–VIRE–AVRANCHES has been captured, the Army will be directed southwards with the object of capturing RENNES and then the *ports of NANTES and ST NAZAIRE* [italicised words crossed out and amended to 'establishing our flank on the R. LOIRE' by hand in Eisenhower's copy].

Second British Army.

To assault to the west of the R. ORNE and to develop operations to the south and south-east, in order to secure airfield sites and to protect the eastern flank of First U.S. Army while the latter is capturing CHERBOURG.

In its subsequent operations the Army will pivot on its left and offer a strong front against enemy movement towards the lodgement area from the east.

First Canadian Army.

This Army will land after the Second British Army and will take over from it the left or northern sector of the lodgement area. The troops of Second British Army in the area so taken over, probably one Corps, will come under command First Canadian Army.

Third U.S. Army.

This Army will land after First U.S. Army and will have the tasks:

(a) of clearing the BRITTANY peninsula and capturing the BRITTANY ports.

(b) as soon as the BRITTANY and LOIRE ports have been captured, of covering the south flank of the lodgement area while the First U.S. Army is directed N.E. with a view to operations towards PARIS.

The Sea-borne Assault.

17. The existing resources in landing ships and craft are contained in five Naval Assault Forces, and two Naval Follow-up Forces. These forces have been allotted in support of Armies as follows:

<u>First U.S. Army</u>

| Two Assault Forces | } | Lift of approximately |
| One Follow-up Force | | 8,700 vehicles. |

<u>Second British Army</u>

| Three Assault Forces | } | Lift of approximately |
| One Follow-up Force | | 10,900 vehicles. |

The total lift is some 20,000 vehicles, all of which will be landed on the first, second, or third tides.

18. The forces to be carried in the initial lift are as follows:

<u>First U.S. Army.</u>

Three Infantry Divisions (Assault)

Five Tank Battalions (Assault)

Two Ranger Battalions.

Army and Corps Tps, and Naval and Air overheads.

<u>Second British Army.</u>

Three Infantry Divisions (Assault).

Three Tank Brigades (Assault)

One Armoured Brigade

One Infantry division (less two Inf Bde Groups)

Two S.S. Bdes.[13]

Army and Corps Tps, and Naval and Air overheads.

19. The assault will take place on D day on an eight Brigades/Regimental Combat Team, front.

H hour will be nautical twilight+90 minutes, but this time may change.

<u>First U.S. Army.</u>

Assaults on a front of three Regimental Combat Teams.

<u>Second British Army.</u>

Assaults on a front of five Infantry Brigades.

Details are shown on the diagram, and Army Comds will explain the plans later.

The Fire Plan.

20. The object of the fire plan is to get the Army on shore and for this purpose the chief requirements are as follows:

(a) the destruction or neutralization of enemy coast artillery batteries that might interfere with the approach of the convoys, or shoot up the anchorages.

(b) the neutralization of enemy strong points and defended localities that might bring fire to bear on the beaches.

Very good naval support is available, as will be explained by the Naval C-in-C. Direct air assistance to the assault is being provided by the Allied Air Forces up to the extent required by the Navy and the Army. All are agreed that the Army must be got on shore and all three services are doing everything in their power to ensure this. The Air C-in-C will explain the air action when he speaks to us.

Commandos and Rangers.

21. First U.S. Army.

Two Bns of Rangers are to land at H hour on the right of 5 Corps sector, to move WEST, and deal with enemy batteries and defences to the EAST of the CARENTAN estuary.

Second British Army.

(a) 4 S.S. Bde with two Commandos will land with 1 Corps at H hour and clean up the area between 3 Canadian and 3 British Divisions. The Commandos will then move inland and seize the bridges over the R. SEULLES which runs between 1 and 30 Corps.

(b) 1 S.S. Bde to land in 3 British Div Sector. One Commando will clean up OUISTREHAM. The remainder of the Bde will move inland, cross the R. ORNE by the bridges at BENOUVILLE, and attack in rear and destroy the enemy coast defences to the east of the R. ORNE up to CABOURG inclusive.

(c) Two Commandos 4 S.S. Bde will be held in reserve.

Airborne Forces.

22. First U.S. Army.

(a) 101 Airborne Div will land in rear of the VARRAVILLE

74

beaches prior to H hour, and will assist 4 Div in capturing its objectives.

(b) 82 Airborne Div will land about *24 hrs after* [italicised words crossed out and amended to 'the same time as' by hand in Eisenhower's copy] 101 Div in the area shown on the diagram, with the object of preventing the movement of reserves into the CARENTAN peninsula.

Second British Army.

6 Airborne Div (less one Bde) will be landed to the East of CAEN prior to H hour. Its task will be to seize the bridges over the R. ORNE at BENOUVILLE and RANVILLE and, in conjunction with 1 S.S. Bde, to dominate the area lying east of CAEN so as to hold up and delay enemy movement towards that place.

23. The problem with airborne troops is to land enough troops to do the job, and to land them in the right place. I have laid down that the smallest number to be landed in any one place, at one time, is a Bde; and far better to land a whole Division. Once airborne troops have done their job, they must be collected into reserve for use again as soon as they are refitted.

24. Once the initial operations are over, airborne troops will be used to keep the battle moving by means of "air hooks" of not less than a Brigade; see para. 28.

25. The whole of 1 British Airborne Div will be in reserve, plus one Bde of 6 Airborne Div.

26. A total of some 1,500 S.A.S. troops will be dropped on the night D–2/D–1 in a belt 40 to 50 miles from the coast from the south of BREST to BELGIUM, with the tasks of attacking Divisional areas and interfering with the movement of reserves.

Development of Operations.

27. You will see from the diagram on the wall how the land battle will be developed.[14]

Phase 1.

28. Phase 1 is shown in GREEN.

In this Phase the First U.S. Army and Second British Army secure the whole area included within the green line. This gives us a good base for subsequent operations. I estimate we may have this area by D+20, and we will fight continuously until we get it. There may then have to be a pause to see how we stand administratively; if not, so much the better.

Phase 2.

29. Phase 2 will then begin, and the operation will be developed as shown by the YELLOW lines.

30. 8 Corps from Third U.S. Army will be brought in through CHERBOURG and will come under First U.S. Army.

First U.S. Army will operate southwards towards *ST NAZAIRE–NANTES–ANGERS–LE MANS* [italicised words crossed out and amended to 'LOIRE' by hand in Eisenhower's copy].

8 Corps (under First U.S. Army) will turn westwards into the BRITTANY peninsula.

31. Second British Army will push its left out towards the general line of the R. TOUCQUES. At the same time the Army will pivot on FALAISE and will swing with its right towards ARGENTAN–ALENCON. This Army will have completed landing by D+17.

32. Third U.S. Army will be brought in after First U.S. Army. There are several alternatives:

(a) through CHERBOURG and/or the VARRAVILLE beaches.
(b) through the LOIRE ports.
(c) through the BRITTANY ports.

Airborne landings may be undertaken to capture BRITTANY ports such as MORLAIX, so as to allow ships to come in. This operation is being worked out now – Operation SWORDHILT.

The task of Third U.S. Army will be to clear the BRITTANY peninsula.

33. I estimate that, if all goes well, we may have the area up to the Yellow line by D+35 to D+40.

This would not include the complete cleaning up of the BRITTANY peninsula; the time for this is not possible to estimate with any likelihood of accuracy; it may take up to D+60. *If we want to have free use of the LOIRE ports it may become necessary for First U.S. Army to secure a bridgehead south of the LOIRE* [italicised words crossed out by hand in Eisenhower's copy].

Phase 3.

34. The positions to which the Armies will be directed is shown in black.

First Canadian Army will have taken over the left, or northern sector. It will then face up to the R. SEINE below ROUEN, will force the crossing of that river and will operate northwards towards ST VALERY so as to cut off and capture HAVRE. This will be called Operation AXEHEAD.

The capture of HAVRE is essential; it is required for the maintenance of the British and Canadian Armies; if not captured fairly soon it will have repercussions on the U.S. build-up.

Second British Army.

This Army will move forward towards the line of the R. SEINE between PARIS and ROUEN; it will protect the right flank of First Canadian Army south of the SEINE, while operation AXEHEAD is in progress.

First U.S. Army.

Will be directed on PARIS, and the SEINE above the city. It will be prepared to cross the river and operate to the N.E.

Third U.S. Army.

Will operate on the right flank of First U.S. Army, and will protect its right or southern flank.

35. We might reach the black line on the diagram by D+90.

36. The weight of air power available to support the development of operations will be very great. After the initial assault the tactical air forces will be directed against enemy reserves, movement on roads, defended centres of resistance, rear maintenance areas, and so on. Given close cooperation between the air forces and the land armies, I do not see how the enemy can stop us from developing the operations as we plan – if only we can get a good lodgement in the first four days and capture CHERBOURG quickly.

Rate of Build-up.

37. The general principle on which the build-up has been planned is to land on the continent the maximum number of fighting formations in the first few days; after that, Divisions are brought in consistent with maintenance and other factors. Flexibility has been

introduced at the earliest possible moment so that the priority of fighting formations, as against overheads of all kinds, can be varied to suit operational conditions as they develop.

Some examples of the number of Divisions on shore in the early stages, and in later phases, are as follows:–

		U.S.	British	TOTAL.
	D Day (incl airborne)	3⅔rds	4	7⅔rds
	D+1	5⅔rds	4⅔rds	10⅓rd
	D+4	8⅓rd	6⅓rd	14⅔rds
	D+12 (excl airborne)	9	9	18
(GREEN)	D+20 "	9	15	24
(YELLLOW)	D+35 "	15	15	30
(BLACK)	D+90 "	20	15	35

Further Airborne Operations.

38. It is hardly possible to forecast airborne operations after the assault. But the following types of operations are envisaged and forces will be held in readiness in England *and/or on the Continent – see para. 14* [italicised words crossed out by hand in Eisenhower's copy]:–

(a) an attack on the BRITTANY ports by up to two airborne Divisions.

(b) airborne operations in conjunction with the crossing of the LOIRE and Operation AXEHEAD.

(c) S.A.S. operations against vital objectives in the enemy's rear.

(d) Airborne landings in conjunction with a large-scale break-through operation.

(e) deep penetration in the event of enemy disintegration.

(f) air "hooks" to keep the battle moving. See para. 15.

Resistance Groups.

39. The launching of the assault will be the signal for action by Resistance Groups in occupied territory. During the assault, and the period immediately following it, action will be directed to hindering the movement of enemy reinforcements and harassing the enemy back areas; these activities will be co-ordinated with those

of the S.A.S. troops in areas where both are operating. As the battle develops it is anticipated that Resistance Groups may be able to seize control of certain areas where the ground and strategical situation is favourable. The co-ordination of Resistance will be in the hands of Special Force H.Q. in LONDON, working under the operational control of SHAEF. Special liaison staffs will be detached to work with Army H.Q.; these have their own W/T communications and can pass to Special Force H.Q. details of the ways in which commanders require their plans to be supported by Resistance Groups.

Engineer Problems.

40. <u>Beaches.</u>
(a) No underwater obstacles have yet been laid where they will be encountered before touch down. Naval and Marine teams are being trained in the removal of such obstacles.
(b) There is so far no evidence of underwater beach mines. If they appear, the BOOKREST[15] will be fired from LCA (HR) in front of the leading waves.
(c) Clay outcrops occur in some sectors of the British front, about 100 yards from the back of the beach. Carpets are being provided to be laid over clay patches.
(d) Heavy steel obstacles are appearing on the coast in some areas, from 50 to 400 yards from the beach i.e. above the point of touch down. These are not obstacles to infantry but may be a serious obstacle to craft of subsequent flights. The technique of clearing these obstacles is being studied i.e. by shooting at them, by charging with tanks, by mechanical equipment and by hand placed charges. More of these obstacles may appear, but the effort involved in their manufacture and transport to the site is very great.
(e) Sea walls varying in height from 6 to 20 feet appear in some sectors. These will be dealt with by hand-placed charges, by assault R.E, and mechanical equipment.

41. <u>Obstacles to advance inland.</u>
Routes inland from the beaches are likely to be canalised by means of flooding, demolitions, craters, and so on. Rivers and streams will cause lateral obstacles.

Tanks and wheeled-vehicles may not find it too easy to debouch quickly from the beaches; but no obstacles that have yet been noticed could stop determined infantry from penetrating inland by the skilful use of ground and manoeuvre; infantry must act in this way, and outflank the enemy posts guarding the defiles.

42. Bridging.

Extensive enemy demolitions are likely and will cause major bridging problems. Between D day and D+60, there will be landed 45,000 tons of bridging equipment.

43. Airfield Construction.

The programme aimed at is:

Date	U.S.	British.
D+3	2	2
D+8	5	5
D+14	8	10
D+24	12	15

These figures are cumulative.

Four Aviation Bns U.S. Eng. ⎱ will be landed
Five Airfield Construction Groups British ⎰ before D+4
One Field Construction Wing, RAF. will be landed before D+30.

Changes in the plan, or in the nature of the country, may well necessitate U.S. Aviation Engineers operating in the British Sector or vice-versa; the former is more likely as there is a good area for airfields south and S.E. of CAEN.

Complete flexibility of employment between British and U.S. Airfield Construction Units is therefore desirable; the problems of control and administration arising from this must be studied by all concerned.

44. General.

It is obvious that the enemy will make every use of obstacle demolitions, and so on, to hamper our landing and to hold up and delay our penetration inland. Commanders must keep very close touch with this aspect of the problem; photography will disclose what is going on. We must not be misled because nothing very serious has appeared so far. All engineers are studying the problems as they arise, and some special types of equipment have been devised. Commanders must realise clearly that this equipment has not yet proved itself in battle. Sub-units of divisional engineers must be well forward and ready to lend a hand. And infantry must be quickly on the scene, using manoeuvre and ground, and so outflanking and by-passing obstacles, and thus making it easier for the engineers to do their work.

MOUNTING ARRANGEMENTS.

General.

45. Responsibilities for mounting arrangements to conform to the operational plan are:–
(a) War Office for British/Canadian troops.
(b) Air Ministry for RAF, except that War Office provides RAF marshalling facilities.
(c) ETOUSA for United States forces.

46. The general procedure for mounting the operation is laid down in the combined pamphlet "Overseas Movement. Instructions for Commanding Officers (Combined Ops – SSV[16])". This procedure is divided into three phases –
(a) Concentration
(b) Marshalling
(c) Embarkation.

Concentration.

47. Concentration is the locating of formations and units in areas from which they can move direct to marshalling areas.

Movement to concentration areas is ordered by 21 Army Group, 2nd TAF and ETOUSA.

The distances between concentration areas and marshalling areas are governed by:–
(a) Restricted mileage permitted after waterproofing.[17]
(b) Movement Control requirement that units must be concentrated within one day's march of marshalling areas.

The concentration plan is not yet firm, but it is anticipated that it will provide for the following:–
(a) All formations (except Allied) being in concentration areas by Y–21.[18]

(b) 10–12 days' estimated flow of Army Group, Army and Corps troops being concentrated by Y - 21.

The assault, follow-up and early build-up formations and units will have a pre-allocation of craft and/or shipping, and will in the majority of cases concentrate in marshalling areas.

Concentration of the subsequent build-up will be ordered by BUCO (see para 59 below) according to the build-up tables or special operational requirements.

Marshalling.

48. In the marshalling areas all troops will be hotel serviced[19] and organised into craft loads ready to be called forward to the embarkation points.

Embarkation.

49. The coast is divided into various embarkation areas, each of which has a headquarters which controls a group of embarkation points.

In embarkation areas are embarkation regulating parks to which coast movement control call forward serials from marshalling areas for embarkation. This park acts as a regulating area to control the flow to embarkation points.

Briefing.

50. Briefing will take place in marshalling areas under strict security arrangements. Special accommodation is provided. The time allowed is 4 days for assault, 24 hours for follow-up and 6–10 hours for build-up formations.

Models for briefing assault and follow-up troops are being made by teams from formations working under 21 Army Group direction.

Maps.

51. The assault, follow-up and early build-up will draw maps from special depots established in and near marshalling areas. Build-up formations and units will use depots in concentration areas. Maps are issued in coded rolls which will be opened as late as possible, and only in marshalling areas prior to H hour.

Residues.

52. Formations and units up to approximately D+17 and possibly later will embark at reduced scales. The portions which are left

behind are known as residues, and are classified as follows, based on a percentage of the vehicle W.E. and approximately 3 personnel to each vehicle:–

(a) Assault formations 40–60% – First Assault residues

(b) Assault formations 60–75% – Second Assault residues

(c) Other formations and units 75% – WE – Last residues.

Special provision is being made for the grouping, accommodation and administration of these various residues.

Command and Control.

53. (a) Commanders and a small command post staff of headquarters down to brigades are not required to pass through the process of marshalling.

(b) Mounting arrangements provide for cars to report to headquarters concerned in concentration areas which will enable commanders and their command post staffs to move about freely.

(c) Waiting rooms adjoining the headquarters of marshalling areas and sub areas and embarkation areas, with suitable communications, are available for them to occupy on their way to embarkation.

Security.

54. The principal security problem is the segregation of personnel who have been briefed prior to H hour. This problem will be further aggravated in the event of a postponement. This responsibility is left to Army Commanders who will order the wiring of camps as they consider necessary.

Postponement.

55. Postponement may be of two types:–

(a) Short postponement of one or two days during a suitable tide and weather period.

(b) A long postponement of about twenty-eight days between two suitable tide and weather periods.

In the event of a short postponement, troops on board LSI and LST will remain on board. Troops on LCI and LCT at alongside berths will be disembarked. Troops on LCI and LCT not secured alongside may be disembarked as determined by conditions prevailing at the time.

In the event of a long postponement, all troops, less maintenance parties for vehicles, will be disembarked and returned to marshalling areas which will be kept empty until the expedition sails. Vehicles will not be disembarked.

Protection.

56. 21 Army Group formations and units will be responsible for their own protection except in so far as AA protection is afforded by 'ADGB'[20] (until arrival in marshalling areas), when it will become the responsibility of Home Commands.

AA defence is the responsibility of 'ADGB', but as many 21 Army Group AA formations and units as possible have been allotted to 'ADGB' until required for embarkation.

Assistance to Home Forces.

57. Two mobile infantry brigade groups from the late build-up are being ear-marked as mobile reserves for Home Forces in case of raids by enemy ground or airborne forces. One brigade group will be located in KENT and the other in SUSSEX.

In the unlikely event of Home Forces requiring further assistance they will apply to HQ 21 Army Group.

CROSSBOW.[21]

58. Home Forces have been asked to release 21 Army Group formations and units from as many of their CROSSBOW commitments as possible, but it is probable that they will have to be accepted so long as formations and units are available. Allowing time for concentration, marshalling, and embarkation this is unlikely to be later than D+9.

Build-up Control Organisation (BUCO).

59. BUCO is a combined and joint organisation of staff officers including representatives of the Service Ministries. Its function is to exercise the detailed control of the build-up which is necessary to implement the Commanders' plan. Broadly speaking it is divided into two parts:–

(a) Representatives of the staffs of the Expeditionary Forces. This portion exercises control.

(b) Representatives of the various movement agencies. This portion, collectively known as MOVCO, will issue the necessary executive movement instructions.

Execution of Mounting Plan.

60. The time table of events leading up to initial embarkation and the build-up priority tables represent the Commanders' authority to Movements to put the general mounting plan into operation on notification to the Director of Movements at the War Office on D day. Any alteration in the build-up tables, as a result of operational requirements, will be submitted by Commanders concerned to BUCO who will put them into effect.

HEADQUARTERS

61. Locations on D day.

Supreme Commander	SOUTHWICK HOUSE or BROOMFIELD.[22] Then to STANMORE.
Commander-in-Chief.	SOUTHWICK HOUSE or BROOMFIELD.
Main Headquarters, 21 Army Group	SOUTHWICK PARK.
Rear Headquarters, 21 Army Group	ST. PAULS.
Main Headquarters, First U.S. Army.	Afloat to land D+1 (Going through Plymouth)
Main Headquarters, Second British Army.	FORT SOUTHWICK.
ANCXF	SOUTHWICK HOUSE.
AEAF	STANMORE.
Second TAF	UXBRIDGE.
9th United States Air Force	UXBRIDGE.

Tactical HQ, 21 Army Group, will accompany Tactical HQ Second British Army overseas on D+1 or D+2, and set itself up in readiness for the arrival of the Commander-in-Chief.

Main HQ, 21 Army Group, will move overseas as soon as conveniently possible after the D+20 phase line is reached. The area selected provisionally is near ST LO, which is central and has good signals facilities.

Rear HQ 21 Army Group will move overseas and establish itself close to Main HQ 21 Army Group as soon as conveniently possible. This is not likely to be before D+21 at the earliest.

COVER PLAN AND DIVERSIONARY OPERATIONS.[23]
Cover Plan.

62. The object of the Cover Plan is to:–

(a) Before D day indicate a D day of D+45 in order to encourage the enemy to reinforce other fronts on which he may be heavily engaged, at the expense of our own front.

(b) From D day onwards make the enemy believe that we have retained in the SOUTH and SOUTH EAST of ENGLAND a force whose task is to attack the PAS DE CALAIS the moment he has withdrawn his reserves from that area in order that we may pin these reserves there for as long as possible.

It is the task of 21 Army Group to implement this plan so far as it is possible with our own forces and the added assistance of Home Forces. The task of indicating a later D day is a difficult one which we have endeavoured to achieve by taking all possible security precautions, as well as by trying to persuade the enemy that our final operation will be yet another rehearsal.

In order to achieve the second object, we shall endeavour to show the enemy that the First Canadian and Third U.S. Army under command of the First U.S. Army Group, are retained in EAST and SOUTH EAST ENGLAND for the purpose of being available to attack the PAS DE CALAIS area. Large numbers of dummy landing craft will be launched and moored in suitable areas in EAST and SOUTH EAST ENGLAND from shortly before until well after D day in order to give this potential threat its means of transport. It will be necessary to carry out a certain amount of wireless activity both by real and imaginary formations, in order to build up a force required for the threat.

Diversions.

63. In order to distract the enemy during the night immediately preceding the assault, it is intended that we carry out the following diversionary operations.

Sea

Three Naval diversions will be executed, these diversions being carried out by a small number of Naval craft whose special apparatus will be able to indicate to the enemy RADAR system, convoys of shipping.

The first diversion will be against the NORTH of the CHERBOURG PENINSULA. The object of this diversion will be to engage the enemy RADAR stations in that area in order to prevent them from being able to gauge the depth and therefore the strength of our assaulting forces. It should also cause the enemy shore batteries to dissipate their effort.

The second diversion is against the coast immediately NORTH of the SEINE, and will have as its object, the retention of the GERMAN forces in that area, and the creating of greater breadth to our assault forces which it is hoped will cause dissipation of the enemy coastal fire and air bombing. This diversion will be linked up with a large-scale Airborne diversion.

The third diversion will be against the PAS DE CALAIS area, and its object will be to confuse the enemy Intelligence in order to delay his knowing that our only effort will be against the NEPTUNE area. It may also cause him to dissipate his bomber force.

All these diversions take place during the hours of darkness.

64. Air Diversions.

In order to retain enemy forces NORTH of the SEINE, and in order to endeavour to encourage the enemy armoured reserve, which is West of the SEINE, to move Eastwards, dummy paratroop droppings to simulate the dropping of one airborne div will be made in the area of LE HAVRE.

A number of smaller dummy airborne operations will take place elsewhere.

MAIN ADMINISTRATIVE POINTS.

65. The administrative problem facing the US forces is entirely different from that of the British. The operational plan envisages the British forces remaining in reasonable proximity to their Advance Base whereas the U.S. forces have got to first make a rapid move to CHERBOURG and then turn South to capture NANTES and the LOIRE Ports. The development of the BRITTANY and LOIRE ports and the railways and roads to effect distribution of stores will put great strain upon the U.S. administration. In view of this no satisfactory comparison can be made between the tonnages required for the British and US forces since stores requirements for the development of the L of C in the U.S. sector are very large.

66. The limiting capacity for the build-up of forces is likely to be the maintenance stores which can be landed. This will be governed by the acceptance capacity on the Continent as it is likely that transportation resources and shipping can be found to ensure that ports, MULBERRIES and beaches are working to capacity. There is, however, a limit to the number of coasters available, and this precludes the use of a number of ports in the BRITTANY Peninsula in which it is impossible to discharge deep draught shipping.

67. Should there be a serious and unexpected break in the weather before D+14, this will have a serious effect on the maintenance of both forces. Plans for emergency maintenance have been made but this will not cover a prolonged spell. Previous experience does not, however, point to the likelihood of there being many days in succession at this time of the year when nothing can be unloaded. Between D+14 and D+90 it is not expected that the weather will be a limiting factor to the forces which can be maintained ashore. After D+90 it must, however, be assumed that the weather will deteriorate and it is not practicable to plan for the British forces to be maintained during the winter months over the beaches. It therefore follows that the British must look to CHERBOURG and to MULBERRY 'A' for their maintenance until such time as the SEINE ports are captured.

68. The build-up of both forces is very rapid and it is essential that the British forces should advance sufficiently far East and South to allow room for the development of the RMA[24] and administrative installations at as early a date as possible. Unless this is done very considerable congestion and some confusion will inevitably occur.

69. The British have no large port in their sector and are, therefore, entirely dependent on the beaches and their MULBERRY. At a later stage it is envisaged that British will take over the US MULBERRY. It therefore follows that the successful maintenance of the British forces, until the capture of LE HAVRE and ROUEN is dependent on the successful construction and operation of these MULBERRIES.

70. It is not economic for the US forces to open all the small ports in the BRITTANY Peninsula and major ports only will be selected for development. It is not expected that maximum development of these will be achieved until after D+60 and the advantage thus obtained will be offset by the necessity of the British use of CHERBOURG and MULBERRY 'A' until such time as these ports can be handed back to the US after capture of LE HAVRE and ROUEN.

It therefore follows that the speed of the subsequent build-up of the US forces depends on the date of capture of LE HAVRE and ROUEN.

In order to maintain their forces in the LE MANS area it will be necessary for the US to develop a long road and rail L of C from the LOIRE and BRITTANY ports in the West of CHERBOURG and the beaches in the North. The speed of the US advance will depend on the speed with which this L of C can be developed.

Note – A large outline sketch map will be prepared to show the main administrative installations.

IWM, Montgomery Papers Part I, BLM 74/4

37
Montgomery's diary notes, 7[–8] April 1944

[Typescript]

7 April.

2. I held a two-day exercise on 7/8 April which was attended by all general officers of the field armies.

My object was to put all senior officers and their staffs completely into the whole OVERLORD picture – as affecting the general plan, the naval problem, and the air action. This was done on the first day, 7 April.

On 8 April I held an exercise when we examined certain situations[25] that might arise in the 'OVERLORD' operation, either during the approach by sea or in the land battle itself.

My address to the officers is filed with this diary (see Brief Summary of Operation 'OVERLORD' as affecting the Army).

3. The British Chiefs of Staff, the Secretary of State for War, and General EISENHOWER all attended the first days work.

The Prime Minister also attended and spoke to all the assembled officers; he looked very tired and worn out, and I fear did not create the inspiring influence I had wanted.

I cannot feel happy about the P.M.; if he cracks up now we shall be in a bad way; it is vital he should keep fit and well; his personality and drive are essential for what we have to do.

IWM, Montgomery Papers Part II, LMD 55/1

38
Memorandum by Montgomery addressed to Commander First US Army and Commander Second British Army[26]

[Typescript]

14 April 1944

1. In operation OVERLORD an uncertain factor is the speed at which the enemy will be able to concentrate his mobile and armoured Divisions against us for counter-attack.

On our part we must watch the situation carefully, and must not get our main bodies so stretched that they would be unable to hold against determined counter-attack; on the other hand, having seized the initiative by our initial landing, we must ensure that we keep it.

2. The best way to interfere with the enemy concentrations and counter-measures will be to push forward fairly powerful armoured-force thrusts on the afternoon of D day.

If two such forces, each consisting of an Armd Bde Group, were pushed forward on each Army front to carefully chosen areas, it would be very difficult for the enemy to interfere with our build-up; from the areas so occupied, patrols and recces would be pushed <u>further</u> afield, and this would tend to delay enemy movement towards the lodgement area.

The whole effect of such aggressive tactics would be to retain the initiative ourselves and to cause alarm in the minds of the enemy.

3. To be successful, such tactics must be adopted on D day; to wait till D plus 1 would be to lose the opportunity, and also to lose the initiative.

Armoured units and Bdes must be concentrated quickly as soon as ever the situation allows after the initial landing on D day; this may not be too easy, but plans to effect such concentrations must be made and every effort made to carry them out; speed and boldness are then required, and the armoured thrusts must force their way inland.

4. The result of such tactics will be the establishment of firm bases well in advance of our own main bodies; if their location is carefully thought out, the enemy will be unable to by-pass them. I am prepared to accept almost any risk in order to carry out these tactics. I would risk even the total loss of the armoured brigade groups – which in any event is not really possible; the delay they would cause to the enemy before they could be destroyed would be quite enough to give us time to get our main bodies well ashore and re-organised for strong offensive action. And as the main bodies move forward their task will be simplified by the fact that armoured forces are holding firm on important areas in front.

5. Army Commanders will consider the problem in the light of the above remarks, and will inform me of their plans[27] to carry out these tactics.

IWM, Montgomery Papers Part I, BLM 89/5

39
Letter to Lieutenant-General Sir Giffard Martel[28]

[Holograph]

17 April 1944

I have your letter, and I sent you a message[29] – which I hope you got.

In your letter you talk about "an appreciation and plan".

But I do not want anything of that sort.

All I would like you to do is to give me any notes you like on how the Russians used their tanks. I definitely do NOT want any appreciation on how I should use my tanks, or armour.[30]

I hope this is quite clear.

IWM, Martel Papers 8/1a

40
Letter from Sir James Grigg

[Holograph]

21 April 1944

The P.M. will not advise the King in favour of your special service[31] so that is the end of it for the time being. He doesn't like using the Coronation regalia anyhow.

Incidentally he asked me to tell you to lay off your "public tours & civic receptions".[32] I pass on this message therefore but you shd know that I have already told the PM that your public addresses to other audiences than your own troops have without exception been undertaken at the request of, and indeed under pressure from Govt. Depts, especially the Ministries of Labour, Supply & War Transport.

I am looking forward to my trip with you.[33]

IWM, Montgomery Papers Part II, LMD 110/2

41
Letter from the Ministry of Supply to Montgomery

[Typescript]

25 April 1944

Now that we have finished our tours to factories, I[34] want to thank you so much not only on my own behalf but for the whole Ministry for what you have done. I feel sure that your visits have been a great inspiration to thousands of workpeople and that production will be enhanced in consequence. You saw for yourself what great enthusiasm you inspired and this will be the subject of conversation in many homes for weeks to come.

I have known for some time that the workpeople of this country were getting somewhat jaded and they needed a topic of conversation to carry them on. You have been good enough to serve as that topic and also as a tonic to them all. My grateful thanks.

IWM, Montgomery Papers Part I, BLM 97/14

42
Montgomery's diary notes, late April/early May 1944

[Typescript]

[Late April/early May][35]

8. April has been a busy month, with exercises, visits to factories, and much travelling. I began to feel somewhat tired by the end of the month; I had had no leave of any sort since I got back from ITALY. The Ministry of Supply wrote me a very nice letter of thanks for my visits to factories.

The large-scale final rehearsals were to take place between 3rd and 5th May, and I determined to go away after that for a week. I was anxious to visit the Home Fleet at SCAPA,[36] and then I wanted to have a few days rest on the Scotch [*sic*] mountains.

9. I have had some interesting conversations with the War Office since I got back from ITALY. When I was an Army Commander with Eighth Army I used often to write home my views on tanks, organisation, and so on.[37]

But no attention was paid to my views.

Since I have been home I have been having <u>personal</u> talks, and I have been very emphatic on certain points. And I have given my views very firmly and clearly; in my diary will be found my D.O. letter on tanks to the D.C.I.G.S.,[38] and my address on artillery at LARKHILL.[39]

The real trouble is that there is no one in the War Office who is a really good soldier; there are many experts, but no good soldier in the wider sense of the word. The great exception is the C.I.G.S. (BROOKE) who is, in my opinion, the best soldier we have ever produced in ENGLAND; but he is far too busy to be able to bother about it.

The V.C.I.G.S. (NYE) is a very clever officer, but he knows nothing whatever about what goes on in battle.

The D.C.I.G.S. (WEEKS) is a very able business man in the T.A.; he knows nothing about what is needed to win battles.

The D.S.D. (STEELE) and the A.C.I.G.S. (EVETTS) are both useless in that respect.

The two people who have to deal with the business are NYE and WEEKS; they do not get their 'general advice' from good soldiers, and are completely in the hands of experts – who are not good soldiers. I keep telling them that they should get 'general advice' from a good soldier, before going to the experts for 'particular advice'.

I have recently made some progress, I think, with WEEKS in this respect; he is the most awfully nice person.

I have also put the whole subject very fully to the Secretary of State for War (Sir James GRIGG); I have the highest opinion of GRIGG; he is a man of firm courage, great integrity, and sterling character, and he has no political axe to grind; he says what he thinks and he stands by it; I like him immensely and would do anything for him.

10. I think a further trouble with those who work in the War Office is that they have not got the time to think the thing out clearly. They go about and get advice from too many people; very often the views they get are conflicting; and then they compromise; and then the trouble begins.

11. I believe that we want in the War Office a really experienced

senior officer to control the Directorates dealing with organisation and weapons. This officer must have had modern battle experience, i.e. in this war, and recently, on a variety of fronts; he must be a really good soldier in the wider sense; he must be a good judge of men; he must have time to think. The man for the job would be HORROCKS, who is now recovering from his wounds; he was a Corps Commander under me in AFRICA and knows his stuff well; on the other hand he is a very good commander and it may be we cannot spare him from the field.[40]

IWM, Montgomery Papers Part II, LMD 55/1

May

43
Letter to Army Commanders[1]

[Typescript]

4 May 1944

During the last four months, i.e, since I got back from Italy, it has been gradually brought home to me that there is a definite gulf in England between the armies and their supporting air forces. Of course I naturally compare the situation in England with that which obtained in the Allied Armies overseas. There the Army concerned and its Air Force were welded into one entity; the two HQ were always adjacent; and the spirit of unity went right down to the individual soldier and airman. These fine results were achieved only by a great deal of "give and take" on both sides; gradually mutual confidence and trust grew up, and the Army and its supporting Air Force became one fighting machine.

2. In England today the problem is somewhat different, since Armies are not actually fighting and being supported by their Air Forces. It is therefore not so easy to link them up into one entity – as one fighting machine.

But they can at least get to know each other, and get that understanding of each others problems which will be the firm foundation of mutual confidence and trust when we begin fighting.

3. From my own experience I am convinced that the following points are important if real unity is to be achieved between an Army and its supporting Air Force or Group:

(a) The two HQ, Army and Air, must be side by side, or adjacent.

(b) Army HQ may on occasions throw off a Tac HQ; but Main Army must always be with Air HQ.

(c) Army HQ must never plan a move of HQ without first consulting Air HQ. The deciding factor in the location of Main

97

Army will be whether it will suit Air HQ. There must be give and take on both sides; but the Army staff must realise that Air HQ requires to have telephone communication to airfields, and this is often the ruling factor in the location of the combined HQ.

(d) Before the Army staff initiates or takes any action the first question must always be: "How will this affect the air?"

The appropriate branch of the staff at Air HQ must be consulted especially on administrative matters.

The Chief of Staff at Army HQ, and the SASO at Air HQ, must be in constant touch at all times.

Similarly for the heads of the operations and intelligence staffs.

(e) This integration must be carried right down the scale to the regimental officers and men. At the lower end, the traffic policeman must recognise at once a flagged Air Force car, and accord it the usual facilities.

Formation and unit commanders, and the regimental officers and men, must be taught to realise that without the help of the air they cannot win the land battle; and they must understand the repercussions that follow from this statement of fact.

(f) On the air side, every pilot in air forces allotted specifically for the support of an Army, must realise that his sole job is to help the Army win the land battle; sometimes this involves fighting in the sky; at other times it involves coming right down and participating in the land battle by shooting up ground targets. This side of the problem is I know being tackled energetically by the air commanders.

4. I feel very strongly on the whole matter, and I know that we can achieve no real success unless each Army and its accompanying Air Force can weld itself into one entity.

Visiting each other occasionally, and having the odd meal together, will never achieve what is wanted; there is far more to it than that. The two HQ have got to set themselves down side by side, and work together as one team; that is the only way.

5. I wish Army Commanders to give this matter their personal attention. There is much to be done and not too much time in which to do it. We must not merely pay lip service to a principle;

we must put into practice the actual methods that will achieve success.

IWM, Montgomery Papers Part II, LMD 55/9

44
Montgomery's notes for 'Address on 15 May 1944: Brief Presentation of Plans before the King'[2]

[Typescript][3]

1. Object of OVERLORD.

2. General Eisenhower has charged me with the preparation and conduct of the land battle.

My HQ is an Allied HQ, exercising operational command and control over the land forces of the Allies.

There are 4 Armies under my command:

First American ⎫
Second British ⎬ Assault Armies.
Third American ⎫
First Canadian ⎬ Follow up.

3. <u>The intention.</u>

To assault simultaneously

(a) immediately north of the CARENTAN estuary.

(b) Between the CARENTAN estuary and the R. ORNE with the object of securing, as a base for further operations, a lodgement area which will include airfield sites and the port of CHERBOURG.

A port is essential for our administration; initially we want CHERBOURG and later HAVRE.

The Enemy.

4. Last February Rommel took command from HOLLAND to the LOIRE. It is now clear that his intention is to deny any penetration; <u>OVERLORD is to be defeated on the beaches.</u> To this end Rommel has:

(a) Thickened up the coastal crust.

(b) Increased the number of infantry divs not committed to beach defence, and allotted them in a lay back role to seal off any break in the coastal crust.

(c) Redistributed his armoured reserve.

5. There are now 60 enemy divisions in FRANCE, of which 10 are Panzer type. 12 are field infantry, mobile.

There are 4 Pz divs in or near the NEPTUNE area:

21 Pz	–	CAEN
12 SS	–	LISIEUX
17 SS	–	RENNES
Lehr Div	–	TOURS

6. The immediate situation is 5 divisions opposing initially:

Two coastal	–	one opposite each Army
One field Inf	–	ST. LO
One field Inf	–	COUTANCE
One Pz	–	CAEN (21)

By 1200 hrs D Day.

The Pz Division from LISIEUX could be on the scene (12 SS)

TOTAL – 6.

By dusk on D Day.

The Pz Div from RENNES could be appearing (17 SS)

(Ourselves 7 ⅔) We should be fighting hard against 6 divisions, with one more Pz Div from RENNES approaching – to be effective on D+1.

7. By dusk on D+1.

Two more Pz divisions can arrive:

One Pz – TOURS (Lehr)

One Pz – NANTES (116)

(Ourselves 10 ⅓) TOTAL 9 of which 5 are Pz.

8. <u>By D+2.</u>

(Ourselves 12)   Same number

But by now OVERLORD will have become an overriding menace requiring the concentration of all available formations that can be spared.
13 divisions may begin moving to the NEPTUNE area:

5 Pz (from AMIENS, TOULOUSE, BORDEAUX, SEDAN, BELGIUM).

8 Inf (from W. BRITTANY and PAS de CALAIS).

9. <u>By D+5.</u>

(Ourselves 15)   The 13 divisions mentioned in para. 8 may not yet all have arrived. But the enemy is beginning to have the necessary ingredients for a full scale counter-attack after proper recce and deployment – with infantry holding essential ground and 10 Pz divisions available for the blow. The full blooded counter-attack is likely at any time after D+6.

10. <u>By D+8.</u>

(Ourselves 18)   The total number of enemy divisions can now be up to 24 – of which 10 are Pz. The majority will be securing the vital ground forward of the lateral which links his front and which controls the essential routes and nodal centres.

The Pz divisions will have the mobile role to push us back into the sea.

11. Rommel is an energetic and determined commander; he has made a world of difference since he took over. He is best at the spoiling attack; his forte is disruption; he is too impulsive for the set-piece battle. He will do his level best to "DUNKIRK" us – not to fight the armoured battle on ground of his own choosing, but to avoid it altogether by

preventing our tanks landing by using his own tanks well forward.

On D Day he will try to:

(a) force us from the beaches.

(b) secure:–

CAEN

BAYEUX

CARENTAN

In relation to NEPTUNE his obsession is likely to be BAYEUX; this important nodal point splits our frontal landings in half.

If he can hold firm in the above three nodal points, we would be awkwardly placed.

12. Thereafter he will continue his counter-attacks. But as time goes on, he will combine them with a roping-off policy, and he must then hold firm on the important ground which dominates and controls the road axes in the "bocage" country.

The areas in question are:

(a) the high ground east of the R. DIVES.

(b) The high ground between FALAISE and ST LO, between the rivers ORNE and VIRE.

(c) The high ground west of the R. VIRE.

The Problem.

13. The enemy is in position, with reserves available.

There are obstacles and minefields on the beaches; we cannot gain contact with the obstacles and recce them.

There are many unknown hazards.

After a sea voyage, and landing on a strange coast, there is always some loss of cohesion.

14. We must time our assault so as to make things as easy as possible for the leading troops. Therefore we shall touch-down so that all obstacles are dry, and so that we have 30 minutes in which to deal with them before the incoming tide reaches them.

The Solution.

15. We have the initiative.

We must then rely on:–

(a) the violence of our assault.

(b) our great weight of supporting fire, from the sea and air.

(c) Simplicity.

(d) Robust mentality.

16. We must blast our way on shore and get a good lodgement before the enemy can bring sufficient reserves up to turn us out. Armoured columns must penetrate deep inland, and quickly, on D day; this will upset the enemy plans and tend to hold him off while we build up our strength.

We must gain space rapidly, and peg out claims well inland.

And while we are engaged in doing this the air must hold the ring, and must hinder and make very difficult the movement of enemy reserves by train or road towards the lodgement area. The land battle will be a terrific party and we will require the full support of the air all the time, and laid on quickly.

17. Once we can get control of the main enemy lateral GRANDVILLE–VIRE–ARGENTAN–FALAISE–CAEN, and the area enclosed in it is firmly in our possession, then we will have the lodgement area we want and can begin to expand.

Army Tasks.

18. First U.S. Army (front of 3 combat teams)

Second British Army (front of 5 Inf Bdes)

First Canadian Army

Third U.S. Army

Commandos and Airborne Troops.

Development of Operations.

19. Up to D+90.

Morale.

20. We shall have to send the soldiers in to this party "seeing red". We must get them completely on their toes; having absolute faith in the plan; and embued [*sic*] with infectious optimism and offensive eagerness. Nothing must stop them. If we send them in to battle in this way – then we shall succeed. Leading troops must be very lightly equipped.

IWM, Montgomery Papers Part II, LMD 55/16

45
Montgomery's diary notes, 15–16 May 1944

[Typescript]

15 May.

20. Supreme H.Q. staged a final presentation of plans on this day.

It was held at my H.Q. in London (St. Paul's School) and was attended by The King, the Prime Minister, General SMUTS, and the British Chiefs of Staff.

I had to explain the general Army plan, and a copy of my address is filed with this diary.

Throughout the day EISENHOWER was quite excellent; he spoke very little, but what he said was good and on a high level. The King also spoke before he left; he made an absolutely first-class speech, quite short, and exactly right.

At the end of the day SMUTS spoke, and also Winston CHURCHILL. The latter was in very good form and seems to have recovered; when I last saw him on 7 April he looked very ill (see para 3);[4] but today he was quite a different person and was full of life.

21. In the evening I had dinner alone with the C.I.G.S. (BROOKE).[5] He put me fully into the picture as to what was going on. He is definitely worried about ALEXANDER[6] in ITALY; the trouble is that ALEXANDER is quite unfit to hold high command and he has to have a very good Chief of Staff who will run the show for him; it seems that HARDING[7] is not good enough and things are not going well.

I gave it as my opinion that the trouble is not HARDING – who is quite first-class. The trouble is ALEXANDER – who is very definitely third-class as a high commander. It will be very interesting to see when the P.M., and others, discover that ALEXANDER is no good. He might be compared with HINDENBERG;[8] he has to have someone to tell him what to do, and then to do it for him; he does not know himself anything about it, he cannot give a decision, and he gives his staff no clear guidance. So long as I was with him I ran the battles for him, and we won; when CLARK[9] of Fifth American Army was fighting the results were poor, as CLARK is not experienced and

ALEXANDER could not help him; the final CASSINO battle[10] was handled by LEESE and EIGHTH ARMY and was a success, as LEESE is very good.

[16 May][11]

22. I had lunch with SMUTS; his son was there, a young Major in the Sappers and a most charming lad.

23. SMUTS is worried that we may lose the peace. BRITAIN, with American aid, won the Great War of 1914/18; but when it was over we were tired and we stood back, allowing FRANCE to take first place in EUROPE; the result was the present war.

We cannot allow EUROPE to disintegrate; EUROPE requires a structure – a framework on which to rebuild itself – and a good structure must have a firm core.

FRANCE has failed dismally.

BRITAIN must stand forward as the corner stone of the new structure; nations that want security and peace must range themselves on the side of BRITAIN; there can be no more neutrals.

It is BRITAIN that stood alone and then, with American help, stemmed the tide. BRITAIN is a continental nation. BRITAIN must remain strong; we must keep up small, but highly efficient forces which are capable of rapid expansion; the keynote of the armed force necessary in peace time must be air power; the Army can be relatively small.

24. SMUTS said that statesmen cannot always say things like this. He said that I had made a great name, and would make a greater one still. I could say practically what I liked; my position with the public in ENGLAND was secure and they would 'swallow' whatever I said.

He was emphatic that, when the war was nearly over, I must speak out and say these things; he said I must give the lead in the matter.

25. This rather startled me. I am not convinced it is right for the soldier to lay down the law on such matters; it is more the sphere of the statesman. However, it gives one food for thought.

IWM, Montgomery Papers Part II, LMD 55/1

46
Letter from Major-General Sir Hastings Ismay to Montgomery

[Typescript]

17 May 1944

The Prime Minister has asked me to tell you that he was much concerned by some of the statements made at last Monday's Conference[12] on the subject of administrative arrangements for OVERLORD. He was told, for example, that 2,000 officers and clerks were to be taken over to keep records, and he was given a statement (copy attached) which shows that at D plus 20 there will be one vehicle to every 4.84 men.

The Prime Minister would like to have a discussion with you and your staff on the whole question of the British tail, and he wonders whether it would be convenient to you to have this before dinner at your Headquarters next Friday, 19th May.[13]

Enclosure:

From: DACOS (Mov. & Tn.)[14]

	U.S.		BRITISH		TOTAL	
	Vehicles	Personnel	Vehicles	Personnel	Vehicles	Personnel
D+20	96,000	452,000	93,000	450,000	189,000	902,000
D+60	197,000	903,000	168,000	800,000	365,000	1,703,000

Plus replacement of casualties

IWM, Montgomery Papers Part I, BLM 120/14

47
Letter from Field Marshal Sir Alan Brooke to Montgomery, forwarding a copy of a letter from Lieutenant-General K. Stuart, Chief of Staff at the Canadian Military Headquarters in London, to Brooke

[Carbon copy]

18 May 1944

I attach a copy of a letter I have just received from Stuart.

The matter he refers to is one which I feel can easily be put right. Could you discuss with Crerar and then have a word with Eisenhower.[15]

Liddell Hart Centre for Military Archives, Alanbrooke Papers 6/2/25

Enclosure:
Letter from Lieutenant-General K. Stuart to Field Marshal Sir Alan Brooke

[Typescript copy]

18 May 1944

I hesitate at this time to worry you with such matters as the subject of this letter and I do so only in the hope that by raising the point now we can avoid any embarrassing incidents occurring in the future.[16]

As you know I am not anxious to tie any strings to Canadian Formations cooperating with those of the U.K. or the U.S. There is one string, however, that we must insist upon and that is the right of reference to the Canadian Government of our senior commander in any theatre. The corollary to this is that in the Western European theatre of operations Harry Crerar serves, in a sense, in a dual capacity. He commands the First Canadian Army and he is also the Canadian national representative in respect to all Canadian Formations and Units serving operationally in that theatre even though some may not be under his operational command. This dual role is inescapable because the Canadian Government quite rightly holds the senior Canadian Commander in any theatre responsible for all Canadian Formations and Units employed operationally in that theatre.

I know that you and your assistants at the War Office understand and recognize our special position in this regard.

A recent event suggests to me that perhaps 21 Army Group and S.H.A.E.F. do not recognize our special position and consider that Harry Crerar has no responsibility for Canadian Formations and Units that are not directly under his operational command.

I refer to a recent visit by General Eisenhower to 3 Cdn Inf Div. This was arranged presumably by 21 Army Group through Second Army and I Corps. Crerar knew nothing about it until he was advised by the Div Comdr.[17] It is quite true that on the grounds of correct military procedure the proper channel of communication was followed, but the mere fact that Crerar was not even notified either by 21 Army Group or S.H.A.E.F. suggests that his special position has not been appreciated by either of the Headquarters mentioned.

The actual event itself is of no importance. I raise it simply because it indicates a position that, I feel, should be corrected before active operations begin.

I hope you do not misunderstand me. As you know Harry and I and the whole Canadian Army have complete confidence in the commanders concerned. All I ask is that Harry's responsibility for all Canadians in the theatre, whether under his actual command or not, be recognised by 21 Army Group and by S.H.A.E.F. The application of this recognition would not involve any interference in the normal chain of command, it would merely call for consultation in the pre-planning stage.

I am sure you will agree that Montgomery should discuss this matter with Crerar at an early date in order to clear up any misunderstanding before the show starts. Montgomery would then be in a position to explain to S.H.A.E.F.

I feel that explanation is all that is necessary, hence the above suggestion.

IWM, Montgomery Papers Part II, LMD 55/23

48
Letter to Field Marshal Sir Alan Brooke

[Typescript]

19 May 1944

1. The implications of the manpower situation on 21 Army Group are going to be very serious. We are already short of over 13,000 men of our WE plus authorised reinforcements even before we commence fighting, and the situation will deteriorate and not improve. In these circumstances I wonder whether the training establishments and schools in this country have been sufficiently rigorously combed to give up all the fit personnel which they could adequately afford to do.

2. In my opinion, once 21 Army Group has gone overseas, it will have little or no need of many schools in this country, and there

will be few, if any, troops in this country to make use of them. For instance I do not consider that the Army Group will require to send any men to Battle Schools. The best training for battle is actual fighting, and I never found in the Eighth Army any necessity for a Battle School, nor did I send personnel away to one. There are undoubtedly other instances of a similar nature.

3. I understand also that there is a certain overlapping between existing schools, such as for instance between the Armoured Corps School and the Recce Corps School. Surely whatever may be the policy after the war, the time has now come for the period at any rate of the present emergency, to close down and amalgamate all schools which overlap, or which will not be fully used. After the war we may be able once more to afford these luxuries.

4. To carry out such a drastic pruning of schools as I consider the seriousness of the present manpower situation would warrant, I suggest that you should appoint an independent and battle experienced officer who will approach the problem from the point of view of the needs of the Army in the field.[18] Such an officer as B.G. Horrocks would do the job very well. He would obviously require suitable terms of reference such as I have outlined above.

5. The gist of the matter is this.

When the army goes overseas in Overlord we cannot possibly want all the schools we now have. Many vested interests are involved.

Therefore, would you consider an investigation by an outside authority?[19]

IWM, Montgomery Papers Part I, BLM 115/3

49
Montgomery's diary notes, 19 May 1944

[Typescript]

<u>19 May.</u>

27. Winston CHURCHILL, the Prime Minister of England, came to dinner. We talked on many subjects and I expressed to him my confidence in the successful outcome of our operations.[20] I gave him a copy of the final talk I am giving to the senior officers of all

the Armies;[21] he was very taken with it and said he would circulate it as a Cabinet paper.

IWM, Montgomery Papers Part II, LMD 55/1

50
Letter to Field Marshal Sir Alan Brooke

[Holograph]

20 May 1944

I have your letter of 18 May, sending me on Stewarts [*sic*] letter re the Canadians. I will talk to Crerar on the subject, and will let Eisenhower know the form.

The "special position" referred to by Stewart is very well realized, and no one would dream of going against it – certainly not myself, who have probably had more experience than most in dealing with Dominion soldiers. I have discussed the whole matter at great length with Mackenzie King, and he agreed completely with my general line of action with Dominion troops.[22]

But the idea that commanders cannot pay friendly visits anywhere they like without advising the whole place is quite frightful. Nor has Crerar any operational responsibility for Canadian troops serving in another Army; nor could he possibly be consulted about it when we are all fighting hard in Europe.

Harry has much to learn about what goes on in battle. I will discuss the whole matter with him.

Yrs ever

Monty.

P.S.

I may say that Harry took Mackenzie King to visit 5 Cdn DIV on 18 May and never told Dempsey!!

Liddell Hart Centre for Military Archives, Alanbrooke Papers 6/2/25

51
Letter to Lieutenant-General K. Stuart

[Typescript]

26 May 1944

I am so glad we had that talk last night; it cleared the air and we now know how we stand.

I understand your viewpoint very clearly. You understand my viewpoint, and I have explained to you my technique of "grouping".

We all want to win the war as soon as we can.

I admit the right of Crerar to refer any point to his Government, whenever he likes – through you I presume.

I admit that Crerar is responsible for the general welfare and administration of all Canadian troops in the theatre of war.

I do NOT admit that Crerar has any operational responsibility for Canadian troops serving temporarily in another Army.

I do NOT admit that Crerar has any special right to be consulted by me when making my plans for battle – apart from the normal consultation I would have with all my Army Comds at any time.

We discussed all this together yesterday and you expressed your complete agreement with the above points.[23]

I am a great friend of Canada and you can trust me to look well after the interests of all Canadian troops. Actually I am not a bad person to trust as I have some small practical knowledge of the business – and Crerar has none!! But the great point is that we are all very good friends and we all want to get this business finished off as soon as we can.

Thank you again for coming to see me.[24]

IWM, Montgomery Papers Part II, LMD 55/23

52
Montgomery's diary notes, 26 May 1944

[Typescript]

26 May.

31. I have had to be firm with STUART, who is Chief of Staff at Canadian Military H.Q. in LONDON. He wrote a letter to the C.I.G.S. about CRERAR's right to be consulted in the planning stages; I have a feeling that CRERAR put him up to it.

In my reply I made it quite clear that I could not admit that CRERAR had any operational responsibility for Canadian troops serving temporarily in another Army.

I have put the correspondence in the file.

There is no doubt that the national and political feeling is very strong in the Canadian senior ranks. My view is that what people really want is victories, and they will put all national feelings into the background till the war is over in order to get victories.

It is victories that win wars and not public opinion.[25]

IWM, Montgomery Papers Part II, LMD 55/1

53

Letter from General Dwight D. Eisenhower to Montgomery
[Typescript]
26 May 1944

I have just read the notes that you use as a basis of your talks to Senior Commanders.[26] To say that I am enthusiastic about them is merely understatement. You have hit exactly the right note and have punched home your points perfectly.

So far I have seen a total of twenty-two divisions and am visiting two or three more on Monday. I have been to twenty-one air fields and visited four major units of the Fleet. I wish I could do more but my commitments simply will not permit. However, no matter where I go I have found the most beneficial results from your own visits, and there is no doubt in my mind that everything that one man can do to make this a success you are doing.[27] I will see you soon.

IWM, Montgomery Papers Part II, LMD 114/1

June

54

Montgomery's diary notes, 1–3 June 1944

[Typescript]

<u>1 June.</u>

36. I had a final conference of my four Army Commanders at 1900. They all stayed to dinner and we had a very cheery evening.[1]

<u>2 June.</u>

37. I addressed all officers of Main H.Q. in the morning, at SOUTHWICK HOUSE, near PORTSMOUTH.

   In the afternoon I drove to LONDON and addressed all officers of Rear H.Q. and the L. of C., in the Kings Theatre, Hammersmith.

38. EISENHOWER dined quietly with me. I do like him tremendously; he is so very genuine and sincere.

   After dinner we went up to SOUTHWICK HOUSE and had a conference with the Met experts[2] on the weather – at 2130 hours. The weather prospects are as follows:

(a) <u>Sea.</u> This is good and calm seas should rule for about a week, with nothing greater than Force 4 to Force 5 – and that only in mid-channel. Winds will be warmer than of late and be from the S.W., so the Neptune beaches should be quite calm.

(b) <u>Air.</u> This is not so good because a depression off ICELAND is likely to produce low clouds, down to about 800 feet, especially in the early mornings from about 0300 hours and up to 1000 hours. This would make the airborne operations difficult, and especially the landing of gliders.

It was decided to lay on the whole operation; the next Met conference to be at 2130 hours on 3 June.

39. The Prime Minister decided to spend the week-end in the PORTSMOUTH area, on his train, and to spend the time visiting everything he could.

I immediately got on to Supreme H.Q. and asked them to try and stop him coming; I also spoke to the C.I.G.S.

The real point is that at this last stage we do all want to be left alone, and no one has any time to devote to organising tours for Prime Ministers. Furthermore, there is the danger of drawing attention to this area; the cover plan is that we are going across the Straits of DOVER to the Pas de CALAIS, and the best place for the P.M. to go would be DOVER – if he cannot stay quietly at CHEQUERS or in LONDON.

He also wants to go to sea in a cruiser and see the assault and the bombardment on D day; wherever he is he must be an embarassment [sic] and a liability, and might compromise success in that area; I hope the Cabinet will not allow him to go.

Quite apart from everything else, he is too valuable and should not take such risks; if anything were to happen to him we should be in a bad position. His own good sense and judgment may prevail over his great fighting spirit, but I doubt it!!

3 June.

40. The Prime Minister arrived yesterday in his train; all attempts to stop him were quite useless. He must know that it was I who tried to stop him, and I shall not be popular!!

41. The weather forecast is not so good. The depression over ICELAND is spreading to the South, and the high pressure system which was coming up this way from the AZORES is now being pushed back. So the chance of a good belt of high pressure over the channel area is now receding.

All this is awkward, and some very big decisions may be necessary. My own view is that if the sea is calm enough for the Navy to take us there, then we must go; the air has had very good weather for all its preparatory operations, and we must accept that it may not be able to do so well on D day.

GENERAL REMARKS.

42. We are now on the eve of the Second Front. The weather forecast does not look too good, and tomorrow, 4 June, will be an interesting day; at 0800 hours tomorrow the final decision must be taken, and once taken must be stuck to; everything will be at sea,

and if it is to be turned back, it must be turned back then. Strong and resolute characters will be very necessary.

43. I came home from the Eighth Army in ITALY in January. The last five months have been a strenuous and very difficult time; few really know how difficult it has been, and one hopes that it never will be known.

Initially I had some friction with the War Office as they did not understand the tempo at which I and my staff are accustomed to work; the robust methods of the Eighth Army were not popular in Whitehall, where indecision generally rules.

Another trouble was there was no one in the War Office, or in fact anywhere else, who really knew much about the battle end of the problem. <u>WE</u> did know, and said what was wanted in no uncertain voice. Certain of my enemies undoubtedly tried to create trouble and friction.

44. But all difficulties and troubles were overcome.

I think that there is no doubt that I and my staff were largely to blame for any friction that arose; we were intolerant and too pushful; though we did have a difficult job and not too much time in which to do it. The Secretary of State for War (GRIGG) and the C.I.G.S. (BROOKE) have both been very good, and have been most helpful and very tolerant of myself. I have tried hard to be restrained, but at times it has been not easy. Now it is all over and we are off on the great adventure; as one thinks back over the last five months it is clear to me that the War Office has been quite first-class in doing what we wanted; WEEKS has been a tower of strength on all occasions. The War Office itself has had its own troubles and difficulties with other Government Departments, and I do not think we always realised that.

45. The great lesson I have learnt is that the War Office, and the C-in-C and his staff, are together a team; they must all pull together, and work in closely with each other.

I wrote a letter to the Secretary of State,[3] and thanked him, and all under him, for what had been done by the War Office; the letter is filed with this diary.[4]

IWM, Montgomery Papers Part II, LMD 55/1

55
Montgomery's diary notes, 4–7 June 1944

[Typescript}

4 June.

1. By 2130 hrs. last night, 3 June, the weather forecast had become very bad; it was the worst forecast we had had since we began to consider the weather 6 weeks ago. It looked as if D day could not be on 5 June; the forecast gave winds of Force 6 and 10/10 of cloud, with many of our airfields put out and the enemy airfields remaining operational.

One Force was already at sea. Another Force was due to sail at midnight 3/4 June.

I urged that we should not definitely postpone until the last moment.

So we decided to meet again at 0430 hrs. today, 4 June.

2. We all met again at 0430 hrs. today. The previous forecast was confirmed and it was now quite clear that the operation could not take place tomorrow;[5] it was therefore postponed 24 hours, i.e., until Tuesday 6 June.

3. I saw the Naval C.-in-C. during the morning, and the Chief of Staff to Eisenhower,[6] and gave my views as follows:

(a) We must try and carry out the operation this week. If we failed to do so it would have to go back to the next favourable tides, i.e. about 18 June which was a dark period with no moon. The troops would all have to be disembarked; they had all been briefed and security would be difficult.

(b) We must decide <u>tonight</u> whether D day was to be 6 June, or to be Wed. 7 June; this extra time would enable the troops to get off the craft, and have exercise.

(c) If 7 June proves impossible I was prepared to carry it out on 8 June or on 9 June.

That gave a range of five days. After 9 June was not possible, as it gave too short a fighting day and para-troops would be too long without assistance.

(d) If we were forced back to the dark period in Mid-June, then we must plan to have a range of six days for the operation. To have only three days is not enough.

4. We met again at 2100 hours to consider the weather. A great change had occurred; the present depression had passed over quickly and the Met experts were prepared to almost guarantee good weather conditions from midnight tonight up to the forenoon of Tuesday 6 June. After that time on 6 June the weather might deteriorate again.

We decided to make D day the 6 of June. This would at least get us on shore and enable us to get our teeth into the enemy. We agreed to meet again at 0415 hrs. 5 June to confirm finally.

5 June.

5. We met at 0415 hrs. There was no change in the weather forecast, except that conditions on 6 June and following days were likely to be better than stated yesterday; the depression that might have caused bad weather was moving away up towards Iceland.

We confirmed D day for 6 June.

6. I went up to Hindhead in the evening and took most of my belongings to Amesbury School (Major and Mrs. Reynolds) which is my home in England. These included my diaries, from the day I arrived in Egypt in August 1942 to command the Eighth Army, up to the 3 June 1944; these diaries cover the whole of the campaign in Africa, the campaign in Sicily, the campaign in Italy up to 31 Dec. 1943, and all the preparations for opening the Second Front; they are very personal and very confidential, and are also very historic.[7]

7. The night 5/6 June was fine and reasonably free from low cloud. The wind dropped and the sea was not too rough for our purposes.

6 June.

8. This is D day.

Airborne landings were carried out as planned; three airborne Divisions were put into France:

$\left.\begin{array}{l} 82 \\ 101 \end{array}\right\}$ U.S. Divisions in COTENTIN peninsula.

6 Br. Division to the N.E. of CAEN.

Parachute Bdes. were dropped first and then each Division had 50 gliders brought in before dawn, with anti-tank guns and H.Q., etc., etc.

All objectives of the airborne troops were secured; and on the east flank the 6 Br. Div. secured the bridges north of CAEN intact – which was excellent. Only 30 aircraft were lost.

9. H hour for the land armies was from 0700 to 0745 hrs.

By 0830 hrs. all the five assault Bdes. of Second British Army were on shore, including the Bde. H.Q., and the build-up was going well. On the American First Army front reports were good, but no firm news came in early as the U.S. Armies do not use J, or Phantom.[8]

10. By the afternoon it was clear that all three British assault Divisions were on shore, and the 4 U.S. Div. on the UTAH beaches.

The situation of 5 U.S. Corps on OMAHA beaches was not so clear – in fact it looked very bad. I decided to cross over to France and take charge of the land battle.[9]

I left Portsmouth at 2230 hrs. in H.M.S. FAULKNOR, a fast destroyer.

7 June.

11. I arrived at 0600 hrs. at the American cruiser AUGUSTA, on which BRADLEY (First American Army Comd.) had his H.Q. He gave me his situation, which was good at UTAH but very bad at OMAHA.

I gave him orders that as the resistance was stronger than expected, and his progress on D day had not been so rapid as had been hoped, he must now work to link up his two lodgement areas by securing CARENTAN and ISIGNY. After that he must thrust west from the UTAH sector and secure LA HAYE DU PUITS, thus cutting off the Cherbourg peninsula. We would then deal with the enemy in the COTENTIN by bombing and go for Cherbourg as a more methodical operation which would take longer than we had previously thought.

12. I then went on and met DEMPSEY (Second British Army Comd.) and Admiral VIAN[10] and had a good talk with them. On Second Army beaches all was going well and the original plan was being worked to; BAYEUX and PORT-EN-BESSIN were captured and 50 Div. got astride the road CAEN–BAYEUX about midway between these places.

CAEN was not captured and it was clear that the enemy intended to hold it strongly and to try and drive in my eastern flank.

13. I went back to see Bradley again in the evening.[11]

   I spent the night on H.M.S. FAULKNOR.[12]

   My cipher messages M1 and M2 give the situation.[13]

IWM, Montgomery Papers Part II, LMD 59/1

56
Message (M1)[14] to Major-General F.W. de Guingand

[Typescript]

7 June, 1130 hours[15]

For Chief of Staff from General Montgomery (.) Have seen BRADLEY and DEMPSEY (.) situation as follows (.) Para 1 (.) UTAH landings good and 4 DIV lodgement area about 5 miles deep with 82 and 101 DIVS further to WEST and SOUTH (.) Para 2 (.) OMAHA not so good and lodgement area about 2 miles deep (.) much fighting took place on the beaches and considerable casualties suffered in personnel and vehicles and craft (.) infantry of five regiments now on shore but short of artillery and supporting weapons (.) Para 3 (.) Second Army situation good (.) 50 DIV yesterday secured area ARRAMANCHES–BAZENVILLE–COULOMBS–VAUX SUR AURE–LONGUES and attacking BAYEUX yesterday (.) Canadians are astride road BAYEUX–CAEN in area BRETTEVILLE 9272 and are moving southwards (.) 3 DIV secured OUISTRHAIN and BIEVILLE and advancing on CAEN today (.) all above Divisions of Second Army complete with artillery and armd bdes (.) 6 Airborne DIV in area BAVENT–ST HONORINE 0971–RANVILLE–AMFREVILLE and has blown bridges at TROARN (.) SS Bde[16] secured VARRAVILLE–FRANCEVILLE and moving on CABOURG (.) Para 4 (.) appears likely 21 Pz DIV intends to hold CAEN (.) Para 5 (.) have given orders as follows (.) BRADLEY to secure his D day objective and in particular to capture CARENTAN and ISIGNY so as to link up his two lodgement areas (.) then to thrust towards LA HAYE DU PUITS and thus cut off the CHERBOURG peninsula (.) meanwhile enemy troops in peninsula to be dealt with by air action (.) CHERBOURG to be captured after above action is completed (.) Para 6 (.) DEMPSEY to proceed relentlessly with the original plan (.) he will hold a flank on the River DIVES and capture CAEN and BAYEUX (.) he will then pivot on CAEN and swing his right forward (.) likely that 51 DIV will cut in behind CAEN moving east of River ORNE (.) Para 7 (.) the two armies to join up at PORT EN BESSIN (.) DO NOT want US troops brought in through Second Army beaches.

IWM, Montgomery Papers Part I, BLM 110/1

57
Message (M3) to General Dwight D. Eisenhower
[Typescript]
8 June 1944, 2000 hours
Personal for EISENHOWER from MONTGOMERY (.) To-day has been spent in repelling attacks in the CAEN sector and in cleaning up centres of resistance still existing inside our lodgement area (.) on the left all our gains have been held (.) in the centre the two armies have now joined hands (.) on the right progress has been made towards ISIGNY and CARENTAN (.) build up is going on well (.) as a guess prisoners total about 6000 and include Germans Russians Poles and some Japanese and two Turks (.) Germans have fought well but the others surrender freely (.) am organising strong thrust south towards VILLERS BOCAGE and EVRECY (.) am very satisfied with situation (.)

IWM, Montgomery Papers Part I, BLM 110/3

58
Letter to Major-General F.E.W. Simpson[17]
[Holograph]
8 June 1944
You may like the following news of our battle.
1. There is no doubt that the Germans were surprised, and we got on shore before they had recovered. The speed, power, and violence of the assault carried all before it.
2. Generally, the beach obstacles presented no difficulty; where they were troublesome it was because of the rough weather – and on some beaches it was pretty rough.

3. <u>D.D. Tanks.</u>

(a) Used successfully on UTAH beaches.

(b) Failed to reach the shore on OMAHA beaches and all sank – too rough.

(c) Were not launched on 50 DIV front as it was too rough; were landed "dry"[18] behind the leading flights; casualties to AVRE sappers high as a result, and to leading infantry.

(d) Landed "dry" on Canadian front.

(e) Used successfully on 3 DIV front.

Generally it can be said that the DD tanks proved their value, and casualties were high when they could not be used.

4. As a guess prisoners about 6000 so far. They consist of Germans, Russians, Poles, Japanese, and two Turks.

5. British casualties about 1000 per assault Division.

American casualties not known.

High proportion of officer casualties, due to sniping behind our front.

Two Inf. Bde. Comds wounded:

Cunningham[19] 9 Bde

Senior[20] 151 Bde

Great many Inf C.O.'s killed, including HERDON,[21] o.c. 2 Warwicks.

No general officers are casualties.

6. The Germans are fighting well; Russians, Poles, Japanese, and Turks, run away; and if unable to do so, surrender.

7. Our initial attack was on a wide front, and there were gaps between landings. The impetus of the assault carried us some way inland and many defended localities were by-passed; these proved very troublesome later. In one case a complete German Bn, with artillery, was found inside 50 DIV area; it gave some trouble but was eventually collected in (about 500 men). There is still one holding out – the radar station west of DOUVRES; it is very strong and is held by stout-hearted Germans.

8. Sniping in back areas has been very troublesome, as a result of para 7.

The roads have been far from safe and we have lost several good officers.

I have been all right myself, though I have toured the area all day.

There have been women snipers, presumably wives of German soldiers; the Canadians shot 4 women snipers.

9. The Germans are doing everything they can to hold on to CAEN. I have decided not to have a lot of casualties by butting up against the place; so I have ordered Second Army to keep up a good pressure at CAEN, and to make its main effort towards VILLERS BOCAGE and EVRECY and thence S.E. towards FALAISE.

10. First US Army had a very sticky party at OMAHA, and its progress at UTAH has not been rapid.

I have therefore ordered it to join up its two lodgement areas and to secure CARENTAN and ISIGNY. It will then thrust towards LA HAYE DU PUITS and cut off the Cherbourg peninsula.

11. The two armies have now joined hands east of BAYEUX.

No time for more.

Yrs. ever

B.L. Montgomery.

P.S.

The country here is very nice; green fields; very good crops; plenty of vegetables; cows & cattle; chickens, ducks, etc.

The few civilians there are appear well fed; the children look healthy; the people have good boots and clothing.

The locals did not believe the British would ever invade France or come over the Channel; they say that the German officers and men thought this also – which may account for the tactical surprise we got.

B.L.M.

0900 hrs

9 June

P.S.

I enclose a copy of a letter sent today to my Chief of Staff. This will give you my situation and my future intentions. It is of course very secret; please acknowledge receipt personally to me by wireless – of M500.[22]

B.L.M.

IWM, Simpson Papers

59
Letter (M500)[23] to Major-General F.W. de Guingand

[Typescript]

9 June 1944[24]

I have your letter 23351 of 8 June, and will deal with your paras first.[25]

Para 1.   Tac HQ now going well.

Para 2.   Bad weather has much delayed build-up through beaches. But situation very satisfactory on the whole.

Para 3 ⎫
Para 4 ⎭   Bomb line situation not easy. Leading troops have been shot up a good deal by our own aircraft, which of course cannot be helped. I think the bomb line has got to be a bit out just at present; enemy facing our troops must be dealt with by artillery, etc.; air must stop enemy build-up.

Later on when air groups get established alongside Army HQ, then the integration will be closer and the bomb line can be brought in. I do not want to force the bomb line issue just at present; the troops are mostly new to fighting and we do not want to create a loss of confidence in the air.

Para 5.   Noted.

Para 6.   Port-en-Bessin is now in our hands.

Para 8 ⎫
Para 9 ⎭   Noted.

Para 10.   Noted.

2. My present situation is as follows:

1 Corps Line
FRANCEVILLE–BAVENT–SANNERVILLE–BIEVILLE–BURON–BRETTEVILLE.

30 Corps Line
BRONAY–BLARY – one mile west of BAYEUX.

5 US Corps
From Bayeux westwards along river line to ISIGNY (not yet captured).

7 US Corps
CARETAN CANAL about 4488–VINDELONDE 3387–
FRESVILLE–ST MARCOUF 3703.

3. The whole line is joined up and is one front from
FRANCEVILLE to ISIGNY. There is still a gap between the two
American Corps across the CARETAN estuary, but I hope this
will be closed by tomorrow.

There is free communication by road through PORT-EN-
BESSIN to V Corps HQ at ST LAURENT-SUR-MER 6789.

4. The enemy is acting as follows:

A. Trying to hold me off from CAEN and drive in my eastern
   flank. He is using for this:
       711 Div
       346 Div
       21 Pz Div
   He is achieving no success and is being held very well; we are
   very firm on this flank and our [*sic*] holding tight.

B. Trying to thrust northwards across the road CAEN–
   BAYEUX about BRETTEVILLE and push me back to the
   R. SEULLES. I have got a lot of armour sitting pretty behind
   the junction of 50 DIV and Canadian DIV and I think we shall
   prevent any enemy penetration here. He is using for this:
       12 Pz Div
       LEHR Div.

C. Further to the West the enemy is not being offensive. He is
   trying to stop the expansion of the lodgement areas of 5 US
   Corps and 7 US Corps – and not very successfully. He is using
   352 DIV but there cannot be much left of this.

D. On the north flank of 7 US Corps he is trying to thrust in
   towards ST MERE EGLISE, but this is being held.

5. My intentions are as follows:

A. On American front.
   To join up the two lodgement areas. To thrust west and capture
   LA HAYE DU PUITS and seal off the CHERBOURG area.
   On 5 Corps front, to thrust south and secure CAUMONT,
   and establish a line from CAUMONT – westwards to the
   R. VIRE about AIREL 5074 – thence across to CARENTAN.

B. <u>On British front – 30 Corps.</u>
To secure the road triangle just east of TILLY-SUR-
SEULLES 8368; this is being done today by 8 Armd Bde.
To launch 7 Armd Div tomorrow southwards through
BAYEUX to secure VILLERS BOCAGE and NOYERS 8762
and then EVRECY; then to exploit to the S.E.

C. <u>On 1 Corps front.</u>
To pass 51 DIV across R. ORNE, through 6 Airborne DIV, to
attack southwards east of CAEN towards CAGNY 1163.

D. To put down 1 Airborne DIV somewhere south of CAEN
as a big air hook, and to link up with it from EVRECY and
CAGNY.
This is being worked out now; I would want the whole
Division, which should get ready to load now; the Bde standing
by to come over at short notice can now be cancelled.

6. I shall work gradually on the intentions given in para 5.

If the Germans wish to be offensive and drive in our lodgement
area between CAEN and BAYEUX, the best way to defeat them
is to be offensive ourselves – and the plan given in B, C and D of
para 5 will checkmate the enemy completely if we can pull it off.

7. It will take a few days to carry out this general plan but I give it
some way ahead so as to show you what I am aiming at.

I do not expect we shall want 1 Airborne DIV for 3 days or
more. I then want to get 6 Airborne DIV home to UK as soon as
possible, ready for use again in 3 weeks or so.

8. I have got Bill's intelligence note.[26]

9. I am very well satisfied with the general situation.

10. Tell Eisenhower my plans.

11. Acknowledge receipt of this by most immediate signal.

IWM, Montgomery Papers Part I, BLM 126/1

60
Message (M6) to General Dwight D. Eisenhower[27]

[Typescript]
9 June 1944, 1930 hours
Personal for EISENHOWER from MONTGOMERY (.) 5 U S
Corps captured ISIGNY and is within two miles of CARENTAN (.)

7 U S Corps within two miles of CARENTAN on north side (.) First Army is doing well (.) am directing left of First Army on CAUMONT (.) Second Army will attack with its right tomorrow to secure area TILLY–EVRECY–VILLERS BOCAGE (.) am very satisfied with the way battle is going.

IWM, Montgomery Papers Part II, LMD 59/3

61
Message (M10) to General Dwight D. Eisenhower[28]
[Typescript]
10 June 1944, 1835 hours
Personal for EISENHOWER from MONTGOMERY (.) lodgement area now 60 miles long from FRANCEVILLE on east to MONTEBOURG 15 miles SE of CHERBOURG (.) today joined up as one continuous front as 5 and 7 Corps have made contact (.) it is being deepened and at same time being extended NW towards CHERBOURG (.) 30 Corps attack towards VILLERS BOCAGE going well (.) am very pleased with todays operations

IWM, Montgomery Papers Part I, BLM 110/7

62
Letter to Major-General F.W. de Guingand
[Holograph]
10 June 1944
I cannot possibly come out to Ramsay's ship tomorrow; nor is there any need for me to do so; for me, beyond the pleasure of seeing Ramsay, it would be a waste of time.[29]

You have my letter sent by Johnnie,[30] and my intentions and plans will now be quite clear to you.

It is quite impossible to send any commandos back yet.[31]

I am directing the left of First Army on CAUMONT as a first priority; then ST LO next.

Everything is going very well and I am well satisfied. The Canadians are a bit jumpy just at present, but they will settle down as they gain experience.

I have issued enclosed Personal Message.[32] Give it to the press your end, and have it given out by the BBC. Send copies to Second

JUNE

Army Main for distribution to Second Army formations still in England; and send a copy to First Canadian Army.

Do not let any V.I.P.'s visit me, or anyone not actually concerned with the operation on land i.e. War Office P.M. 'B'[33] etc, etc. I have two Army Commanders[34] who have never commanded Armies in battle before, and a large number of inexperienced Divisions and Generals, and my time is very fully occupied; I have no time to spare for visitors. I would like to see Miles Graham, and also Slap White.[35]

The roads have been far from safe, due to snipers left behind by the enemy. So far 8 women snipers have been killed.

Night bombing is going to be a nuisance; we had a very near miss at Tac HQ last night, and Sgt Ship[36] had a narrow escape in the Mess tent.

Yrs ever

B.L. Montgomery.

If you want to discuss things come over and see me.

The National Archives, WO 205/5G

63
Montgomery's diary notes, 10 June 1944

[Typescript]

10 June.

19. A somewhat better day as regards the weather.

20. I had a conference of Army Commanders at PORT-EN-BESSIN and gave out my orders for future operations.[37]

21. As far as Second British Army was concerned my plan was to hold very firmly on the left and in the CAEN sector; 1 Corps would do this; it was vital not to lose the bridgehead gained by 6 Airborne Div. over the R. ORNE.

While holding firm, 1 Corps would pass 51 Div. across the ORNE and use it to operate southwards, east of the river, towards CAGNY.

The right of the Second Army, i.e., 30 Corps, was to swing forward to secure VILLERS-BOCAGE–NOYERS–EVRECY, and then to operate to the S.E. and secure the crossings over the R. ORNE from incl. THURY-HARCOURT northwards.

127

1 Airborne Div., now ready in U.K., would be held ready to be put down in between the pincer movement being carried out by 1 and 30 Corps; before we do this it would be necessary to create such a favourable battle situation as would make this operation a good possibility; meanwhile we would work to create this favourable situation; if things went very well we might not want to use the Airborne Division at all.

There were great possibilities about this right "swing" by 30 Corps, and it might trap Pz. LEHR division and possibly 12 S.S. Div. 22. First American Army was to capture CARENTAN and get reasonable depth at the junction of its two Corps; it must hold CARENTAN firmly.

Its next priority was to establish its left at CAUMONT, in conformity with the move of Second Army on VILLERS BOCAGE, and to hold CAUMONT firmly. Next it was to secure COUTANCE. Finally, and later on, it was to advance south on VILLEDIEU and VIRE, and AVRANCHES and MORTAIN. And all the time it was to extend its lodgement in the COTENTIN peninsula towards LA HAYE DU PUITS and CHERBOURG.

23. First U.S. Army did very well today. The two Corps joined up north of, or behind, CARENTAN; 7 Corps on the right made progress northwards towards CHERBOURG and reached MONTEBOURG; 5 Corps on the left made progress southwards and reached AIREL and BALLEROY.

24. Second Army held firm on the east flank against repeated enemy thrusts east of the R. ORNE and west of CAEN.

On its right the movement of 30 Corps against VILLERS BOCAGE began to develop.

25. By this evening the total lodgement area in France was over 60 miles wide; it varied in depth from 8 to 12 miles; it was joined up as one continuous front.

My policy was to gain depth and to deepen the lodgement area, and at the same time to extend it N.W. towards CHERBOURG.

26. In general I planned to draw all German reserves on to Second British Army, so as to make it more easy for First U.S. Army to press on to the south, and to capture CHERBOURG – in accordance with the original plan.

Two other things were important:

(a) to increase our own build-up.

(b) to do all in our power to interfere with the enemy build-up against us, by air action and all other means.

IWM, Montgomery Papers Part II, LMD 59/1

64
Message (M15) to Field Marshal Sir Alan Brooke

[Typescript]

11 June 1944, 0900 hours

TOPSEC (.) Personal for CIGS from General Montgomery (.) First Army going very well and have reached AIREL and BALLEROY (.) my general policy is to pull the enemy on to Second Army so as to make it easier for First Army to expand and extend the quicker (.) looking forward to your visit[38]

IWM, Montgomery Papers Part I, BLM 110/10

65
Message (M21) to Major-General F.W. de Guingand

[Typescript]

12 [?11][39] June 1944, 1900 hours

TOPSEC (.) For Chief of Staff from General Montgomery (.) do NOT understand refusal of LM to carry out airborne operation (.)[40] I am working to create such favourable conditions as would make the dropping of one airborne DIV in EVRECY area a good operation of war and one which if successful would pay a good dividend (.) Conditions have not yet been created but may well be created by 14 June (.) LM should come over and see me and ascertain the true form before he refuses to carry out an operation (.) He could get here by air in 30 minutes (.) meanwhile I want planning to go ahead so that when conditions are favourable the operation can be laid on quickly (.) am sending BROWNING[41] to see you tomorrow leaving here by air at 1000 hrs (.) inform LM as above (.)

IWM, Montgomery Papers Part I, BLM 109/1

66

Memorandum by Montgomery headed 'Some notes on the battle in NORMANDY between 6 and 12 June', and dated 12 June 1944[42]

[Typescript]

1. Our attack on D day (6 June) definitely achieved tactical surprise. Civilians say that they had been told by German officers and men that an Allied landing in these parts was not possible.

2. The coastal crust east of the CARENTAN estuary had been strengthened by bringing 352 DIV up from its layback area about ST LO. This Division was actually carrying out a "stand to" exercise on the coast when the attack of 5 US Corps went in on the OMAHA beaches; it was a good Division and fought very well.

3. The weather was bad and the sea rough. But troops were landed in good heart at the right places.

4. The beach obstacles and minefields presented no difficulties and were dealt with easily. The few exceptions were when the rough sea caused the landing craft to smash into the obstacles.

The beaches generally were not mined.

Taken as a whole the beach obstacles were very amateur, and were easily dealt with by our sappers.

5. There were many strong concrete pill boxes along the coast and these caused us great trouble; our initial casualties came chiefly from stout-hearted Germans in these pill boxes.

6. The attack was put in on the beaches with great power and violence, and it swept ashore on all beaches, <u>except one</u>, and penetrated inland. Many defended localities were by-passed, and later had to be cleared up; these caused considerable casualties.

For two or three days the lodgement area was full of enemy snipers, who took toll of our soldiers before they were all rounded up; we lost some good officers and men in this way; there were several cases of women snipers.

7. The one beach where enemy resistance held up the assault was OMAHA, the beach of 5 US Corps. Here there was a long dogfight on the beach and 5 Corps suffered heavy casualties in craft, personnel, and vehicles; by dark on D day the beachhead was only about 200 yds deep and the beach was under heavy mortar

and small arms fire. The situation here was very awkward and at one time it seemed as if no success would be possible. Eventually we pulled through by the gallantry of the American soldiers, by good supporting naval fire, and by brave work by fighter-bomber aircraft.

8. The air support by bombing before and during the assault was very good, and the enemy were not in very good shape after it – except at OMAHA where it seems to have gone wrong.[43]

9. The bad weather and rough sea delayed the build-up on D plus 1 and following days. LST's had to anchor and wait for the wind to drop.

By D+3 (9 June) we were 36 to 48 hours behind our time-table. This meant that we were not able to exploit fully the initial success we had gained, and this gave the enemy more time to bring up reserves and to build-up against us.

10. But slowly and relentlessly we made ground and extended the lodgement area.

On D+1 we were 5 to 6 miles inland.

By D+4 (10 June) the lodgement area was 60 miles long, and varied in depth from 8 to 12 miles; it was firmly held.

It was joined up into one continuous whole – from FRANCEVILLE on the east to MONTEBOURG 15 miles S.E. of CHERBOURG. It was being deepened, and at the same time being extended NW towards CHERBOURG.

11. I estimate we have had 11,000 casualties up to D+4 i.e. in five days fighting:

First US Army	6,000
Second Br Army	5,000

12. Prisoners

First US Army	6,500
Second Br. Army	5,500
	12,000

A very great many Germans have been killed.

The prisoners taken include Germans, Poles, Russians, some Japanese, and two Turks. The Germans fight well and bravely; the others run away if they can, otherwise they surrender freely.

13. DD Tanks

The DD tanks proved their worth. At OMAHA beach a great many were drowned in the rough sea; some were landed dry and did good work.

At some beaches it was considered too rough to launch them; in these cases they were landed dry but behind the leading AVRE and infantry, and as a result the RE and infantry suffered considerable casualties owing to the absence of tanks.

Where they could be used in their proper role they proved their worth, and saved casualties to foot soldiers. The flails were very useful.

14. The French Civilians

The French civilians in Normandy are in no way depressed. The Germans were quite good to them. There seems to be plenty of food; cattle, goats, etc are plentiful; there are plenty of vegetables; the crops are very good. The people are well clothed and have good boots and shoes; the children look healthy.

They are very co-operative.

In Port-en-Bessin the fishermen helped us to get the port cleared and in working order.

On the whole they are glad to see the Germans go; but I do not think they like us overmuch.

The Anxious Time

15. I was definitely somewhat anxious on the evening of D day, and on D+1 day.

The situation on OMAHA beach was very bad and our several lodgements were not joined up. I crossed over to France myself on evening of D day and took charge of the battle, as I could definitely do no good sitting in Portsmouth.

Things slowly got better and by D+4, i.e. 10 June, all anxiety had passed; the lodgement area was one whole, British and Americans were all joined up, and we were very strong on shore. I am convinced that the commander in the theatre of war has got to grip the battle; if he does then all is well.

Reflections on the Past.

16. When the planning of OVERLORD began in England there were few officers if any, from the C-in-C (Paget) downwards who had any idea as to how to stage the operation or as to the operational repercussions of any particular line of action.

It was considered that tactical surprise was impossible; it was considered that the beach obstacles would be almost insurmountable; unknown hazards assumed alarming proportions, and when in doubt everyone took counsel of their fears and played for safety.

The robust mentality, and fresh air, of the battle was conspicuous by its absence.

17. When I came into the party in January 1944, and took over from Paget, I brought in my own "team" of experienced staff officers. We found we had to recast the operational plan, the administrative plan, and in fact practically everything.

The operation has worked out to be a complete success and we are definitely justified in having torn-up and disregarded all the previous plans.

Allied and Enemy Build-up.

18. The attached Appendix 'A' gives some figures regarding the respective build-up of ourselves and the enemy, prisoners, casualties, etc.[44]

France

12–6–44

IWM, Montgomery Papers Part II, LMD 59/5

67
Message (M22) to Major-General F.W. de Guingand

[Typescript]

12 June 1944, 2230 hours

TOPSEC (.) For Chief of Staff from General Montgomery (.) advance of 7 Armd DIV met strong opposition just WEST of TILLY from PZ LEHR DIV (.) thrust line was switched quickly further to WEST and DIV moved south through LA BELLE EPINE and leading troops reached BRIOQUESSARD at 1900 hrs and will move on VILLERS BOCAGE[45] and NOYERS tomorrow (.) joint patrols of First and Second armies are in CAUMONT (.) all this is very good and PZ LEHR may be in grave danger tomorrow (.) inform EISENHOWER and DMO[46] at War Office (.)

IWM, Montgomery Papers Part I, BLM 110/11

68
Montgomery's diary notes, 12 June 1944

[Typescript]

<u>12 June.</u>

28. I was visited by The Prime Minister, the C.I.G.S., and General Smuts. They all arrived at 1215 hrs. in a DUCK[47] on MIKE beach;[48] I met them, drove them to my H.Q., and explained the general situation and my intentions.[49]

They re-embarked at 1500 hrs. to return to their warship.

The P.M. was in very good form; and he was quite prepared to obey orders and do what he was told – which was a great change!!

29. The thrust by 7 Armd. Div. southwards towards VILLERS BOCAGE met strong opposition just west of TILLY; this was from Pz. LEHR division. The thrust line was switched quickly further to the WEST; the whole Division disengaged and moved south through LA BELLE EPINE and by 1900 hrs. the leading troops were in BRIOQUESSARD. Joint patrols of First and Second Armies reached CAUMONT. This was all very good and things were working out as we wanted.

IWM, Montgomery Papers Part II, LMD 59/1

69
Letter to Major-General F.W. de Guingand

[Holograph]

12 June 1944

Had the P.M., C.I.G.S., and Smuts, here today; all in very good form; the P.M. very obedient and I pushed him away at 1500 hrs and would not let him go beyond my H.Q.

I sent you a wire last night re L.M.[50] and his refusal to drop 1 Airborne DIV. The favourable conditions I am working up to are that the D.Z. would be within range of the artillery of 7 Armd

Div in the VILLERS BOCAGE area; if we then drop the Airborne DIV in EVRECY area we would be very well placed and might get a big "scoop".

The real point is that L.M. sitting in his office cannot possibly know the local battle form here; and therefore he must not refuse my demands unless he first comes over to see me; he could fly here in a mosquito in ½ hour, talk for one hour, and be back in England in ½ hour. Obviously he is a gutless bugger, who refuses to take a chance and plays for safety on all occasions. I have no use for him.

We must get a proper air service laid on, to come over here. We have got two very good airfields now and Douglas machines come over regularly. I have told Kit to send over my C/47. The Miles 38 came over today in one hour and landed in a field 100 yds from my caravans – where it now lives.

Officers can fly over on business for the day.

I have told Miles[51] to tell you my views about accommodation, messes, etc, at Tac HQ. It is not designed for a large crowd, nor do I want one.

I have decided that the only major-generals to be members of my Mess will be yourself and Miles; the others are all to go elsewhere. I will not have a crowd in my mess; my personal staff, chief of staff, head A/Q, – and no more.

You must set up another mess down the road. I cannot have B Mess at Tac over-crowded.

In fact Tac HQ has got to remain small and self-contained.

We have not the transport here to supply vehicles to officers from Main; a pool must be kept over here for them or they must bring their own.

The P.M. is very anxious that The King should come over here; just to land for two hours, have lunch with me, and go away. I said I would agree to that. The date may be Friday this week, or Saturday.[52]

Whatever date is settled, keep anyone else away on that day i.e. warn Eisenhower off if he proposes to come the same day. I cannot deal with more than one V.I.P. – and told the P.M. today he must not come again just yet.

___

13 June

I have told Bradley to get 1 US DIV firmly established in CAUMONT area, and to push strong recces thence further to the south so as to help Bimbo's[53] thrust – see my M22[54] sent you last night. He is then to operate with his left Corps towards ST LO, and capture that place; I expect he will use 2 US Armd DIV for this.

___

Meanwhile 51 DIV is quietly working southwards with its right flank on the R. ORNE i.e. east of the ORNE.

___

Lay on very strong air (other things being equal) to assist:
(a) First US Army to hold CARENTAN against counter–attack.
(b) Left Corps of Bradley to capture ST LO.
(c) Second Army thrust from CAUMONT area towards VILLERS BOCAGE and NOYERS and EVRECY.
Of these I think (c) is the most important.

We are very strong now astride the road CAEN–BAYEUX about junction of 3 DIV and 3 Canadian DIV, and if the enemy attacks here he should be seen off; I have 400 tanks there. Any such enemy attack here would be good, so long as we see it off and the right flank of Second Army swings round to NOYERS and EVRECY.

Yrs ever

B.L. Montgomery

I am enjoying life greatly and it is great fun fighting battles again[55] after 5 months in England.

The National Archives, WO 205/5D

70
Montgomery's diary notes, 13 June 1944

[Typescript]

13 June.

30. 7 Armd. Div. got on the move at dawn and by 0800 hrs. its leading troops were in VILLERS BOCAGE.

The Division established a firm base there of two armoured Regts., one Inf. Bn., and 5 R.H.A.

It then sent out strong patrols and reconnaissances towards NOYERS and EVRECY and AUNAY-SUR-ODON.

I gave orders that the right of Second Army, i.e., 30 Corps, was to swing forward, and that it was important to secure intact the crossings over the R. ORNE between THURY-HARCOURT and AMAYE-SUR-ORNE.

I ordered First U.S. Army to establish its left Division (1 U.S. Div.) firmly at CAUMONT, and to gain touch with the right flank of Second Army.

31. During the late afternoon 2 Pz. Div. appeared in the area CAUMONT–VILLERS BOCAGE. This Division had come from TOULOUSE and we kept touch with its move; from the direction of the move, and its detraining station, it was clearly intended to be put into the battle in the CAEN section; but our break-in in the area CAUMONT–VILLERS BOCAGE has pulled it over to plug the hole we made, which is excellent. So long as Rommel has to use his strategic reserves to plug holes, then we have done well.

32. 2 Pz. Div. put in a furious attack against 7 Armd. Div. at VILLERS BOCAGE. The attack was beaten off but both Divisions got very mixed up and parties of Germans got in between bodies of our troops. When dark came the situation was very obscure.

IWM, Montgomery Papers Part II, LMD 59/1

71
Letter (M501) to Field Marshal Sir Alan Brooke

[Typescript]

13 June 1944

The situation is developing very favourably on my eastern flank, and in the centre.

Eastern Flank.

2. The thrust of 7 Armd DIV of 30 Corps southwards towards VILLERS BOCAGE met strong opposition immediately west of TILLY.

So yesterday, 12 June, the thrust line was moved further west; the Division disengaged and moved south through LA BELLE EPINE and via BRIOQUESSARD.

Soon after dawn today the leading troops reached VILLERS BOCAGE.

A firm base was built up there of about 100 tanks, one Inf Bn, and 5 RHA, and plans made to push strong recces and patrols out in all directions.

3. 7 Armd DIV was now in a good position to get right in behind Pz LEHR DIV.

I ordered Second Army to operate with the Division so as to secure AUNAY-SUR-ODON and EVRECY, and to seize the crossings over the R. ORNE from THURY-HARCOURT northwards to AMAYE-SUR-ORNE.

4. In rear of 7 Armd DIV the right wing of Second Army was to swing forward; this meant 50 DIV and 49 DIV (now about to enter the battle) pivoting on TILLY and swinging round in a south-easterly movement.

5. Pz LEHR DIV are somewhere in the middle and we want to stop them from getting away. We may get some of them; it is too early to say yet; I expect they will pull out tonight.

6. Away to the east, 51 DIV is developing operations to the east of the R. ORNE, north-east of CAEN.

The Division is moving southwards with its right flank on the ORNE; this movement is slow as just at present it cannot be given any tanks.

7. So my pincer movement to get CAEN is taking good shape, and there are distinct possibilities that the enemy Divisions may not find it too easy to escape; especially Pz LEHR.

21 Pz and 12 S.S. could escape easily, but would have to pull out soon – unless they can hold up the western half of the pincers i.e. 30 Corps swing.

8. At the present moment the Armd Recce Regt of 7 Armd DIV (8 H) is moving on NOYERS; there are a lot of enemy, including some TIGER tanks, milling about in the triangle HOTTOT–NOYERS–VILLERS BOCAGE. The situation will clarify later!!

Centre.

9. The wheel of the right flank of Second Army is taking it away from CAUMONT, where is the left flank of First US Army.

I have ordered Bradley to establish his left Division (1 US Inf DIV) firmly at CAUMONT and to push out strong patrols and recces south-east towards COULVAIN and southwards to ST MARTIN-DES-BESACES.

10. Bradley's left Corps, 5 US Corps, is getting rather stretched and he has had to send some armour over from 2 Armd DIV to lend a hand at CARENTAN.

So I have told him to hang on firmly to CAUMONT vide para 9 above, and not to push the right of the Corps forward to ST LO until he feels he can safely do so. 30 DIV will be coming in through the beaches tomorrow and then the Corps will be able to move on again.

Right Flank.

11. CARENTAN is being attacked by the enemy. It is important we should not lose it and I have told Bradley that he must concentrate all available resources on holding it.

There is a strong naval force that is giving good covering fire from the sea, but it is bad weather for good air support.

12. Further to the north we hold MONTEBOURG and 7 US Corps is slowly pushing northwards.

13. I have just heard (1700 hrs 13 June) that the Germans have got back into CARENTAN; this is a nuisance.

Future Intentions.

14. Working from the east my future intentions are as follows:

Second Army.

(a) To capture CAEN and establish a strong eastern flank astride the R. ORNE from the sea as far south as THURY-HARCOURT.

(b) Gradually to push this flank eastwards.

(c) To establish 8 Corps in the area about FALAISE.

(d) To establish 30 Corps in the area about MT PINCON and FLERS.

First US Army.

(e) To hold on firmly to CAUMONT; to recapture CARENTAN and to hold it firmly.

(f) To capture ST LO and then COUTANCE.

(g) To thrust southwards from CAUMONT towards VIRE and MORTAIN; and from ST LO towards VILLEDIEU and AVRANCHES.

(h) All the time to exert pressure towards LA HAYE DU PUITS and VALOGNES, and to capture CHERBOURG.

15. Later, the First Canadian Army will take over the northern part of the eastern flank – including 1 Corps in situ, and possibly certain other troops.

16. It is not quite clear yet exactly where 12 Corps will be employed. This will emerge in a few days, as the situation develops. Meanwhile I have phased back the Guards Armd DIV of 8 Corps, and am bringing in 43 DIV (from 12 Corps) in its place. We have got plenty of armour, and want more infantry.

17. 19 Corps of First US Army is in process of coming in now. It is probably <u>that</u> Corps which will thrust south towards VILLEDIEU and AVRANCHES vide para 14(g).

Administrative.

18. We are in a very reasonable position in Second British Army. Over and above full echelons we have in reserve:

> 12,000 tons of ammunition.
>
> 5 days rations
>
> 50 miles of petrol for every vehicle.

12,000 tons came in through the beaches yesterday.

19. The American situation is not quite so good. They are roughly 50% behind in all unloading i.e. they have on shore only half the maintenance stores they should have.

There are a great many ships off the beaches but no one knows what is in them; the Americans have no Movement Staff, which is a weak point in their organisation; they have no "manifests" showing what each ship contains.[56]

But they are alright and have the following in reserve:

(a) Ammunition for two days at intense rates.

(b) 4 days rations.

(c) Plenty of petrol.

They are short of 105[57] artillery ammunition but Second Army has plenty and can transfer some.

The American "mulberry" is very nearly finished, and they have made a fine job of it.[58]

General.

20. I consider we have now got our teeth well into the Germans and if we don't let go, and avoid mistakes, we ought to be in a very good position in another week or two.

Once we get CAEN, and can establish a strong flank astride the ORNE from the sea to THURY-HARCOURT, we will be very well placed to develop the operations as originally planned – and as outlined in para 14.

21. The first vital moment in the battle was, I think, on the afternoon and evening of D day when the left American Corps had a beachhead of only 100 yds after fighting all day.

Other parts of the lodgement area were not linked up, and we were liable to defeat in detail.

The answer to invasion from across the sea is a strong counter-attack on the afternoon of D day, when the invading force has no proper communications and has lost certain cohesion.

That was Rommel's chance.

It was not taken, and we were given time to recover – thank goodness. If you saw OMAHA beach you would wonder how the Americans ever got ashore.

22. The turning point of the battle was I think on 12 June, when the thrust line of 7 Armd DIV was switched after meeting strong opposition near TILLY, and we broke through and reached VILLERS BOCAGE on morning 13 June. We were then in a position to be able to force a German withdrawal, and to make any attack by the enemy astride the road CAEN–BAYEUX very hazardous.

23. To get the best results we are very dependent on good weather.

Bad weather affects our build-up through the beaches.

And bad weather means we do not get the full power of the very great air strength we possess.

24. Today 13 June has been a very wet and cloudy day.

I am told that from tomorrow onwards we are in for a long spell of fine weather; that would be excellent.

Casualties.

25. So far as I can make out our casualties to date are as follows:

First US Army	13,000
Second British Army	8,000
	21,000

This is far less than we had allowed for.

Prisoners.

26. The total is about 13,000.

Yrs ever

B.L. Montgomery

Field Marshal Sir Alan F. Brooke, GCB, DSO,
CIGS, The War Office.

Maj-Gen F.E.W. Simpson, CB, MC,
DMO, The War Office.

Further Notes.

Later 0900 hrs 14 June

27. Late last evening (13 June) 2 Pz DIV came into the battle; it counter-attacked 7 Armd DIV in the VILLERS-BOCAGE area and we took some prisoners.

A real good dogfight went on all the evening. The village itself is in low ground and finally 7 Armd DIV withdrew and occupied firmly the high ground immediately to the west – which dominates the village.

The situation in that area is still a bit confused.

28. The arrival of 2 Pz DIV at this place puts a different complexion on the problem.

I have got to be very certain of my position, step by step; I must at all costs remain well balanced and able to handle easily any situation that may develop as the enemy reserves come into the battle.

29. I am now very strong defensively on the left of Second Army, in the CAEN sector; I would be stronger still if I had CAEN itself, but I am quite well positioned as things are at present.

I have not yet sufficient strength to be <u>offensive</u> on both flanks of Second Army.

I have therefore decided to be <u>defensive in the CAEN sector</u> on the front of 1 Corps, but aggressively so. I am going to put all my offensive power, ammunition, and so on, into the offensive by 30 Corps on the right of Second Army. That is – 30 Corps will operate offensively in the VILLERS BOCAGE area with:

7 Armd DIV

50 DIV   *33 Armd Bde will be ready on shore*

49 DIV   *by evening 15 June and will join this party.*[59]

8 Armd Bde

The general idea will be to establish ourselves very firmly in the VILLERS-BOCAGE area, and swing towards the area EVRECY– THURY HARCOURT–AUNAY SUR ODON, keeping close touch with the left of First US Army all the time.

30. The offensive movement of 51 DIV vide para 6 above will now be piped down.

31. The Americans are back again in CARENTAN. Thank God!!

I see the SHAEF communique said yesterday the town had been "liberated". Actually it has been completely flattened and there is hardly a house intact; all the civilians have fled. It is a queer sort of liberation!!!

32. The intake over the beaches is going on well in Second Army. On 12 June we had in 14,500 tons.

33. My general policy remains unchanged. It is as follows:

(a) To increase and improve our own build-up through the beaches.

(b) To do everything possible to hamper and delay the enemy build-up, by air action and other means.

(c) To pull the Germans on to Second British Army, and fight them there, so that First US Army can carry out its task the easier.

34. I shall hold strongly, and fight offensively, in the general area CAUMONT–VILLERS BOCAGE i.e. at the junction of the two armies.

Enemy reserves look like coming in here – *in fact where we broke in.*

It is here that 2 Pz DIV has come in, and it attacked the Americans at CAUMONT last evening as well as 7 Armd DIV at VILLERS BOCAGE.

35. The general line up of Pz Divisions is now, from east to west:

21, 12 S.S., Pz LEHR, 2 Pz.

2 S.S. Pz (ex TOULOUSE) may appear soon.

Later 1000 hours 14 June

36. Have spoken to BRADLEY.

He is quite happy about CARENTAN and is strongly positioned now, some 2000 to 3000 yards to the west and south of the town.

His left Corps (5 Corps under GEROW)[60] is getting rather stretched. So he is putting in 19 Corps (CORLETT)[61] at 1200 hrs today to take over the sector between ST LO and CARENTAN.

37. Bradley is strongly positioned at CAUMONT. He beat off the attack of 2 Pz DIV there last night, and will hold that area firmly.

B.L. Montgomery

1100 hrs 14 June[62]

IWM, Montgomery Papers Part I, BLM 126/2

72
Montgomery's diary notes, 14–17 June 1944

[Typescript]

14 June.

33. It was decided during the morning to withdraw 7 Armd. Div. to a more rearward position, so that it could get disentangled from the enemy and could re-organise. It was to begin to withdraw at dusk. But in the evening 2 Pz. Div. put in a further terrific attack against the Division; the Germans seemed to be desperate and to have lost all reason; they suffered very heavily and it is estimated they must have lost 600 killed and at least 40 tanks.

That quietened 2 Pz. Div., and it withdrew. 7 Armd. Div. then proceeded to carry out its own withdrawal to its selected area.

34. General de Gaulle visited me today. He is a poor fish and gives out no inspiration. I gave him every facility to go where he liked, but asked him to leave the lodgement area before dark – and this he did.

His general reception in BAYEUX and other places was lukewarm; his staff had to keep shouting "General de Gaulle" and pointing to him.

35. I sent letter M501[63] to the C.I.G.S. This explains my ideas at the moment.

36. Leigh-Mallory, Air C.-in-C., came to see me[64] and was anxious to use the air power of the heavy bombers in closer relation to the land battle. I was delighted and he proposed a scheme for doing it.

He brought with him a large staff of some 8 officers, imagining that I would get down to it with them and work out the details. I would not see them.

But we arranged that he should send over a planning staff tomorrow to work out details with Second Army.

15 June.

37. It is quite clear that 2 Pz. Div. has had a "bloody nose", and I don't think we should have any more offensive action from that Division. This means that the situation in the CAUMONT–VILLERS BOCAGE area is now well in hand, and all is ready for the offensive of 30 Corps which is due to start on 17 June. See letter M501, para. 29.

38. I went over to see First U.S. Army and spent the day examining the situation in the COTENTIN.

The thrust due west across the peninsula to cut off CHERBOURG is going well; the thrust line chosen by Bradley is towards ST. SAUVEUR so that he can use the R. DOUVE as a flank facing south.

I would have preferred a thrust line towards LA HAY DU PUITS, as once we have captured that place we have got the Cherbourg area sealed off; but the detail of the operation is a matter for Bradley to decide.[65]

South and S.E. of CARENTAN the First Army is working to gain more depth and elbow room.

Between ST. LO and CAUMONT the front is a holding one for the moment.

I directed Bradley that, as the German main effort was being exerted on the front of Second British Army, and most of his troops were over that way, he was to go all out to capture CHERBOURG.

39. I saw Dempsey in the evening.

I said that, as we had the VILLERS BOCAGE situation well in hand and the offensive there was ready to begin on 17 June, I wanted him now to examine <u>again</u> the question of an attack southwards from the bridgehead east of the area, i.e., towards BOURGEBUS, so as to get in behind CAEN.

My general idea was that he should put 8 Corps (O'Connor) in on that thrust line.[66]

40. Eisenhower and Tedder came to see me at 1600 hrs.

It appears that Leigh-Mallory's ideas vide para. 36 have been turned down completely by Tedder, Harris, and Coningham as being quite impracticable. I feel there is possibly some intrigue going on in "air" circles. There is definitely something in what Leigh-Mallory proposes, and he is prepared to try out anything to win the war. But Coningham and Harris do not like him.

Coningham is a very jealous person and I am beginning to feel that he is anti-army; he says one thing to your face and another thing behind your back; he is not a loyal member of the team.

Coningham would prefer to get L-M. to trip up, rather than to win the battle.

<u>16 June.</u>

41. The King came to Normandy and had lunch with me at my H.Q. He had a bit of a party getting on shore as it was very windy and rough; he arrived finally somewhat late and not in a very good temper. However he very soon recovered and was charming. He held an investiture after lunch and decorated 7 officers and men.[67]

<u>17 June.</u>

42. The Americans are racing across the peninsula and should reach the west coast by dawn tomorrow. We will then have CHERBOURG cut off; as a guess I would say there are possibly 40,000 enemy in there – probably a pretty mixed bag.

IWM, Montgomery Papers Part II, LMD 59/1

73
Letter from General Dwight D. Eisenhower to Montgomery
[Typescript]

18 June 1944

Recently I sent you a message by General deGuingand [*sic*] saying that I was going to forbid, for the time being, any further visits by V.I.P.'s to the battle area.[68] I won't have you bothered at this time by people who are not in a position to help you directly in the battle effort and unless you personally desire to approve such visits I am quite certain that no further ones are necessary or desirable. I have just been told that you have approved a visit by the Secretary of State for War and if so that is all right with me.[69] However, if any other person submits a request directly to you and you find yourself in an embarrassing position to find a legitimate excuse for refusal, simply lay the blame on me. You can state that I have raised the question myself, and make my attitude as firm as you desire.

The Chief of Staff tells me that the attack is to start tomorrow morning after a forty-eight hour delay. I can well understand that you have needed to accumulate reasonable amounts of artillery ammunition but I am in high hopes that once the attack starts it will have a momentum that will carry it a long ways. As I agreed when I saw you last,[70] I have been putting a lot of steam behind phasing up fighting units and ammunition at the expense of all other types of personnel and stores. We are making some progress but these things, of course, always seem to move much more slowly than one would desire.

I thoroughly believe you are going to crack the enemy a good one. You certainly have every reason to be proud of your troops to date.

Right now I am counting on running over to see Bradley for a short time on Tuesday.[71] I will probably go by destroyer so as not to interfere with operations from any of the air fields during your present battles.

With good luck and warm personal regards.

IWM, Montgomery Papers Part II, LMD 114/3

74
Letter to Mrs Phyllis Reynolds

[Holograph]

18 June 1944

Have just got your letter[72] of 11 June – the day Kit Dawnay took Timothy up to you. He is a most delightful dog and I am very fond of him; he will grow into a really good pet. It is a great thing to know that he is safely housed with you.

The King was here on Friday; but you saw that in the papers I have no doubt. Dawnay is over here with me now, having brought over the balance of my personal camp – including the two Rolls Royce cars!! I have sent Noel Chavasse[73] over in my aeroplane today to England to get some spare parts for my small Miles aeroplane – which got hit by falling shrapnel two nights ago and was put out of action. Incidentally he has taken my laundry over to some Nuns near Portsmouth – who wash for me. I have told him to telephone you. I shall continue to send my laundry to England just at present.

I told The King that I did not think the people of Normandy had any wish to be liberated. When you read in the paper that another town has been "liberated" it really means that heavy fighting has taken place around it and that it has been destroyed – that not one house is left standing – and that a good many of the civilian inhabitants have been killed. Such is the price the French are now paying. When they chucked their hand in in 1940 they thought they could avoid all this – but they cannot.

My love to you all, and to Tim.

Yrs ever

Monty

P.S. I have seen some very good cartoons of myself in the newspapers recently – Daily Express, Sunday Pictorial, and others. I hope you are collecting them. The Daily Express one of 12 June is good; then there is one of me in a sweater in a picture gallery of generals in full dress.[74]

B.L.M.

I enclose a good selection of photos for you.

IWM, Montgomery's letters to the Reynolds

75
Directive (M502) to Lieutenant-General Omar N. Bradley, First US Army, and Lieutenant-General Miles Dempsey, Second British Army[75]

[Cyclostyle]

18 June 1944

1. To-day is D plus 12, and we have now been fighting since 6 June. During this time we have been working on the original directive issued by me in England, and we have:

(a) gained a good lodgement area in Normandy.

(b) linked up all our different thrusts to form one whole area, and made the area we hold quite secure.

(c) kept the initiative, forced the enemy to use his reserves to plug holes, and beaten off all his counter-attacks.

(d) replaced our casualties in personnel and tanks, etc, so that Divisions and armoured units are up to strength again.

(e) placed ourselves in a sound position administratively.

2. After the very great intensity of the initial few days we had to slow down the tempo of operations so as to:

(a) ensure we could meet the enemy counter-attacks without difficulty.

(b) build up our strength behind the original assault divisions.

And while doing this we had to continue our offensive operations in order to get well positioned for the next moves, and also to ensure that we kept the initiative.

3. All this is good, But we are now ready to pass on to other things, and to reap the harvest. I give below my view of the general situation.

The General Situation.

4. The enemy mobile reserves are becoming exhausted. He can still milk divisions in BRITTANY, and he can milk Southern FRANCE of such reserves as are mobile. But he still lacks good infantry to release his Panzer divisions so that the latter can be grouped for a full-blooded counter-attack.

The enemy infantry in the CHERBOURG peninsula will be written off sooner or later, and he will then have to make a decision as to whether he will continue to fight for CHERBOURG.

In Normandy the enemy has never had the initiative; but he has been in sufficient strength to stage local counter-attacks and these have delayed the full expansion of our plans.

5. The enemy administrative situation, and his command set-up, are both disorganised; this will continue. His HQ are bombed daily, his communications are disrupted, and his mobility in his own area is restricted.

As the policy of forcing back his detraining areas gathers more momentum, so this restricted mobility, coupled with a growing shortage of fuel, is going to cost him dear. The activities of the S.A.S. units are paying a good dividend,[76] and these will now be brought further northwards so as to be more closely related to the operations which we ourselves are about to undertake.

6. Once we can snap the enemy "roping off" policy, he is going to find it very difficult to gather the stuff to stabilise again. The old policy of "stretch", which beat him in SICILY, then begins to emerge.

7. At present out [sic] own armies are facing in different directions. Once we can capture CAEN and CHERBOURG, and all face in the same direction, the enemy problem becomes enormous.

The actual threat in Normandy then becomes his big anxiety, and it will probably take precedence of other potential threats, e.g. the PAS DE CALAIS.[77]

It is then that we have a mighty chance – to make the German army come to our threat, and to defeat it between the SEINE and the LOIRE.

8. I consider that we have got the enemy into a very awkward situation, and we ourselves are ready to take advantage of his predicament.

9. It is clear that we must now capture CAEN and CHERBOURG, as the first step in the full development of our plans.

CAEN is really the key to CHERBOURG; its capture will release forces which are now locked up in ensuring that our left flank holds secure.

10. By Wednesday 21 June the Second Br Army and First US Army will both have fresh reserves ready.

We will now strike again, in accordance with the following directive.

Second British Army.

11. The immediate task of this Army will be to capture CAEN, and provide a strong eastern flank for the Army Group.

12. The operations against CAEN will be developed by means of a pincer movement from both flanks.

The object will be to establish the 8 Corps, strong in armour, to the S.E. of CAEN in the area BOURGUEBUS 0761–VIMONT 1561–BRETTEVILLE-SUR-LAIZE 0553.

13. From VIMONT northwards the flank of the army will be established on the general line TROARN – thence along the R. DIVES to the sea at CABOURG.

14. The right flank of the Army, forming the western half of the pincer movement against CAEN, will swing south-eastwards through AUNAY-SUR-ODON 8351 and EVRECY 9259 towards the bridges over the R. ORNE between incl THURY-HARCOURT 9447 and AMAY-SUR-ORNE 9757.

15. While carrying out the operation outlined in para 14 it will be essential to ensure firm touch with the left of First US Army.

16. The above operations will be begun on 18 June, and will work up to a crescendo on 22 June – on which date 8 Corps will pass through the bridgehead east of the R. ORNE on its task vide para 12.

First US Army.

17. The immediate task of this Army is to capture CHERBOURG.

18. The first stage will be to isolate the peninsula from further reinforcement from the south. This is now being done by means of a thrust westwards through ST SAUVEUR towards the sea at BARNEVILLE.

19. The "roping off" line will be held securely.

The right wing of the Army will then thrust hard towards CHERBOURG by the shortest route through VALOGNES, will capture the town and port, and will clear the peninsula of the enemy.

20. The left wing of the Army, now in the CAUMONT area, will maintain the closest touch with the right of Second Army vide para 15. It will be prepared to advance its positions so as to afford a measure of protection to the right flank of 7 Armd DIV as that Division moves on AUNAY.

21. Between CARENTAN and CAUMONT the left wing of the Army will hold its present positions, as a first priority.

It will endeavour, as a second priority, to make progress towards ST LO and to secure the high ground east of the R. VIRE which overlooks and dominates the town.

22. 15 US Corps (of three infantry divisions) will be brought in through the OMAHA beaches beginning 24 June.

When this Corps is ready the left wing of the Army will be prepared to strike south and south-west through the front ST LO–CAUMONT.

23. The bringing in of a fifth Corps to the American sector will impose a certain strain on the administrative services.

In order to ease this strain it will be necessary to capture CHERBOURG in the next 10 days, i.e. by 27 June.

General.

24. The operations outlined above will be carried out with the greatest drive and energy. The enemy divisions are weak, and he has nothing "in the kitty". We are up to strength, are strong in armour, and have a great weight of air power to support us.

25. I shall hope to see both CAEN and CHERBOURG captured by 24 June.

IWM, Montgomery Papers Part I, BLM 126/3

76
Montgomery's diary notes, 18 June 1944

[Typescript]

<u>18 June.</u>

43. I issued M502, my directive to Army Commanders. In it I give my views on the situation, and lay down that we must now capture CAEN and CHERBOURG.

It is filed with this diary.

44. First U.S. Army reached the west coast of the peninsula at midnight last night. It has done very well, and Collins[78] of the 7 Corps has great drive.

A re-grouping is being carried out and 7 Corps will move on Cherbourg tomorrow with 4, 79, and 9 Divs.

45. The Secretary of State for War (Grigg) came to see me and we had a long talk.[79] I sent M503[80] back by him.

46. I have now had to give up 4 days to visitors, none of whom need really have come at all:

> The P.M. and party.
> General de Gaulle.
> The King.
> S. of S. for War.

I have spent many hours waiting on the beach for guests to arrive; it is all a very great waste of my time and I have made it quite clear that I cannot go on with it.

47. I have been thinking a lot on the problem now in front of us. I am not altogether convinced that I was right about launching 8 Corps from the bridgehead east of the ORNE – vide para. 39 above.

There is very little room there and before undertaking any large scale operations in that area I feel we have first got to push the enemy back eastwards, and establish our own flank on the R. DIVES.

This will take time and would require another Division of infantry, and at the moment we have not got one.

I went to see Dempsey at 1830 hrs. and gave him my views as above.[81]

I suggested that he should transfer 8 Corps to the right or western pincer of the movement, and make <u>that</u> the main effort of the Army in its task of capturing CAEN.

48. I also talked to Dempsey about his Chief of Staff – Brigadier Chilton.[82] He is a very nice chap but he knows nothing whatever about how to handle air power and the air staff of No. 83 Group have no confidence in him. He will think over the matter.

49. Our casualty figures to date are interesting:

	<u>K.</u>	<u>W.</u>	<u>M.</u>	<u>Total.</u>
British.	1838	7835	3611	13284
U.S.	2538	12395	7243	22181
	4376	20230	10859	35465

50. Total prisoners as follows:

British zone. 5500
U.S. zone.   9500
              15000

IWM, Montgomery Papers Part II, LMD 59/1

77
Directive (M504) to Lieutenant-General O.N. Bradley, First US Army, and Lieutenant-General M.C. Dempsey, Second British Army

[Cyclostyle]
19 June 1944
Ref M502 dated 18–6–44.

Second British Army.

1. Detailed examination of the problem has revealed that the difficulties of forming up 8 Corps in the bridgehead east of the R. ORNE, and of launching it from that bridgehead as the left wing of the pincer movement against CAEN, are very great.[83]

The enemy is strongly posted on that flank and certain preliminary operations would be necessary; these would take time, and we do not want to wait longer than we can help.

It has therefore been decided that the left wing of the pincer movement, from the bridgehead over the ORNE, shall be scaled down and be only of such a nature as can be done by the troops of 1 Corps already there.

2. 8 Corps will be switched to form part of the right, or western, wing of the pincer movement – see para 14 of M502. The final objective of 8 Corps will remain as given in para 12 of M502, but the Corps will advance to this objective on the general thrust line:

ST MAUVIEU 9269–ESQUAY 9460–AMAYE SUR
ODON 9757.

3. Para 16 of M502 will be amended to read as follows:

"The above operations will be begun at or about dawn on 22 June. 8 Corps will be launched on its task on the morning of 23 June."

First US Army.

4. It is important that the Army should not wait till CHERBOURG is actually captured before extending its operations to the south-west.

5. As soon as they can be organised, operations will be developed against LA HAYE DES PUITS and against COUTANCE.

Later, as more troops become available, these operations will be extended towards GRANVILLE, AVRANCHES, and VIRE.

Third US Army.

6. A study is being made of the possibility of seizing ST MALO by airborne operations from ENGLAND, and then bringing in to that port a Corps of Third US Army.

7. If this can be done it would enable the whole tempo of the operations to be speeded up, since Third Army would be in close touch with First Army and everything would thus be more simple.

IWM, Montgomery Papers Part I, BLM 126/5

78
Letter to Major-General F.E.W. Simpson

[Holograph]

19 June 1944

I send you M504; this will show you how I have had to change the thrust line for 8 Corps. A certain re-grouping is taking place and for the attack 8 Corps will consist of:

    15 DIV
    43 DIV
    11 Armd DIV
    4 Armd Bde
    31 Armd Bde *33? Tank?*[84]

It will be a blitz attack supported by all available air power – on the lines of EL HAMMA.[85] The trouble in Second Army is that there is no one at Army HQ who knows anything about the practical side of air cooperation in the land battle; so I am lending Charles Richardson to Dempsey as a BGS (Air) to teach them all.[86] I fear that Chilton is not really fit to be Chief of Staff to a large Army; however, we will try and teach him.

First US Army will thrust towards LA HAYE DES PUITS and COUTANCE, beginning on 21 June.

Bad weather has, and is, delaying our build-up; today everything is closed down, even the Mulberries. It is most unlucky as every days delay helps the Germans.

Yrs ever

<u>B.L. Montgomery</u>

Please ACK M504, and the copy I am sending to C.I.G.S.

IWM, Simpson Papers

79
Letter to Lieutenant-General Sir Richard O'Connor

[Holograph]

19 June 1944

I am grateful to you for the very clear exposition on the problems of the attack from the existing bridgehead <u>east</u> of the ORNE. I considered the problem after leaving you and told Bimbo to chuck it; 8 Corps instead to deliver its blow on the EVRECY flank.[87]

When you have got your plans thought out for the new thrust line, do come & see me and explain them – or I will come & see you.

Liddell Hart Centre for Military Archives, O'Connor Papers 5/4/9

80
Montgomery's diary notes, 19 June 1944

[Typescript]

19 June.

51. I issued M504 in which 8 Corps is transferred to the right, or western, pincer of the movement against CAEN. See para. 47.[88]

52. I have arranged with Dempsey that Charles Richardson, my B.G.S. (Plans), shall be attached to Second Army H.Q. as a B.G.S. (Air). He is a great expert on the whole question of air cooperation in the land battle.

We want the attack of 8 Corps on 23 June to be a complete blitz attack, supported by all the air power we can lay on.

Richardson will have to teach Chilton. See para. 48.[89]

53. The weather today is vile – raining hard and a high wind.

We are now several days behind in our build-up.

Everything we want for the resumption of the offensive on 22 June (vide M504) is lying in ships off the beaches, but it is too rough to unload it. If this weather goes on we may have to postpone the attack of Second Army; they must get 43 Div. on shore and more ammunition.

54. I have just seen in the English papers an account of The King's visit; the route followed by The King from the beach to my H.Q. is given, villages on the route being named, and it says I live in a chateau 6 miles from the front.

I am informed that this was done by the press man from Buckingham Palace, who came in the party; of course the real culprit is the censor at SHAEF who should have stopped it.

It may be a coincidence, but a chateau a few miles away was destroyed by enemy bombing on 18 June; the King came on 16 June.

I have now left my bedroom caravan at night, and sleep below ground. I have written to Lascelles on the subject, saying that these things must not happen.[90]

55. First U.S. Army is going very well towards Cherbourg, and are only now about 5 miles from the town.

IWM, Montgomery Papers Part II, LMD 59/1

81
Message (M25) to Major-General F.W. de Guingand
[Typescript]
20 June 1944, 2015 hours

TOPSEC (.) Personal for Chief of Staff from General Montgomery (.) The continued rough weather has put us now 5 days behind in our planned build up (.) Essential portions of 15 Div. and 43 Div. and essential artillery ammunition waiting at anchor to be unloaded (.) Given calm weather for unloading tomorrow and Thursday will deliver blitz attack of 8 Corps on Sunday 25 June and that is now the earliest date (.) Each further day of bad weather will mean a further postponement of one day (.) Inform Eisenhower and D.M.O.[91] at War Office for C.I.G.S.

IWM, Montgomery Papers Part I, BLM 110/12

82
Letter to Major-General F.W. de Guingand

[Holograph]

23 June 1944

I am just back from visiting 7 Corps in the Cherbourg area. Both 4 and 79 DIVS are right through the main defences of the fortress on the land side; and I think 79 DIV will tonight be looking right down into the town. MONTEBOURG and VALOGNES have been "liberated" in the best 21 Army Group style i.e. they are both completely destroyed!! I think VALOGNES probably wins; it is worse than YPRES in the last war.

2. I have ordered Bradley as follows:

(a) capture (or liberate!!) Cherbourg with all speed.

(b) regroup so that he can operate strongly on the axis:

> LA HAYE DU PUITS
> LESSAY
> COUTANCE
> GRANVILLE–VILLEDIEU

This thrust to begin as early as possible. Bradley does not think it can begin till 4 days after Cherbourg falls.

(c) The whole front of the Army Group that faces southwards, i.e. from east of CAEN westwards to the sea south of BARNEVILLE, is to burst into flames on the day 8 Br. Corps attack goes in. Some parts of the front have little arty ammunition and cannot do very much; but everyone can do something, and that "something" must be the maximum possible with the resources he has.

3. The attack of 8 (British) Corps is at present fixed for Sunday 25 June. But it may have to be delayed till 26 June.

4. I have explained to Miles my views re further troops. The order is:

12 Corps	53 DIV
	59 DIV
	Gds Armd DIV (but Inf. Bde. of this DIV to come as soon as possible).
2 Cdn Inf DIV.	

I am not going to have Canadian Army HQ over here, with all its Army troops, until we really have enough room.

I will if necessary have over 2 Cdn Corps HQ, and put it in Second Army.[92]

The National Archives, WO 205/5B

83
Letter from Field Marshal Sir Alan Brooke to Montgomery
[Holograph]

23 June 1944

Very many thanks for your letter[93] and for the copies of orders, all of which I have found most useful to keep me in your picture.

This bad weather has been a real tragedy in delaying build up and deployment of your forces, it looks however like improving at last. I do hope that you will now be able to get your Caen attacks going.

The Cherbourg side is going well & from all indications Schlieben[94] does not seem very happy about the morale of his troops!

I like your St Malo proposal[95] and hope you will be able to manage something of this kind.

If I can escape I hope before long to fly over for a talk with you, but at present am very busy about the future of Alex's operation and fixing up Far East strategy.[96]

The flying bombs have been producing a warlike atmosphere in London,[97] and I shall soon be asking you to send over officers to gain battle experience on the London front!

Hope you are keeping fit. It meant a great deal to me the other day to shake hands with you again on the soil of France![98] It brought back floods of memories of our early times together in 1940, and all the slow & laborious work we have put in to arrive back again in a position to give the old Bosh a final kick in the pants, and that day should not be too far distant now!

Very best of luck to you in your great task.

IWM, Montgomery Papers Part I, BLM 1/99

84
Letter to Lieutenant-General Sir Oliver Leese[99]

[Holograph]

24 June 1944

I was delighted to get your long letter of 11 June,[100] and to hear all your news. I am so glad George[101] has got a C.B., and John Harding a K.C.B. Please congratulate them both from me.

2. I think the best way to give you my news is to send you a copy of the notes I used when I addressed all General officers of Second Army on 22 June.[102] These will tell you exactly what has happened, the lines on which I have been working, and how things are working out. I have now 23 Divisions on shore and in the battle, and some 2500 tanks; this is not too bad

There are 12 more Divisions to come along. Our present strength is round about ¾ of a million – all put on shore <u>over the beaches</u> in under three weeks – not a bad effort. Our total will go up to two million!!

3. The Americans are doing awfully well. Bradley is first class as an Army Comd and is very willing to learn; the same with Bimbo. Both are very inexperienced, especially on the air side, but both are anxious to learn and are doing so.

I have grave fears that Harry Crerar will not be too good; however, I am keeping him out of the party as long as I can.

George Patton may be a bit of a problem when he comes into it!!

4. I have had only one really anxious moment. After fighting all day on D day we had a bridgehead of only 100 yards on the beaches of 5 American Corps. Very awkward. However they pulled it through somehow and the Bosche cracked.

The American soldier is without doubt a very brave chap; the more I see of him the more I like him.

5. The reinforcement situation has worked well. The total casualties are over 40,000 all told, British and American, but today all units are up to strength.

Incidentally the casualties are less than half what we had thought was likely. I put this down to the fact that we achieved tactical surprise for the initial assault.

6. We have suffered rather heavily in casualties to C.O.'s, and we have lot [sic] some very good ones. We have been lucky in generals; only

one slightly wounded i.e. Thomas Rennie of 3 DIV who was blown up on a mine, but is not bad. I have given 3 DIV to Bolo Whistler.[103]

7. 50 DIV under Douglas Graham[104] have been superb; they have had a lot of casualties. 51 DIV have not been so good under Bullen-Smith; but I have no doubt the Division will be all right when it settles down, and when Bullen is more in the saddle.[105]

3 Canadian DIV started well, but then became rather jumpy; the Bosche snipers in our own back areas rather upset them.

8. Once we were firmly established on shore, everyone in England wanted to come to Normandy. In one week I had:

> The PM ⎫
> C.I.G.S. ⎬ all the same day
> Smuts ⎭
> De Gaulle.
> The King.
> Secretary of State for War.

I finally said I would not have it and got Eisenhower to forbid any more visitors to come.

In any case it was not safe, as all HQ are within range of longe [sic] range guns – and the odd Bosche plane nips over frequently. The Press that came with The King gave away the area of my HQ; I was in the gardens & grounds of a chateau.[106] A nearby chateau was destroyed by bombing two nights later; and heavy gun fire was opened on my HQ two days after that, and I had one killed & two wounded. I then decided to move my HQ, and am having no more visitors!!!

9. Freddie is very well. The gall stones are in hand;[107] but may return to activity at any time if he takes to drink. So he now sinks a good deal of water!

Good luck to you all.

IWM, Leese Papers

85
Message (M29) to Major-General F.W. de Guingand
[Typescript]
24 June 1944, 1940 hours
TOPSEC (.) For Chief of Staff from General Montgomery (.) Have got your letter sent by ADLS (.)[108] Have issued orders

forbidding the writing of any further reports by G1 Liaison officers (.) Have also forbidden officers to send reports on operations or equipment to anyone except through the accepted channels (.) 6 Gds. Tank Bde.[109] to be kept U.K. till asked for by me (.) Now definitely settled that attack of 8 Corps goes in Monday 26 June (.) 30 Corps attacks with 49 Div. early tomorrow Sunday (.)

IWM, Montgomery Papers Part I, BLM 109/2

86
Memorandum to Lieutenant-General Sir Miles Dempsey[110]

[Typescript]

25 June 1944

<u>CONFIDENTIAL</u>

<u>Comd, Second Army.</u>

1. In accordance with their terms of reference and instructions, the GSO1's Liaison with Corps and Divisions are sending in "Immediate Reports" about the battle, and giving their views on operations, equipment, and so on.

2. At this early stage such reports can be of little value; they are bound to be influenced by local conditions, and are unlikely to be the carefully considered views of those whose opinions are of real value.

In cases where adverse comment is made on British equipment such reports are likely to cause a lowering of morale, and a lack of confidence among the troops.

It will generally be found that when the equipment at our disposal is used properly, and the tactics are good, we have no difficulty in defeating the Germans.

3. I have therefore decided that GSO1's Liaison will write no more reports for the present. You will issue orders at once that further reports are forbidden until I give permission.

4. You will also issue orders that under no circumstances whatsoever will commanders or staff officers forward their written views on operations, or equipment, to anyone other than to their immediate superior.

Such views will always be <u>most welcome</u>; but they must be made through the accepted channel of command and responsibility.

5. At a time like this, with large forces employed and great issues at stake, we must be very careful that morale and confidence are maintained at the highest level.

Alarmist reports, written by officers with no responsibility and little battle experience could do a great deal of harm.

There will therefore be no reports, except those made through the accepted channels of command.

6. Please ensure that the above orders are communicated to all commanders now serving in France, and to all others as they arrive in France.

Copy to: Comd, First Canadian Army.
             Comd, 79 Div (for compliance)
             Chief of Staff, 21 Army Group.

IWM, Montgomery Papers Part II, LMD 59/12

87
Message from General Dwight D. Eisenhower to Montgomery

[Typescript]

25 June 1944

I LEARN THAT YOUR ATTACK ON THE EAST FLANK STARTED THIS MORNING PAREN TO GENERAL MONTGOMERY FROM EISENHOWER UNPAREN ALL THE LUCK IN THE WORLD TO YOU AND DEMPSEY PARA PLEASE DO NOT HESITATE TO MAKE THE MAXIMUM DEMANDS FOR ANY AIR ASSISTANCE[111] THAT CAN POSSIBLY BE USEFUL TO YOU PD [period] WHENEVER THERE IS ANY LEGITIMATE OPPORTUNITY WE MUST BLAST THE ENEMY WITH EVERYTHING WE HAVE PARA I AM HOPEFUL THAT BRADLEY CAN QUICKLY CLEAN UP THE CHERBOURG MESS AND TURN AROUND TO ATTACK SOUTHWARDS WHILE YOU HAVE GOT THE ENEMY BY THE THROAT ON THE EAST PD I AM SURE THAT BRADLEY UNDERSTANDS THE NECESSITY OF HITTING HARD AND INCESSANTLY PD AGAIN GOOD LUCK.

IWM, Montgomery Papers Part I, BLM 108/6

88
Message (M30) to General Dwight D. Eisenhower
[Typescript]

25 June 1944, 1930 hours

TOPSEC (.) Personal for General EISENHOWER from MONTGOMERY (.) Thank you for your message to myself and DEMPSEY (.) have now moved my HQ into the American area as am satisfied that the eastern flank is now secure and we can turn over to the offensive in the CAEN sector (.) am in very close touch with BRADLEY and he will attack southwards as soon as he can (.) Attack of Second Army began today[112] with advance to limited objectives by 30 Corps (.) so far all objectives captured (.) blitz attack of 8 Corps goes in tomorrow at 0730 hrs and once it starts I will continue the battle on the eastern flank till one of us cracks and it will NOT be us (.) if we can pull the enemy on to Second Army it will make it easier for First Army when it attacks southwards (.) we want all the air that can usefully be employed and I will not hesitate to ask

IWM, Montgomery Papers Part I, BLM 110/13

89
Message (M31) to General Dwight D. Eisenhower
[Typescript]

26 June 1944, 2240 hours

TOPSEC (.) Personal for General Eisenhower from MONT-GOMERY (.) Attack of Second Army went in today (.) weather very bad with heavy rain and low cloud (.) but very good progress made and leading troops of 8 Corps now on railway line at COLLEVILLE 9264 (.) fighting will go on all day and all night and I am prepared to have a show down with the enemy on my eastern flank for as long as he likes (.) it can be accepted that CHERBOURG is now in First Army hands and the enemy commander has been captured

IWM, Montgomery Papers Part I, BLM 110/14

90
Montgomery's diary notes, 26 June 1944

[Typescript]

<u>26 June.</u>

72. The First U.S. Army captured the enemy commander at Cherbourg and organised resistance then ceased. Isolated parties of Germans continued to fight on, especially in the arsenal area. But the town can now be said to have been captured.

The total U.S. prisoners of war now come to about 20,000.[113]

73. Second Army attack, which began yesterday, was continued today when 8 Corps was launched in a strong attack – on a very narrow front. The attack is in great depth and is intended to go right through to the bridges over the ORNE and the LAIZE, in order to establish an armoured force astride the road CAEN–FALAISE.

The weather today is very bad, with heavy rain and low cloud; the air is grounded. However, good progress was made; but nothing like what we could have made if we had had the air behind us. By the evening attack of Second Army had reached the main road CAEN–VILLERS BOCAGE.

IWM, Montgomery Papers Part II, LMD 59/1

91
Letter to Field Marshal Sir Alan Brooke[114]

[Typescript]

27 June 1944

I was glad to hear from you.[115] Do fly over and have a talk some day; I would love it. It is quite easy for me if you fly over, have lunch and a good talk, and then fly back to U.K. But it is NOT easy when large parties come, who want to go about and see things; we will be fighting very hard now for some weeks, and all commanders will be very busy.

2. It is a great pity the weather went bad on us just when we wanted it to be fine. I had planned to get Second Army offensive launched on 20th June, and given fine weather we would have done it – and the Germans would not have had the extra time <u>they have now had</u> to bring up more stuff.

We got it launched yesterday (Monday); it was a bad day, with rain and low cloud, and our air was grounded; the air plays a big part in the plan and there were attempts to postpone the operation; but the troops were all ready formed up and I ordered it to go, air or no air; and it went – successfully. I cannot give Rommel any more time to get himself organised.

3. I think my general broad plan is maturing quite reasonably well. All the decent enemy stuff, and his Pz and Pz.S.S. divisions, are coming in on the Second Army front – according to plan. That has made it much easier for the First U.S. Army to do its task; and once that Army had collected its balance after the initial dogfights, then it very quickly "roped off" the peninsula and advanced to Cherbourg.

4. I tried very hard to get First U.S. Army to develop its thrust southwards, towards COUTANCE, at the same time as it was completing the capture of Cherbourg. And I have no doubt myself that it could have been started in a small way, and gradually developed. But Bradley didn't want to take the risk; there was no risk really; quick and skilful re-grouping was all that was wanted.

I have to take the Americans along quietly and give them time to get ready; once they are really formed up, then they go like hell. I have got to like them very much indeed, and once you get their confidence they will do anything for you. In the end I think it will work out all right; Second Army attack, now launched, may pull some more stuff over to the CAEN sector from the ST. LO area, and then First U.S. Army will have an easier party when its attack southwards is begun.

5. My main anxiety these days is the possibility that we should not get the full value from our great air power because of jealousies and friction among the air "barons". The real "nigger in the woodpile" is Mary Coningham;[116] I know him well and he is a bad man, not genuine, and terribly jealous. There is constant friction between him and L-M. L-M. does not know much about it; but he is a very genuine chap and will do anything he can to help win the war; he has not got a good staff and he fiddles about himself with a lot of detail he ought to leave alone; but he does play the game.

Mary spends his time in trying to get L-M to "trip-up", and

putting spokes in his wheel; he would prefer to do this rather than win the war quickly; he <u>does</u> know his stuff, but he is a most dangerous chap. The man who ought to keep the whole show on the rails is Tedder; but he is very weak and does nothing about it; actually he and Mary are in the same camp, and <u>both of them</u> combine against L-M.

So L-M is fighting hard to hold his own. I myself am determined to keep right clear of the whole dirty business; but I am also determined not to lose the battle; and the chap who will do anything to help in that respect, and who does not spend his time trying to "trip-up" other people, is L-M.

We manage all right so far. But several hours every day are wasted in argument with the opposing camps, and in ensuring that "air jealousies" do not lose us the battle.

It is a curious world, is it not? But I expect you could add very considerably to the above sordid story, as I am sure similar happenings are of daily occurrence in your circles!!!

6. I have had to stamp very heavily on reports that began to be circulated about the inadequate quality of our tanks, equipment, etc., as compared with the Germans.[117] It all arose over alarmist reports written by Bowring – G1 (L) with 30 Corps;[118] he is a very unbalanced officer and his views are of no value. Furthermore his experience is confined to the "bocage" country – which is not tank country – it is infantry country.

The Panther is not reliable mechanically, and is very vulnerable to penetration from a flank; the 17 pr will go straight through the front, and so will the 6 pr (Sabot)[119] at 400 yards; we have had tests.

If our armour is used properly we have nothing to fear from enemy tanks; in close country we have had cases of infantry "doing in" the Panther with a Piat mortar.[120]

I think we want to pep up our gun power in the tank, and the best way is to increase our "Fireflies"[121] (17 pr in tanks) to two per troop – and get the H.E. good for the 17 pr. This I imagine is being done. Eventually have all 17 prs.

I enclose a copy of the letter I have sent out on the subject of alarmist reports.[122]

7. The battle is going very well.

(a) Cherbourg is now definitely captured; the enemy commander was collected yesterday afternoon (26 June) and that ended organised resistance.

(b) On Second Army front the 8 Corps has broked [*sic*] through the enemy positions on a 4000 yd front between LE-MESNIL-PATRY and NORREY-EN-BESSIN.

On the first day (26 June) it reached the line GRAINVILLE–MOUEN, on the railway line from VILLERS BOCAGE to CAEN.

Today (27 June) 15 DIV is moving forward to the ODON valley, and I hope to see 11 Armd DIV at ESQUAY tomorrow (28 June).

(c) On the right of 8 Corps, 30 Corps has advanced 49 DIV (its left Division) to the line VENDES–RAURAY, and this Division is advancing on NOYERS.

(d) It is again very bad weather, wet with low clouds – today is also bad.

8. I am keeping my eyes very firmly directed to the suspected enemy concentration of three S.S. Pz divisions in the area ALENCON–EVREUX. That may mean dirty work ahead, in the shape of a full-blooded counter stroke. However, we will see.

9. I have got my British strength well built up now, and am prepared to go on fighting on my eastern flank for as long as the Germans like.

I shall have the following additional incoming British Divisions "operational" by the dates stated:

53 DIV	30 June
59 DIV	2 July
Gds Armd	3 July
34 Armd Bde	7 July
2 Canadian Inf DIV }	10 July
2 Canadian Corps HQ }	

10. On my western flank, having captured Cherbourg and thereby released considerable forces for other jobs, I am also now very strong. First U.S. Army will get cracking to the southwards on Saturday 1 July.

11. So the whole situation is now becoming most interesting. It requires all my time and attention, and a close grip on the battle, to ensure that the battle swings the way I want.

At the moment my tender spot is the bridgehead east of the R. ORNE, containing 51 DIV and 6 Airborne DIV. As soon as 8 Corps has got to the ORNE via EVRECY and ESQUAY, then we will get busy on 1 Corps front and push eastwards to the R. DIVES.

12. The forecast of grouping in Second Army is as given in attached Appendix 'A'. That will be worked to, and as soon as 1 Corps can be constituted as stated, then I will send 6 Airborne DIV and the S.S. Bdes back to UK for refitting.

13. I lost John Curry [*sic*][123] killed yesterday; he was my best Armd Bde Comd (4 Armd Bde), and is a great loss.

TOP SECRET
APPENDIX "A".
SECOND BRITISH ARMY.
Forecast of Grouping.

1 Corps	–	3 Div
	–	51 Div
	–	53 Div (30 June)
	–	or 59 Div (2 July)
	–	27 Armd Bde
CDN Corps (10 July)	–	2 Cdn Div (10 July)
	–	3 Cdn Div
	–	Cdn Armd Bde
8 Corps	–	11 Armd Div
	–	Gds Armd Div (3 July)
	–	15 Div
	–	43 Div
	–	4 Armd Bde
	–	31 (Churchill) Armd Bde.

30 Corps	–	<u>7 Armd Div</u>
	–	49 Div
	–	50 Div
	–	8 Armd Bde
	–	56 Inf Bde

12 Corps	–	53 Div (30 June)
(Army Reserve)	–	or 59 Div (2 July)
	–	33 Armd Bde
	–	34 (Churchill) Armd Bde
		(7 July).

IWM, Montgomery Papers Part II, LMD 59/13

92
Montgomery's diary notes, 27 June 1944

[Typescript]

<u>27 June.</u>

74. The attack of 8 Corps progressed further and reached the R ODON. That is good. Steps are now being taken to hold firm bridgeheads over the river and to push an armoured force up on to the high ground about ESQUAY.

75. I had a conference with Army Commanders[124] at 1630 hrs. The situation is good; but we must be careful on Second Army front; there are indications of strong German reinforcements moving this way – enemy air cover over certain areas gives me cause to think this is so.

The main job of Second Army is to draw the enemy reserves on to our EASTERN flank, and to capture CAEN; but the over-riding factor is that there must be no set-back.

First U.S. Army will deliver a strong attack southwards on Saturday 1 July.

76. Our prisoners now total 41,000.

77. I sent a personal letter to the C.I.G.S. by my M.A. (Lt.-Col. Dawnay). A copy of it is filed with this diary (No. 1093 dated 27 June 1944).[125]

IWM, Montgomery Papers Part II, LMD 59/1

93
Montgomery's diary notes, 28 June 1944

[Typescript]

<u>28 June.</u>

78. 11 Armd. Div. crossed the R. ODON and secured the high ground about ESQUAY vide para. 74.[126]

The enemy launched counter-attacks against the flanks of the corridor which we had pushed into his positions; but these were beaten off.

79. The success of our attack forced the enemy to draw on other areas for reserves and 2 S.S. Pz. Div. appeared on the ODON front, having come over from ST. LO. This is good.

IWM, Montgomery Papers Part II, LMD 59/1

94
Message (M33) to the Prime Minister

[Typescript]

29 June 1944, 1300 hours

TOPSEC (.) Following personal for PRIME MINISTER from General Montgomery with copy for CIGS (.) begins (.) thank you for your message (.)[127] since offensive began on eastern flank on 26 June we have pulled two extra Panzer Divisions in to that flank (.) they are 1 SS and 2 SS (.) have now six Panzer Divisions involved in trying to hold my advance west and south-west of CAEN (.) have since D day worked on the general policy of getting enemy heavily involved on eastern flank so that my affairs on the western flank could proceed the easier (.) so am well satisfied with present situation (.) am regrouping on western flank and strong offensive over that side begins on Saturday 1 July on general thrust line COUTANCE–AVRANCHES–VIRE (.) total prisoners now 41000 (.) ends (.)

IWM, Montgomery Papers Part I, BLM 110/16

95
Letter from Field Marshal Sir Alan Brooke to Montgomery

[Holograph]

29 June 1944

Very many thanks of your letter.[128]

Delighted that your attack is going so well, & do hope you will now have some better weather.

I was very interested in what you said about friction amongst Air Commanders. I shall do what I can from this end. I have known for a long time about Coningham as I had already discovered his failings when he was with you in the advance on Tripoli![129] It is rather delicate ground but I shall do what I can for you from this end. Delighted to see the instruction you sent out about equipment.[130] There is far too great a tendency in the Army now to go on complaining of its tools instead of getting on with the job.

Hope to manage a lunch with you soon, but at present am engaged in a serious war with our American friends in Washington who are doing their best to stop us from deriving full advantage from Kesselring's blunders![131] The situation is strained at present to say the least of it.

Write and let me know how you get on & if there is anything I can help about.

Best of luck to you.

IWM, Montgomery Papers Part I, BLM 1/100

96
Letter from Lieutenant-General Omar N. Bradley to Montgomery[132]

[Typescript]

29 June 1944

As I intimated to you over the telephone last evening I find that it is essential that I put off my attack until Monday.[133] The storm in the UK has delayed the sailing of VIII Corps troops so that we will be lucky if we have them available by Monday. I hope to have enough by that time to jump off. In addition, it has taken longer to clean up the Cherbourg peninsula than I had hoped. The 4th Division finished its operations this morning. However, they have sustained approximately 6,000 casualties and, of course, this includes a large number of officers and non-commissioned officers. They have also lost a lot of equipment. It will take several days to put them in shape, as to personnel and equipment, ready for another operation.

From the progress made by the 9th Division today in their attack on the Cap de Hague it may take them several days to clean up that peninsula. They have also been fighting for many days and have suffered severe casualties.

By waiting until Monday we will be able to attack with the 79th and 90th Divisions in the VIII Corps and with the 8th Division in reserve. The latter should be operational by Wednesday. This should be as soon as this division is needed by the VIII Corps.

Either the 9th or 4th should be ready to back up the 83rd in its attack in the VII Corps by Tuesday or Wednesday.

I am very sorry to have to make this postponement but I feel that we must be set for this next attack so that when we once break his present defensive lines we will give him no chance to get set but can keep right on pushing until we get at least to the base of the peninsula. In fact, I would like to keep right on around the corner. I feel that this is entirely feasible due to the fact that he has placed so much of his strength in front of Dempsey.[134]

IWM, Montgomery Papers Part II, LMD 115/1

97
Montgomery's diary notes, 29 June 1944

[Typescript]

29 June.

80. Three more additional Pz. divisions appeared on the ODON front today: 1 S.S., 9 S.S., 10 S.S. That makes a total of eight Pz. divisions all involved in trying to stem my advance west and southwest of CAEN; this is excellent.

81. The problem is now becoming clearer. Para. 75[135] applies, and there must be no reverse. I instructed Second Army to pause in its advance, to get cohesion and balance, and get all set to receive a strong attack.

This was done, two good bridgeheads were formed over the R. ODON, each of one Inf. Bde., and the Armd. Bde. of 11 Armd. Div. was brought back to the north of the river from ESQUAY.

82. I addressed the senior officers of 53 Div.[136] This Division is now complete and ready for battle, and has been given to 8 Corps.

IWM, Montgomery Papers Part II, LMD 59/1

98
Montgomery's Directive (M505) to Lieutenant-General
O.N. Bradley, First US Army, and Lieutenant-General Sir
Miles Dempsey, Second British Army

[Cyclostyle]

30 June 1944

The General Situation.

1. My broad policy, once we had secured a firm lodgement area, has always been to draw the main enemy forces in to the battle on our eastern flank, and to fight them there, so that our affairs on the western flank could proceed the easier.

2. We have been very successful in this policy. Cherbourg has fallen without any interference from enemy reserves brought in from other areas; the First US Army is proceeding with its re-organisation and re-grouping, undisturbed by the enemy; the western flank is quiet.

All this is good; it is on the western flank that territorial gains are essential at this stage, as we require space on that side for the development of our administration.

By forcing the enemy to place the bulk of his strength in front of the Second Army, we have made easier the acquisition of territory on the western flank.

3. Our policy has been so successful that the Second Army is now opposed by a formidable array of German Panzer Divisions – eight definitely identified, and possibly more to come.

The more recent arrivals seem to have come from far afield. The Divisions identified between CAUMONT and CAEN are as follows:

> 21 Pz
> 2 Pz
> 1 SS
> 2 SS
> 9 SS
> 10 SS
> 12 SS
> LEHR

21 Pz is on the CAEN front; 2 Pz is on the CAUMONT front; the remaining six divisions are collected round the 8 Corps penetration in between.

4. It is not yet clear whether Hitler proposes to concentrate great strength in N.W. Europe so as to annihilate the Allied forces in Normandy. He may decide that this is a good proposition; and in order to achieve success he may be quite prepared to give ground gradually on the Russian front, and to accept reverses in that theatre.

His policy in this respect will emerge in due course.

5. For the present it is quite clear that he has reinforced the Normandy front strongly, and that a full-blooded counter-attack seems imminent. We welcome such action.

6. Our tactics must remain unchanged. Briefly, they are as follows:–

(a) <u>To retain the initiative.</u>
We shall do this only by offensive action. On no account must we remain inactive. Without the initiative we cannot win.

(b) <u>To have no set-backs.</u>
This is very important on the eastern flank; the enemy has concentrated great strength here and he must not be allowed to use it successfully. Any set-back on the eastern flank might have direct repercussions on the quick development of our plans for the western flank.

(c) <u>To proceed relentlessly with our plans</u>.
These will be based on the broad policy indicated in para 1 above.

We must retain such balance and poise in our dispositions that there is never any need to re-act to enemy moves or thrusts; the enemy can do what he likes; <u>we</u> will proceed with <u>our</u> plans.

Plan in Outline.

7. To hold the maximum number of enemy divisions on our eastern flank between CAEN and VILLERS BOCAGE, and to swing the western or right flank of the Army Group southwards and eastwards in a wide sweep so as to threaten the line of withdrawal of such enemy divisions to the south of PARIS.

The bridges over the SEINE between PARIS and the sea have been destroyed by the Allied air forces, and will be kept out of action; a strong Allied force established in the area LE MANS–ALENCON would threaten seriously the enemy concentration in the CAEN area and its "get-away" south of PARIS.

Second British Army.

8. Tasks as follows:

(a) To hold the main enemy forces in the area between CAEN and VILLERS BOCAGE.

(b) To have no set-backs.

(c) To develop operations for the capture of CAEN as opportunity offers – and the sooner the better.

9. A full-blooded enemy counter-attack seems likely, put in somewhere between CAEN and VILLERS BOCAGE; the main axis of such an attack is not yet apparent. In order to provide a mobile reserve in the hands of the Army Commander, the 7 Armd DIV, now holding the right divisional sector, will be relieved tomorrow by First Army and that divisional sector will be included in First Army area; the inter-army boundary to be adjusted accordingly.

10. The careful attention of the Army Commander is drawn to para 6.

First US Army.

11. To develop an offensive southwards on the right flank, beginning on Monday 3 July.

12. The Army to pivot on its left in the CAUMONT area, and to swing southwards and eastwards on to the general line CAUMONT–VIRE–MORTAIN–FOUGERES.

13. A strong thrust to be made eastwards from VIRE to secure the important intercommunication centre of FLERS.

14. On reaching the base of the peninsula at AVRANCHES, the right hand Corps (8 Corps) to be turned westwards into BRITTANY and directed on RENNES and ST MALO.

This Corps to consist of three infantry divisions and one armoured division.

15. As regards the remainder of the Army.

Plans will be made to direct a strong right wing in a wide sweep, south of the bocage country, towards successive objectives as follows:

    (a)   LAVAL–MAYENNE.

    (b)   LE MANS–ALENCON.

16. It is highly important that when the above operations begin on 3 July, vide para 11, they should be carried out with the greatest drive and energy.

There must be no pause until the Army has swung up on to the line CAUMONT–FOUGERES, vide para 12; thereafter, the less delays the better.

17. The Army will extend its left flank tomorrow, 1 July, to include the sector now held by 7 Armd DIV of Second Army – vide para 8.

IWM, Montgomery Papers Part I, BLM 126/6

99
Montgomery's diary notes, 30 June 1944

[Typescript]

<u>30 June.</u>

83. I decided that Second Army must have a good reserve, as the thrust line of the expected full-blooded enemy counter-attack was not certain.

So I ordered First U.S. Army to be prepared to relieve 7 Armd. Div., the right Division of Second Army – using 2 U.S. Armd. Div. for the purpose. The whole Div. sector to pass to First U.S. Army. Recces. to begin accordingly; final decision this evening.

84. I had a conference of Army Commanders (Bradley and Dempsey) in the evening. I gave out my orders for the next phase.

Briefly my plan is this:

(a) We have got all the main German strength involved in the battle on our eastern flank.

(b) Second British Army will have the job of holding it there.

(c) First U.S. Army will pivot on its left flank, and swing southwards and eastwards; it will finally develop a strong easterly movement south of the bocage country.

The operations of First Army to begin on 3 July.

I had hoped to begin on 1 July, but Bradley could not get ready by this date.

85. After the conference I issued M505,[137] the directive on the next phase; this is filed in the diary.

IWM, Montgomery Papers Part II, LMD 59/1

July

100
Message (M38) to Field Marshal Sir Alan Brooke

[Typescript]

1 July 1944, 1815 hours

TOPSEC (.) Personal for C.I.G.S. from General Montgomery (.) Understand from DAWNAY that EISENHOWER has stated that I support his views regarding ANVIL (.)[1] Want to make it quite clear that I have had no discussion with him about ANVIL and do NOT know what his views are (.) Above is for your personal information (.) Do you consider I should discuss the matter with EISENHOWER who is coming this way tomorrow Sunday.

IWM, Montgomery Papers Part I, BLM 115/6

101
Message from Field Marshal Sir Alan Brooke to Montgomery[2]

[Holograph (of a clerk)]

1 July 1944, 2340 hours

TOPSECRET (.) personal for General MONTGOMERY from C.I.G.S. (.) your M.38[3] 1 July (.) I note what you say but consider you should NOT discuss matter with EISENHOWER (.)[4] That may do more harm than good at this stage

IWM, Montgomery Papers Part I, BLM 115/7

102
Message (M39) to Major-General F.E.W. Simpson

[Typescript]

2 July 1944, 1440 hours

TOPSEC (.) Personal for General Simpson D.M.O. from General Montgomery (.) Your 435 dated 30 June received (.)[5] Would like you to come over here Thursday next 6 July and stay night (.) Will send my aeroplane for you to NORTHOLT (.) You should leave NORTHOLT 1400 hrs. 6 July (.) Will fly you back to London on morning 7 July (.) Let me know if above possible (.) Saw EISENHOWER today[6] and he opened the subject of operations in Mediterranean theatre and asked me for my views (.) Gave him my personal views as follows (.) First (.) We should continue the battle in ITALY as long as we get a good dividend and can destroy German divisions (.) Second (.) When we no longer get a dividend in Italy then an ANVIL would help us here (.) Third (.) It seemed to me that we would not do much good operating over and beyond the ALPS in winter but my opinion on this matter was not of much value as I did not know the various pros and cons (.)

IWM, Montgomery Papers Part I, BLM 115/8

103
Letter to Sir James Grigg

[Typescript with holograph addition][7]

2 July 1944

I have had to withdraw 6 DWR[8] from 49 Division as it is no longer fit for battle. This battalion has seen some heavy fighting and has suffered very heavy casualties especially among key personnel, and as a result it is no longer able to assimilate the reinforcements sent up to it. I have therefore withdrawn the battalion from 49 Division and have replaced it in the Division by 1 Leicesters from 162 Bde.

I enclose a report[9] which the new C.O. of the 6 DWR has made on the present state of this unit, which I think you may like to see. *I consider the C.O. displays a defeatist mentality and is not a "proper chap".*

Churchill Archives Centre, Grigg Papers 9/8/12(a)

104
Letter (M508) to Field Marshal Sir Alan Brooke

[Typescript]

7 July 1944

Simpson will take this letter to you and will give you my latest news.[10]

PRESENT OPERATIONS.

2. I am working quietly on the general plan contained in my Directive M.505[11] dated 30 June. We must keep the initiative and not let the enemy "dig in."

3. The American offensive on my western flank is gathering momentum slowly. When it began on 3 July the weather was too awful; driving rain, mist, low cloud, no visibility; and since then we have had fine periods only, and no continued spell of good weather. The country over that side is most difficult; it is very thick and approximates to jungle fighting. However the Americans are gaining ground gradually, and shortly will go much quicker I think. At the time of writing this they have got past LA HAYE DU PUITS, and are pushing southwards.[12]

In order to help the western flank I am going to set things alight on my eastern flank, beginning tomorrow; the enemy is very sensitive to thrusts eastwards in the CAEN sector, and I shall make use of that fact.

4. And so, on my eastern flank, I have ordered Second Army to develop operations so as to get CAEN[13] this week-end, i.e., by Monday, 10 July. I want first that part of CAEN which lies north of the river, and I think it might be got by Monday.

The phases on this flank would be as follows:

(a) To get our front positions up on to the line of the ORNE through CAEN, and thence along the R. ODON to VIRSON. I shall begin this tomorrow 8 July.

(b) To get that part of CAEN which lies south of the ORNE, and to organise operations to push S.E. on that axis.

(c) To extend our positions up the ORNE to about AMAYE, and get bridgeheads over the ORNE from AMAYE northwards.

We will do (a) first, beginning tomorrow; then (b) and (c) simultaneously.

5. The show which begins tomorrow in the CAEN sector will be a big operation, designed to get CAEN and eventually to get an armoured force out into the good going to the S.E. of the town.

This will tend to draw attention away from my western flank.

Also, we cannot be 100% happy on the eastern flank until we have got CAEN. We have pulled such a weight of enemy on to our eastern flank that I want to get 100% happy there!!

THE AIR PROBLEM.[14]

6. The situation with regard to the air "barons" is as follows.

Tedder came to see me and I tackled him squarely on the subject of Coningham.[15] I put the following points to him:

(a) The Army was beginning to have a lack of confidence in Coningham.

(b) The Army knows that Coningham says unpleasant things about it – behind its back.

(c) The Army is having difficulty in getting its full value from the available air support because of the friction between Coningham and Leigh-Mallory.

(d) The Army is beginning to wonder if Coningham is a loyal member of the team.

I said that I would weigh in 100% to try and put things right. But the only person who can really prove that the above is not the case – is Coningham himself.

7. Tedder spoke to Coningham; I do not know what took place.

But Coningham came straight over to see me. I told him what I had told Tedder, and put to him the points given in para. 6 above.

Coningham was almost in tears.

Since then his attitude has been very different, and his advances almost an embarassment [sic]!!

8. I have to proceed very carefully.

And I have had long talks with Dempsey on the subject.

Dempsey and his staff do not know a very great deal yet about how to wield air power; and Dempsey himself has slipped up once or twice in the matter. Coningham knows this and will seize on any opportunity to make capital over it for his own purposes.

So I am watching over this very carefully myself, and Dempsey keeps in close touch with me about air matters; I have explained to him the pitfalls and the dangers.

He is very teachable and will soon get "the form"; just at present he is inclined to rush his fences somewhat and to be impatient; whereas the only real answer is to proceed very carefully, and to lead "the air" down the garden path – but we must always be right, and remember that the path is a bit slippery.

THE FUTURE.

9. I am interested in the way my name seems to have been taken in vain in connection with ANVIL.

I said nothing about it; but when Eisenhower came to see me on 1st July[16] he gave tongue on the whole subject, and asked me for my views.

I then gave him my views, as follows:

(a) So long as we are getting a really good dividend in Italy, surely we must go on there. It is madness to close down on a good thing, and to open up another front with all its administrative problems; you may find that the new front takes a very long time to pay any dividend at all.

(b) The business in Italy is helping us here very much; therefore go on with it.

(c) When the business in Italy begins to cease paying a dividend, and it is clear that it is not helping us to any extent, then switch the thrust line.

And it may well be <u>then</u> that an ANVIL is the best proposition. But I personally am not in full possession of all the facts, and my opinion as to the best thrust line for a new venture is not now of much value; I am far too busy keeping a tight grip on the battle in Normandy.

10. I hope that para. 9 is in general accordance with your own views.[17] I would be glad to know this as I feel I must be careful on this point. And you can be quite certain that I will never give out any views without first checking up on whether it is in general accord with you.

11. I do not believe the enemy has got the stuff to prepare and man the PISA–RIMINI line; it seems as if Alex may flush it with luck.

12. In general, I see the picture as follows:

Phase 1. In Hitler's eyes, the WEST has priority.

Phase 2. The Russians get too near to Germany proper to remain second priority.

Phase 3. The Germans decide which Allies to lose the war to.

We are now only beginning Phase 1. It is possible that if the Russians continue at their present rate they may jump the enemy into Phase 2; that would be very good.

SYSTEM OF COMMAND IN FRANCE.[18]

13. There is great pressure at SHAEF to get the U.S. Army Group in operation, commanding the two U.S. armies; the pressure comes chiefly from the younger element. I am keeping right clear of all discussion on this subject.

14. But I have explained very clearly to Eisenhower that the direction and control of the land battle in France is a whole-time job for one man; the battle can very easily become untidy and the armies become unbalanced; it takes me all my time to keep the battle swinging our way, to ensure that we retain the initiative, and to ensure there is no possibility of a set-back; we are up against a skilful and desperate enemy and we must not give him any opportunity to deal us a blow which might unsettle us.

15. I have then explained that if he forms a U.S. Army Group, and SHAEF wants to take direct charge of the battle, he himself must come over here and devote his whole and undivided attention to the battle. Any idea that he could run the land battle from England, or could do it in his spare time, would be playing with fire.

16. Eisenhower himself has, I fancy, no delusions on this subject.

He has now decided to form the U.S. Army Group, with Bradley in command, and to put it under me.

I will then command:

First U.S. Army Group.
Second British Army.
First Canadian Army.

And I see no difficulty in this.

I do not think very much of Hodges[19] who will take over First U.S. Army from Bradley. But I shall deal with Bradley; we know each other well now, and he is most co-operative.[20]

MEMORANDUM ON ARMOUR.[21]

17. I have been working for some days on a memorandum on armour and tanks. It is meant to provide ammunition to shoot down people who say that our tanks are no good. And it gives my views on future tank policy.

I have sent copies to Weekes [sic] and I hope you will find it of use.

I shall be interested to know if the War Office will agree to do what I suggest; also whether my views here are in general accord with opinion from other fronts.

CANADIANS.

18. I am not too happy about the Canadians. Keller[22] has proved himself to be quite unfit to command a Division; he is unable to get the best out of his soldiers – who are grand chaps.

If he was a British Div. Commander I would have removed him before this. But I am putting 2 Cdn. Corps into the line on or about 10 July, and I think it is best that Guy Simmonds [*sic*] should remove Keller, i.e., let the Canadians do it themselves.[23]

19. Harry Crerar once suggested to me that Keller would be the next for a Corps. The idea is quite absurd. A Bde. Comd. is his ceiling.

20. I fear very much that Harry Crerar will be quite unfit to command an Army; I am keeping him out of it as long as I can. He is a most awfully nice chap, but he is very prosy and stodgy, and he is very definitely not a commander.

He commanded the 1st Cdn. Corps for two years, and when it went into battle in Italy the Corps H.Q. proved to be quite untrained – so Oliver Leese tells me.

21. The only really good senior officer in the Canadian Army is Guy Simmonds; he is quite 1st Class.

CASUALTIES.

22. These are as follows:

	K.	W.	M.	Total.
British.	3,501	16,308	5,716	25,525
U.S.	5,757	26,300	5,425	37,482
				63,007

23.PRISONERS OF WAR.

These now total 51,000.

24.MY PRESENT TANK STRENGTH.

British.   2,316

U.S.   <u>1,466</u>

           <u>3,782</u>

IWM, Montgomery Papers Part I, BLM 126/9

105
Letter from General Dwight D. Eisenhower to Montgomery[24]

[Typescript]

7 July 1944

Since returning here[25] I have been studying our existing situation and future prospects, particularly in consultation with G-2[26] and the Air Commanders.[27]

When we began this operation we demanded from the air that they obtain air superiority and that they delay the arrival of enemy reinforcements in the NEPTUNE area. Both of these things have been done. In the meantime, in spite of storms and hard luck, our ground build-up has proceeded rapidly and on the British side we are approaching the limit of our available resources. Very soon, also, we will be approaching the limit in the capacity of the ports now in our possession to receive and maintain American troops. Thereafter it is possible for the enemy to increase his <u>relative</u> strength; actually he seems to be doing so, already.

These things make it necessary to examine every single possibility with a view to expanding our beachhead and getting more room for maneuvering so as to use our forces <u>before</u> the enemy can obtain substantial equality in such things as infantry, tanks and artillery. On the left we need depth and elbow room and at least enough territory to protect the SWORD beach from enemy fire. We should, by all means, secure suitable air fields. On the right we need to obtain additional small ports that are available on the north side of the Brittany coast and to break out into the open where our present superiority can be used.

I am familiar with your plan for generally holding firmly with your left, attracting thereto all of the enemy armor, while your right pushes down the Peninsula and threatens the rear and flank of the forces facing Second British Army. However, the advance on the right has been slow and laborious, due not only to the nature of the country and the impossibility of employing air and artillery with maximum effectiveness, but to the arrival on that front of reinforcements, I believe the 353d Div. In the meantime, I understand from G-2 that some infantry has arrived on the front opposite the British Army allowing the enemy to withdraw certain Panzer elements for re-grouping and establishing of a reserve.[28]

It appears to me that we must use all possible energy in a determined effort to prevent a stalemate or of facing the necessity of fighting a major defensive battle with the slight depth we now have in the bridgehead.

We have not yet attempted a major full-dress attack on the left flank supported by everything we could bring to bear. To do so would require some good weather, so that our air could give maximum assistance. Through Coningham and Broadhurst[29] there is available all the air that could be used, even if it were determined to be necessary to resort to area bombing in order to soften up the defense. On the right, about the only way I could visualize helping out would be by an airborne operation against St. Malo. At one time this was reported to me as impracticable because of the strength of the defensive garrison at that point. I am having the matter re-examined in the light of information that the enemy has thinned out very considerably in that region. The First British Airborne Division is now available and if it could seize the port and a U.S. Infantry Division could follow in quickly by sea, they could, from that position, assist materially in getting your right flank rapidly down the Cotentin Peninsula.

Because of the transfers that we have to make to the Mediterranean to help out in ANVIL,[30] I think we cannot put on a full-scale three or four division airborne attack before early September. We are planning for this eventuality but in the meantime we will have the lift for more than a full division and the moon will again be right for such operations along about August 3rd or 4th.

I know that you are thinking every minute about these weighty questions. What I want you to know is that I will back you up to the limit in any effort you may decide upon to prevent a deadlock and will do my best to phase forward any unit you might find necessary. For example, if you could use in an attack on your left flank an American armored division, I would be glad to make it available and get it in to you as soon as possible.

Beedle[31] tells me that he was prevented by weather from dropping in to see you the other day, but will be coming over soon. Possibly he will bring this letter. In the meantime, please be assured that I will produce everything that is humanly possible to assist you in any plan that promises to get us the elbow room we need. The air and everything else will be available.

If you get a chance to talk to Beedle, please give him any views you have on these matters, so whatever duties or planning may devolve on my headquarters can be expeditiously carried out.

With best of luck.

IWM, Montgomery Papers Part I, BLM 126/10

106
Letter (M509)[32] to General Dwight D. Eisenhower

[Typescript]

8 July 1944

Thank you for your letter of 7 July.

2. I am, myself, quite happy about the situation. I have been working throughout on a very definite plan, and I now begin to see daylight.

3. Initially, my main pre-occupations were:

(a) to ensure that we kept the initiative,

 and,

(b) to have no setbacks or reverses.

It was not always too easy to comply with these two fundamental principles, especially during the period when we were not too strong ourselves and were trying to build up our strength.

But that period is now over, and we can now set about the enemy – and are doing so.

4. I think we must be quite clear as to what is vital, and what is

not; if we get our sense of values wrong we may go astray. There are three things which stand out very clearly in my mind:

(a) <u>First.</u>

We must get the Brittany peninsula. From an administrative point of view this is essential; if we do NOT get it we will be greatly handicapped in developing our full potential.

(b) <u>Second.</u>

We do not want to get hemmed in to a relatively small area; we must have space – for manoeuvre, for administration, and for airfields.

(c) <u>Third.</u>

We want to engage the enemy in battle, to write-off his troops, and generally to kill Germans. Exactly where we do this does not matter, so long as (a) and (b) are complied with.

5. The first thing we had to do was to capture CHERBOURG.

I wanted CAEN too, but we could not manage both at the same time and it was clear to me that the enemy would resist fiercely in the CAEN sector.

So I laid plans to develop operations towards the R. ODON on the Second Army front, designed to draw the enemy reserves on to the British Sector so that the First US Army could get to do its business in the west all the easier. We were greatly hampered by very bad weather and the offensive towards the ODON did not begin till 26 June, on which date the enemy commander at CHERBOURG was captured and the port was practically in First Army hands.

But this offensive <u>did</u> draw a great deal on to it; and I then gave instructions to the First Army to get on quickly with its offensive southwards on the western flank. There were problems of reorganisation, and re-grouping, and bad weather on the beaches; and First Army offensive could not begin before 3 July.

6. The First Army advance on the right has been slower than I thought would be the case; the country is terribly close, the weather has been atrocious, and certain enemy reserves have been brought in against it.

So I then decided to set my eastern flank alight, and to put the wind up the enemy by seizing CAEN and getting bridgeheads over the ORNE; this action would, indirectly, help the business going on over on the western flank.

These operations by Second Army on the eastern flank began today; they are going very well; they aim at securing CAEN and at getting our eastern flank on the ORNE river – with bridgeheads over it.

7. Having got our eastern flank on the ORNE, I shall then organise the operations on the eastern flank so that our affairs on the western flank can be got on with the quicker.

It may be that the best proposition is for the Second Army to continue its effort, and to drive southwards with its left flank on the ORNE; or it may be a good proposition for it to cross the ORNE and establish itself on the FALAISE road.

Alternatively, having got CAEN and established the eastern flank on the ORNE, it may be best for Second Army to take over all the CAUMONT area – and to the west of it – and thus release some of Bradley's divisions for the southward "drive" on the western flank.

8. Day to day events in the next few days will show which is best.

The attack of Second Army towards CAEN, which is going on now, is a big show; so far only 1 Corps is engaged; 8 Corps takes up the running on Monday morning (10 July). I shall put everything into it.

It is all part of the bigger tactical plan, and it is all in accordance with para 4 above.

9. I am not anxious to seize ST MALO by an airborne operation, if it can be avoided. I would much prefer to take it from the land and this is what I hope to do – vide my M505[33] dated 30 June. But it may happen that Bradley's southward move is very slow and requires help to get down the Cotentin peninsula; in this case an air and sea move against ST MALO might become necessary, and it is being planned in case it is needed.

10. I am very anxious to secure the Quiberon Bay area so that we can get a move on with developing it for our administrative needs.

This would be done sometime about the first week in August – when I hope 8 U.S. Corps will have turned the corner and be heading for RENNES and ST MALO.

This operation is being planned.

11. I do not need an American armoured division for use on my eastern flank; we really have all the armour we need. The great

thing now is to get First and Third U.S. Armies up to a good strength, and to get them cracking on the southward thrust on the western flank, and then to turn Patton westwards into the Brittany peninsula.

12. To sum up.

I think the battle is going very well. The enemy is being heavily attacked all along the line; and we are killing a lot of Germans.

Of one thing you can be quite sure – there will be no stalemate.

If the enemy decides to concentrate very great and overwhelming strength against us, that will take a considerable time; and during that time we will relentlessly get on with <u>our</u> business; we are very strong now and need not delay any longer for build-up purposes.

I shall always ensure that I am well balanced; at present I have no fears of any offensive move the enemy might make; I am concentrating on making the battle swing our way.

IWM, Montgomery Papers Part I, BLM 126/10

107
Message (M45) to Field Marshal Sir Alan Brooke

[Typescript]

8 July 1944, 2215 hours

TOPSEC (.) Personal for CIGS from General Montgomery (.) leading troops of Second Army now in outskirts of CAEN and pushing on tonight towards centre of city and the river line (.) operations were developed rapidly from the NE by 3 Div and from the NW by 3 Cdn Div and it is these two Divisions that are now in the outskirts of the city (.) considerable numbers of enemy still north of city facing 59 Div and these are likely to be cut off (.) am now directing Second Army to operate southwards with its left flank on the R ORNE securing bridgeheads at suitable places (.) its objective will be the general line THURY HARCOURT– AUNAY–CAUMONT (.) have decided on this line of advance for Second Army as being the best way to help First US Army forward (.) it is very necessary for us to get the BRITTANY Peninsula for admin reasons

IWM, Montgomery Papers Part I, BLM 110/18

108
Montgomery's diary notes, 8 July 1944

[Typescript]

<u>8 July.</u>

13. The attack to secure CAEN,[34] and get our eastern flank on the R. ORNE, went in at 0500 hrs. It had very heavy artillery support.[35]

It at once made good progress and by the afternoon it was quite clear that we were going to capture CAEN.

14. The earliest success was gained on the N.E. of the city by 3 Div., and so it was on that flank that armoured and other reserves were flung in.

On the N.W. of the city the Canadians did not do well initially; eventually they came along better.

Then the two flanks of the attack went in towards the city and the Germans opposing 59 Div. in the centre got cut off.

15. During the day I received a letter from Eisenhower,[36] expressing concern at our lack of progress. This is the first time he has ever expressed any views on the battle; and it arrived at a rather unfortunate time – just as we were about to capture CAEN!!!

I sent him an answer – M.509.[37]

16. I received letters today from Dempsey on the subject of Keller,[38] reporting privately that he was not fit to command a Division. I sent them on to Crerar, saying that I agreed.

In my opinion Keller is not fit to command 3 Canadian Div. But the Division goes into 2 Cdn. Corps very soon and it is better that Canadian Generals should handle the matter.

I fear that Crerar himself has no real qualifications that fit him to command an Army; he is not a commander and inspires no confidence.

The only really good general in the Canadian forces is Simmonds [*sic*].

The letters about Keller are filed in this diary.

IWM, Montgomery Papers Part II, LMD 60/1

109
Message (M46) to General Dwight D. Eisenhower

[Typescript]

9 July 1944, 2130 hours

Personal for EISENHOWER from MONTGOMERY (.) thank you very much for your message (.)[39] operations on eastern flank have proceeded entirely according to plan and will continue without a halt (.) 8 British Corps joins in tomorrow (.) have ordered Second Army to operate southwards with left flank on ORNE to secure general line THURY HARCOURT–MONT PINCON feature–LE BENY BOCAGE (.) all this will help to expedite affairs on western flank (.) have had good conference with Bradley today and he will crack ahead hard tomorrow

IWM, Montgomery Papers Part I, BLM 110/19

110
Montgomery's diary notes, 9 July 1944

[Typescript]

9 July.

17. I addressed[40] the senior officers of:

    H.Q. First Canadian Army.

    H.Q. 2 Canadian Corps.

    2 Canadian Inf. Div.

18. The capture of CAEN was completed and the whole city north of the river was in our hands by 1600 hrs.

19. I saw Bradley and Dempsey[41] and went carefully into the situation on the whole battle front. Now that we have CAEN the problem is much easier. Affairs on the western flank are not going quick enough, and I can see that the main operations of Second Army must be directed in a more S.W. thrust so as to affect directly the battle on the western flank.

IWM, Montgomery Papers Part II, LMD 60/1

III
Montgomery's Directive (M510) to Lieutenant-General O.N. Bradley, First US Army, Lieutenant-General Sir Miles Dempsey, Second British Army, Lieutenant-General G. Patton, Third US Army, and Lieutenant-General H.D. Crerar, First Canadian Army

[Cyclostyle and holograph][42]
10 July 1944

THE GENERAL SITUATION.

1. Now that CAEN has been captured our tactical situation is very good on the eastern flank. The general problem confronting us is now much simplified and we can continue the work of implementing our policy with greater force.

2. My broad policy remains unchanged. It is to draw the main enemy forces in to the battle on our eastern flank, and to fight them there, so that our affairs on the western flank may proceed the easier.

   See para 1 of M505 dated 30 June 44.[43]

3. But the enemy has been able to bring reinforcements to oppose the advance of the First Army. It is important to speed up our advance[44] on the western flank; the operations of the Second Army must therefore be so staged that they will have a direct influence on the operations of the First Army, as well as holding enemy forces on the eastern flank.

4. The following points are now very important:

(a) <u>First</u>

   We must gain possession of the Brittany peninsula. From an administrative point of view this is essential; if its capture is long delayed we will be greatly hampered in developing our full potential.

(b) <u>Second</u>

   Having captured CAEN and thus secured a sound position on our eastern flank, we must now gain depth and space in our lodgement area. We require space for manoeuvre, for administrative purposes, and for airfields.

(c) Third

We must engage the enemy in battle unceasingly; we must "write-off" his troops; and generally we must kill Germans.

5. We are now so strong, and are so well situated, that we can attack the Germans hard and continuously in the relentless pursuit of our objectives.[45]

This will be done by both First and Second Armies.

So long as we capture or kill the enemy troops in large numbers we are doing what is needed. In the LA HAYE DU PUITS sector alone the 8 US Corps has taken 2000 prisoners and actually buried 500 dead Germans in the last week; many more still remain to be buried; all this is excellent.

Second British Army.

6. CAEN will be held securely, and our positions in the bridgehead east of the R. ORNE to the north of CAEN will be maintained, and improved as opportunity offers.

The FAUBERG DE VAUCELLES, lying on the south side of the ORNE opposite CAEN, will be secured and a bridgehead thus gained, if this can be done without undue losses; I am not prepared to have heavy casualties to obtain this bridgehead over the ORNE, as we shall have plenty elsewhere.

7. To the south of CAEN the Army will immediately operate strongly in a southerly direction, with its left flank on the ORNE.

Objective: the general line THURY HARCOURT–MONT PINCON feature–LE BENY BOCAGE.

8. During its progress southwards the Army will secure bridgeheads to the east of the R. ORNE at selected places.

9. The Army will retain the ability to be able to operate with a strong armoured force east of the ORNE in the general area between CAEN and FALAISE.

For this purpose a Corps of three armoured divisions will be held in reserve, ready to be employed when ordered by me.

The opportunity for the employment of this Corps may be sudden and fleeting; therefore a study of the problems involved will be begun at once.

10. The Army will relieve 6 Airborne DIV, and 1 and 4 S.S. Bdes,

in the bridgehead over the ORNE to the north of CAEN, as early as possible.

When relieved these formations will be returned at once to the U.K.

11. The Army will be prepared to take over the front now held by the left division of First Army, i.e. 2 US Armd DIV, so that this division can be available for offensive operations on the western flank or elsewhere as desired by First Army.

C.G. First Army will give 48 hours notice of his desire to hand over this front.

12. 2 Canadian Corps is placed under command Second Army. The Army will be re-grouped in conformity with its new tasks and objectives.

13. As the Army operates southwards, it will be prepared to offer a strong front eastwards against enemy attempts to interfere with its intentions and plans.

The eastward front will become gradually longer.

A study will be made as to when the northern portion of the eastward front, i.e., from the sea as far as CAEN and possibly south of CAEN, could profitably be transferred to First Canadian Army.

First Canadian Army will study to what extent command of this eastward front so transferred could be exercised at an early date with comparatively limited resources in Army troops.

The result of these studies will be reported verbally to me; meanwhile no action will be taken as to phasing forward units of First Canadian Army H.Q. or Army Troops until I have further considered the problem.

FIRST U.S. ARMY.

14. The right wing of the Army will operate strongly southwards.

The whole Army will pivot on its left and will swing southwards and eastwards on the general line LE BENY BOCAGE–VIRE–MORTAIN–FOUGERES.

The left flank of the Army will operate southwards and gain touch with Second British Army at LE BENY BOCAGE.

15. On reaching the base of the peninsula at AVRANCHES,

the right hand Corps (8 Corps) will be turned westwards into BRITTANY and directed on RENNES and ST. MALO.

This Corps to consist of three infantry divisions and one armoured division.

16. As regards the remainder of the Army.

Plans will be made to direct a strong right wing in a wide sweep, south of the bocage country, towards successive objectives as follows:

(a) LAVAL–MAYENNE.

(b) LE MANS–ALENCON.

17. 82 and 101 Airborne Divisions will be returned this week to England for refit and re-organisation.

THIRD U.S. ARMY.

18. The H.Q. of this Army will be stepped forward in rear of 8 Corps, so that it can take direction and control of the operations on the extreme western flank when so ordered.

OTHER OPERATIONS.

19. Planning is proceeding for operations in areas as follows:

(a) ST. MALO.

(b) QUIBERON BAY.

20. The troops available for the spearhead of these operations are:

1 British Airborne Div.

52 (Lowland) Div.

21. I do not want to have to use these troops for an operation against ST. MALO; I prefer to take ST. MALO from the land vide para. 15.

22. These troops will then be available for the operation of seizing the VANNES area, and subsequently of operating to secure QUIBERON BAY, or LORIENT.

23. Subsequently all operations in BRITTANY will come under the direction and control of Third U.S. Army, which Army will have the task of clearing the whole of the BRITTANY peninsula.

Copies of M510[46]

1 Bradley	*9 C-in-C*
2 Dempsey	*10 Leigh-Mallory*
3 Crerar	*11 Coningham*
4 Eisenhower	*12 C.I.G.S.*
5 Bedel [sic] *Smith*	*13 D.M.O.*
6 Chief of Staff	*14 Tac Ops*
7 Personal Diary	*15 File*
8 Personal Diary	*16 M.G.A.*

IWM, Montgomery Papers Part I, BLM 126/11

112

Letter from General Dwight D. Eisenhower to Montgomery
[Typescript with holograph addition][47]
10 July 1944
I received your letter of the 8th as well as the message you sent on the evening of the 9th.[48]

Your letter, of course, sets forth the obvious fact that we must have space for maneuver, administration and for airfields, and I emphatically agree that one of the areas we need for these purposes, particularly for administration, is the Brittany peninsula. It is unfortunate that before Bradley's attack to the southward could get into full swing, some of the Panzer elements had time to shift to his front and other reinforcements arrive from the South. However, I am gratified to see the energetic way in which he is applying the full force he can bring to bear.

I was quite sure that you did not feel a need for additional armor on your left flank; in my letter[49] I merely cited that as an example of the type of thing we are prepared to do in order to carry out any aggressive plan you might have in mind.

As you and I have agreed from the beginning, the ideal situation would have come about had we been able to obtain the entire coastal area from Havre to Nantes, both inclusive. With such a broad avenue of entry we could have brought into the area every single soldier the United States could produce for us, and we would have had little if any interest in ANVIL, since under those conditions we could also have brought in troops from the Mediterranean. With such a development out of the question – at least under present conditions – we must obtain and perfect the greatest number of small ports that we can, both on the right and on the left. Like you, I would rather take St. Malo by land if we can do so. Moreover, I hear from the Naval Planners that we are likely to be disappointed in its possibilities as a port. Its sea defences are very strong.

Today, Monday, I will be watching with keen interest the progress made by the VIII Corps of Dempsey's Army. Somewhere along the line the enemy is going to show the effect of our continued pressure and we are going to make a real advance and gain a tactical victory. As you say, we now have the strength to keep on attacking – and in the long run the enemy can't stand it.

I had a long talk with General Alexander,[50] who is in his usual good form. Also an hour yesterday with the P.M.[51] He had lots of questions, most of which I answered by saying we were going to the offensive all along the line and would gain room and would kill Germans. I didn't have your letter at the time. But I outlined for him the general scheme very similarly as you did in your letter.

Good luck and good hunting! Thank you for the clear exposition of your ideas which I am bound to say seem to me perfectly sound and practicable.

Sincerely
Ike

P.S. As soon as I get confirmed information that Caen is definitely ours, I want to send you a message for Dempsey & his army. You have a real job, but you're doing it as I knew you would. Again – good luck!
DE

IWM, Montgomery Papers Part II, LMD 114/4

113
Letter from Field Marshal Sir Alan Brooke to Montgomery
[Holograph]
11 July 1944
Very many thanks for your last letters[52] which have been full of interest, and most useful. Also my <u>very</u> best congratulations about

Caen, it is a relief off my mind to see you in that place as I had told you when we met.[53]

I had made all plans to come & lunch with you next Friday[54] & had already written out the wire when Winston ordered a Staff Conference on Pacific Strategy for Friday morning & asked me out to Chequers that evening to meet Stimson.[55] I am now trying to arrange for Wednesday 19th. There are several matters I want to discuss with you,[56] the behaviour of some of our air friends amongst others.

I am very worried about what you say about Keller of 3rd Can Div![57] The Canadian Corps Commander in Italy[58] has also been found wanting & at one moment it was suggested Keller might replace him!! It is evident that the Canadians are very short of senior Commanders, but it is equally clear that we shall have to make the best of the material we have. I had about 1½ intimate years with the Canadians in the last war[59] & know well what their feelings are. They will <u>insist</u> that Canadian forces should be commanded by Canadians. I have already had MacNaughton kicked out[60] & if we don't watch it we shall be accused of thinning out Canadians to try and make room for British Commanders. For that reason I want you to make the best possible use of Crerar,[61] he must be retained in command of the Canadian Army, and must be given his Canadians under his command at the earliest convenient moment. You can keep his Army small & give him the less important jobs, and you will have to teach him.

We had just the same trouble in the last war and had to replace Bing [sic] by Currie[62] although the latter was a very medium commander. We can discuss the whole matter when I come over.

Riddell Webster[63] is not very happy about the lines on which control of the Mulberry projects are developing. He has written to Graham (letter dated 8th). Look into the matter, & if you are not happy about it let me know so that we can take it up here.[64]

With <u>very</u> best of luck to you.

IWM, Montgomery Papers Part I, BLM 1/101

JULY

114
Message (M47) to the Prime Minister, copy to Field Marshal Sir Alan Brooke

[Typescript]

11 July 1944, 1930 hours

Following for Prime Minister from General Montgomery with copy to CIGS (.) begins (.) Thank you for your message (.)[65] we wanted CAEN badly (.) we used a great weight of air power to ensure quick success and the whole battle area leading up to CAEN is a scene of great destruction (.) the town itself also suffered heavily (.) all today 9 and 10 SS PZ divisions have been attacking furiously to retake PT 112 to the NE of EVRECY and PZ LEHR have been assaulting 30 US division to the NW of ST LO (.) very heavy losses have been inflicted on all three divisions and the more they will attack us in this way the better (.) all goes well (.)

IWM, Montgomery Papers Part I, BLM 110/20

115
Message (M49) to General Dwight D. Eisenhower[66]

[Typescript]

12 July 1944, 2010 hours

TOPSEC (.) EYES ONLY for General EISENHOWER from MONTGOMERY (.) Reference my M.510[67] dated 10 July para. 9 (.) This operation will take place on Monday 17 July (.) Grateful if you will issue orders that the whole weight of the air power is to be available on that day to support my land battle (.) We must have the air to ensure success so good weather is essential and we will wait for it if Monday is bad (.) My whole eastern flank will burst into flames on Saturday and the operation on Monday may have far reaching results (.)[68] Most grateful if you will see no visitors come to me or to the armies just at present as this next business will require all our attention (.)[69] Please keep information of the intended operation VERY SECRET.

IWM, Montgomery Papers Part I, BLM 108/7

116
Message (OA 305) from General Dwight D. Eisenhower to Montgomery

[Typescript]

13 July 1944, 1325 hours

SECRET. FOLLOWING PERSONAL GEN MONTGOMERY FROM GEN EISENHOWER. QUOTE. RECEIVED YOUR SECRET MESSAGE TO ME THIS MORNING. WILL IMMEDIATELY MAKE SURE THAT YOU GET WHAT YOU ASK AND WILL KEEP VISITORS AWAY FROM ARMY COMDRS. GOOD LUCK. UNQUOTE.

IWM, Montgomery Papers Part I, BLM 108/8

117
Message from General Dwight D. Eisenhower to Montgomery

[Typescript]

13 July 1944, 1830 hours

PERSONAL FOR GENERAL MONTGOMERY EYES ONLY FROM GENERAL EISENHOWER. BIGOT.[70] TOPSECRET.

WE ARE ENTHUSIASTIC ON YOUR PLAN (.)[71] I THINK THAT CONINGHAM HAS ALREADY GIVEN YOU THE ASSURANCE YOU DESIRE CONCERNING AIR (.)

ALL SENIOR AIRMEN ARE IN FULL ACCORD BECAUSE THIS OPERATION WILL BE A BRILLIANT STROKE WHICH WILL KNOCK LOOSE OUR PRESENT SHACKLES (.) EVERY PLANE AVAILABLE WILL BE READY FOR SUCH A PURPOSE (.)

I EARNESTLY HOPE THAT EVEN IF CONDITIONS ARE SUCH AS TO PREVENT THE PERFECTION OF AIR SUPPORT BEST DESIRABLE YOU WILL STILL FIND WAYS AND MEANS OF CARRYING OUT YOUR PLAN (.) IN ANY CASE, EXCEPT IN THE MOST ADVERSE CONDITIONS, A VERY CONSIDERABLE PORTION OF THE AIR CAN ALWAYS OPERATE EFFECTIVELY (.)

WE ARE SO PEPPED UP CONCERNING THE PROMISE OF THIS PLAN THAT EITHER TEDDER OR MYSELF OR

BOTH WILL BE GLAD TO VISIT YOU IF WE CAN HELP
IN ANY WAY (.)

PLEASE MAKE REPLY DIRECT TO AIR CHIEF
MARSHAL TEDDER SHAEF MAIN SINCE MY WHERE-
ABOUTS FOR THE NEXT TWENTY-FOUR HOURS WILL
BE UNCERTAIN.

IWM, Montgomery Papers Part II, LMD 60/14

118
Message (S 55476) from Air Chief Marshal Tedder to Montgomery

[Typescript]

[13 July 1944], 1830 hours

TOPSEC (.) FOR GENERAL MONTGOMERY PERSONALLY
FROM AIR CHIEF MARSHALL [*sic*] TEDDER (.) HAVE
SPOKEN TO EISENHOWER AND FULLY ENDORSE HIS
SIGNAL TO YOU (.) IN PARTICULAR CAN ASSURE YOU
THAT ALL THE AIRFORCES WILL BE FULL OUT TO
SUPPORT YOUR FAR-REACHING AND DECISIVE PLAN
TO THE UTMOST OF THEIR ABILITY

IWM, Montgomery Papers Part II, LMD 60/15

119
Message (M51) to General Dwight D. Eisenhower

[Typescript]

13 July 1944, 2000 hours

TOPSEC (.) EYES ONLY for General EISENHOWER from
MONTGOMERY (.) Am going to launch two very big attacks next
week (.) Second Army begin at dawn on 16 July and work up to the
big operation on Tuesday 18 July when 8 Corps with three armoured
divisions will be launched to the country east of ORNE (.) Note
change of date from 17 to 18 July (.) First Army launch a heavy attack
with six divisions about 5 miles west of ST. LO on Wednesday 19 July
(.) The whole weight of air power will be required for Second Army on
18 July and First Army on 19 July (.) have seen CONINGHAM and
explained what is wanted (.) Thank you for your OA.305 sent today.[72]

IWM, Montgomery Papers Part I, BLM 108/9

120
Montgomery's diary notes, 13 July 1944

[Typescript]

13 July.

27. I decided that the time had now come to strike really heavy blows designed to knock loose the present enemy shackles that are hemming us in.

On the Second Army front we must fight the enemy armour in the open country to the S.E. of CAEN and damage it so greatly that it is no longer effective; then aim at isolating the enemy troops between EVRECY and CAUMONT.

On the First Army front a heavy blow west of ST. LO must aim at "writing off" all the enemy troops between that place and the west coast of the peninsula; having broken in, fresh divisions must pass through and swing right-handed towards COUTANCES and GRANVILLE.

28. I saw Dempsey and Bradley and got them working on these plans.[73] Actually, they have both been working up to these battles for some time, and the business we now want to do is merely in accordance with my directive M.510[74] dated 10 July.

It was essential that we had the whole weight of the air in to help in these two battles.

I exchanged telegrams with General Eisenhower and A.C.M. Tedder on this subject; see M.49, M.51, and M.53[75] – all filed in this diary.

The Second Army operations were fixed to begin on night 15/16 July, and on 18 July the 8 Corps of three armoured divisions would be launched into the country S.E. of CAEN.

The First Army operation was fixed for 19 July.[76]

IWM, Montgomery Papers Part II, LMD 60/1

121
Message (M53) to Air Chief Marshal Sir Arthur Tedder

[Typescript]

14 July 1944, 0830 hours

TOPSEC (.) Personal for Air Chief Marshal TEDDER from Montgomery (.) Your S.55476[77] received for which many thanks

(.) Three things important (.) First (.) To hold the ring between now and 18 July and delay enemy moves towards lodgement area to greatest extent possible (.) Second (.) To examine every means so that the air can play its part on 18 and 19 July even if weather is not 100 per cent what is wanted (.) Third (.) Plan if successful promises to be decisive and therefore necessary that the airforces bring full weight to bear (.) No need for you to come over unless you wish (.) Chief of Staff returns today and will give you full details (.) Please thank IKE for his signal[78] and show him this if you think suitable.

IWM, Montgomery Papers Part I, BLM 109/3

122
Letter from General Dwight D. Eisenhower to Montgomery
[Typescript]
14 July 1944

Through our recent exchange of telegrams[79] I clearly understand the proposed timing of the impending operations.

With respect to the plan, I am confident it will reap a harvest from all the sowing you have been doing during the past weeks. With our whole front line acting aggressively against the enemy so that he is pinned to the ground, O'Connor's plunge[80] into his vitals will be decisive. I am not discounting the difficulties, nor the initial losses, but in this case I am viewing the prospects with the most tremendous optimism and enthusiasm. I would not be at all surprised to see you gaining a victory that will make some of the "old classics" look like a skirmish between patrols.

I saw your message today to Arthur,[81] sent in response to mine of yesterday. My only thought in suggesting that he or I come over was that there might be some particular point in which you wanted assurance from your rear. I know that the Air will be full out for you, day and night. I am sure, also, that when this thing is started you can count on Bradley to keep his troops fighting like the very devil, twenty-four hours a day, to provide the opportunity your armored corps will need, and to make the victory complete.

I have been going after the Cherbourg thing[82] for the last two weeks. Prospects are some better, and Ramsay is over there today.

You may be sure that we are using every facility and every talent on which we can lay our hands.

May good fortune attend you; I am looking forward to the happy chore of telling about your accomplishments as soon as we have put this one over. I hope you will forgive me if I grow a bit exuberant.

Warm regards.

IWM, Montgomery Papers Part II, LMD 114/5

123
Letter (M511) to Field Marshal Sir Alan Brooke

[Typescript]

14 July 1944

I have your letter of 11 July,[83] for which many thanks.

The Canadians.

2. Do not worry about this.

All Canadian Troops in France are now under Canadian command, i.e., 2 Canadian Corps has taken over the CAEN sector and has both Canadian divisions in it.[84]

3. It would definitely be wrong at this stage to introduce another Army (i.e., Canadian Army) into the British sector in France. It is a one-man battle and is all leading up to a great fight on the CAEN–FALAISE road; this latter is scheduled to begin on 18 July (not 17th as previously notified).

4. When I hand over a sector to Crerar I will certainly teach him his stuff, and I shall give him tasks within his capabilities. And I shall watch over him carefully. I have a great personal affection for him; but this must not be allowed to lead me into doing unsound things.

5. I only wanted to make it clear to you[85] that the Canadian senior commanders are not good. They have some good officers; but their top commanders are bad judges of men – and Harry Crerar is no exception, and does not know what a good soldier should be.

The great exception is Simmonds [*sic*]; he is far and away the best general they have; he is the equal of any British Corps Commander, and is far better than Crerar. And he now commands all the Canadians in France; so that is good and should satisfy Canadian national feeling.

The Mulberry.

6. I have not seen the letter Riddel-Webster [*sic*] sent to Graham. But I gather the gist of it is that the Q.M.G. considers things are not going too well; that we are probably inclined to give way too much to the Navy; that when the Navy insist on doing something we think is wrong, we must make a protest in writing – presumably to cover the Army if there is a disaster!!

7. I could not possibly agree to the question of protests in writing; it would cut right across the whole spirit of the way we are working here. Nor is there any need for such action.

8. Actually we here are very satisfied with the way the matter is going. The soldiers who are in the business (Duke and Walters)[86] work in well with the Navy and there is complete agreement on any action that is taken. McMullen and Grove-White[87] may NOT agree, and possibly they have told the Q.M.G. that all is not well.

I know that the War Office have a certain responsibility in this matter, and so has the Admiralty.

Perhaps the Director of Transportation could come over and look into his side of it, and satisfy himself that all is well – or give me any comments he has to make.

9. What I do not want to do is to generate bad feeling and trouble in the team that is working on it here. And this would happen at once if we start protests in writing.

10. To sum up. I am quite happy about it, and I suggest you take no action your end. But do send the Director of Transportation over, if Q.M.G. would like this. And do please ask him not to stir up friction in what is now a very friendly party!!

If he has any acid comments, could he give them quietly to me.

GENERAL OPERATIONAL POLICY.[88]

11. I have been considering the problem very carefully. Both armies are working on the general instructions contained in my M.510[89] dated 10 July.

Eastern Flank.

12. The Second Army is now very strong; it has in fact reached its peak and can get no stronger; it will in fact get weaker as the manpower situation begins to hit us. Also the casualties have affected the fighting efficiency of divisions; the original men were very well trained; the reinforcements are not so well trained; and this fact is beginning to become apparent and will have repercussions on what we can do. The country in which we are fighting is ideal defensive country; we do the attacking and the Bosche is pretty thin on the ground; I would say we lose three men to his one in our infantry divisions.

13. But the Second Army has three armoured divisions, 7, 11, and Gds. These are quite fresh and have been practically untouched. A fourth armoured division will be complete in here by 27 July, i.e., the Canadian Armd. Div.

14. Having got CAEN, my left flank is now firm; my whole lodgement area is very secure and is held by infantry divisions. And available to work with the infantry I have eight independent armoured Bdes:

2 Cdn.	6 Gds.
27	31
4	33
8	34

with a tank strength of over 1000 tanks.

15. And so I have decided that the time has come to have a real "show down" on the eastern flank, and to loose a Corps of three armoured divisions in to the open country about the CAEN–FALAISE road.

We shall be operating from a very firm and secure base.

The possibilities are immense; with 700 tanks loosed to the S.E. of CAEN, and armoured cars operating far ahead, anything may happen.

And the air will have an absolute field day.

This operation will be launched on Tuesday 18 July, from the existing bridgehead east of the ORNE to the north of CAEN.

The air will play such a big part in it that we must have good "air weather"; and if 18 July is bad flying weather, we shall have to postpone it day by day until we get a good day.

Western Flank.

16. First U.S. Army has been battling its way since 3 July through very difficult country, thickly wooded and very marshy; and with canalised avenues of approach to enemy positions. The Americans have had very heavy casualties; but they have stuck it well and have killed a great many Germans, and have severely mauled the enemy divisions facing them.

17. The First Army is nearly through this country. Once it can get a footing on the road PERIERS–ST. LO, it will be able to launch a real "blitz" attack with fresh troops. This attack would break in on a narrow front with great air support, and fresh divisions would pass through the gap.

18. I have discussed the problem with Bradley and this operation will be launched on 19 or 20 July.

Generally on both Flanks.

19. During the past weeks we have been fighting "for position."

On the eastern flank I had to be careful what I did until I could get CAEN and establish my flank on the ORNE; that has now been done.

On the western flank we had to get Cherbourg, and then fight our way through the marshy country in the area LA HAYE DU PUITS–CARENTAN–ST. LO–LESSAY; that has now been done.

20. During all this time we have stretched the Germans very greatly.

The time has now arrived to deliver terrific blows, designed to "write off" and eliminate the bulk of his holding troops; I doubt if he can collect more troops to rope us off again in the west, and it is in the west that I want territory, i.e., I want Brittany.

Second Army Plan.

21. Night 15/16 July.
(a) 30 Corps will attack with 59 Div., due south to capture the high ground about NOYERS.
(b) 12 Corps will attack with 15 Div., to capture the high ground N.W. and S.E. of EVRECY.

22. 16 and 17 July.
Above attacks continued.

Generally Second Army works on the orders it has received to operate southwards, with its left flank on the ORNE.

23. Tuesday 18 July.

(a) 8 Corps carry out a "blitz" attack southwards, from the bridgehead over the ORNE to the N.E. of CAEN.

(b) The heavy bombers will blot out, and render impassable, a belt on the eastern flank: TOUFFREVILLE–SANNERVILLE–BANNEVILLE

and

a belt on the western flank: COLOMBELLES–GIBER-VILLE–MONDEVILLE.

(c) 8 Corps will be assembled in the BENOUVILLE area, west of the ORNE, having moved there by night.

The bombing in (a) will be as soon after dawn as possible. As soon as it starts 8 Corps will cross the ORNE by four bridges and routes, and will pass between the two bombed belts, being preceded by very heavy artillery fire and air action with fragmentation bombs.

Composition: 7 Armd. Div.

                      11 Armd. Div.

                      Gds. Armd. Div.

(d) Gds. Armd. will lead, will turn left handed, and will make the general area CAGNY–MOULT.

11 Armd. will come next, will turn right handed, and will make for the general area FONTENOY–BRETTEVILLE.

7 Armd. will pass between these two and will be directed on FALAISE.

Armoured cars will streak ahead and shoot up everything they see, and block all approaches over the rivers on the general line MEZIDON–FALAISE–CONDE.

(e) 1 Corps establish a division (probably 3 Div.) in the TROARN area.

(f) Canadian Corps will have the task of capturing FAUBERG DE VAUCELLES, of completely clearing up that place, and of opening through communication from CAEN – across the river – and down the FALAISE road.

24. The operations of 8 Corps on 18 July and following days may

have far reaching results. Anything may happen.

We may "muck up", and write off, a great many of the enemy troops east of the ORNE.

Given good weather the air forces should have a complete field day.

I shall watch over the battle very carefully myself; we must be certain that we neglect no chance of inflicting a real heavy defeat on the enemy; we must also be certain that we do nothing foolish, and so lay ourselves open to a German come back which might catch us off balance – and lead to a set-back.

The basic fundamentals of the policy are as stated in paras. 2, 3, 4, 5, of M.510, and the BRITTANY peninsula is essential for us; but we may well get it by a victory on the eastern flank.

25. The general aim in this battle will be to destroy all possible enemy troops in the general area CAEN–MEZIDON–FALAISE–EVRECY, and to see if we can cut off those in the general area between EVRECY and CAUMONT. Whether we can do all this remains to be seen; but we will have a good try.

26. Remember that the attack of 8 Corps is fixed for Tuesday 18 July. But good "air weather" is essential; if the weather on 18 July is such that the air cannot play, then the attack will be postponed day by day until we get a good day.

First Army Plan.

27. The Army plan vide para. 17 cannot be developed until a footing has been established on the PERIERS–ST. LO road. A pause of 48 hours is then necessary.

It is hoped to reach this line by Sunday; 48 hours pause is then wanted.

The Second Army has the air power on Tuesday.

So First Army attack is fixed for Wednesday 19 July.

28. An area of about 8000 yds. wide by 2000 yds. deep will be completely blitzed by heavy bombers, using instantaneous fuses and fragmentation bombs.

The centre of this area will be about LA CHAPELLE EN JUGER 4064, five miles west of ST. LO.

On the flanks of this area are the main roads running south to MARIGNY and ST. GILLES.

29. Through this blitzed area two infantry divisions will attack, and break into the enemy positions.

Four divisions will then be passed through the gap; two armoured and two infantry.

Three divisions will turn westwards towards COUTANCES and GRANVILLE, and one will turn eastwards.

30. This plan aims at writing off all the enemy troops in the area LESSAY–ST. LO–GRANVILLE.

There is little in it that can go wrong, and it will not require the same careful watching as will the battle on the eastern flank. I think it should succeed.

The VANNES Operation.

31. I am planning to land a force by air at VANNES and capture the QUIBERON BAY area; we want this for an American base.

I do not think there should be much resistance down that way.

This operation will I hope take place during the first week in August; I do not want to launch it until the First Army has got down to about AVRANCHES and have turned the corner towards RENNES and ST. MALO.

Cherbourg.

32. Something seems to have gone wrong up that way. I captured the port on 26 June. Today is 14 July and we are still unable to use the port; the Navies seem unable to get it open for use.

Possibly the Admiralty could ginger up someone about it; I understand the harbour is full of some new type of mine.

I have not been there myself.

Director of Infantry.

33. The M.S. has written to me re a Div. Comdr. to succeed Wilson as Director of Infantry.[90]

The man I would like to give you is Bullen-Smith.

34. There is something wrong with the Highland Division. I have examined it from every angle and have discussed it at length with Neil Ritchie.

I am now certain that Bullen-Smith is not the man for that Division; they must have a Highlander. I want to put Rennie in there; he is nearly fit again. He is very good; he was a Brigadier in that Division; he is the man for the job.

35. I am convinced they will never be the same chaps until Rennie gets there. Bullen-Smith does not "go down" with them.

36. Will you agree to this?

I think Bullen-Smith would be O.K. as Director of Infantry, and recommend him for the job.

Your visit.

37. Do come over and see me.

You mention Wed. 19 July. That would suit me and the battle may be in a very interesting position by then.

IWM, Montgomery Papers Part I, BLM 126/12

124
Memorandum by Montgomery headed 'Notes on Second Army Operations 16 July–18 July'[91]

[Typescript with holograph addition]

15 July 1944

1. Object of this operation

To engage the German Armour in battle and "write it down" to such an extent that it is of no further value to the Germans as a basis of the battle.

To gain a good bridgehead over the ORNE through CAEN, and thus to improve our positions on the eastern flank.

Generally to destroy German equipment and personnel, as a preliminary to a possible wide exploitation of success.

2. Affect [sic] of this operation on the Allied policy

We require the whole of the Cherbourg and Brittany peninsulas.

A victory on the eastern flank will help us gain what we want on the western flank.

But the eastern flank is a bastion on which the whole future of the campaign in NW Europe depends; it must remain a firm bastion; if it became unstable the operations on the western flank would cease.

Therefore, while taking advantage of every opportunity to destroy the enemy, we must be very careful to maintain our own balance and ensure a firm base.

3. The enemy

There are a lot of enemy divisions in the area SE of CAEN:

21 Pz   272
1 SS   16 GAF
12 SS

Another one is coming and will be here this week-end.

4. Operations of 12 Corps and Cdn Corps – 16 & 17 July

Advantage must be taken of these to make the Germans think we are going to break out across the ORNE between CAEN and AMAYE.

5. Initial Operations of 8 Corps

The three armoured divisions will be required to dominate the area BOURGUEBUS–VIMONT–BRETTEVILLE, and to fight and destroy the enemy.

But armoured cars should push far to the south towards FALAISE, and spread alarm and despondency, and discover "the form".

6. Canadian Corps

While para 5 is going on, the Canadians must capture VAUCELLES, get through communication, and establish themselves in a very firm bridgehead on the general line FLEURY–CORMELLES–MONDEVILLE.

7. Later Operations 8 Corps

When 6 is done, then 8 Corps can "crack about" as the situation demands. But not before 6 is done.

8. To sum up for 8 Corps

Para 5.

Para 7.

9. Finally

Para 6 is vital.

Above given to General Dempsey on 15 July. He gave a copy to General O'Connor, 8 Corps.[92]

B.L. Montgomery

General

15–7–44

IWM, Montgomery Papers Part II, LMD 60/19

125
Montgomery's diary notes, 15 July 1944

[Typescript]

<u>15 July.</u>

32. I visited 8 Corps and 1 Corps. I also had a long talk about the coming battle with General Dempsey (Second Army).

I gave Dempsey a paper[93] giving my views on the coming battle on the eastern flank, as affecting the whole battle front in Normandy.

He agreed, and will act on it.

The paper is filed in this diary.

33. It is clear that 51 (Highland) Div. is not battleworthy. The Division is "down" and will not fight. We shall have to get a new Div. Commander. It is very regrettable that this fine division should have sunk to such a level.

See my telegram to C.I.G.S. – M.54 dated 15–7–44.[94]

IWM, Montgomery Papers Part II, LMD 60/1

126
Message (M56) to the Prime Minister, copy to Field Marshal Sir Alan Brooke

[Typescript]

17 July 1944, 1015 hours

Following personal for Prime Minister from General Montgomery with copy to CIGS (.) begins (.) Thank you for your message (.)[95] general conditions for big attack tomorrow now very favourable as main enemy weight has moved to WEST of ORNE as was intended to oppose my attacks in EVRECY area and these attacks will be continued today and tonight (.) for complete success tomorrow good flying weather essential (.) am determined to loose the armoured divisions tomorrow if in any way possible and will delay zero hour up to 1500 hrs if necessary

IWM, Montgomery Papers Part I, BLM 110/22

127
Letter from General Dwight D. Eisenhower to Montgomery
[Typescript]
17 July 1944

Beetle tells me that your Headquarters has requested our cooperation in suppressing early news of your forthcoming attack, particularly as to its size. Naturally you have my complete and full support in this purpose, especially since the newspapers, recently, in the absence of spectacular news, have been doing a lot of speculating that has been uncomfortably close to the truth. However, the general situation in that flank is rather obvious to both sides and any attempt to stop speculation would have been futile.

I had to allow our Secretary of War[96] to visit Bradley briefly. I told him he would have to stay out of the Second Army Sector and Bradley had already informed me he could take care of this particular visitor without embarrassment.[97] One of your own VIP's[98] is soon to take a naval trip along the Channel. He promised to do nothing but inspect ports so there will be no occasion for you, your Army Commanders and other fighting men to be bothered.

There is one item of censorship in which the War Office policy has never been quite the same as that of the U.S. War Department. This applies to the release of the designation of regiments and of the names of commanding officers within a Division that has already been identified on the battle front. Our War Department has always insisted on doing this because, in our country, at least, this produces a personality in the news that brings the war closer to the people. For the past two years I have made a great effort to keep all these policies on an absolute level throughout my Allied Commands. I have officially supported the British view, not particularly because I believe in it, but in order to have uniformity even in this detail.

The time has come when I must fall in with the U.S. demands along this line, so far as U.S. troops are concerned.[99] Beetle is taking the matter up in detail with Freddie DeGuingand [*sic*].

Security will not be involved. Under the American system the regiments in a Division do not change. Consequently, after a

Division has been clearly identified on a front, there is, so far as I can see, no objection to publishing the names and designations of subordinate units when there appears to be any definite news reason for doing so. Naturally, stories of this kind would not be allowed to go out until the lapse of sufficient time to avoid any help to the G-2 System[100] of the enemy, but news stories of unusual accomplishment by battalions, regiments, and their commanding officers, will begin to go to the United States out of Divisions whose designations have already been released.

I think the War Office itself appears to be considering some change in its policies along this line. I personally hope so because of the tremendous efforts I have made during the past two years to keep everything absolutely level, even including the intricate problems of public relations and censorship.

Good luck for tomorrow!

IWM, Montgomery Papers Part II, LMD 114/6

128
Memorandum by Montgomery headed 'SITREP FOR 9 p.m. NEWS. 18 July 1944'

[Typescript]

18 July 1944

Early this morning British and Canadian troops[101] of the Second Army attacked and broke through into the area east of the ORNE and S.E. of CAEN. The attack was preceded and supported by a very great weight of air power organised by the A.E.A.F. The town of VAUCELLES, lying on the south side of the ORNE opposite CAEN, is being cleared of the enemy and strong armoured and mobile forces are operating in the open country further to the S.E. and south. Heavy fighting continues. General Montgomery is well satisfied with the progress made in the first day's fighting of this battle.

IWM, Montgomery Papers Part II, LMD 60/22

129
Message (M58) to Field Marshal Sir Alan Brooke

[Typescript]

18 July 1944, 1620 hours

TOPSEC (.) Personal for C.I.G.S. from General Montgomery (.) Operation this morning a complete success (.)[102] The effect of the air bombing was decisive and the spectacle terrific (.) 8 Corps advanced at 0730 hours (.) Present situation as follows (.) 11 Armd. Div. reached area TILLY 0760–BRAS 0663 (.) 7 Armd. Div passed area DEMOUVILLE 1067 and moving on LA HOGUE 0960 (.) Gds. Armd. Div. passed CAGNY and now in VIMONT (.)[103] 3 Div. moving on TROARN (.) Have ordered the armoured car Regts. of each Division supported by armd. recce. Regts. to recce. towards and secure the crossings over the DIVES between MEZIDON and FALAISE (.) Canadians fighting hard in VAUCELLES (.) Have issued a very brief statement for tonights 9 p.m. B.B.C. news and am stopping all further reports today (.) Situation very promising and it is difficult to see what the enemy can do just at present (.) Few enemy tanks met so far and no mines.

IWM, Montgomery Papers Part I, BLM 110/23

130
Message (M60) to General Dwight D. Eisenhower

[Typescript]

18 July 1944, 1940 hours

TOPSEC (.) EYES ONLY for General Eisenhower from MONTGOMERY (.) Am very well satisfied with todays fighting on eastern flank (.) We definitely caught the enemy off his balance and our operations on 16 and 17 July made him think the main attack was coming from the EVRECY area (.) The weight of air power used was very great and its effect was decisive (.) Second Army has three armoured divisions now operating in the open country to the south and S.E. of CAEN and regts. of armoured cars supported by tanks are being directed to the crossings over the DIVES between MEZIDON and FALAISE (.) First Army has made much better progress today with 7 and 19 Corps and I hope to get their big attack launched on Friday 21 July.

IWM, Montgomery Papers Part I, BLM 110/24

131
Montgomery's diary notes, 18 July 1944

[Typescript]

<u>18 July.</u>

42. Everything went beautifully. The weather was clear at 0530 hrs. and the whole bomber effort was terrific; nothing could live under it.

First the night bombers of Bomber Command; then the heavy day bombers of Eighth Air Force; then the mediums and fighter bombers.

And at about 0900 hrs. it began to get hazy!!

43. The armoured divisions of 8 Corps went through in the following order:

11 Armd. Div. – swung right-handed, and made for the area ST. ANDRE–FONTENAY.

Gds. Armd. Div. – swung left-handed and made for the area CAGNY–VIMONT.

7 Armd. Div. – went in between to the area LA HOGUE–ROQUANCOURT.

44. I directed General Dempsey to push armoured car Regts. of divisions, each supported by an armoured recce. regt., to secure the crossings over the R. DIVES from MEZIDON to FALAISE. We would then study the form.

45. There is no doubt that the attacks of 12 and 30 Corps, southwards, gave the enemy the impression that we intended to break out over the ORNE from the EVRECY direction.

And to meet such an attack he put all his main forces over to the <u>west side</u> of the ORNE.

Having got them there, our attack emerged in great strength from the bridgehead over the ORNE to the N.E. of CAEN; it drove hard due south into the open country on the <u>east side</u> of the ORNE.

IWM, Montgomery Papers Part II, LMD 60/1

132
Message (M61) to General Dwight D. Eisenhower

[Typescript]

19 July 1944, 0730 hours

TOPSEC (.) Personal and EYES ONLY for General Eisenhower from Montgomery (.) am anxious to discuss some points with you and in particular the air set up (.) could you come and see me tomorrow morning 20 July (.) grateful if you would come alone (.)[104]

IWM, Montgomery Papers Part I, BLM 108/11

133
Message from General Dwight D. Eisenhower to Montgomery

[Typescript]

19 July 1944, 1115 hours

TOPSECRET (.) FROM GENERAL EISENHOWER FOR GENERAL MONTGOMERY (.) WILL COME TO SEE YOU THURSDAY MORNING WEATHER PERMITTING (.)

PRIME MINISTER HAS BEEN INSISTING FOR SEVERAL DAYS ON VISIT TO BEACHHEAD FINALLY MAKING ISSUE OF MATTER BECAUSE OF MY EFFORT TO RESTRICT HIM TO PORTS ONLY (.)[105] I HAVE FELT COMPELLED TO AGREE SUBJECT TO HIS STATEMENT THAT HE DOES NOT REPEAT NOT WANT TO SEE YOU OR ARMY COMMANDERS OR ANY OTHER PERSON BUSY WITH THE BATTLE (.) CONSEQUENTLY HIS TRIP WILL BE IN HANDS OF AIR AND NAVY AND LINE OF COMMUNICATIONS (.) HE WILL BE IN CHERBOURG OTHER PORTS AND REAR AREAS THURSDAY TO FRIDAY (.) I HAVE EXPLAINED TO HIM THAT RESTRICTIONS UPON VISITORS MADE ON MY RESPONSIBILITY TO PROTECT MY BUSY COMMANDERS ENGAGED IN BATTLE

IWM, Montgomery Papers Part II, LMD 60/24

134
Letter to the Prime Minister[106]

[Photocopy of a holograph letter]

19 July 1944

I have just heard from the C.I.G.S. that you are proposing to come over this way shortly; this is the first I have heard of your visit. I hope you will come over here whenever you like; I have recently been trying to keep visitors away as we have much on hand.

But you are quite different, and in your capacity as Minister of Defence you naturally are above all those rules. So as far as I personally am concerned I hope you will visit Normandy whenever you like; and if I myself am too busy to be with you I will always send a staff officer. And if you ever feel you would like to stop the night do come and stay in one of my caravans – which will be held ready for you at any time.[107]

The National Archives, Prem 3/339/11

135
Montgomery's diary notes, 19–20 July 1944

[Typescript]

19 July.

46. The really important thing in this operation has been to get through and safe communication from CAEN – over the river to VAUCELLES – and down the FALAISE road to link up with the divisions of 8 Corps. This means that 2 Cdn. Corps must clear VAUCELLES quickly and get both of its divisions over the river and firmly established in a good bridgehead area – which would be a firm and secure base from which 8 Corps could operate and be supplied.

But 3 Cdn. Div. has been very slow, and Keller has had to be gingered up by Simmonds [sic] (the Comd. 2 Cdn. Corps). If Crerar had acted on my advice and replaced Keller[108] on the reports I sent him on 8 July, we should have got on quicker in VAUCELLES yesterday and this would have helped to quicken up the whole business.

47. However Simmonds and 2 Cdn. Corps got very busy today and made good progress. The 2nd Cdn. Div. came into the picture

and was put on a thrust line from CAEN southwards with its right flank on the ORNE and it did well.

Elsewhere it was a day of heavy fighting for the three armoured divisions of 8 Corps; the enemy resistance began to stiffen, as he got 1 S.S. and 10 S.S. Panzer Divs. into line to oppose our advance; so the armoured divisions made little material gains.

48. The total tank casualties in this battle which began on Tuesday 18 July are now available and are as follows:

	Lost.	Runners today.
11 Armd. Div.	140	126
7 Armd. Div.	6	240
Gds. Armd. Div.	33	240
27 Armd. Bde.	20	
33 Armd. Bde.	20	
	219	

49. I have arranged with Bradley that the attack of First Army, west of ST. LO, will go in on Friday 21 July. ST. LO itself was completely in our hands last night 18/19 July.

For his attack he will have the whole weight of the air power; see paras. 27 and 28.[109]

50. The C.I.G.S. came to see me and we had a long talk.

Eisenhower has been telling the Prime Minister that I will not allow him to visit Normandy; as a result the P.M. is very angry with me. Actually, I have asked Eisenhower to keep visitors away just at present as no one has time to deal with them; see my M.49[110] dated 12 July. So I wrote a letter[111] for the C.I.G.S. to take back and give the P.M.; in the letter I explained the situation and said that as Minister of Defence he could of course come and go as he liked, that I would be delighted to see him, and that if he ever wanted to stay the night I would have one of my caravans reserved for him. He sent me a telegram thanking me for my letter.[112]

51. The C.I.G.S. told me that there was talk in certain circles that the Americans were doing all the fighting and having all the casualties, and the British were not doing their fair share.

This is amazing.

The bigger American casualties are due to their lack of skill in fighting.

This may be the inner reason for Eisenhower's letter to me of 7 July; see M.509, and my reply dated 8 July.[113]

My attacks on 8 July to get CAEN, and on 18 July to get a bridgehead beyond CAEN, should dispel that nonsense.

52. I discussed the air situation with the C.I.G.S. The Army has no trust or confidence in Coningham, and is beginning to distrust Tedder.

It is very important that Leigh–Mallory should remain as Air C.-in-C.

When planning in England we did not think very highly of L–M; but we all agree now that he is the only "air lord" who will do anything to help the army win the war; and he is completely genuine and sincere.

Coningham is untrustworthy and no one likes him, and he is out for himself. I thought Tedder was all right, but from what the C.I.G.S. said I have now certain doubts.[114]

Portal, Chief of the Air Staff, seems to be our great hope; he is 100 per cent genuine and I like him very much.

53. I saw all the Press today – British, Canadian, and American – and talked to them on the great need to avoid speculation about the future; I gave examples of how our plans were nearly jeopardised by the Press.

I then talked to them about the war; and other matters, and generally tried to help them.[115]

20 July.

54. I went over to First U.S. Army and saw Bradley, and got his detailed plan for the attack tomorrow. The weather does not look too good.

He will accept a zero hour up to 1200 hrs.

I said that for future days he must accept a zero hour up to 1500 hrs.

It is very important to get this attack launched.

I gave him orders re the future.

55. In the afternoon I went to see Second British Army and gave Dempsey my orders about his front.[116] I had been thinking over

the problem and it was clear to me that there was no real objective at the moment away to the S.E. of CAEN; we now had the bottleneck of CAEN, and a good bridgehead over the ORNE, and this gave us the ability to operate strongly towards FALAISE when a good opportunity was created.

The important thing <u>now</u> was to swing the western flank forward, and all our efforts must go to that.

I decided therefore to re-group, to put Canadian Army in on a one Corps front, and to make Second Army take over some front from First U.S. Army so that that Army could have more resources for its attack.

56. I got back to my H.Q. and found Eisenhower there,[117] and told him of my plans.

I also told him my views about Coningham, 2nd T.A.F., and how much disliked he was in the Army. I said he must keep Leigh-Mallory as Air C.-in-C., as he was a very genuine chap – possibly the only one in our team. See para. 52.

57. Eisenhower told me further details of the P.M.'s anger against me; see para. 50. I told him of my letter to the P.M.[118]

IWM, Montgomery Papers Part II, LMD 60/1

136
Montgomery's Directive (M512) to Lieutenant-General O.N. Bradley, First US Army, Lieutenant-General Sir Miles Dempsey, Second British Army, Lieutenant-General G. Patton, Third US Army, and Lieutenant-General H.D.G. Crerar, First Canadian Army

[Cyclostyle]
21 July 1944

The General Situation.

1. Since the attack of Second Army on 18 July, our general position on the eastern flank has become greatly improved. We now hold a good and firm bridgehead beyond the ORNE in the CAEN sector; and we thus have the ability to operate strongly in that sector, when desired, in an easterly, south-easterly, or southerly direction.

In the last three days we have not only improved our positions on the eastern flank, but in doing so we have "written off" a large amount of enemy personnel and equipment.

2. Operations will be continued intensively on the eastern flank until the following general line is in our possession:

> The R. DIVES from the sea
> southwards to BURES
> thence along the R. MUANCE
> to ST. SYLVAIN – thence
> CAUVICOURT–GOUVIX–EVRECY –
> NOYERS–CAUMONT.

3. Having gained this general line we will be well positioned on the eastern flank, and ready to take quick advantage of any situation that may suddenly develop.

4. It is now vital that the western flank should swing southwards and eastwards, and that we should gain possession of the whole of CHERBOURG and BRITTANY peninsulas. The whole weight of the Army Group will therefore be directed to this task; we require the BRITTANY ports so that we can develop the full resources of the Allies in western Europe, and we must get them soon.

And while carrying out this task we must improve, and retain firmly, our present good position on the eastern flank, and be ready to take quick action on that flank vide para 3.

5. The tasks of armies will be given in the following paragraphs.

<u>First Canadian Army.</u>

6. This army will take over from Second British Army the sector at present held by 1 British Corps.

Command to pass at 1200 hrs 22 July [amended by hand to 23 July].[119]

7. Boundary between First Canadian and Second British armies, incl First Canadian Army: the line of the railway from CAEN to MEZIDON.

8. All troops <u>under command</u> 1 Corps will pass to command First Canadian Army. The divisions to be transferred will be:

> 3 DIV
> 49 DIV
> 51 DIV
> 6 Airborne DIV (incl 1 and 4 SS Bdes).

9. The immediate task of First Canadian Army will be to advance its left flank eastwards so that OUISTREHAM will cease to be under close enemy observation and fire, and that use can then be made of the port of CAEN. To achieve this it will be necessary to push the enemy back to the east side of the R. DIVES, and to occupy such positions as will ensure that all territory to the west of the river is dominated by our troops.

10. Thereafter, the army will operate so as to secure the general line defined in para 2, within the army boundaries.

11. Orders regarding air support and co-operation for the army are being issued by the Air C-in-C. Pending such orders, it has been arranged that air support as may be necessary will be provided by 83 Group.

Second British Army.

12. The left Corps sector will be handed over to First Canadian Army as ordered in paras 6, 7, and 8.

13. The army will operate intensively so as to secure the general line defined in para 2, within the army boundaries, and to hold it firmly. Having gained this line, that part of the army front to the east of the R. ORNE will be kept as active as is possible with the resources available; the enemy must be led to believe that we contemplate a major advance towards FALAISE and ARGENTAN, and he must be induced to build up his main strength to the east of the R. ORNE so that our affairs on the western flank can proceed with greater speed.

14. The army will keep in reserve a Corps, containing at least two armoured divisions, which will be held ready to operate east of the R. ORNE towards FALAISE and ARGENTAN when ordered by me.

15. The army will take over the left divisional sector of First US Army in the CAUMONT area; this sector is at present held by 5 US Inf DIV.

Relief to be complete by 0600 hrs 24 July.

The inter-army boundary to be adjusted accordingly.

First US Army.

16. The immediate task of this army is to secure the whole of the CHERBOURG peninsula, up to the base of the peninsula in the AVRANCHES area.

17. To achieve this task the army will pivot on its left, and will swing its right flank southwards and eastwards on to the general line VIRE–MORTAIN–FOUGERES.

18. On reaching the base of the peninsula in the AVRANCHES area, the right hand Corps (8 Corps) will be turned westwards into BRITTANY and directed on RENNES and ST MALO.

19. As regards the remainder of the army.

Plans will be made to direct a strong right wing in a wide sweep, south of the bocage country, towards successive objectives as follows:

(a) LAVAL–MAYENNE.

(b) LE MANS–ALENCON.

20. The army will shorten its present front, so as to have more resources available for its immediate task, and will hand over the left divisional sector to Second British Army vide para 15.

Third US Army.

21. The HQ of this army will be stepped forward in rear of 8 Corps, so that it can take direction and control of the operations on the extreme western flank when so ordered.

22. The task of the army will be to clear the whole of the BRITTANY peninsula.

12 Army Group.

23. Under orders issued by General Eisenhower, this Army Group will be formed to take command of the American Armies in France.

12 Army Group is to be commanded by Lt-Gen. Bradley, and its operations will for the present be under the general direction and control of 21 Army Group.

24. Lt-Gen. Bradley will decide when the moment has come to form the Army Group, which will consist initially of First and Third US Armies.[120]

25. General Eisenhower has commanded that, until the Army Group is formed, all operations in the American sector will be under the direction and control of Lt-Gen. Bradley.

26. The fact that the Third US Army, commanded by General Patton, is to form part of 12 Army Group for operations in BRITTANY is to be kept TOP SECRET and will not be disclosed below Army Commanders in the British and Canadian Armies.

Air Operations.

27. The Air C-in-C has been asked to direct the weight of the available air power to further the operations on the western flank of the Army Group, as outlined in paras 16 to 20.

General.

28. The attention of Army Commanders is directed, finally, to paras 1 to 4 above.

The policy on which we will now work, and to which all our efforts must be directed, is as laid down in para 4.

IWM, Montgomery Papers Part I, BLM 126/13

137
Letter ('M513')[121] from General Dwight D. Eisenhower to Montgomery

[Typescript]

21 July 1944

Since returning from your Headquarters yesterday I have been going over the major considerations that, in my mind, must guide our future actions. This letter is to assure myself that we see eye to eye on the big problems.[122]

I think that from the military side the case was well summed up in your letter of 8th July.[123] There are also serious political questions involved, but in my mind they parallel, for the moment at least, the military factors. You said:

"1. We must get the Brittany Peninsula. From an administrative point of view this is essential.

2. We do not want to get hemmed into a relatively small area. We must have space for maneuver, for administration and for airfields.

3. We want to engage the enemy in battle to write off his troops and to kill Germans."

(To this last one you might well have added "We should like to kill them in big packets by means of breaking through his positions and cutting him off in sizeable elements.")

You stated this last thought in clear language in your M-510[124] of 10th July in Paragraph 5. You said:

> "We are now so strong and are so well situated that we can attack the Germans hard and continuously in the relentless pursuit of our objectives. This will be done by both First and Second Armies."

This is my view exactly. I think that so far as we can foresee we are at this moment relatively stronger than we can probably hope to be at any time of the near future. Time is vital. We must not only have the Brittany Peninsula – we must have it quickly. So we must hit with everything.[125]

In late June, when First Army was cleaning up the Cherbourg Harbor area, Second Army was attempting to prevent any movement of German troops from the Eastern to the Western flank, in order that when First Army turned southward it would have the best possible conditions for a rapid advance to the base of the Peninsula. But because it had also to hold a firm defensive line, Second Army was not entirely successful in this – it could not have been done except by a definite, continuing, offensive. In any event, Bradley's advance to the southward has been disappointingly slow, even though he has kept everlastingly on the attack with everything he can bring into action.

Then, a few days ago, when Armored Divisions of Second Army, assisted by tremendous air attack, broke through the enemy's forward lines, I was extremely hopeful and optimistic. I thought that at last we had him and were going to roll him up.[126] That did not come about.

Now we are pinning our immediate hopes on Bradley's attack, which should get off either tomorrow or on the first good day. But the country is bad, and the enemy strong at the point of main assault, and more than ever I think it is important that we are aggressive throughout the front.

The recent advances near Caen have partially eliminated the necessity for a defensive attitude, so I feel that you should insist that Dempsey keep up the strength of his attack. Right now we have the ground and air strength and the stores to support major assaults by both armies simultaneously. As Bradley's attack starts Dempsey's should be intensified, certainly until he gains the space and airfields we need on that flank. In First Army, the whole front comes quickly into action to pin down local reserves and to support the main attack. Dempsey should do the same. The enemy has no immediately available major reserves. We do not need to fear, at this moment, a great counter offensive.

I am sure that in this way we will secure the greatest results in the quickest possible time, which is our basic objective. Moreover, I am convinced that in this way we will have in the long run the least number of casualties. I realize the seriousness of the reinforcement problem for Dempsey. That is another reason, in my mind, for getting the business straightened out quickly. Eventually the American ground strength will necessarily be much greater than the British. But while we have equality in size we must go forward shoulder to shoulder, with honors and sacrifices equally shared.

I have taken up the air matters you suggested to me.[127] We must preserve our organization, because the air, in the whole campaign, has performed splendidly, in support of the ground, in spite of adverse weather conditions.

Good luck!

IWM, Montgomery Papers Part I, BLM 126/14

138
Montgomery's diary notes, 21 July 1944

[Typescript]

<u>21 July.</u>

58. I drafted a new directive, M.512,[128] and sent it out. This was based on my orders given to Army Commanders vide paras. 54 and 55.[129]

59. The Prime Minister came to see me.[130] I tackled him about

his anger with me, and everything was made clear. I told him that whenever he got angry in future he was to send me a telegram and find out the truth. He promised he would do so.

I gave him a bottle of French brandy as a peace offering; and I asked him to lunch tomorrow, and said I would take him to CAEN.
60. The weather has been ghastly; pouring rain all day.

The attack of First U.S. Army could not take place, and is cancelled for tomorrow.

It is hoped that Sunday 23 July will be fine, and the attack is now fixed for that day.

IWM, Montgomery Papers Part II, LMD 60/1

139
Message (M65/'M513')[131] to General Dwight D. Eisenhower

[Typescript]

22 July 1944, 1955 hours

TOPSEC (.) Personal and EYES ONLY for General Eisenhower from Montgomery (.) Have received your letter dated 21 July (.) There is not and never has been any intention of stopping offensive operations on the eastern flank (.) For that reason I have regrouped and given the sector facing due east in the close country to Canadian Army (.) Second Army can then devote its main attention to offensive action towards FALAISE and a strong attack by its left Corps will be delivered on 25 July (.) See para. 14 of M.512[132] which provides for a force to exploit any success gained (.) Does above assure you that we see eye to eye on the main military problem (.) If NOT do please let me know.

IWM, Montgomery Papers Part I, BLM 126/14

140
Memorandum by Montgomery headed 'NOTES FOR MINISTER OF DEFENCE'[133]

[Typescript]

22 July 1944

1. Taken all round the equipment of the army in the field has proved to be what was required.

There is often a tendency to de-cry equipment and weapons

instead of getting on with the job and making the best of the tools provided.

I doubt if the British War Office has ever sent an Army overseas so well equipped as the one now fighting in Normandy.[134]

When the tactics are good, and weapons and equipment are properly used, we have found no difficulty in defeating the Germans in battle – other things being equal.

2. I would like to express my appreciation of the air forces, controlled and directed by the A.E.A.F. under General Eisenhower.

These have many tasks and the main work of the heavy bombers, and other long range types, often lies far afield. But with centralised control, the flexibility of air forces can be exploited to the full; and this is now being done – one day the main weight of air power is aimed at the heart of Germany, and the next day it is co-operating intimately in the tactical battle in Normandy.

3. The medical services have been quite 1st Class. A soldier is back in England 24 hours after he is wounded, the fullest use being made of air transport.[135] The mortality amongst the wounded in hospitals in Normandy is about 1 per cent; this very low rate is due to skilled surgery, blood transfusion, devoted nursing by our hospital sisters, and by the general high standard of our medical organisation.

4. I started very early a sound system by which our dead are buried initially in certain large cemeteries, instead of in little packets all over Normandy with difficult exhumation problems after the war.

The local French authorities have been most helpful and have presented the ground.

We now have about 6 cemeteries in convenient centres – one being Canadian. The Imperial War Graves Commission have helped me enthusiastically.

5. Casualties are slowly mounting. As the war proceeds the manpower situation will necessitate that some units and formations have to be disbanded.

I am in very close touch with the War Office in this matter, and when it becomes necessary to disband units the policy will be to take first the war formed units.

No regular or Territorial unit will be disbanded; if the men of any such units are required, the units would be reduced to a cadre basis and be kept "in being."

IWM, Montgomery Papers Part II, LMD 60/28

141
Montgomery's diary notes, 22 July 1944

[Typescript]

<u>22 July.</u>

61. The Prime Minister came to lunch and I took him to visit CAEN and Second Army H.Q. – where he met Dempsey and all Corps Commanders.

62. Eisenhower wrote me a letter which expressed concern at my stopping operations on the eastern flank. Some very curious undercurrents must be going on; I have no intention of stopping operations on the eastern flank. See M.513 for his letter, and my reply.[136]

IWM, Montgomery Papers Part II, LMD 60/1

142
Letter from the Prime Minister to Montgomery

[Photographic copy of holograph letter][137]

23 July 1944, 0025 hours

<u>H.M.S. Enterprise</u>

Cd you kindly arrange to let General Ismay visit either Dempsey or one of yr Corps Commanders on the front we saw today & thence be given an officer to take him & his companions on my staff (Tommy & John Martin)[138] for a drive or a ride. The Navy is providing the car & all that is needed is yr permission.

General Ismay is one of the most important of the officers in the Chiefs of Staff & Minister of Defence's circle & I am anxious he shd see as much as possible, subject of course to battle exigencies & other like considerations.[139]

I enjoyed my day with you enormously & only hope that fruitful results will come from my more intimate impressions of the war scene, & from another opportunity of having a good talk with you.

You can send word here via Naval Officer in charge of fl[eet] movement by telephone at any time.

IWM, Montgomery Papers Part I, BLM 93/5

143
Message ('M513')[140] from General Dwight D. Eisenhower to Montgomery

[Typescript]

23 July 1944, 1444 hours

TOPSECRET. PERSONAL FOR GENERAL MONTGOMERY FROM GENERAL EISENHOWER. THANKS FOR YOUR MESSAGE.[141] MY LETTER TO YOU[142] WAS WRITTEN BEFORE RECEIPT OF YOUR M-512.[143] WE ARE APPARENTLY IN COMPLETE AGREEMENT IN CONVICTION THAT VIGOROUS AND PERSISTENT OFFENSIVE SHOULD BE SUSTAINED BY BOTH FIRST AND SECOND ARMIES.[144] GENERAL OFFENSIVE ACTION IS FURTHER INDICATED AT THIS MOMENT BECAUSE OF EVIDENCE THAT ENEMY MUST UTILIZE SS TROOPS TO INSURE EFFECTIVENESS IN OTHER UNITS. THERE IS OBVIOUSLY SOME CONFUSION AND DOUBT IN RANKS OF ENEMY[145] THAT WE SHOULD EXPLOIT

IWM, Montgomery Papers Part I, BLM 126/14

144
Letter (M514) to General Dwight D. Eisenhower

[Typescript]

24 July 1944

The weather here has been quite frightful; we have not seen the blue sky for days on end, there is 10/10ths cloud, and air operations have been practically closed down. The heavy rain turned the area S.E. of CAEN into a complete sea of mud, and everything came to a stop. Today it is still cloudy and misty, and we could not get Brad's attack launched.

2. I sent you M.512,[146] which gives my broad plan. The following paragraphs will show you in more detail how it will work out.

First U.S. Army.

3. This army is all lined up to attack.

The opening gambit is an attack by three divisions west of ST.

LO, under a great air bombardment. The objective of this "break-in" is the general line MARIGNY–ST. GILLES. Three more divisions then pass through, turn right-handed, and make for COUTANCE and GRANVILLE.

The general idea is to cut off all the enemy in the area PERIERS–LESSAY.

It is a large scale operation and, once we can get it launched, I am sure it will go well; it has great possibilities, and Collins is a grand leader.

8 Corps, with five more divisions in the LESSAY area, takes up the battle on the second day.

Second British Army.

4. We have now got the bottleneck of CAEN behind us, have cleared the debris of the D day bombing, and made good routes over the river.

We have also got a good bridgehead area over the ORNE to the S.E. of CAEN.

5. It is very necessary that, while Third U.S. Army is swinging southwards and eastwards on the western flank, Second Army should fight hard on the eastern flank so as to draw the enemy attention and strength over to that side – keep the enemy pinned down in the CAEN sector – and constitute the definite and continuous threat of an advance on FALAISE and ARGENTAN. See para 13 of M 512.

6. Second Army will carry out its part in the plan as follows:

(a) First. An attack by Canadian Corps east of the ORNE to capture FONTENAY – Pt 122 on the FALAISE road – GARCELLES. This attack will go in before dawn tomorrow, 25 July.

(b) Second. An attack by 12 Corps west of the ORNE to capture the area EVRECY–AMAYE. This attack will go in on 28 July and will be supported by the artillery of Canadian Corps as well as by its own Corps artillery.

(c) Third. An operation by 8 Corps east of the ORNE and through Canadian Corps, down the FALAISE road and then towards ST SYLVAIN and CONTEVILLE – in order to cover the capture by Canadian Corps of the wooded area between GARCELLES and CHICHEBOVILLE. 8 Corps will probably use two armoured divisions; if the general form is good they will stay out; if the general form is bad, they might be withdrawn back through Canadian Corps.

I hope this will be done on 30 July.

See para 14 of M 512.

(d) <u>Fourth.</u> All the above operations are preliminary to a very large scale operation, by possibly three or four armoured divisions, which I want to launch towards FALAISE. See para 14 of M 512.

The object would be to create complete chaos in the FALAISE area, destroy everything seen, and generally to put the wind up the enemy.

What might happen finally cannot be foretold. My aim would be to "crack about" and try to bring about a major enemy withdrawal from in front of Brad.

If the general form was not too good, we can always withdraw into our own lines of the Canadian Corps firm base, and repeat the operation a few days later.

I would like to get this off about 3 or 4 August.

Summary.

7. What it all really amounts to is that I am planning to fight the enemy really hard on both flanks simultaneously.

8. The really big victory is wanted on the western flank, and everything will be subordinated to trying to make it so.

9. But the enemy must be assaulted <u>also</u> on the eastern flank, and I have ordered Second Army to do a series of "left–right–left" blows, east–west–east of the ORNE, so as to keep him guessing. And then a really heavy blow towards FALAISE with up to three or four armoured divisions.

10. It may well be that we shall achieve our object on the western flank by a victory on the eastern flank.

11. Brad's attack could not be launched today because of the weather; it may not even be launched tomorrow if the weather stays bad. But I have told Brad he must accept a later zero hour if by so doing we can get the attack launched; he has agreed to accept a zero hour up to 1800 hours.

12. I am not going to hold back or wait on the eastern flank. I have ordered Dempsey to loose his forces tomorrow <u>anyhow</u>, and the Canadian Corps attack will begin at 0330 hrs. tomorrow 25 July.

> That will be para. 6(a).
> Para. 6(b) – 28 July.
> Para. 6(c) – 30 July.
> Para. 6(d) – difficult to say exactly, but I shall work up to do it in the first week in August.

13. I thought you might like to have above details of how my plan in M.512 is being implemented.

IWM, Montgomery Papers Part I, BLM 126/15

145
Letter from Lieutenant-General H.D.G. Crerar to Montgomery

[Typescript]

24 July 1944

I regret that, at the commencement of my operational career[147] under you, I must call upon you for aid, but, as you will understand from the attached memoranda,[148] the present situation is not one that can be allowed to continue.

I must add that Crocker gave me the immediate impression, at the commencement of the interview, that he resented being placed under my command and receiving any directions from me. This impression was accentuated as the discussion proceeded. I do not know whether this attitude is personal, or because of the fact that I am a Canadian – but it certainly showed itself. There was no tact, nor desire to understand my views, shown on his part.

As I know you believe in frankness, I shall say, at once, that I am quite convinced that Crocker is temperamentally unsuited to be one of my Corps Comds. He will never "play up" as one of my subordinates. He does not like the position.[149]

I am therefore going to ask if you will transfer him to 12 or 30 Corps,[150] and let me have Ritchie, or Bucknall, in his place. I know both these Corps Comds, well. Ritchie was in MO1 with me at the War Office, years ago, and Bucknall was my GSO 2 when I was Commandant at the RMC, Kingston, before the war.[151] Either of them will work well with me, I know. Crocker never will, that I now know.[152]

IWM, Montgomery Papers Part II, LMD 60/30

146
Letter to Sir James Grigg

[Holograph]

24 July 1944

The P.M. spent a good deal of his time with me and I gave him every facility to do what he wanted. We talked about many things and he asked me for some facts which he could "work into" his speech in the House on 2nd August.[153]

I told him that in his speech he must pay a great tribute to the War Office; such a tribute has never yet been paid, and it is high time it should be paid – publicly.

He said he would do so.[154]

Churchill Archives Centre, Grigg Papers 9/8/17

147
Montgomery's diary notes, 25 July 1944

[Typescript]

25 July.

70. The attack of Canadian Corps[155] on the eastern flank went in at 0330 hrs., using field searchlights to illuminate the battle area. Initially good progress was made; but enemy resistance stiffened towards the evening and some determined counter-attacks were put in.

The enemy is now very strong on the front to the S.E. of CAEN; 2 Pz. Div. from CAUMONT has now come over there, having been relieved in the CAUMONT area by an Inf. Div. He has taken all his S.S. and Pz. Troops there from the west side of the ORNE.

This front is now very tight, and progress here will be slow and costly.

71. The attack of First U.S. Army to the west of ST. LO went in at 1100 hrs.[156] A considerable number of bombs were dropped on their own troops and there were many American casualties, including General McNair.[157]

Very heavy fighting went on all day and little progress was made initially. But towards evening the enemy was gradually overcome and a considerable advance was made.

72. Eisenhower came to see me. He had received my M.514.[158]

He talked a good deal about public opinion in America and he hinted that there was a feeling that the U.S. troops were doing more than the British troops; this was proved, to their own satisfaction, by the fact that they had had more casualties and captured more prisoners.

He was very pleasant about everything.

I assured him that the British troops on the eastern flank would not stop but would continue hard.

IWM, Montgomery Papers Part II, LMD 60/1

148
Letter to Lieutenant-General H.D.G. Crerar

[Typescript with holograph addition][159]

26 July 1944

I have seen Crocker.

I have told him:

(a) he has got to be a loyal subordinate in every way.

(b) he has got to lead the way in 1 Corps in saying what an honour it is to serve in the Canadian Army.

(c) when there is a clash of opinions, and things get difficult, he must remember that we are all trying to win this war – and he will not contribute to winning it by "sticking his toes in" when it does not really matter.

(d) he must assemble his whole staff and say that all bickering with Canadian Army is forbidden.

2. On your part I suggest you should remember the following:

(a) An Army Commander should give his Corps Commanders a task, and leave it to them as to how they do it.

(b) He will naturally keep in touch with what they are doing, and will intervene only if he thinks it is not going to be a success.

(c) An Army Commander must stand back from the detailed tactical battle; that part is the province of his Corps Commanders.

(d) Para. 1(c) is applicable to an Army Commander.

3. I hope you will try and cut down paper in the field. You will get the best results by dealing verbally with your Corps Commanders.

I suggest it would be a good thing to tell Crocker that you sent him several copies of your Tactical Directive[160] only in case he wanted to send them on to his subordinates, and that there is no need to send them on unless he so wishes; I consider that <u>in the field</u> it is wrong to send tactical directives to anyone except your immediate subordinates – as <u>they</u> are responsible to you, and <u>their</u> subordinates are responsible to them; I have expressed this opinion many times.

If you inform Crocker as I suggest, I am sure it will help to ease the situation.

4. It takes all sorts to make a good Army. John Crocker is a very experienced fighting commander; he has done very well in Normandy, and he knows his stuff.

He is possibly somewhat stubborn, and you cannot drive him; there are many like that; I am certainly like that myself, and so are you. I have learnt by hard experience in battle that once you can get the confidence and trust of your subordinates, then you have a pearl of very great price; and you will not get it without a very great deal of hard work, and very considerable subordination of self.

I offer you this friendly advice. There are great issues at stake and I have no time to settle quarrels between my generals.

Yours *ever*

<u>B.L. Montgomery</u>

Lt-Gen Crerar

Comd. First Canadian Army

P.S. – When an Army Comdr. has only one Corps in his Army he will, unless he is careful, find that he is trying to command that Corps himself in detail; he has to exercise great patience and restraint; he has not enough to do and is inclined to become involved in details which are the province of his subordinates.

I have been through it all myself. It is not easy; but let us see if you can pull it off. *I am sure you can. I hope you will take the above*

in the spirit in which it is meant. It is only what I told you personally yesterday; don't let it upset our friendship.
B.L.M.

IWM, Montgomery Papers Part II, LMD 60/31

149
Letter from Lieutenant-General H.D.G. Crerar to Montgomery

[Holograph]
26 July 1944

Thanks for your personal note of this morning. Your remarks, and the action you have taken, have helped me – and I appreciate the spirit behind them. I'll make a go of it with Crocker, if he'll half meet me or even less than half.

Our friendship was never firmer.

IWM, Montgomery Papers Part II, LMD 60/32

150
Letter to Field Marshal Sir Alan Brooke

[Holograph]
26 July 1944

Harry Crerar has started off his career as Army Comd by thoroughly upsetting everyone; he had a row with Crocker the first day, and asked me to remove Crocker. I have spent two days trying to restore peace; investigating the quarrel, and so on. As always, there are faults on both sides. But the basic cause is Harry; I fear he thinks he is a great soldier and he was determined to show it the very moment he took over command at 1200 hrs on 23 July. He made his first mistake at 1205 hrs; and his second after lunch.

I have had each of them to see me – separately of course.

I have told Harry in quite clear terms that in my opinion the basic fault lies with him, in this quarrel.

I have seen Crocker, and told him he must play 100%.

Finally I sent Harry the attached letter.[161]

And I now hope I can get on with fighting the Germans – instead of stopping the Generals fighting amongst themselves!!

I am tee-ing up a big party which will involve up to four armoured divisions. If successful it would "write off" for the time being up to about four enemy divisions i.e. it would damage them so much that they would require a major refit.

It would also, if successful, bring about a major withdrawal by the enemy on the front CAUMONT–AUNAY–EVRECY.

I have explained it to Archie.[162]

The First US Army attack began very stickily; their bombing killed a good many chaps, in their own units, including one very high ranking General from the States who should NOT have been up near the front line. However it is going better now.

I have got to fight very hard on the eastern flank while the Americans are battling on the western flank. From one or two things Ike said yesterday when he was here, there is no doubt that public opinion in America is asking why the American casualties are higher than the British – and why they have captured so many more prisoners.

Liddell Hart Centre for Military Archives, Alanbrooke Papers 6/2/28

151
Letter from General Dwight D. Eisenhower to Montgomery
[Typescript]
26 July 1944

This noon I had lunch with the Prime Minister.[163] I reported to him your general plan for continuing attack in the Eastern Sector and he was delighted to know that you will have attacks on both flanks in that Sector supporting the main effort down the middle. I told him further that Leigh-Mallory was going to see you today[164] in order to be ready to put on whatever air show you will need when you get your four Armored Divisions ready to break out to the South. He was very pleased. He repeated over and over again that he knew you understood the necessity for "keeping the front aflame", while major attacks were in progress.

My news this evening on Bradley's attack is very sketchy and I have none at all on what is going on in the Second Army front.

However, I know the troops are fighting for all they are worth and I am certain the enemy will somewhere crack under the pressure. I think we have conclusively demonstrated, in spite of some faulty technique, that when we apply the full power of our air, we can crack the enemy's position at will. When we put on the next all-out effort, let's use everything that the weather will permit, and be sure to carry the bombing effort to sufficient depth to cover the enemy's complete gun area. On the American front 4 uninjured enemy tanks put up the white flag as the result of bombing – this shows what the stunning effect was. I am convinced that if we would make a concerted intensive effort with our whole air force, possibly keeping mediums and lights in reserve for emergency help, we could break through his entire defense system on a selected front. I am not going to admit that among us we have not the brains to work out the technique that will do the job![165] We are going to get a great victory, very soon.

Best of luck!

IWM, Montgomery Papers Part II, LMD 114/7

152
Message (63324) from the Prime Minister to Montgomery ('A')[166]

[Typescript]

26 July 1944

TOP SECRET. PERSONAL FOR GENERAL MONTGOMERY FROM PRIME MINISTER. I WISH YOU ALL SUCCESS IN YOUR IMPENDING VENTURE. I AM VERY GLAD THAT THE AMERICANS HAD A GOOD SUCCESS TODAY. IT WOULD BE FINE IF THIS WERE MATCHED BY A SIMILAR BRITISH VICTORY. I REALIZE THAT YOU HAVE THE MAIN WEIGHT OF ENEMY AGAINST YOU AND I AM SURE THAT YOU WILL OVERCOME THEM. THIS IS THE MOMENT TO STRIKE HARD.

THANK YOU SO MUCH FOR YOUR KINDNESS AND HOSPITALITY.

IWM, Montgomery Papers Part II, LMD 60/33

153
Montgomery's diary notes, 26 July 1944

[Typescript]

<u>26 July.</u>

73. The V.C.I.G.S. came to see me (NYE).[167]

74. I have been having trouble with Crerar.

As soon as Canadian Army took over its sector, Crerar began to throw his weight about and at once had a row with Crocker (1 Corps).

I have spent a lot of time trying to make peace between them.

The real trouble is that Crerar wants to show at once that he is a great soldier; he made a sad mess of the whole business; the truth of the matter is that he is a very poor soldier, and has much to learn.

I finally sent him a letter this morning, which put the matter quite clearly; he took it very well.

The whole correspondence is filed in the diary.

75. The First U.S. Army is doing splendidly and is making good progress. I really think the Americans will get through to COUTANCE and cut off a lot of Germans to the north.

76. The attack of Second Army to the S.E. of CAEN has come up against very strong opposition and has been brought to a stop.

The enemy strength there is now too great for us to be able to make progress; he has six Pz. and S.S. divisions in the line from NOYERS eastwards.

I decided to keep them there, and to switch the main thrust of Second Army to its right wing, and strike hard southwards from the CAUMONT area. This thrust from CAUMONT will be very important as the enemy will undoubtedly try to pivot on CAUMONT for his new line, and hold up the First U.S. Army on the line CAUMONT–AVRANCHES. We will smash this plan by driving hard from CAUMONT towards VIRE.

IWM, Montgomery Papers Part II, LMD 60/1

154
Message from the Prime Minister to Montgomery ('B')[168]

[Typescript]

27 July 1944, 1115 hours

Special Unnumbered Signal.

Prime Minister to General MONTGOMERY.

Personal and private, also Top Secret.

1. It was announced form [*sic*] SHAEF last night that the British had sustained "quite a serious set-back".[169] I am not aware of any facts that justify such a statement. It seems to me that only minor retirements of say a mile have taken place on right wing of your recent attack, and that there is no justification for using such an expression. Naturally this has created a good deal of talk here. I should like to know exactly what the position is, in order to maintain confidence among wobblers or critics in high places.

2. For my private most secret information I should like to know whether the attacks you spoke of to me, or variants of them, are going to come off. It certainly seems very important for the British Army to strike hard and win through, otherwise there will grow comparisons between the two Armies which will lead to dangerous recrimination and affect the fighting value of Allied organization. As you know I have the fullest confidence in you and you may count on me.

IWM, Montgomery Papers Part II, LMD 60/34

155
Message to Prime Minister, copy to Field Marshal Sir Alan Brooke ('C')[170]

[Holograph draft]

27 July 1944, 1900 hours

Personal for Prime Minister from General Montgomery with copy to C.I.G.S.

TOPSECRET and Private.

I know of no "serious set-back". Enemy has massed great strength in the area south of CAEN to oppose our advance in that quarter. Very heavy fighting took place yesterday and the day before and as a result the troops of Canadian Corps were forced back 1000 yds.

from the furthest positions they had reached. The places we could not secure were MAY and TILLY; we hold ST MARTIN and VERRIERES.

My policy since the beginning has been to draw the main enemy armoured strength on to my eastern flank and to fight it there so that our affairs on the western flank could proceed the easier. In this policy I have succeeded; the main enemy armoured strength is now deployed on my eastern flank to the east of the R. ODON, and my affairs in the west are proceeding the easier and the Americans are going great guns.

As regards my future plans.

The enemy strength south of CAEN astride the FALAISE road is now very great, and greater than anywhere else on the whole Allied front. I therefore do not intend to attack him there. Instead I am planning to keep the enemy forces tied to that area and to put in a very heavy blow with six divisions from the CAUMONT area where the enemy is weaker.

This blow will tend to make the American progress quicker.

IWM, Montgomery Papers Part II, LMD 60/35

156
Letter to Field Marshal Sir Alan Brooke

[Holograph]

27 July 1944

The situation has changed very greatly. This new directive[171] will show you my revised plans.

2. It is not good for the morale of British troops in Normandy to see headlines in the English Newspapers:[172]

> Set-back in Normandy
> etc.
> etc.

I wonder if Grigg could have lunch with some leading editors and get this across to them.

From the very beginning it has been my policy to try and pull the main enemy strength, and especially his main armoured strength, on to the British Second Army on the eastern flank so that our affairs on the western flank could proceed more easily. After a very great deal of hard fighting, we got the main enemy armoured strength deployed on the eastern flank when the big American blow was struck in the west on 25 July at 1100 hrs. This was not a bad achievement. Very heavy fighting took place south of CAEN on 25 and 26 July and on the front of 2 Cdn DIV, which was fighting its first battle in Normandy, we were forced back 1000 yds in two places i.e. at MAY and at TILLY.[173]

I would give 5 miles on the eastern flank if I could thereby get the whole of the Cherbourg and Brittany peninsulas!!

Yrs ever

Monty

See attached from Harry.

Copy of Letter from Harry Crerar to me on 26 July[174]

My dear Monty

Thanks for your personal note of this morning.

Your remarks, and the action you have taken, have helped me – and I appreciate the spirit behind them.

I'll make a go of it with Crocker, if he'll half meet me – or even less than half.

Our friendship was never firmer.

Yrs ever

Harry.

So I hope this now ends the matter, and that Harry will sail ahead on an even keel!!

B.L.M.

Liddell Hart Centre for Military Archives, Alanbrooke Papers 6/2/28

157
Montgomery's Directive (M515) to Lieutenant-General O.N. Bradley, First U.S. Army, Lieutenant-General Sir Miles Dempsey, Second British Army, Lieutenant-General G. Patton, Third U.S. Army, and Lieutenant-General H.D.G. Crerar, First Canadian Army.

[Cyclostyle]
27 July 1944

THE GENERAL SITUATION.

1. As a result of our having got the bottleneck of CAEN behind us and having gained a good bridgehead beyond it, the enemy has brought a very powerful force across to the east of the ORNE to oppose our further advance southwards in the direction of FALAISE.

He is so strong there now that any large scale operations by us in that area are definitely unlikely to succeed; if we attempt them we would merely play into the enemy's hands, and we would not be helping on our operations on the western flank.

2. On the western flank the First U.S. Army has delivered the main blow of the whole Allied plan, and it is making excellent progress.

Anything we do elsewhere must have the underlying object of furthering the operations of the American forces to the west of ST. LO, and thus speeding up the capture of the whole of the Cherbourg and Brittany peninsulas; it is ports we require, and quickly.

3. By our operations on the eastern flank we have pulled the main enemy strength on that side in to the area east of the ORNE and astride the FALAISE road. The enemy has tried hard to relieve his armoured divisions with infantry divisions, and to hold his armour in reserve for counter-attack. But he has failed in this; on the front of the Second British Army we now find that he has six Pz. and S.S. divisions holding the line, and all these are to the east of NOYERS.

We will now take advantage of this situation.

There are no Pz or SS formations to the west of NOYERS, and therefore the situation is favourable for a very heavy blow to be delivered by the right wing of the Second British Army in the CAUMONT area.

While this blow is being organised and prepared, it will be necessary for the Second Army to do everything possible to keep the enemy forces pinned down in the general area to the east of NOYERS, and especially in the area east of the ORNE.

4. Along the whole front now held by the First Canadian and Second British Armies it is essential that the enemy be attacked to the greatest degree possible with the resources available. He must be worried, and shot up, and attacked, and raided, whenever and wherever possible; the object of such activity will be to improve our own positions, to gain ground, to keep the enemy from transferring forces across to the western flank to oppose the American advance, and generally to "write off" German personnel and equipment.

The main blow on the eastern flank will be delivered in great strength by the right wing of the Second British Army.

5. The tasks of armies as laid down in M 512[175] dated 21–7–44 will be modified as indicated below.

First Canadian Army.

6. No change.

It is realised that resources are limited, and this may prevent the full implementation of paras 9 and 10 of M 512 at the present time.

7. The Belgian and Dutch contingents of the Allied forces will shortly arrive in Normandy from the U.K., and these will be placed in the Canadian Army.

Second British Army.

8. On the left wing of the Army, operations will be conducted so as to hold in the CAEN sector the strong enemy forces now there.

9. The lodgement we have secured, by hard fighting, in the open country to the south and southeast of CAEN must be held firmly, so that we retain the ability to thrust strongly towards FALAISE should we wish to do so.

The left Corps sector will contain not less than:

  One Armd. Div.

Two Inf. Divs.

Two Independent Armd. Bdes.

10. The Second Army will regroup[176] and will deliver a strong offensive on its right wing with not less than six divisions.

The offensive will be delivered from the general area about CAUMONT.

The initial objective will be the area ST. MARTIN DES BESACES–LE BENY BOCAGE–FORET L'EVEQUE, and a strong force will be held ready for quick exploitation towards VIRE.

11. The sooner this offensive can be launched the better. The latest date, consistent with good weather, will be 2nd August.

First U.S. Army.

12. No change from M.512.

13. The operations of the Second British Army vide para. 9 will have a very direct effect on the general situation on the western flank and should tend to ease the problem for the First U.S. Army.

If Second Army can establish its right flank about FORET L'EVEQUE–LE BENY BOCAGE, and seize VIRE, then the wheel of the First U.S. Army vide para. 17 of M.512 will be greatly facilitated and its front will be shortened.

14. In order to link up with Second Army, First U.S. Army will, on its left flank, direct a strong thrust towards TORIGNY-SUR-VIRE, and towards the high ground about the cross roads Pt. 286 five miles to the S.E. in square 5946.

Third U.S. Army.

15. No change from M.512.

12 Army Group.

16. No change from M.512.

17. 12 Army Group will examine the problem of seizing the MORLAIX area on the north coast of the BRITTANY peninsula, and will plan this operation – vide discussions held personally by me with Lt.-Gen. Bradley.

General.

18. The present period is a critical and important time. The summer is drawing on and we have not many more months of good campaigning weather; there is still much to be done; we must secure the Brittany ports before the winter is on us.

19. The armies have been fighting "for position" during the past weeks. We have come through that period successfully and have gained the positions we wanted.

The main blow of the whole Allied plan has now been struck on the western flank; that blow is the foundation of all our operations, and it has been well and truly struck.

The armies on the eastern flank must now keep up the pressure in the CAEN area; and Second British Army must hurl itself into the fight in the CAUMONT area so as to make easier the task of the American armies fighting hard on the western flank.

In this connection see para. 4.

IWM, Montgomery Papers Part I, BLM 126/16

158
Message (M67) to Field Marshal Sir Alan Brooke

[Typescript]

27 July 1944, 2300 hours

TOPSEC (.) Personal for C.I.G.S. from General Montgomery (.) It begins to look as if the policy we have been working on for so many weeks is now going to pay a dividend (.) When the American attack went in west of ST. LO at 1100 hrs. on 25 July the main enemy armoured strength of six panzer and S.S. divisions was deployed on the eastern flank opposite Second British Army (.) that was a good dividend (.) the Americans are going well and I think things will now begin to move towards the plan outlined in M.512 (.)[177] Have decided to shut down on strong attacks towards FALAISE as enemy is very strong in that quarter (.) Instead am planning a big attack with six divisions southwards from CAUMONT towards VIRE and hope to get it launched not later than 2 August (.) New directive M.515 should reach you tomorrow evening.

IWM, Montgomery Papers Part I, BLM 110/25

159
Montgomery's diary notes, 27 July 1944

[Typescript]

<u>27 July.</u>

77. I went over to 3 Div. to see the 2nd Bn. of my regiment.[178]

78. I issued a new directive: M.515. See para. 75.[179] Copies filed with this diary.

79. I got two nessages [*sic*] from the Prime Minister. One sent on 26 July, expressing gladness at the American progress and hoping for a similar British advance. Marked A.

The other sent on 27 July and expressing alarm at reports in London of "quite a serious set-back" sustained by the British.[180]

The whole thing is very curious.

I sent him a message in reply giving the facts. Marked C.

80. The whole matter is quite simple.

My policy since the beginning has been to pull the main enemy weight, and especially his armoured weight, on to the Second British Army and to fight it there so that our affairs on the western flank could proceed the more easily.

This has been done and we got Cherbourg easily by that means.

Then the Americans re-grouped and got ready for their big attack southwest; this went in at 1100 hours on 25 July and at that time the main enemy strength, including six Panzer and S.S. divisions, was deployed opposite the British Army.

Very heavy fighting went on to the south of CAEN, where the enemy was very strong, and during it the Canadians were pushed back 1000 yds. This seems to have been interpreted as "a serious set-back."

I would gladly lose 5 miles in the east, and come back behind the ORME [*sic*], if thereby we could get what we want in the west the quicker!!

81. I wrote to the C.I.G.S.[181] and asked if the S. of S. could talk to editors of papers in England and explain the facts. Alarmist reports, and sensational headlines in the papers, are liable to affect the morale of the soldiers fighting in Normandy.

I sent the C.I.G.S. a signal about the situation and my change in plans. See M.67.[182]

82. The First U.S. Army made very good progress. Leading elements got down near COUTANCE and a very considerable number of prisoners were roped in – certainly 2000.

IWM, Montgomery Papers Part II, LMD 60/1

160
Message (M68) to General Dwight D. Eisenhower

[Typescript]

28 July 1944, 1730 hours

TOPSEC (.) Personal and EYES ONLY for General Eisenhower from Montgomery (.) Ref. M.515[183] para.11 (.) Date for this will be Sunday 30 July and it will go without air if the weather is bad (.) I have ordered DEMPSEY to throw all caution overboard and to take any risks he likes and to accept any casualties and to step on the gas for VIRE (.)[184] On west flank the battle is going splendidly and Bradleys troops are in COUTANCE (.) it begins to look as if the general plan on which we have been working for so long is at last going to pay a dividend.

IWM, Montgomery Papers Part I, BLM 110/26

161
Letter from Field Marshal Sir Alan Brooke to Montgomery[185]

[Holograph]

28 July 1944

The trouble between you & the P.M. has been satisfactorily settled for the present, but the other trouble[186] I spoke to you about is looming larger still and wants watching very carefully.

Ike lunched with P.M. again this week and as a result I was sent for by P.M. and told that Ike was worried at the outlook taken by the American Press that the British were not taking their share of the fighting and of the casualties. There seemed to be more in it than that and Ike himself seemed to consider that the British Army could and should be more offensive.

The P.M. asked me to meet Ike at dinner with him which I did last night, Bedel [sic] was there also.[187]

It is quite clear that Ike considers that Dempsey should be doing more than he does, it is equally clear that Ike has the very vaguest conception of war! I drew his attention to what your basic strategy had been, ie to hold with your left and draw Germans onto the flank whilst you pushed with your left [holograph amendment inserted here by Montgomery: right!]. I explained how in my mind this conception was being carried out, that the bulk of the Armour had continuously been kept against the British.

He could not refute these arguments, and then asked whether I did not consider that we were in a position to launch major offensives on each Army front simultaneously. I told him that in view of the fact that the German density in Normandy is 2½ times that on the Russian front, whilst our superiority in strength was only in the nature of some 25% as compared to 300% Russian superiority on Eastern front, I did not consider that we were in a position to launch an all out offensive along the whole front. Such a procedure would definitely not fit in with our strategy of opening up Brest by swinging forward Western flank.

Evidently he has some conception of attacking on the whole front which must be an American doctrine judging by Mark Clark with 5th Army in Italy!

However, unfortunately this same policy of attacking (or "engaging the enemy") along the whole front is one that appeals to the P.M. – Ike may therefore obtain some support in this direction.

I told Ike that if he had any feelings that you were not running operations as he wished he should most certainly tell you, and express his views. That it was far better for him to put all his cards on the table and that he should tell you exactly what he thought.

He is evidently a little shy of doing so, I suggested that if I could help him in any way by telling you for him I should be delighted. He said that he might perhaps ask me to accompany him on a visit to you! So if you see me turn up with him you will know what it is all about.[188]

Now as a result of all this talking, and the actual situation on your front, I feel personally quite certain that Dempsey must attack at the earliest possible moment on a large scale. We must not allow German forces to move from his front to Bradley's front or we shall give more cause than ever for criticism.

I shall watch this and keep you informed, but do not neglect this point it is an important one at present.

So sorry you had that trouble with Harry and Crocker[;] hope all is well now.

Very best of luck to you.

IWM, Montgomery Papers Part I, BLM 1/102

162
Message (M69) to Field Marshal Sir Alan Brooke

[Typescript]

28 July 1944, 1905 hours

Personal for C.I.G.S. from General Montgomery (.) Your letter received 1830 hrs (.) Ref. M.515[189] para.11 this will go in on Sunday 30 July (.) It will be on the largest scale and everything will be thrown in (.) Gave orders to DEMPSEY this morning that the attack is to be pressed with utmost vigour and all caution thrown to the winds and any casualties accepted and that he must step on the gas for VIRE (.) Americans are going great guns and with Second Army driving south from CAUMONT I think the results may be good.

IWM, Montgomery Papers Part I, BLM 110/27

163
Message from General Dwight D. Eisenhower to Montgomery

[Typescript]

28 July 1944

AM DELIGHTED THAT YOUR BASIC PLAN HAS BEGUN BRILLIANTLY TO UNFOLD WITH BRADLEYS INITIAL SUCCESS (.) I HAVE JUST READ YOUR M-515[190] WITH WHICH I ENTIRELY AGREE AS BEING CALCULATED TO EXPLOIT THE SITUATION BEFORE THE ENEMY CAN REINFORCE, WHICH HE IS TRYING DESPERATELY TO DO (.) I PARTICULARLY AGREE WITH YOUR PARAGRAPH FOUR AND BEG OF YOU TO INSIST THAT CANADIAN AND SECOND BRITISH ARMIES CARRY OUT THEIR ASSIGNMENTS WITH

VIGOR AND DETERMINATION SO THAT BRADLEY MAY BRING YOUR PLAN TO FULL FRUITION (.) MOREOVER, THEIR EFFORTS MAY WELL PRODUCE UNFORESEEN OPPORTUNITY (.) IN ADDITION, I SUGGEST TO YOU THE ADVISEABILITY OF SPEEDING UP THE MAIN BLOW OF THE SECOND ARMY IN THE CAUMONT AREA (.) ON THAT TEN MILE FRONT THE ENEMY NOW HAS ONLY FOUR REGIMENTS AND AN OCCASIONAL DUG-IN TANK (.) THE ATTACK SHOULD BE IN JUST AS QUICKLY AS DEMPSEYS ASSAULT UNITS CAN BE HURRIED INTO LINE (.) I FEEL VERY STRONGLY THAT A THREE DIVISION ATTACK NOW ON SECOND ARMYS RIGHT FLANK WILL BE WORTH MORE THAN A SIX DIVISION ATTACK IN FIVE DAYS TIME (.) FOLLOW-UP UNITS, IF NEEDED, CAN REACH THE SCENE WHILE THE INITIAL BREAK THROUGH PROGRESSES AS NOW AS NEVER BEFORE OPPORTUNITY IS STARING US IN THE FACE (.) LET US GO ALL OUT ON THE LINES YOU HAVE LAID DOWN IN YOUR M-515 AND LET US NOT WASTE AN HOUR IN GETTING THE WHOLE AFFAIR STARTED (.) NEVER WAS THE TIME MORE VITAL TO US AND WE SHOULD NOT WAIT ON WEATHER OR ON PERFECTION IN DETAIL OF PREPARATION (.) THE ENEMY MUST HAVE NO TIME FOR READJUSTMENT OF LINES, FOR SHIFTING OF UNITS AND FOR BRINGING UP RESERVES (.) ABOVE ALL THE DISLOCATION OF ENEMY FORCES YOU HAVE ENGINEERED ON YOUR EXTREME RIGHT MUST BE EXPLOITED TO THE FULL (.) I AM COUNTING ON YOU AND AS ALWAYS WILL BACK YOU TO THE UTTERMOST LIMIT.

IWM, Montgomery Papers Part II, LMD 60/40

164
Montgomery's diary notes, 28 July 1944

[Typescript]

<u>28 July.</u>

83. The enemy is beginning to react to our attacks.

There are signs of two divisions moving up from the south of France; that is good from the ANVIL aspect.[191]

There are signs of one division moving across the SEINE from the Pas de Calais area.[192]

What we must try and ensure is that the stuff coming up from the south of France is put in to the COUTANCE sector, and the stuff coming from the Pas de Calais is put in to the CAEN sector. Our attack in the CAUMONT sector should then go well.

84. The Americans are going great guns on the western flank.

I had a conference at H.Q. First U.S. Army with Bradley and Dempsey.[193] The troops of First Army are spreading out and pushing well ahead; the enemy must be losing masses of equipment and stores, and have lost all cohesion.

I ordered Dempsey to launch his attack from the CAUMONT area on Sunday 30 July; all caution to be thrown overboard, every risk to be taken, and all troops to be told to put everything into it.

If this is done I believe we have the Germans beaten.

85. First U.S. Army took over 4000 prisoners today.

86. The C.I.G.S. sent me a long personal letter[194] by special fast Spitfire on the subject of Eisenhower and public opinion in America. There is no doubt the Americans have the feeling that the British are not doing enough; they say our casualties are far lighter than theirs, and so on. The letter is a very interesting sidelight on the whole matter, and is filed in this diary.

IWM, Montgomery Papers Part II, LMD 60/1

165

Letter from General Dwight D. Eisenhower to Montgomery
[Typescript]
29 July 1944

Thank you very much for the message you sent me last night.[195] I am perfectly positive that you are doing exactly the right thing and it is easily possible that the most tremendous results will follow. You will still have plenty of strength on your extreme left flank to take advantage of any opportunity that may arise; I understand that the Polish Armored Division is now loading up to join you.[196]

A few days of good weather at this juncture would be a Godsend. Not only would it make the ground attack easier, but if our fighter bombers could really work at maximum strength for a few days simultaneously with strong attacks all along the front, we would possibly find the enemy Divisions exhausted both of fuel and ammunition and could capture and destroy them in place. This, of course, is what you have been aiming toward for a long time and I must say that you deserve the luck of having a bit of good weather at such a critical time.

I tried to go to France today just to drop in on you and possibly Dempsey and Bradley. I am grounded but will come as soon as the weather clears up.[197]

IWM, Montgomery Papers Part II, LMD 114/8

166
Message (M70) to General Dwight D. Eisenhower
[Typescript]
29 July 1944, 0755 hours
TOPSEC (.) Personal for General Eisenhower from Montgomery (.) thank you for your message[198] which got here late last night (.) expect you have got my M 68[199] saying that attack from CAUMONT area goes in tomorrow Sunday (.) two divisions can reach that area by then and others will be thrown in to the battle as they arrive (.) BRADLEY DEMPSEY and myself met together yesterday afternoon[200] and drew up agreed plans to complete the dislocation of enemy and on eastern flank CRERAR will play his part (.) have great hopes we shall win a great victory and achieve our basic object

IWM, Montgomery Papers Part I, BLM 110/28

167
Montgomery's diary notes, 29–31 July 1944
[Typescript]
29 July.
87. I am told that the Americans are today quite happy. The basic plan on which I have been working for so many weeks, is now beginning to unfold and mature.

The attack by Second Army tomorrow from CAUMONT should clinch the matter.

88. I decided to transfer Canadian Corps, and the sector to the S.E. of CAEN, to First Canadian Army; command to pass at 1200 hrs. on 31 July. The set-up will then be:

Second British Army.	First Canadian Army.
8 Corps.	1 Corps.
12 Corps.	2 Cdn. Corps.
30 Corps.	

89. I went over to see Bradley at First U.S. Army H.Q. Eisenhower was there, and we had a talk. Ike is not an easy person to have "listening in" when you are having a conference with your subordinates; he cannot stop "butting in" and talking – always at the top of his voice!! He is so keen that you cannot be angry with him; but it is a nuisance. I like him very much but I could never live in the same house with him; he cannot talk calmly and quietly.[201]

The First U.S. Army is going very well. Enemy resistance is stiffening somewhat on its left flank about TESSY. But on its right the progress is rapid; the leading troops are past GRANVILLE and will soon be turning the corner at AVRANCHES into BRITTANY.

30 July.

90. Attack of Second Army southwards from CAUMONT went in at 0830 hrs.[202]

I visited the HQ of 8 and 30 Corps and impressed on everyone the need for great drive and energy.

I had tea at Second Army H.Q. and told the Army Comd. he must put everything in.

91. I ordered Canadian Army to stage an operation on the front S.E. of CAEN tomorrow, so as to make the enemy think we were going to come out from there.

92. I ordered Canadian Army to pull two Inf. divisions into reserve west of the ORNE, and said I wanted 3 Div. and 51 Div. These might be wanted for the offensive battle now going on, and must be out in reserve so that they could be available quickly.

<u>31 July.</u>

93. The First U.S. Army has reached AVRANCHES, which is excellent.

94. The attack of Second Army from CAUMONT progressed about 6 miles yesterday, and today reached LE BENY BOCAGE and the high ground to its west; this was 11 Armd. Div.

Gds. Armd. Div. was passed through on the left and directed on LE TOURNEUR, which it reached by dark.

7 Armd. Div. was yesterday moved closer up so as to be ready to enter the battle; it was launched at dawn this morning towards AUNAY.

95. I visited Second Army and said I considered Armd. Divisions should be directed as follows:

11 Armd. – VIRE.

Gds. Armd. – VASSY.

7 Armd.– AUNAY-SUR-ORNE and then CONDE.

96. I impressed on Dempsey the great need for vigorous action. If we could get strong armoured columns thrusting forward to areas as in para. 95, then we would have cut the enemy forces in two – to the east, those forces between NOYERS and CAEN – to the west, those forces at the base of the Cherbourg peninsula.

Bucknall of 30 Corps is very slow; he does his stuff in the end but he is always 24 hours late; I have several times told Dempsey he must drive him along; if he cannot be quicker he will have to go.

I am also becoming suspicious of Erskine, 7 Armd. Div; he is too cautious and will not fight his division all out; he may have to go too.

IWM, Montgomery Papers Part II, LMD 60/1

August

168
Letter from Sir James Grigg to Montgomery[1]

[Typescript]

1 August 1944

I have had your two messages[2] about the Press and their alarmist stuff. The trouble for me is to know whether it comes from your side or from SHAEF. The particular item which infuriated you[3] was from SHAEF and the Prime Minister has himself taken it up with Eisenhower and Bedell Smith (Brooke being present).[4] I also spoke to Bracken about it. The worst of it is, however, that both Bracken and Eisenhower seem to exist to give the journalists what they think they want and to support them against the soldiers at all costs. So nobody but the P.M. can do much there. However you can rely on C.I.G.S. and me beavering away at the old man, and I will certainly speak to the more reputable editors and proprietors – but individually, I think, and not in a formal conference.

What happens on your side I don't know. They are a pretty scurvy lot anyhow but perhaps now that you have got Neville[5] over there you may be able to induce them to be no more than a minor misfortune.

But none of this in my view goes to the root of the matter. The Americans at the best of times would do their damnedest to write down our effort and write up their own, to laud others and diminish you. But an election year[6] isn't the best of times anyhow. And further I am convinced that Conyngham [*sic*][7] is continuing to badnam[8] you and the Army and that what he says in this kind is easily circulated in SHAEF via Tedder and again that Bedell – who seems to have become very conceited and very sour – listens too readily to the poison. If I am right then you will have no comfort until you have demanded and obtained the removal of Conyngham from any connection with OVERLORD whatever. He is a bad and treacherous man and will never be other than a plague to you.

If I may presume further I should force Eisenhower to come out into the open the next time you see him and refuse to put up with dark and fearful hints. Indeed I should make the accusation that the rumours are started in his own headquarters.[9]

However giving advice is easy. You want me to <u>do</u> something. I will. I will try to get the SHAEF news arrangements right mechanically. At present the American No.1 is sick[10] and the British No.2 is a bogus airman who is, I think, a relation of Archie Sinclair's.[11] And I will also disseminate some wheat among the tares.

God bless you and may your enemies be scattered – as well as your false friends.

IWM, Montgomery Papers Part II, LMD 110/7

169
Letter to Sir James Grigg[12]

[Holograph]
2 August 1944
My dear P.J.

May I address you thus in my more personal letters. I will be very correct and official on other occasions!! I have your letter of 1 August. It is quite 1st Class and I had a real good hearty laugh when reading it; a good "lash out" all round is an excellent thing. What we really need is an extensive use of weed killer; we would then progress rapidly towards the end of the war.

Here, the broad basic plan, on which we have been working for so many weeks, is now unfolding in the exact way in which it was intended.

This is very gratifying. There were some difficult moments; that must always happen in battle, and it takes a little time to get the enemy where you want him so that you can hit him a colossal crack <u>somewhere else</u>.

It was the same at Alamein.

And it is at that time that the commanders in the field want to be supported and encouraged, and the soldier's morale kept high.

In this case it was <u>at that time</u> that the Press began a campaign which might have done great harm.

This is one great battle, directed by one commander, and designed to produce a great dividend. But one cannot tell them what you are trying to do, or how the battle is being forced to swing; the need for secrecy is too great.

However, we are off now and I think the Bosche will find it very difficult to stop us from bringing the full plan into effect i.e. the swing of the right flank right up to Paris, and pushing the enemy armies up against the Seine between Paris and the sea. And while this is going on we open up Brittany.

Do come over and stay the night.

That is the best time. I have to be out by day a good deal.

I would send my aeroplane to Northolt for you any time, and return you to London in the morning in time for work.

Churchill Archives Centre, Grigg Papers 9/8/20(a)

170
Letter to Major-General F.E.W. Simpson

[Holograph]

2 August 1944 [13]

The battle goes well and completely according to plan.

RENNES is now ours – and ST MALO.[14]

I doubt if there are many Germans in the whole of Brittany, except base wallahs, etc. George Patton should be in BREST in a day or two.

The broad plan remains unchanged.

I shall swing the right flank round, and up towards PARIS. And while this is going on I shall try to hold the enemy to his ground in the CAEN area. Then I hope to put down a large airborne force, including 52 DIV, somewhere in the CHARTRES area and cut off the enemy escape through the gap between PARIS and ORLEANS.

The big idea would be to push the enemy up against the Seine – and get "a cop".

However these things don't always work out quite as planned!! Although the present operations are absolutely as planned.[15]

Can I count on having 52 DIV?

I fear I shall have to remove Erskine[16] from 7 Armd DIV. He will not fight his division and take risks.

It was very easy in the desert to get a "bloody nose", and a good many people did get one. The old desert divisions are apt to look over their shoulder, and wonder if it is all O.K. behind, or if the flanks are secure, and so on.

7 Armd DIV is like that. They want a new General, who will drive them headlong into, and through, gaps torn in the enemy defence – not worrying about flanks or anything.

The big mass of German soldiery want an opportunity to surrender, and they must be given it; this does not apply to the SS troops.

Great vistas are opening up ahead, and we want Generals now who will put their heads down and go like hell.

I have also got to remove Bucknall[17] from 30 Corps. It is no use trying to make him change his character; he is too slow for this mobile business.

Please show this letter to C.I.G.S.

IWM, Simpson Papers

171
Montgomery's diary notes, 2 August 1944

[Typescript]

<u>2 August.</u>

101. The plan is unfolding.

8 Corps (of Third Army) has 4 Armd. Div. in RENNES.

ST. MALO is invested, and DINAN, and FOUGERES have been captured.

102. In the centre the Second British Army is approaching VIRE and ESTRY.

On the east flank the Canadians have not had much success in the CAEN sector, but they are playing their part by keeping the Germans there on the alert.

103. I visited H.Q. Second Army.

Dempsey says that Erskine (Comd. 7 Armd. Div.) is not fighting his Division and has missed some good chances.

I agree, and Erskine must be removed.

But I also consider that Bucknall (Comd. 30 Corps) has failed to show the great drive and energy required in the semi-mobile battle; he is too slow.

I put this to Dempsey and said in my opinion Bucknall was not fit to command a Corps in battle.

I had in fact taken with me an adverse report on Bucknall.

Dempsey accepted this.

I have asked the War Office to send Horrocks out at once – to relieve Bucknall. I saw Bucknall this evening.

I am putting VERNEY to command 7 Armd. Div. vice Erskine; he has done very well in command of 6 Gds. Armd. Bde. (Churchills).

IWM, Montgomery Papers Part II, LMD 60/1

172
Message from the Prime Minister to Montgomery[18]

[Typescript]

3 August 1944, 0745 hours[19]

I am delighted that the unfolding of your plan, which you explained to me, has proceeded so well. It is clear that the enemy will hold on to his eastern flank and hinge with desperate vigour. I am inclined to feel that the BREST Peninsula will mop up pretty cheaply. I rejoice that our armour and forward troops have taken VIRE. It looks on the map as if you ought to have several quite substantial cops. Naturally I earnestly desire to see 2nd Army armour which cannot be far short of 2,500, loose on the broad plains. In this war by-passing has become a brand-new thing on land as well as at sea. I may come to you for a day in the course of the next week, before I go to ITALY.[20] Every good wish.

IWM, Montgomery Papers Part II, LMD 60/43

173
Message to the Prime Minister, copy to Field Marshal Sir Alan Brooke

[Holograph draft][21]

4 August 1944

1. Thank you for your message.

2. I fancy we will now have some heavy fighting on the eastern flank and especially on that part from VILLERS BOCAGE to VIRE which faces due east. The enemy has moved considerable strength to that part from the area south and SE of CAEN.

3. I am therefore planning to launch a heavy attack with five divisions from the CAEN area directed towards FALAISE. Am trying to get this attack launched on 7 August.

4. I have turned only one American corps westwards into BRITTANY as I feel that will be enough.[22] The other corps of Third US Army will be directed on LAVAL and ANGERS.

The whole weight of First US Army will be put into the swing round the south flank of Second Army and directed against DOMFRONT and ALENCON.

5. Delighted to welcome you here next week or at any time.[23]

6. Hope you enjoyed the bottle of brandy and the cheeses.

IWM, Montgomery Papers Part II, LMD 60/45

174
Letter from Field Marshal Sir Alan Brooke to Montgomery
[Holograph]
4 August 1944

I am <u>delighted</u> that your operations are going so successfully and conforming so closely to your plans.

For the present all the "mischief making tongues" are keeping quiet, I have no doubt they will start wagging again and am watching for them!

I hear from Ronnie Weeks that you are now a little doubtful about O'Connor ever making an Army Commander,[24] and that should anything happen to Bimbo you might be asking for Kirkman.[25] I should not be very happy to let you have him, he has only had a Corps for a very short time, and I have heard one rumour that he was inclined to be a bit sticky, but I am not certain about this.

I would sooner you took Dick McCreery[26] who has now had a Corps for a long spell & done very well with it. He has also got the broader Army aspect of the job by having done Chief of Staff to Alex.

Personally I know him well & have a high opinion of him, he has both brains and dash, his only fault is that he is a bit short in the temper, but has lately kept that well under control. Let me know what you think about him.

Horrocks went off in great form & should do well.[27] I am glad you are taking Mackeson for a Brigadier.[28] I have a high opinion of him.

I asked Simbo[29] to-day to get in touch with you to ask you to send me <u>personally</u> a short daily situation report.[30] I can get no news out of S.H.A.E.F. Alex sends me a short daily report which I find most useful.

<u>Very</u> best of luck to you.

IWM, Montgomery Papers Part I, BLM 1/103

175
Montgomery's Directive (M516) to 12 Army Group, Second British Army and First Canadian Army

[Cyclostyle]
4 August 1944

General Situation.

1. The general situation is very good.

We have now unloosed the shackles that were holding us down, and have knocked away the "key rivets". The enemy front is now in such a state that it could be made to disintegrate completely.

2. But to achieve this great result, very determined and energetic action is necessary on the part of us all.

Once a gap appears in the enemy front we must press into it, and through it, and beyond it into enemy rear areas.

Enemy personnel and equipment must be written off in large quantities. Everyone must go all out, all day and every day.

Second British Army.

3. Having broken through the enemy defences in the CAUMONT area, the Second Army is now swinging southwards and eastwards pivoting on its left Corps (12 Corps).

4. Its centre Corps (30 Corps) has the task of securing and dominating the general area AUNAY–MT PINCON–DANVOU 7944.

It will then thrust towards THURY-HARCOURT.

5. Its right Corps (8 Corps) is directed on the area CONDE–FLERS–TINCHEBRAY–VASSY. Its subsequent operations will be in the direction of ARGENTAN.

12 Army Group.

6. First US Army is swinging eastwards round the southern flank of Second British Army. Its left will operate on the general axis DOMFRONT–ALENCON.

7. Third US Army has turned 8 US Corps westwards into BRITTANY, and that Corps has been given the task of clearing the Brittany peninsula.

The remaining Corps of the Third Army are being directed towards LAVAL and ANGERS.

Task of First Canadian Army.

8. To launch a heavy attack from the CAEN sector in the direction of FALAISE.

9. Object of the operation.

(a) To break through the enemy positions to the south and south-east of CAEN, and to gain such ground in the direction of FALAISE as will cut off the enemy forces now facing Second Army and render their withdrawing eastwards difficult – if not impossible.

(b) Generally to destroy enemy equipment and personnel, as a preliminary to a possible wide exploitation of success.

10. The attack to be launched as early as possible and in any case not later than 8 August – dependent on good weather for air support. Every day counts, and speed in preparing and launching the attack is very necessary.

Every endeavour will be made to attack on 7 August if this is in any way possible.

11. It is obvious that if the right wing of Second Army is established at CONDE, vide para 5, and the attack of Canadian Army vide para 8 reaches FALAISE, then the enemy in between will be in a very awkward situation.

12. In order to preserve balance and poise in our dispositions on the eastern flank, Canadian Army must ensure that the front from the CAGNY area northwards to the sea is held securely.

General Note.

13. The broad strategy of the Allied Armies is to swing the right flank round towards PARIS, and to force the enemy back against the SEINE – over which river all the bridges have been destroyed between Paris and the sea.

14. Plans are being worked on to place a strong airborne, and air-portee,[31] force in the CHARTRES area at a suitable moment – thus blocking the gap between the Seine at PARIS and the LOIRE at ORLEANS.

IWM, Montgomery Papers Part I, BLM 126/17

176
Montgomery's diary notes, 4 August 1944

[Typescript]

4 August.

109. I issued M.516,[32] giving the operational situation and my directive for subsequent action.

110. This section of the diary can now be closed.

The main features of what has happened are contained in the summary.

111. The really interesting point is that the operations are proceeding exactly as they were meant to do; we have forced the battle to swing our way.

If we examine the map[33] I used in England when expounding to all General officers the development of the land battle in Normandy, it will be seen that the battle has followed almost exactly the course prescribed.

And in point of time we are about what we said might happen; at one time, i.e., the end of July, we were badly behind; but we have caught up.

There is a good chance that by D+90 we may be up on the line of the SEINE.

SUMMARY

1. This seems a convenient moment to end this section. It deals with the second month in Normandy, which has been a very momentous period. The definite phases are given below.

269

2. Three things were necessary before we could strike the blow that would unloose the shackles that were holding us in:

(a) We had to get the bottleneck of CAEN behind us, so that we had the ability at any time to "drive" hard south-east towards FALAISE.

(b) We had to get the American First Army through all the marshy country in the general area LA HAYE DU PUITS–CARENTAN–ST. LO–PERIERS, and lined up on the road PERIERS–ST. LO; the main blow could then be delivered and could maintain its momentum.

(c) We had to keep the main enemy strength over on the eastern flank while (b) was going on, and actually when the blow was being delivered.

3. Obviously, July was going to be a period of heavy fighting for the British and Canadian Forces on the eastern flank. And this section of the diary reveals that this was so.

Fierce fighting took place on the ODON, and about CAEN, and to the south and S.E. of CAEN. At one time six enemy Pz. and S.S. divisions were kept fully occupied on the eastern flank.

And all this time the First U.S. Army was relentlessly fighting its way forward to its jumping off line for the big blow.

4. The big blow was struck to the west of ST. LO on 25 July. And on the same day the left of the Second British Army attacked to the S.E. of CAEN, in order to hold the enemy to his ground in that area.

5. The enemy line in the west was bent southwards by the Americans, and he tried to form a "hinge" at CAUMONT.

I at once switched the main effort of the Second Army from its left at CAEN over to its right at CAUMONT; a heavy blow was struck at CAUMONT on 30 July, and that smashed the CAUMONT "hinge".

6. Meanwhile the Americans were making great progress. Their right Corps reached AVRANCHES on 31 July, turned westwards into Brittany, and had got to RENNES by 2 August.

7. The Germans tried to make a new "hinge" on the R. ORNE. But the left wing of Second Army then moved forward and pushed the Germans back almost to THURY-HARCOURT; that finished the ORNE "hinge".

8. There remains now the CAEN "hinge". If that goes I consider the Germans will be in a bad way.

9. Towards the end of this period the Americans got right across to the R. LOIRE, practically cleared the whole Brittany peninsula, and progressed eastwards as far as MORTAIN, DOMFRONT, MAYENNE and LAVAL.

10. This period, 3 July–4 Aug., has been one of great interest. We prepared very carefully for the big blow which was to unloose the shackles that were holding us in. The battle, once begun on 25 July, became a process of knocking out the "key rivets" of the enemy holding ring.

The "key rivets" were:

    ST. LO.

    CAUMONT.

    The ORNE.

11. And the next important "hinge" is the CAEN–FALAISE road.

12. We are now ready to deal with that, and to launch the operations that are designed to destroy the German forces between the SEINE and the LOIRE.

13. The next section will show how these tasks were done.

B.L. Montgomery

General

5/8/44

IWM, Montgomery Papers Part II, LMD 60/1

177
Montgomery's Directive (M517) to 12 Army Group, Second British Army and First Canadian Army

[Cyclostyle]

6 August 1944

General Situation.

1. The battle continues to go well.

2. In BRITTANY, American troops have cut right across the peninsula, have reached the sea at VANNES and other places, and are rapidly completing the capture of the whole peninsula.

In the centre, other American troops are moving eastwards through DOMFRONT, MAYENNE and LAVAL.

To the SW of CAEN, British troops are closing in on THURY-HARCOURT and CONDE.

To the east and SE and south of CAEN, British and Canadian troops are in close contact with the enemy who appears to be holding his ground; the CAEN "hinge" would seem to be important to him just at present; he might be in an awkward situation if within the next day or two he lost his positions astride the FALAISE road to the SE of BRETTEVILLE-SUR-LAIZE, and if he lost FALAISE itself.

3. From the general trend of enemy movement it appears he is falling back, unwillingly, to some new line; but there is no evidence yet to show exactly where that line is – though he is definitely trying to pivot on the CAEN area.

There are a series of good delaying positions in the line of advance to the SEINE of the First Canadian Army. It will help our plan if the enemy decides to make use of these positions; he cannot hold a long and extended front strongly everywhere, and, if he holds strongly in the north as he may well do, that is the chance for our right flank to swing round his southern flank and thus cut off his escape.

4. But whatever the enemy may want to do will make no difference to us. We will proceed relentlessly, and rapidly, with our plans for his destruction.

We must be prepared to attack the enemy quickly, whenever and wherever he may stand to fight; he must not be given time to "settle in" on any positions.

We must follow him up with speed whenever he withdraws, and allow him no respite.

Intention.

5. To destroy the enemy forces in that part of France contained in the following area:

The R. SEINE from the sea to PARIS – thence southwards to ORLEANS – thence the R. LOIRE from ORLEANS westwards to the sea.

Plan in Outline.

6. (a) To pivot on our left, or northern flank.

(b) To swing hard with our right along the southern flank and in towards PARIS, the gap between PARIS and ORLEANS being closed ahead of our advance.

(c) To drive the enemy up against the R. SEINE, all bridges over which between PARIS and the sea will be kept out of action.

PLAN IN DETAIL.
Boundaries forward to the SEINE.

7. Between First Canadian and Second British Armies.
All inclusive Second Army:
FALAISE–VIMOUTIERS–ORBEC–BERNAY–LES ANDELYS.

8. Between Second British Army and 12 Army Group.
All inclusive Second Army:
TINCHEBRAY–ARGENTAN–LAIGLE–DREUX– MANTES – CASSICOURT.

Note. Tracings showing the above boundaries in greater detail have been issued to Commanders.

First Canadian Army.

9. Canadian Army will launch a strong attack from the CAEN sector towards FALAISE on night 7/8 August, in accordance with orders already issued. See paras 8 to 12 of M516[34] dated 4–8–44.

10. If possible, FALAISE will be secured and held so as to assist the forward move of the right flank of Second Army. Thereafter, FALAISE is within the boundary of the Second Army vide para 7.

11. In the advance eastwards to the SEINE the main thrust of the Army will be on the axis LISIEUX–ROUEN.

Second British Army.

12. The Second Army will advance eastwards to the SEINE with its main weight initially on its right, or southern, flank through ARGENTAN and LAIGLE.

13. It will then direct its movement on DREUX and EVREUX, and will make contact with the SEINE below MANTES.

It will be prepared to force the crossing of the SEINE at selected places between inclusive MANTES and LES ANDELYS.

<u>12 Army Group.</u>

14. The BRITTANY peninsula will be cleared of the enemy. No more troops will be used for this task than are necessary, as the main business lies to the east.

15. A strong "rear protection" will be formed in the general area RENNES–LAVAL–ANGERS–NANTES, so as to guard against interference to our administrative areas from the south.

16. In the advance eastwards to the SEINE, the Army Group will move on a broad front with its main weight on its right or southern flank.

Plans will be made for the right flank to swing rapidly eastwards, and then north-eastwards towards PARIS; speed in this movement is the basis of the whole plan of operations.

17. Plans will be made for a strong airborne, and air-portee, force to be used to secure the CHARTRES area ahead of the main advance, so as to block the escape gap for the enemy between PARIS and ORLEANS.

This force will be launched when the forward move of the Army Group has crossed the general line LE MANS–ALENCON.

The following British formations are available as the spearhead of the force:

      1 British Airborne DIV.

      52 (Lowland) DIV.

18. As the eastward move progresses, the flank to the south will be guarded on the general line of the R. LOIRE, and in particular at the following main crossing places:

      SAUMUR.

      TOURS.

      BLOIS.

      ORLEANS.

<u>Air Support.</u>

19. The Air C-in-C has been asked to direct the air effort so as to further the general plan outlined above.

In particular he has been requested:

(a) to direct his main power to help the rapid swing of our right flank forward to the SEINE.

(b) to prevent all enemy movement across the SEINE between PARIS and the sea, so far as is possible.

General.

20. Our general situation is very good; the enemy situation is far from good, and he is definitely very stretched and in a bad way.

21. It must be impressed on all commanders that now is the time to press on boldly and to take great risks.

If we can achieve the intention as given in para 5 above, and achieve it quickly, we shall have hastened the end of the war.

22. ACKNOWLEDGE.

IWM, Montgomery Papers Part I, BLM 126/18

178
Letter to Field Marshal Sir Alan Brooke

[Holograph]

6 August 1944

I am sending Dawnay over with my directive[35] for the advance to the SEINE, and he will take this letter.

2. All goes very well. In fact everything is working out so much according to plan that one wonders, sometimes, whether it isn't a bit too good!! On the other hand we have been through our difficult days, as you know. And if we had faltered in those days we might well not be where we are now.

3. I would like to thank you for your firm support at all times. It makes a great difference to me to know that you stand like a firm rock behind us, and your faith in what we are trying to achieve is constant.

4. I wrote you a note re Dick McCreery.[36] I agree that he would make an Army Comd. He would probably require a helping hand; but we are all the same in that respect.

5. Bucknall has written me a letter,[37] and sent a map; a sort of apologia. As you may be seeing him, I send it to you. There is nothing to it. I have told Dempsey to take no action, and to get on with his battle.

6. Horrocks has taken over 30 Corps and a great change, and impetus, took place very quickly.

7. Verney has taken over 7 Armd DIV, and <u>that</u> has had excellent results also. I suggest that Erskine might be given a rest for a month, and might then be a very suitable commandant of the Staff College. Wimberley[38] has now done one year in the job, which is enough for most chaps in war time; and Erskine would take there some very up-to-date experience.

However you may have some other work for him.

8. I have your note of 4 August re looting.[39] It is a very vague accusation and your letter to Cadogan hits the nail right on the head. We have a huge bunch of chaps over here now, well over 1½ million; with destroyed villages, houses, etc, it may well happen that cases of looting do occur. I have heard nothing on the subject myself. But I will ask M. Coulet about it,[40] and see what he says; he is a very decent chap and is bound to know if there has been "far too much of it" – as Cadogan suggests.

I will let you know further.

9. The P.M. sent me a message[41] that he was coming over to see me yesterday 5 August, bring [*sic*] Andrew Cunningham, to discuss some important matters; one of the matters was the question of bringing the whole ANVIL party up to this front.[42]

I have no information as to whether he had previously discussed this question with Ike; possibly NOT, as his message said that on leaving me he was going on to see Ike.

It looks as if he was trying "to sell" the idea to me first, and then to tell Ike that I agreed with him!!! However, bad weather intervened and he never appeared;[43] possibly this is just as well!!

It may well happen that my name will <u>again</u> be taken in vain over this matter.[44] So may I tell you my views on that now:

(a) I have had no discussion with Ike on the subject, and have no idea what his views may be on that subject.

(b) I am not in close touch here with the wider stratagical or political issues that might be involved in such a discussion.

(c) My immediate reactions are that to try and switch ANVIL <u>at this stage</u> would be most unsound. Furthermore I doubt if we could handle the party administratively.

(d) It was decided, rightly or wrongly, to put ANVIL in on the southern front; it is just about to go in; I am all for leaving it at that.

(e) I suggest that the operational direction of the ANVIL effort should come under Ike, once the party is on shore and ready to advance.

10. Dawnay will explain to you the more detailed battle picture.[45]

Liddell Hart Centre for Military Archives, Alanbrooke Papers 6/2/29

179
Message (M81) to Field Marshal Sir Alan Brooke

[Typescript]

7 August 1944, 2230 hours

TOPSEC (.) Personal for CIGS from General Montgomery (.) Enemy attack in MORTAIN area[46] has been well held by the Americans and all positions intact (.) The Americans hold strongly VIRE on the north side of attack and BARENTON on the south side and advanced 4 kilometres southwards from VIRE today (.) When the attack developed three American divs were moving southwards between MORTAIN and AVRANCHES and these were halted this morning to provide additional security in this gap (.) I have no fears whatever for the security of this part of the front and am proceeding with my offensive plans elsewhere without change (.) There is no change in the American front from DOMFRONT southwards (.) I have no confirmation of BBC reports that the garrison of LORIENT surrendered to the Americans (.)[47] 8 Corps on the right of 2 Army has been heavily attacked during the last 24 hours presumably to keep this front secure while the MORTAIN attack went in (.) These enemy attacks have all been repulsed with heavy loss to the enemy but they have caused some dislocation in the attack planned by 8 Corps towards FLERS which attack will not now take place for about 48 hours (.) Tomorrow 30 Corps attacks strongly from MT PINCON area towards CONDE (.) Cdn Army attack goes in tonight and will be continued tomorrow and succeeding days (.) The objective is FALAISE (.) I have considerable hopes that within the next 36 to 48 hours we shall reach FALAISE and CONDE and we should then be in a very good position

IWM, Montgomery Papers Part I, BLM 110/33

180
Message (M82) to Field Marshal Sir Alan Brooke

[Typescript]

7 August 1944, 2315 hours

TOPSEC (.) Personal for CIGS from General Montgomery (.) Following my M81 my LO[48] has just returned from the LAVAL front and reports that the leading troops of 15 US Corps have reached LOUE which is only about 15 miles from LE MANS (.) this is very good news and it is quite possible that this Corps will reach LE MANS tomorrow (.) there has been no advance eastwards as yet from MAYENNE but this will begin tomorrow (.) if only the Germans will go on attacking at MORTAIN for a few more days it seems that they might not be able to get away

IWM, Montgomery Papers Part I, BLM 110/34

181
Montgomery's diary notes, 7 August 1944

[Typescript]

<u>7 August</u>

8. The Americans were heavily counter-attacked in the MORTAIN area last night and today; up to four Pz. divisions were used. The First U.S. Army held firm; BARENTON was strengthened and an advance made southwards from VIRE. I put the whole of 2nd T.A.F. on to help deal with the attack; pilots of 9th Air Force and 2nd T.A.F. claimed 120 tanks destroyed.

The enemy attacks achieved no success.

The purpose presumably was to drive across to AVRANCHES and cut the U.S. forces in two; there were three divisions of Third U.S. Army moving southwards east of AVRANCHES today, and these were halted temporarily as a precaution and to avoid any risk of a German success.

The enemy attack achieved no success.

The divisions he used were:

    1 S.S.
    2 S.S.
    116 Pz.
    2 Pz.

This enemy concentration at MORTAIN, and attack westwards towards AVRANCHES, is a real mistake; if he persists here I will turn the southern wing up northwards to ALENCON and ARGENTAN, and get in behind him.

9. 8 Corps, on the right wing of Second Army, have been heavily attacked all day; presumably the Germans want to keep us fairly quiet on the front VIRE–ESTRY while their attacks at MORTAIN are going on.

But 12 Corps on the left of Second Army managed to get across the ORNE to the north of THURY-HARCOURT, and were heavily counter-attacked there by 12 S.S. Div. during the afternoon; the attack was beaten off.

I was delighted to hear this news as it meant that both 1 S.S. and 12 S.S. had now left the area between CAEN and FALAISE; this was going to make things much easier for the Canadian Army attack tonight.

10. The P.M. visited me at 1500 hrs. and stayed for one hour. He was anxious to get my agreement to switching ANVIL (now called DRAGOON) from the Mediterranean to Brittany.[49] I made it clear that I was not well acquainted as to the political and strategical aspects of such a switch, that we had not yet got the Brittany ports in which to bring the expedition, that it was due to be launched on 15 August in the Mediterranean area.

Therefore, conditions being as they were, it seemed to me to be very unwise to make any changes.

Lastly, such a proposition would probably produce a row with the Americans and the Combined Chiefs of Staff in Washington; we do NOT want any rows at present.

Therefore, leave the thing alone.

11. I visited H.Q. Canadian Army and checked up that all was well for their battle tonight.[50]

IWM, Montgomery Papers Part II, LMD 61/1

182
Message (M84) to Field Marshal Sir Alan Brooke

[Typescript]

8 August 1944, 2250 hours

TOPSEC (.) Personal for CIGS from General Montgomery (.) Situation in the Brittany Peninsula remains unchanged (.) heavy fighting is going on in the outskirts of ST MALO [,] BREST and LORIENT (.) These places are not yet in our hands (.) on the MORTAIN front the enemy has ceased all his attacks westwards (.) patrols from BARENTON have penetrated northwards to points about five miles due east of MORTAIN without interference and there are some grounds for thinking the enemy may be pulling out from this front (.) further to the south we have pushed eastwards about five miles from MAYENNE and my last reports were that American troops were very close to the outskirts of LE MANS (.) a strong force of four divisions will operate tomorrow northwards from the LE MANS area towards ALENCON (.)[51] on the Second Army front there has been heavy opposition all day to any advance southeastwards and the enemy has been counter-attacking heavily the 12 Corps bridgehead over the ORNE north of THURY HARCOURT (.) Canadian Army has advanced six miles since its attack started early this morning and the leading troops have now reached BRETTEVILLE SUR LAIZE and the village of HAUTMESNIL on the main road due east of it (.) this advance is being continued tonight and Canadian Army have been ordered to fight its way forward to FALAISE (.) I am trying to get FALAISE and ALENCON as the first step to closing the ring behind the enemy

IWM, Montgomery Papers Part I, BLM 110/35

183
Montgomery's diary notes, 8 August 1944

[Typescript]

<u>8 August</u>

12. Canadian Army attacked at midnight last night after a very heavy bombing by Bomber Command. The infantry divisions (2 Cdn. and 51) made good progress and got their objectives.[52]

A further bombing by Fortresses of Eighth Air Force took place at 1300 hrs. today; this was very badly done, the bulk of the bombs fell in and around CAEN and some even west of the ORNE; the Cdn. A.G.R.A. and Tac. H.Q. 3 Cdn. Div. were hit, and KELLER was badly wounded.[53] The target area was not properly bombed.

However 4 Cdn. Armd. Div., and Polish Armd. Div., went through; but they made little progress.

280

13. I went to Canadian Army H.Q. at 1600 hrs. and had a conference with Dempsey and Crerar. I impressed on Crerar that the Canadian Army must fight its way to FALAISE; having got there it was to operate strongly westwards towards CONDE and southwards towards ARGENTAN.

14. As regards the American front. Third U.S. Army (Patton) was approaching LE MANS.[54] I ordered Bradley to halt that spearhead there, and then to operate strongly with 3 or 4 divisions northwards to ALENCON.[55]

15. It was clear that if we could secure FALAISE and ALENCON, the German troops facing Second British and First U.S. armies might not get away. See para. 8.[56]

16. The enemy attacks in the MORTAIN area have ceased and there are signs that the enemy is beginning to pull out from that front. See para. 8.

For this reason FALAISE and ALENCON now assume great importance.

If we can gather in the prisoners here, and get "a cop", our advance to the SEINE will be easy.

IWM, Montgomery Papers Part II, LMD 61/1

184
Letter to Field Marshal Sir Alan Brooke

[Typescript with holograph additions][57]

9 August 1944

Simbo takes this and will give you our news.

1. The enemy attack at MORTAIN was just what we wanted; it was held without difficulty; I put the 2nd T.A.F. onto it, as well as the 8th Air Force, and the pilots all had a great day. They claimed "120 flamers";[58] but I doubt that.

2. On the left, the Canadian attack is aimed at FALAISE. I have ordered them to hold that place securely, and from it to operate southwards towards ARGENTAN and westwards towards CONDE.

8 Corps, the right wing of Second Army, is moving on TINCHEBRAY today, but I do not expect this advance to progress far. Its main task is to hold the enemy to his ground.

3. The right wing of 12 Army Group, 15 U.S. Corps, is at LE MANS, where it will secure a bridgehead. I have ordered it then to operate northwards to ALENCON; this is a very important thrust.

4. I am aiming at closing in behind the Germans.

The Canadians should be able to fight their way to FALAISE; they will not have the easy time they fancied, but they should get there; at present their forward movement is not making rapid progress.

The Germans will fight hard for FALAISE I think. I don't think the Americans will have any difficulty in getting to ALENCON, as there is nothing there to oppose them.

If we can get FALAISE, and can also hold ALENCON strongly, we should then be able to close the gap in between – and that would be very excellent.

But the Germans will fight hard; it is good defensive country and we must not expect things to go too rapidly.

So far the Poles have not displayed that dash we expected, and have been sticky.

5. The midday bombing yesterday by Eighth Air Force (Fortresses) on the Canadian front was most inaccurate.[59] Bombs fell in 12 Corps area west of the ORNE, in CAEN itself, behind CAEN, east of CAEN, in the area of Canadian A.G.R.A., and on Tac. H.Q. 3 Canadian Div.

A few fell in the target area.

The Canadians had about 300 casualties in personnel, had about 12 guns knocked out, had a good many vehicles destroyed, and KELLER (Comd. 3 Cdn. Div.) was wounded (*will be out of action for about 6 months*).

The same thing happened on 25 July west of ST. LO; the Americans had 500 killed and wounded, and General McNAIR was killed.

It now seems clear that Eighth Air Force must never come down into the tactical battle.

6. Harry Crerar is fighting his first battle and it is the first appearance in history of a Canadian Army H.Q. He is desperately anxious it should succeed. He is so anxious that he worries himself all day!!

I go and see him a lot and calm him down.

He will be much better when he realises that battles seldom go completely as planned, that great patience is required, that you keep on at it until the other chap cracks, and that if you worry you will eventually go mad!!

He seemed to have gained the idea that all you want is a good initial fire plan, and then the Germans all run away!!

7. Rumours keep reaching me of bad influences at work at SHAEF.

My own feeling is that Bedel [*sic*] Smith is all right and not bad in that way. He is intensely "national"; but I would say he is a good member of the Allied team.

His intense national pride may be at work to try and make it appear that the war in Normandy is being fought by two separate parties – a British party and an American party, with no connection between the two.

If this were so, we would NOT be where we are today.

It is of course one party, working on one plan, and controlled and directed by one HQ. IKE is quite clear on this aspect of the matter.

8. But I hear rumours that Gale[60] is bad, in that he openly runs down the War Office, and the QMG by name, at conferences at SHAEF. I shall check up on this, and if it is true I will tackle him on the matter.

I believe Morgan[61] is suspect too, *but have no evidence.*

The senior British officers at SHAEF must realise that, in addition to being good allied chaps, they have definite loyalties to their own side of the house; and, in our side of the house, we must all pull together.

9. The P.M. visited me on Monday, and stayed one hour.

He asked me about his idea to switch DRAGOON.

I told him as follows:

(a) I was not in touch with the strategical and political issues involved.

(b) The date for DRAGOON was 15 August and that is only 7 days off.

(c) We have not yet captured the ports in Brittany in to which the ships could come. The ports may be all mined, as was Cherbourg.

(d) From the purely military aspect it seemed to me to be too late to attempt a switch.

(e) From other aspects it would probably mean a quarrel with the Americans, and that would do us no good.

(f) Taken all round, I was in favour of deciding well ahead what we wanted to do – and then doing it. You cannot make big changes at the last moment.

10. The P.M. struck me as looking old and tired; he seemed to find it difficult to concentrate on a subject for more than a few moments; he seemed restless, and unable to make his mind up about anything.

11. I hear Dicky Mountbatten is in England. I would like to see him before he goes back, and hear his news about the war in S.E. Asia.[62]

12. Ike came to see me last night. We discussed DRAGOON and I gave him my views as in para 9.

Yours ever

Monty.

P.S. Latest reports are that 4 Cdn Armd DIV is well on. The Poles are still on their start line & thus exposing the eastern flank of the Cdn spearhead. I have told Harry to give the Poles a kick in the fork.

Liddell Hart Centre for Military Archives, Alanbrooke Papers 6/2/29. (A carbon copy in the Montgomery Papers Part II, LMD 61/3, does not include the holograph postscript.)

185
Message (M85) to Field Marshal Sir Alan Brooke

[Typescript]

9 August 1944, 2300 hours

TOPSEC (.) Personal for C.I.G.S. from General Montgomery (.) situation in BRITTANY peninsula remains unchanged and heavy fighting is going on in the outskirts of ST MALO BREST and LORIENT (.) there is considerable pressure from outside sources[63] that more troops should be sent into the peninsula to get the ports cleared up quickly (.) I do not agree with this myself and consider that the main business lies to the east (.) have instructed BRADLEY to concentrate against each port in turn dealing first with ST MALO then MORLAIX then BREST then LORIENT and so on (.) on front of 12 Army Group we now hold LE MANS and strong forces are moving from that area towards firstly ALENCON and secondly ARGENTAN (.) the enemy has been attacking today in the MORTAIN area where his attacks have been easily held (.) on the front of second army there has been no offensive action on the part of the enemy and there are in fact signs that his resistance to our advance is slackening (.) the advance of 30 Corps towards CONDE has now reached the high ground Pt 229 in 8539 and will be continued tomorrow towards CONDE (.) 8 Corps is regrouping and will attack on Friday towards TINCHEBRAY (.) on 12 Corps front the enemy is pulling out from the unpleasant position he was in between the ORNE and the LAIZE about CLINCHAMPS and in the big woods to the south of it (.) Canadian Army has done well today (.) 4 Cdn Armd Div is firmly established on the high ground Pt 180–Pt 195 on the west side of the main FALAISE road about half way between BRETTEVILLE-SUR-LAIZE and FALAISE (.) on the east side of the road the Poles have now reached ESTREES LA CAMPAGNE and high ground Pt 140 southeast of it (.) FALAISE itself is in reach of our guns and so is CONDE (.) there are great possibilities in the present situation (.) if we can get to ALENCON ARGENTAN and FALAISE fairly quickly we have a good chance of closing the ring round the main German forces and I am making all plans to drop an airborne division at GACE about 15 miles east of ARGENTAN in order to complete the block (.) should the Germans escape us here I shall proceed quickly with the plan outlined in M517.[64]

IWM, Montgomery Papers Part I, BLM 110/36

186
Montgomery's diary notes, 9 August 1944

[Typescript]

<u>9 August</u>

17. I instructed Bradley that, while operating with his right towards ALENCON, he must be ready to strike quickly from LE

MANS towards CHARTRES and PARIS. If the Germans slipped out between ALENCON and FALAISE, then we must swing our right forward to PARIS quickly – as in M.517.[65]

18. The Cdn. Armd. Div. made good advances in the moonlight last night and got to the commanding ground Pt. 190–N.W. of FALAISE and west of the main road. This was very good.

But the Polish Division was very disappointing and lacked dash and enterprise; at dawn it was still on its start line. I told Crerar to give it a tremendous jerk up, and push it on. This he did; the Poles re-acted violently and by dark today the Division was up level with the Canadians, on the east of the main road.

19. I had a conference with Dempsey and Crerar at 12 Corps H.Q. at 1700 hrs. We examined the situation.

I impressed on them the need to be able to dominate the road centres of CONDE and FALAISE by night with artillery, and to secure these two places as soon as possible. See M.85 to C.I.G.S.[66]

IWM, Montgomery Papers Part II, LMD 61/1

187
Message (M86) to Field Marshal Sir Alan Brooke
[Typescript]
10 August 1944, 2220 hours

TOPSEC (.) Personal for CIGS from General Montgomery (.) situation in BRITTANY peninsula unchanged except that it is reported our troops have now captured ST MALO and NANTES (.)[67] on the 12 Army Group front the enemy has been putting in small attacks in the MORTAIN area today and there are certain indications that he intends a big attack tomorrow between DOMFRONT and MORTAIN (.) on the other hand there have been signs this evening of enemy movement eastwards from MORTAIN (.) I do not really know what is likely to happen on that front tomorrow or in the future (.) a strong advance by four divisions began this morning northwards from LE MANS and my present information is that this movement has now reached the general line MAROLLES BEAUMONT half way to ALENCON (.) First Canadian Army has not made any progress today but the attack towards FALAISE is being resumed tonight (.) I have ordered Second British Army to transfer its main weight to its left flank and to operate strongly towards FALAISE in conjunction with Canadian Army (.) I am sure we must secure FALAISE early and having done so I have ordered Canadian Army to be prepared to operate with armoured forces towards TRUN and ARGENTAN

IWM, Montgomery Papers Part I, BLM 110/37

188
Montgomery's diary notes, 10 August 1944

[Typescript]

<u>10 August</u>

20. The advance of 15 U.S. Corps from LE MANS northwards to ALENCON began this morning. I have told Bradley to push on to ARGENTAN.

Canadian Army must get FALAISE.

Second Army must get CONDE.

We then would have a ring drawn round all the German troops south of the SEINE.

21. I met Dempsey and Crerar at H.Q. 12 Corps at 1700 hrs. and we studied the situation, and co-ordinated the action of the Second and Canadian armies.

22. There is a big concentration of German armoured divisions, six in all, assembling in the MORTAIN area and it looks as if the enemy was going to stage <u>another</u> attack to get through to AVRANCHES. See para. 8.[68] He has added 9 Pz. and 11 Pz. to the four mentioned in para. 8. He is now doomed; see paras. 15 and 16.[69]

See M.86 to C.I.G.S.[70]

IWM, Montgomery Papers Part II, LMD 61/1

189
Montgomery's Directive (M518) to 12 US Army Group, First Canadian Army and Second British Army

[Cyclostyle]

11 August 1944

<u>General Situation.</u>

1. Since the issue of M517[71] it begins to look as if the enemy intends to fight it out between the SEINE and the LOIRE.

2. A strong armoured force, up to six armoured divisions, has been identified on the front between DOMFRONT and MORTAIN, and determined efforts have been made to break through to AVRANCHES and thus cut in between the Cherbourg and Brittany peninsulas. All these enemy attacks have been well held by 12 Army Group.

3. On other parts of the front the enemy is endeavouring to hold firm, especially on the northern portion between VIRE and FALAISE.

On the southern portion of the front, on the LOIRE and in the LE MANS area, we are making definite progress.

4. The bulk of the enemy forces are west of the general line LE MANS–CAEN.

All their supplies, petrol, etc, must come from the east.

But the gap through which this must come is narrowing; in the north we are approaching FALAISE and in the south we are approaching ALENCON.

Obviously, if we can close the gap completely we shall have put the enemy in the most awkward predicament.

5. (a) As the gap narrows the enemy is certain to re-act.

(b) He will possibly bring in additional divisions from the east.

(c) His armoured and mobile forces in the MORTAIN area are likely to operate to break out eastwards, as it is in that direction they will find petrol and supplies. Should this happen, I consider they are more likely to operate in the general area DOMFRONT–ARGENTAN–ALENCON, so as to have the benefit of the difficult "bocage" country. Their object would be to hold off the right wing of 12 Army Group, and generally to try to facilitate the withdrawal of their forces on the FALAISE–VIRE front.

6. It is definitely beginning to look as if the main battle with the German forces in France is going to be fought between the SEINE and the LOIRE.

This will suit us very well.

7. The enemy force that will require to be watched carefully is the main concentration of armour now in the MORTAIN area; it is a formidable force, and must be well looked after.

<u>Intention.</u>

8. This remains unchanged, and as given in para 5 of M517. Clearly our intention must be to destroy the enemy forces between the SEINE and the LOIRE.

<u>Plan in Outline.</u>

9. For the present the full plan outlined in M517 will be modified as indicated below. We will now concentrate our energies on closing the gap behind the main enemy forces, so that we can possibly destroy them where they are now.

<u>First Canadian Army.</u>

10. Canadian Army will capture FALAISE. This is a first priority, and it is vital it should be done quickly.

11. The Army will then operate with strong armoured and mobile forces to secure ARGENTAN.

12. A secure front must be held between FALAISE and the sea, facing eastwards.

<u>Second British Army.</u>

13. Second Army will advance its left to FALAISE.

   This is a first priority, and a vital one. Sufficient forces will be allotted to the left Corps to ensure that it can fight its way forward to FALAISE, and quickly.

14. When FALAISE is captured, either by Second Army or Canadian Army, it will be held by Second Army.

15. From FALAISE, operations will be developed by Second Army westwards and southwards.

<u>12 U.S. Army Group.</u>

16. 12 Army Group will swing its right flank forward from the LE MANS area up to ALENCON, and then on to the general line SEES–CARROUGES.

<u>General.</u>

17. The attention of commanders is drawn to paras 5, 6 and 7.

18. We must be ready to put into execution the full plan given in M517 should it appear likely that the enemy may escape us here. 12

Army Group will therefore continue to plan the airborne operation against the CHARTRES area as referred to in para 17 of M517; this may have to be put into execution at short notice, and it must therefore be on very simple lines.

19. <u>ACKNOWLEDGE.</u>

IWM, Montgomery Papers Part I, BLM 126/19

190
Message (M87) to Field Marshal Sir Alan Brooke

[Typescript]

11 August 1944, 2245 hours

TOPSEC (.) Personal for CIGS from General Montgomery (.) Have no further information about situation in the BRITTANY peninsula (.) There are now definite indications that the enemy Panzer divisions are pulling out eastwards from the MORTAIN front and we have actually ourselves made some definite advances in that area (.) It is I suppose possible that he is regrouping so that he can deliver a better blow (.) As I said in M86[72] I am not really clear as to what the enemy intends to do on that front (.) The move northwards from LE MANS towards ALENCON has made good progress today (.) Recce elements have reached LA FERTE BERNARD about 20 miles northeast of LE MANS and MORTAGNE about 20 miles east of ALENCON (.) Main bodies of Armoured Divisions are on a general line 6 miles south of ALENCON and reconnaissance elements are reported as having reached ALENCON itself and pushed beyond it (.) On the Second Army front there has been very heavy fighting today on the fronts of all three Corps and each one has made definite advances (.) On the front of Canadian Army no progress has been made today (.) I have now ordered Canadian Army to operate with one division on the west side of the LAIZE River and Second Army to concentrate its weight on its left (.) I have ordered Second and Canadian Armies to go all out on their inner flank in order to get FALAISE within the next 48 hours (.) I sent you M518[73] today (.) I have instructed BRADLEY to collect a fresh Army Corps of three divisions in the LE MANS area and to hold it ready to push quickly through towards CHARTRES if and when we suddenly put M517[74] into operation (.) MS enquired today if I could spare Brigadier MURRAY[75] from 51 Division to command 6 Armoured Division (.) MURRAY is available and can be sent to UK whenever you like

IWM, Montgomery Papers Part I, BLM 110/38

191
Montgomery's diary notes, 11 August 1944

[Typescript]

<u>11 August</u>

23. The American right, 15 U.S. Corps, is going well and today its recce. elements reached LA FERTE BERNARD, MORTAGNE, and ALENCON. The main bodies of leading armoured divisions reached a line about six miles south of ALENCON.

24. The enemy attack in the MORTAIN area did not mature. See para. 22.[76]

25. I met Dempsey and Crerar at H.Q. 12 Corps at 1700 hrs. and discussed their situation. Second Army is attacking on the fronts of all three Corps; I have ordered Dempsey to put his weight on his left and go all out for FALAISE.

Canadian Army advance is halted north of FALAISE; I have ordered Crerar to operate with one Division west of the LAIZE, in close touch with the left of Second Army.

I impressed on both Army Comds. the vital need to get FALAISE, and quickly; I said I must have it in the next 48 hours.

26. I spoke on the phone to Bradley, and said he must begin to collect a new Corps of two or three Divisions in the LE MANS area – ready to push through to CHARTRES quickly vide. M.517[77] if and when it seems that the enemy may elude us in the present area.

27. The present situation is fascinating. If we can get quickly FALAISE, ARGENTAN, and ALENCON, then the enemy is finished.

He may escape us; but then if we hold ALENCON strongly, and push out quickly to CHARTRES, we shall head him off again.

28. I issued M.518,[78] giving my orders.

29. I issued a personal message[79] to the Armies.

30. See M.87 to the C.I.G.S.[80]

31. Casualties to date:

British and Canadian	68,000
U.S	102,000
	170,000

Prisoners taken:

British and Canadian	18,000
U.S.	92,000
	110,000

Tank Strengths:

British and Canadian	2,100
U.S.	3,200

IWM, Montgomery Papers Part II, LMD 61/1

192
Message (M89) to Field Marshal Sir Alan Brooke
[Typescript]

12 August 1944, 2220 hours

TOPSEC (.) Personal for CIGS from General Montgomery (.) The main news that I can give you tonight is that the thrust of 15 US Corps northwards from LE MANS has reached and passed ALENCON and the leading elements are now reported in the ARGENTAN area (.) The main body of the Corps is firmly established on the general line SEES CARROUGES and elements north of that line are at present only recce units (.) This means that the ring is very nearly closed round the Germans except that we have not yet got FALAISE in the north and the Germans are resisting very desperately in that area (.) 30 Corps is now only 4000 yards from CONDE (.) It is not possible to say what German forces are still inside the ring and what have passed eastwards so far (.) but there is no doubt that there is a great mass of the more immobile formations still west of the line FALAISE ARGENTAN and we are actually in close contact with the enemy on the general line FALAISE CONDE VIRE MORTAIN DOMFRONT (.) Second and Canadian Armies are straining every nerve to get to FALAISE quickly (.) There has been an obvious general withdrawal eastwards of enemy forces all day and the tactical air forces have had tremendous fun (.) The whole weight of the AEAF is being used tonight tomorrow and every day and every night in the task of destroying the enemy forces (.) Our great object will be to see that whatever part of the enemy forces escapes us here does not get back over the SEINE without being so mangled that it is incapable of further action for many days to come

IWM, Montgomery Papers Part I, BLM 110/39

193
Montgomery's diary notes, 12 August 1944

[Typescript]

<u>12 August</u>

32. I again met Dempsey and Crerar at H.Q. 12 Corps at 1700 hrs. and discussed the situation.

The situation is that the Americans have now reached ARGENTAN; all indications point to a large scale withdrawal; we must get FALAISE soon.

I ordered Second and Canadian armies to operate intensively day and night, to secure FALAISE.

33. The air squadrons have had a great day. The whole of the A.E.A.F. have been put on to attack the enemy ground forces by day and night.

34. It is now quite clear that the main enemy forces are almost surrounded; there is a small gap between ARGENTAN and FALAISE and through this the enemy is trying to escape.[81]

There is no doubt that a good deal of his light forces will escape to the east; but his heavy stuff, tanks, and so on, should never get away. Whatever forces do get away to the east will without doubt have to try and get back over the SEINE, and "firm up" on that line; there is no where else they could recover; and they have not enough troops to hold a long defensive line except behind a big river – and that not for long.

35. See M.89 to the C.I.G.S.[82]

IWM, Montgomery Papers Part II, LMD 61/1

194

Letter from Field Marshal Sir Alan Brooke to Montgomery

[Holograph]

13 August 1944

I am sorry not to have answered your letter[83] sooner, but have had a bad week with the P.M. – we had 14 hours in two days[84] with him trying to get a decision on the Pacific Strategy!!! We got one of a sort at last, but you would have been surprised if you had listened to some of his arguments.

Your telegrams are of great value & help to keep me in the situation which is not easy as Shaef are usually very badly informed.

I have been watching your battle with enormous interest. There are wonderful possibilities and I do hope that fortune may favour us, and that you succeed in dealing him a crippling blow S.W. of the Seine.

You can go on relying on my firm support, my dear old Monty. We have now been working together for a long time, and in some unpleasant places, where we have been able to appreciate each other properly. If I do talk plainly to you at times it is because I know that I can help you by doing so. There are people who don't understand you and I have had some pretty stiff battles on your behalf at times. I know therefore the type of actions that are calculated to raise the criticism that must be countered and prevented.

You can therefore go on relying on me to the utmost to watch your rear for you. I have complete confidence in your ability to beat the Bosch. Unfortunately there are a lot of jealous, critical, narrow minded individuals in this world. They can succeed in making the easiest things difficult, & in perverting the truth in a marvellous way. Waging war may well be difficult, but waging war under political control becomes at times almost impossible!!

I am off to Italy for a few days[85] on Friday, but may have a chance of looking you up bef. starting.

<u>Very</u> best of luck to you in your great task.

IWM, Montgomery Papers Part I, BLM 1/104

195
Message (M90) to Field Marshal Sir Alan Brooke

[Typescript]

13 August 1944, 2235 hours

TOPSEC (.) Personal for C.I.G.S. from General Montgomery (.) The ring is gradually being drawn tighter round the German forces (.) Two Armoured Divisions of 15 US Corps are now firmly established at ARGENTAN (.)[86] 7 US Corps of four divisions is moving northeast from MAYENNE and its leading armoured division has reached CARROUGES (.) Tomorrow at 1200 hours Canadian Army launches a strong attack with powerful air support towards FALAISE[87] and I am fairly confident that they will reach that place tomorrow night (.) There has been considerable enemy movement by day going on but my view is that only administrative echelons have so far passed eastwards through the gap FALAISE ARGENTAN (.) My Intelligence Staff consider that the fighting portion of five German Army Corps are still west of the road FALAISE ARGENTAN and that it is doubtful if they can move out of the ring owing to shortage of petrol (.) The tactical air forces have today been operating intensively with excellent results (.) I am continuing operations on the assumption that the bulk of the enemy forces are still inside the ring as stated by my Intelligence Staff (.) But in order to head off any who get through the gap 20 US Corps is being directed east of 15 US Corps towards LAIGLE and 12 US Corps is being assembled at LE MANS ready for any action that may be necessary in an easterly or northeasterly direction (.) I would like to finish by telling you that 51 Division have done very well under their new commander[88] in the fighting north of FALAISE and I hope that the division will now have no more setbacks

IWM, Montgomery Papers Part I, BLM 110/40

196
Montgomery's diary notes, 13 August 1944

[Typescript]

13 August

36. I had a long talk with Leigh-Mallory, the Air C.-in-C., who is with me during this period.

37. Eisenhower came to see me at 0915 hrs.

38. We had our church service in the church of CERISY-LE-FORET, a very fine old church.

39. I had a conference at 1200 hrs. at my H.Q. with Bradley and Dempsey.[89] Crerar was too busy to come; he came to tea and I gave him my plans then.

The net is closing round the enemy.

12 Army Group is launching 7 Corps from MAYENNE towards ARGENTAN; and also 20 Corps from LE MANS on the east side of 15 Corps, directed on LAIGLE and DREUX.

I made some notes after the meeting which show the grouping and tasks of Corps; these are given below.

First U.S. Army

5 Corps	2 Div.	Moving east, pushing the enemy in front of them, and preventing his disengagement and quick withdrawal.
	29 Div	
19 Corps	28 Div.	
	30 Div.	
	2 Armd.	

7 Corps	1 Div.	Moving N.E. from MAYENNE towards Argentan.
	4 Div.	
	9 Div.	
	3 Armd.	

None of the above Divisions will cross the boundary between 12 Army Group and Second Army.

Third U.S. Army

15 Corps	79 Div.	In area ALENCON–SEES–ARGENTAN
	90 Div.	
	2 French Armd.	
	5 Armd.	

<u>20 Corps</u>	5 Div. 35 Div. 7 Armd. ⎫⎬⎭	Moving northwards on the east flank of 15 Corps, and directed on LAIGLE and DREUX.
<u>12 Corps</u>	80 Div. 4 Armd. ⎫⎬⎭	Forming at LE MANS, ready to move east towards CHARTRES, or elsewhere as necessary.
<u>8 Corps</u>	In Brittany. 6 Armd. 8 Div. 83 Div.	

<u>12 Army Group:</u> 21 Divisions.
<u>Second British Army</u>

<u>8 Corps</u>	3 Div. 11 Armd. Gds. Armd. ⎫⎬⎭	Very wide front; holding the enemy; moving on TINCHEBRAY
<u>30 Corps</u>	43 Div. 50 Div. 7 Armd. ⎫⎬⎭	Moving on CONDE
<u>12 Corps</u>	15 Div. 53 Div. 59 Div. ⎫⎬⎭	Moving on FALAISE

<u>First Canadian Army</u>

<u>2 Cdn. Corps</u>	2 Cdn. Div. 3 Cdn. Div. 4 Cdn. Armd. 1 Polish Armd. ⎫⎬⎭	Moving on FALAISE

297

1 Corps	49 Div.	
	51 Div.	Very wide front. Holding role,
	6 Airborne	facing east.
	Div.	

21 Army Group: 16 Divisions
Total Allied Armies: 37 Divisions.
40. See M.90 to the C.I.G.S.[90]
IWM, Montgomery Papers Part II, LMD 61/1

197
Letter to Field Marshal Sir Alan Brooke

[Holograph]

14 August 1944

Things really do seem to be going very well. We have a ring round the enemy forces and the only way out is now between FALAISE and ARGENTAN. What actually is inside the ring, one cannot tell. How much has so far got away eastwards, one cannot tell. But I very much doubt if he can "firm up" again this side of the Seine.

I had a conference yesterday with Bradley, Dempsey, and Crerar, and we have our plans well tied up – for any eventuality.

I enclose you a note showing the present grouping,[91] by Corps, and in general what they are doing. Dawnay will explain further details.

The Dutch & Belgians are over here. Prince Bernhard[92] is wanting to come over and see them; they have been here only two days and the present state of the battle is such that Crerar cannot be bothered with odd Princes going about in his Army area. He has asked me to get Bernhard to delay his visit till things are easier. Can you fix this for me. He is quite a decent chap, but just at the moment he must stay away.

The present week may well see great happenings.

Ike is apt to get very excited and to talk wildly – at the top of his voice!!! He is now over here;[93] which is a very great pity. His ignorance as to how to run a war is absolute and complete; he has all the popular cries, but nothing else.[94] However, I manage to compete somehow. He is such a decent chap that it is difficult to be angry with him for long. One thing I am very firm about; he is never allowed to attend a meeting between me and my Army Commanders and Bradley!

Liddell Hart Centre for Military Archives, Alanbrooke Papers 6/2/30

198
Message (M93) to Field Marshal Sir Alan Brooke

[Typescript]

14 August 1944, 2240 hours

TOPSEC (.) personal for C.I.G.S. from General Montgomery (.) fighting has gone on all day on the general line TURNEBU CONDE TINCHEBRAY DOMFRONT against determined resistance (.) the thrust northeast from MAYENNE has reached the main road between FLERS and ARGENTAN and is pressing on to PUTANGES (.) in the North First Canadian Army attacked at 1200 hours today and the last reports were that leading troops had reached ERNES SASSY and OLENDON and were pushing on towards FALAISE (.) considerable chaos was caused to the attack when about twenty per cent of heavy bombers dropped their bombs well inside our lines on attacking divisions (.) there is no doubt that a good many enemy are still inside the ring (.) it is my opinion that a good many enemy have managed to pass eastwards out of the ring (.) I have ordered 12 Army Group to direct 20 U.S. Corps on the axis LA FERTE BARNARD through NOGENT LE ROTROU on DREUX as it is important to stop the enemy from turning southeast (.) we want those who have escaped us here to be pushed up against the SEINE

IWM, Montgomery Papers Part I, BLM 110/41

199
Montgomery's diary notes, 14 August 1944

[Typescript]

14 August

41. I moved my Tac. H.Q. from CERISY-LE-FORET to near LE BENY BOCAGE.

42. I visited 8 Corps and 30 Corps.

43. Our situation regarding reinforcements, especially infantry, is

very bad and we shall have to break up 59 Div. I sent a wire to the C.I.G.S. requesting permission to do this. See M.92.[95]

44. Canadian Army attacked at 1200 hrs. towards FALAISE.[96] Some chaos was caused when the heavy bombers of Bomber Command dropped about 20 per cent of the load on attacking divisions. However the attack went in and made progress. By dark it had not, however, reached FALAISE as I had hoped.

45. It is not yet clear what enemy divisions are in the ring, and what have got out. I have told my Intelligence staff that I must have the answer to this by the morning.

46. See M.93 to the C.I.G.S.[97]

IWM, Montgomery Papers Part II, LMD 61/1

200

Message (M94) to Field Marshal Sir Alan Brooke

[Typescript]

15 August 1944, 2230 hours

TOPSEC (.) Personal for CIGS from General Montgomery (.) It now seems quite clear that the enemy has decided to pull out from the area west of the road FALAISE ARGENTAN (.) In this area we have made considerable advances in all parts today against very slight opposition in the north (.) Leading troops of Canadian Army are within 1500 yards of FALAISE and should get that place tonight (.) We have also cut the CONDE FALAISE road east of CONDE and are in VASSY and TINCHEBRAY and DOMFRONT and the line now runs through those places (.) In the south the 15 US Corps is up against determined resistance astride ARGENTAN (.) The general picture in this area is of a full scale withdrawal by the enemy to get eastwards out of the pocket (.) Further to the east the whole of Third US Army is on the move (.) Troops of 20 US Corps are within 5 miles of DREUX and within 10 miles of CHARTRES (.) 12 US Corps has begun its movement eastwards from LE MANS towards CHATEAUDUN (.) the general picture in this part of the front is that PATTON is heading straight for PARIS and is determined to get there and will probably do so (.) The air forces have throughout the day operated at full intensity and this has facilitated the operations of the armies

IWM, Montgomery Papers Part I, BLM 110/42

201
Montgomery's diary notes, 15 August 1944

[Typescript]

<u>15 August</u>

47. My Intelligence Staff have told me they consider that the main fighting portion of the German Army is enclosed in our ring.

One, or possibly two, Panzer divisions are in the gap and are trying to push the Americans south from ARGENTAN; and certain administrative echelons have passed eastwards <u>through</u> the gap. The remainder of the German forces south of the SEINE are west of the road FALAISE–ARGENTAN and are enclosed in our ring. It is a fascinating picture.

48. The enemy has moved two divisions across the SEINE to BERNAY and CONCHES; he possibly hopes to form a line of sorts on the R. RISLE. He is also moving some divisions up from the south of FRANCE, through the gap between PARIS and ORLEANS; I presume these are intended to form a line on the southern flank.

49. I propose to proceed relentlessly with my plans. I saw all Army Commanders, and Bradley, and said that three points were now very important:

(a) We must close the gap and stop any more enemy getting away.

(b) We must keep up the pressure all round the circle, and make it difficult for him to disengage and get away quickly.

(c) We must ensure that any enemy who pass through the gap are headed off to the N.E., and pushed up against the SEINE; they must not get away to the S.E.

I explained that the whole of the Air Forces would be on the job of stopping large scale movements.

50. I ordered Canadian Army to capture FALAISE; it must be done by tonight. At the same time an armoured force was to be directed on TRUN. FALAISE and TRUN were to be strongly held, and all escape routes to the east blocked. Time is vital.

51. I ordered Bradley to extend his main forces to the east from ARGENTAN, and to prevent any enemy movement away to the S.E.

Consequent on this order he is:

(a) moving two divisions from the ARGENTAN area eastwards to LAIGLE.

(b) moving 20 Corps, of two divisions, from the LE MANS area through NOGENT LE ROTROU towards DREUX.

(c) forming 12 Corps, of two divisions, at LE MANS and will move it eastwards to CHATEAUDUN and ORLEANS, so as to face up to the enemy movement westwards through the gap PARIS–ORLEANS.

52. The general picture now is as follows:

(a) On the north, Canadian Army is attacking southwards to secure FALAISE and TRUN.

(b) On the south, First and Third U.S. Armies are strongly positioned on the general line BRIOUZE–ECOUCHE–ARGENTAN–GACE–LAIGLE; and soon I hope 20 Corps will be at DREUX.

(c) There is at present a gap between FALAISE and ARGENTAN, and through this gap the enemy is trying to withdraw eastwards – being pushed hard from the north and west by Second Army.

(d) The bulk of the German forces in N.W. Europe are to the west of the gap FALAISE–ARGENTAN, and inside the ring.

(e) The enemy is trying to move fresh divisions through the PARIS–ORLEANS gap, up to the battle. 12 Army Group is moving 12 Corps to CHATEAUDUN to deal with this.

53. The Secretary of State for War (Grigg) arrived to stay the night.

54. See M.94 to C.I.G.S.[98]

IWM, Montgomery Papers Part II, LMD 61/1

202
Message (M97) to Field Marshal Sir Alan Brooke

[Typescript]

16 August 1944, 2245 hours

TOPSEC (.) Personal for CIGS from General Montgomery (.) On the northern side of the pocket Second Army have advanced steadily all day but against much increased enemy resistance (.) The right of Second Army is now swinging forward through FLERS and eastwards to PUTANGES and ARGENTAN and has now reached the general line FLERS CONDE (.) Canadian Army is in FALAISE and is developing operations southeastwards down the ARGENTAN road (.) The Poles have crossed the DIVES River south of ST PIERRE SUR DIVES and are advancing south with their right on the river with the objective TRUN and have reached MORTEAUX COULIBOEUF (.) I have now directed Canadian Army to develop a thrust towards LISIEUX and have transferred 7 Armd Div to that army (.) This thrust will be developed in a northeasterly direction from ST PIERRE SUR DIVES where a bridgehead has already been obtained (.) There are good grounds for thinking that six panzer and SS divisions are still inside the pocket and elements of five of these divisions are trying to break out eastwards between ARGENTAN and SEES (.) I think the Americans are strong enough in the ARGENTAN area to hold this attack (.) If we can get the Second Army tomorrow to PUTANGES and the left wing of 2 Canadian Corps to TRUN we shall be very well placed (.) Third US Army is now pretty firm in CHARTRES and DREUX and it is reported but not confirmed that a column is within 10 miles of ORLEANS (.) I am swinging detachments from 20 US Corps from DREUX up on to the SEINE between VERNON and MANTES (.) The general picture today is of stubborn enemy resistance as we close in on his troops still west of the FALAISE ARGENTAN road (.) A great many prisoners are being collected in from all parts of the front and yesterday men from seventeen different divisions were captured by 5 and 19 US Corps (.) The total of prisoners is now about 140,000 (.) As has been the case throughout the whole of this campaign the air forces have been quite magnificent and have operated today with the greatest intensity (.) In the early part of the day the weather was not suitable for heavy operations but later in the day they got cracking

IWM, Montgomery Papers Part I, BLM 110/43

203
Montgomery's diary notes, 16 August 1944

[Typescript]

<u>16 August</u>

55. I took Grigg to see 8 Corps and Gds. Armd. Div.

56. The Adjutant-General (ADAM) came to dinner.

57. The enemy picture is now clearer. In the pocket we are pressing in on him from the west and north and, as we do so, his resistance is stiffening in desperate efforts to keep the pincers from closing in on him.

But he cannot keep us back.

We now hold FALAISE–CONDE–FLERS, and the right flank of Second Army is swinging forward to PUTANGES and ECOUCHE.

The First U.S. Army is holding firm at ARGENTAN, though they do not hold the town itself.

Canadian Army have the Polish Armd. Div. over the R. DIVES at ST. PIERRE-SUR-DIVES, and are moving south on TRUN and CHAMBOIS; they have reached COULIBOEUF.

4 Cdn. Armd. Div. is over the R. DIVES at DAM-BLAINVILLE, and is moving on TRUN via the main road from FALAISE.

The absolutely vital thing now is to get two armoured divisions to TRUN and CHAMBOIS – and quickly.

58. Once the enemy tumbles to what is on, he will without doubt try to pull out; he will try to use the river lines of the ORNE and DIVES to delay us; but both the ORNE and the DIVES are now turned from the north.

59. I transferred 7 Armd. Div. today from Second Army to Canadian Army, and ordered Canadian Army to develop at once a thrust on LISIEUX. If the enemy manages to slip any troops through the gap about TRUN, then a thrust through LISIEUX to BERNAY is the indicated.

60. See M.97 to C.I.G.S.[99]

IWM, Montgomery Papers Part II, LMD 61/1

204
Message (M98) to Field Marshal Sir Alan Brooke

[Typescript]
17 August 1944, 2255 hours

TOPSEC (.) Personal for CIGS from General Montgomery (.) the best news I can give you tonight is that the gap has now been closed[100] and the Polish Armoured Division has reached TRUN and is pushing on to CHAMBOIS (.) on the SEINE all barges and ferries have been openly moved in daylight to the south bank and are waiting at points where the roads lead to the river (.) this has never been done before and seems to be a sure sign that the Germans are going to attempt a major breakout tonight (.) it is really impossible to say exactly what is inside the ring and what has escaped so far to the east (.) it seems quite clear that the best part of five Panzer divisions are still west of the road FALAISE ARGENTAN together with a good mass of immobile infantry (.) we now sit astride the main roads leading east but have not had time to organise definite blocks on every avenue of exit (.) if a major breakout is attempted during tonight it is quite possible that elements will get through and we shall not know what the situation is until later tomorrow (.) the First U.S. Army is now facing north between BRIOUZE and LAIGLE (.) the Third U.S. Army is facing east between DREUX and ORLEANS (.) we hold DREUX CHARTRES and ORLEANS and recce elements have been pushed eastwards from DREUX and CHARTRES some fifteen miles towards PARIS (.) the roll [sic] of the Third Army has been to stop the enemy escaping through the PARIS ORLEANS gap and the intention now is to wheel the northern flank of this army up to the SEINE about VERNON (.) but the Corps at DREUX and the one at CHARTRES are in a very difficult administrative situation and it is doubtful at the moment whether they can move very far until the situation improves (.) air action against the enemy inside the pocket has been difficult today as the net was drawn tighter but air forces have been active all day and have inflicted a great deal of damage on the enemy (.) the first priority for the air tonight are the barges and ferries on the SEINE

IWM, Montgomery Papers Part I, BLM 110/44

205
Montgomery's diary notes, 17 August 1944

[Typescript]

<u>17 August</u>

61. I rang up Crerar on the telephone at 0700 hrs. and impressed on him the vital need to get two armoured divisions to TRUN–CHAMBOIS area today. If he can do so, the enemy is caught and we may capture over 100,000 Germans; if he does not do so, many Germans may escape.

62. I flew over to 12 Army Group, north of FOUGERES, to discuss the situation with Bradley.

We have to think ahead and be clear what we want to do when we have got to the SEINE and PARIS.

I explained my views as follows:

(a) 12 and 21 Army groups must operate together as a strong mass, which need fear nothing.

(b) 21 Army Group must be on the west flank, and must move north and clear the channel coast, the Pas de Calais, West Flanders, and secure ANTWERP.

(c) 12 Army Group to form the eastern flank of the movement, and to move with its right on the ARDENNES – being directed on AACHEN and COLOGNE.

(d) The basic objects would be to destroy the German forces on the channel coast, and to establish a powerful air force in Belgium – from where it could dominate Germany.

(e) Second British and First Canadian armies to cross the SEINE about MANTES, and below it. Canadian Army then to clear the HAVRE peninsula, while Second Army moved north.

(f) The Americans to cross the Seine astride Paris, the main weight being directed south of the city.

63. Bradley agreed entirely with my outline plan.[101]

I have not discussed it with Eisenhower yet; he is not likely to have any great objections, and he will I think undoubtedly accept what we say. I shall suggest to him that the force coming up from south France should be directed to METZ and NANCY, and in to the SAAR.

64. See my M.99 to C.I.G.S. and his reply[102] – both dated 18 Aug.

65. See my M.98 to the C.I.G.S.[103] for the general picture.

66. Grigg left.

General Kennedy, A/C.I.G.S.(Ops) at War Office, arrived to stay the night.[104]

IWM, Montgomery Papers Part II, LMD 61/1

206
Message (M99) to Field Marshal Sir Alan Brooke
[Typescript]

18 August 1944, 0830 hours

TOPSEC (.) Personal for CIGS from General Montgomery (.) have been thinking ahead about future plans but have NOT yet discussed subject with IKE (.)[105] my views are as follows (.) after crossing SEINE 12 and 21 Army Groups should keep together as a solid mass of some 40 divisions which would be so strong that it need fear nothing (.) the force should move northwards (.) 21 Army Group should be on western flank and should clear the channel coast and the PAS DE CALAIS and WEST FLANDERS and secure ANTWERP (.) the American armies should move with right flank on the ARDENNES directed on BRUSSELS AACHEN and COLOGNE (.) the movement of the American armies would cut the communications of enemy forces on the channel coast and thus facilitate the task of the British Army Group (.) the initial objects of the movement would be to destroy the German forces on the coast and to establish a powerful air force in BELGIUM (.) a further object would be to get the enemy out of V1 or V2[106] range of ENGLAND (.) BRADLEY agrees entirely with above conception (.)[107] would be glad to know if you agree generally (.) when I have got your reply[108] will discuss matter with IKE

IWM, Montgomery Papers Part I, BLM 115/19

207
Montgomery's diary notes, 18–20 August 1944
[Typescript]

<u>18 August</u>

67. Today was a day of destruction.

The enemy S.S. and Panzer divisions decided yesterday to endeavour to get away; they abandoned the immobile infantry and tried to break out to the east last night and today.

I have no doubt a great many troops got away. But a great many did NOT, and the day was a record of destruction and killing from the air and ground.

The whole area FALAISE–VIMOUTIERS–ARGENTAN–PUTANGES became a mass of burning tanks and M.T.; at a conservative estimate we destroyed 200 tanks and 5000 vehicles.

Prisoners were taken by 30 Corps from 12 different divisions, thus showing the complete state of disorganisation in enemy circles.

See M.100[109] to the C.I.G.S.

68. The air forces had a splendid day. Our own troops suffered a good deal as the pilots shot up friend and foe,[110] and I received many complaints especially from Canadian Army.

19 August

69. Another day of destruction and killing, in and about the Normandy pocket. It is now estimated that elements of fourteen divisions were more in than out of the pocket; all of them were very badly battered; many of them have been killed. These divisions are mostly infantry; but 21 Pz. and 10 S.S. seem to be there.

The divisions more out than in are the S.S. and Pz. divisions; all of these, also, are badly mauled.

70. I had a conference of Commanders at 1000 hrs. to issue orders for the future operations. This was attended by:

Bradley.	12 Army Group.
Hodges.	First U.S. Army.
Dempsey.	Second British Army.
Crerar.	First Canadian Army.

71. Kennedy left in my plane for U.K.

72. I moved my H.Q. from LE BENY BOCAGE to CONDE.

73. See M.103[111] to the C.I.G.S.

74. I had better explain here a very curious incident that took place recently.[112]

The B.B.C. 9 p.m. news on 15 August contained a statement that Eisenhower had taken over personal command in France, and that he had under him two Army Groups – No. 12 U.S. Group commanded by Bradley and No. 21 Group commanded by me. This gave the impression that I had been deposed from command of the land battle under Eisenhower, and a good deal of comment took place.

The B.B.C. 7 a.m. news on 16 August had a statement correcting the one of the night before, and saying that I was still in overall charge of the land operations.

The Daily Mirror of 17 August had a leading article demanding that an apology be made to me!! It also had an amusing cartoon.[113]

The whole affair is probably a slip-up by someone; or it may have been done on purpose by someone at SHAEF.

It will NOT do IKE any good; people will say that just as I am about to win a big victory, he tried to step in and scoop the reward. Actually IKE is far too decent a chap to do anything of the sort; but there are many on his staff who would love to do so.

20 August

75. I issued M.519,[114] my directive for the future operations.

76. It can now be said that the battle of Normandy is over – and that it has been decisively won.

The German armies in N.W. Europe have received a terrific hammering; they have suffered grievous losses in men and equipment; all divisions have been badly mauled; what can get away is in full retreat to the SEINE and beyond. PARIS is at our mercy.

We could take the capital any time we like; but I am after the field army troops; as I wired to the Prime Minister:

Seek ye first THE COP, and everything else will be added unto you.[115]

77. As Second Army moved forward today, eastwards up the pocket or "bottle", they discovered large enemy forces in the FORET DE GOUFFERN, S.E. of FALAISE. These turned out to be the main portions of five S.S. and Pz. divisions – 1 S.S., 2 S.S., 9 S.S., 10 S.S., 2 Pz. They tried to break out to the east and N.E., and the Poles who were holding the CHAMBOIS area had some very heavy fighting; the enemy was held, and his fate is certain. A very great many were killed in the area about ST. LAMBERT and CHAMBOIS.

78. Meanwhile Second Army began to move forward on its right

flank towards GACE, and Canadian Army on its right flank towards LISIEUX and ORBEC.

Once we can get the "pocket" cleaned up, then the whole of 21 Army Group will go hard for the SEINE.

But meanwhile, 15 and 19 U.S. Corps are moving northwards from the general line MANTES–DREUX–BERNEUIL; this movement will go forward to the sea, thus creating a second "pocket", and cutting off the escape of any further enemy across the SEINE. The victory is going to be a very decisive one.

79. See M.104[116] to the C.I.G.S.

80. Anthony Eden came to dinner and gave me the political form.[117] I like him.[118]

IWM, Montgomery Papers Part II, LMD 61/1

Appendix

Four letters of appreciation sent to Montgomery at the conclusion of the Battle of Normandy

208
Letter from Sir James Grigg to Montgomery

[Holograph]

24 August 1944

I have been meaning to write to you ever since I got back but have put it aside thinking that there was so much that I wanted to say. But I have come to the conclusion that there are really only two things I want to say & that those can be said quite shortly.

The first is to pay tribute to one of the few men of genius that I have met in my varied and amusing existence – & incidentally the only man of genius in any of the British (and I suspect all the other) Services to-day.

The second is to say how glad I am that the War Office is now in unison with the fighting armies & how grateful to you for your very considerable share in producing this.

Oh! there was a third – to express the hope that these personal & national jealousies will not operate to prolong the war or to filch from you the credit for your masterly campaign.

God bless!

IWM, Montgomery Papers Part I, BLM 1/89

209
Letter from Lieutenant-General Sir Richard O'Connor to Montgomery

[Holograph]

24 August 1944

I feel I must write & congratulate you on what seems likely to be one of the most decisive battles in the world's history. It has in every way justified your strategy & tactics, which I well remember you expounding long before we left England. How we were to bear the brunt of the battle for the first few weeks by constantly attacking the enemy, never giving him any rest, & never letting him have a chance of regaining the initiative, all this to take the pressure off the Americans so that they might achieve, what in fact they did achieve, & are achieving.

But apart from that side of it, your own courage & confidence has done such a tremendous lot to keep up the morale of the officers & men serving under you. It has been worth many Army Corps.

I have never before served under anyone whose judgement I trusted in everything.[1] It is a very pleasant change.

IWM, Montgomery Papers Part I, BLM 97/31

210
Letter from Field Marshal Sir Alan Brooke to Montgomery
[Holograph]
1 September 1944
I cannot tell you what joy it gives me writing to congratulate you on becoming a Field Marshal – never has this distinction been better earned.

I knew your value and merits were bound to be recognised, and have fought many battles for you with some who had not got sufficient vision to appreciate your true value. I personally have never had any doubt of it ever since we went through those difficult days from Louvain to Dunkirk![2]

You may perhaps have thought during the last 5 years that I was occasionally unnecessarily rude to you. If I was I can assure you that it was only because I wanted to guard you against the effect of some of your actions which are incorrectly judged by others & lead to criticism which might affect your progress, a matter which has been of <u>great</u> concern to me.

I should like at this moment of your triumph to offer you one more word of advice. Don't let success go to your head & remember the value of humility.

"If you can meet with triumph & disaster
and treat both those impostors just the same

– – – – – –

Yours is the world and everything that's in it,
And what's more you will be a man my son."

I have found the above lines from Kipling a great help during this war.[3]

Well, God bless you Monty old boy, few things have given me more pleasure than to-day's recognition of the great work you have done for your country.[4]

IWM, Montgomery Papers Part I, BLM 1/105

211

Letter from the Prime Minister to Montgomery

[Typescript]

2 September 1944

My dear Field Marshal,

– to use your new rank for the first time –

It gave me the greatest pleasure to make the recommendation to The King, and I am sure no such step has been better earned. There is of course a little reaction in American circles, but here everyone is delighted.

This is to explain to you that I did not intend by this promotion to put you permanently over the head of Alexander, for that I think would be unfair. The occasion of your appointment was fixed by the march of historic events. Presently Alexander will certainly receive the baton, and I propose to date it from the capture of Rome[5] which I am sure will be quite agreeable to you. Thus the old order of seniority will be restored. This can make no difference in practice to anybody. It is in fact the normal practice in respect of special promotions in ranks up to and including that of Major General.

How wonderful it is to see our people leaping out at last after all their hard struggles.

IWM, Montgomery Papers Part II, LMD 108/3

Biographical Notes

Adam, General Sir Ronald ('Bill') (1885–1982). Commanded 3 Corps, 1939–40; and Northern Command, 1940–1. Adjutant-General to the Forces, 1941–6.

Alanbrooke, Field Marshal Viscount (1883–1963). Commanded 2 Corps, 1939–40; and Home Forces, 1940–1. Chief of the Imperial General Staff, 1941–6.

Alexander, Field Marshal Earl (1891–1969). Commanded 1st Infantry Division and 1 Corps, 1939–40. Sent to Burma, and withdrew troops to India, 1942. GOC-in-C, Middle East, 1942–3. Eisenhower's Deputy Land Force Commander, Mediterranean, 1943–4 (18th Army Group and 15th Army Group). Supreme Allied Commander, Mediterranean, 1944–5.

Bedell Smith, General Walter (1895–1961). US Secretary to the Combined Chiefs of Staff, 1942. Eisenhower's Chief of Staff, 1942–5.

Bracken, Brendan, Viscount (1901–58). MP for Paddington North, 1929–45. Churchill's Parliamentary Private Secretary, 1939–41. Minister of Information, 1941–5. First Lord of the Admiralty, 1945.

Bradley, General of the Army Omar Nelson (1893–1981). Commanded US 2 Corps, 1943; US First Army, 1943–4; and US 12th Army Group, 1944–5.

Broadhurst, Air Chief Marshal Sir Harry (1905–95). Senior Air Staff Officer to the AOC, Western Desert, 1942. AOC, Allied Air Forces, Western Desert, 1943. Commanded 83 Group, Allied Expeditionary Air Force, North-West Europe, 1944–5.

Bucknall, Lieutenant-General Gerard (1894–1980). Commanded 5th Infantry Division in Sicily and Italy, 1943–4; and 30 Corps in Normandy, 1944. GOC, Northern Ireland, 1945–7.

Bullen-Smith, Major-General David Charles (1898–1970). Commanded 15th (Scottish) Infantry Division, 1942–3; and 51st (Highland) Infantry Division in Sicily and North-West Europe, 1943–4.

Coningham, Air Marshal Sir Arthur (1895–1948). Commanded Desert Air Force, 1941–3; 1st Allied Tactical Air Force in the Mediterranean, 1943; and 2nd Tactical Air Force in North-West Europe, 1944–5.

Crerar, General Harry (1888–1965). Canadian Chief of General Staff, 1940–1. Commanded 2nd Canadian Infantry Division, 1941–2; 1 Canadian Corps, 1942–4; and First Canadian Army, 1944–5.

Crocker, General Sir John (1896–1963). Commanded 6th Armoured Division, 1940–1; 2nd Armoured Group, Eastern Command, 1941–2; 9 Corps in Tunisia, 1943; and 1 Corps in North-West Europe, 1944–5.

Cunningham, Admiral of the Fleet Viscount (1883–1963). C-in-C, Mediterranean, 1939–42 and 1943. Head of Naval Delegation in Washington, 1943. First Sea Lord, 1943–6.

De Guingand, Major-General Sir Francis (1900–79). Director of Military
  Intelligence, Middle East, 1942. BGS (Operations), Eighth Army, 1942. Chief
  of Staff, Eighth Army and 21st Army Group, 1942–5.
Dempsey, General Sir Miles (1896–1969). Commanded 42nd Armoured
  Division, 1941–2; 13 Corps, 1942–3; and Second Army in North-West
  Europe, 1944–5.
Duncan-Sandys, Baron (1908–87). Conservative MP and Churchill's son-in-law.
  Parliamentary Secretary, Ministry of Supply, Feb. 1943–Nov. 1944. Minister
  of Works, 1944–5. Chaired a War Cabinet Committee concerned with defence
  against German V-weapons.
Eisenhower, General of the Army Dwight David (1890–1969). Allied C-in-C for
  Operation TORCH and the Mediterranean Theatre, 1942–3. Supreme Allied
  Commander, North-West Europe, 1944–5.
Erskine, General Sir George (1899–1965). Commanded 69th Infantry Brigade,
  1941–2. BGS, 13 Corps, 1942–3. Commanded 7th Armoured Division in
  North Africa, Italy and Normandy, 1943–4.
Grigg, Sir James (1890–1964). Permanent Under-Secretary of State for War,
  1939–42. MP for East Cardiff, and Secretary of State for War, 1942–5.
Harding, Field Marshal Baron (1896–1989). Commanded 7th Armoured
  Division, 1942–3, until wounded January 1943. Alexander's Chief of Staff,
  1944–5. Commanded 13 Corps, 1945.
Horrocks, Lieutenant-General Sir Brian (1895–1985). Commanded 10 and 13
  Corps in Eighth Army, 1942–3; and 9 Corps in First Army. Badly wounded in
  an air raid shortly before invasion of Sicily. Commanded 30 Corps in North-
  West Europe, 1944–5.
Ismay, General Baron (1887–1965). Secretary, Committee of Imperial Defence,
  1938–9. Chief of Staff to the Minister of Defence (Churchill), 1940–5;
  Deputy Secretary (Military) to the War Cabinet (1940–5).
Keller, Major-General Rod (1900–54). Commanded 1st Canadian Infantry
  Brigade, 1941–2; and 3rd Canadian Infantry Division, 1942–4. Wounded by
  'friendly fire' in Normandy, 8 August 1944.
King, William Lyon Mackenzie (1874–1950). Leader of the Liberal Party in
  Canada, 1919–48. Prime Minister of Canada, 1921–6, 1926–30 and 1935–48.
Leese, Lieutenant-General Sir Oliver (1894–1978). Commanded Guards
  Armoured Division, 1941–2; 30 Corps in Eighth Army, 1942–3; Eighth Army,
  1944; and Allied Land Forces, South-East Asia, 1944–5.
Leigh-Mallory, Air Chief Marshal Sir Trafford (1892–1944). Commanded
  No 11 (Fighter) Group, 1940–2; Fighter Command, 1942–3; and Allied
  Expeditionary Air Force, 1943–4. Killed in an air crash on 14 November 1944
  en route to take up the post of Air C-in-C South East Asia Command.
McCreery, General Sir Richard (1898–1967). Chief of Staff to General
  Alexander, 1942–3. Commanded 10 Corps, 1943–4; and Eighth Army, 1944–5.
Martel, Lieutenant-General Sir Giffard (1889–1958). Commanded 50th Infantry
  Division in the BEF, 1939–40. Commanded Royal Armoured Corps, 1940–2.
  Head of the British Military Mission to the Soviet Union, 1943–4.
Morgan, Lieutenant-General Sir Frederick (1894–1967). Chief of Staff to the

Supreme Allied Commander (Designate), 1943. Deputy Chief of Staff, SHAEF, 1944–5.

Mountbatten, Admiral of the Fleet Earl (1900–79). Chief of Combined Operations, and member of the Chiefs of Staff Committee, 1942–3. Supreme Allied Commander, South-East Asia, 1943–6.

Nye, Lieutenant-General Sir Archibald (1895–1967). Director of Staff Duties, War Office, 1940–1. Vice-Chief of the Imperial General Staff, 1941–6.

O'Connor, General Sir Richard (1889–1981). Commanded Western Desert Force/13 Corps 1940–1. Taken prisoner April 1941; escaped December 1943. Commanded 8 Corps in North-West Europe, 1944; Eastern Command, India, 1944–5; and North Western Army, India, 1945–6. Adjutant-General to the Forces, 1946–7.

Paget, General Sir Bernard (1887–1961). Commanded South-Eastern Command, 1941; Home Forces, 1941–3; 21st Army Group, 1943; and Middle East Forces, 1944–6.

Patton, General George (1885–1945). Commanded Western Task Force in TORCH landings, 1942; US 2 Corps in Tunisia, 1943; US Seventh Army in Sicily, 1943; and US Third Army in North-West Europe, 1944–5.

Portal, Marshal of the RAF Viscount (1893–1971). Commanded RAF Bomber Command, 1940. Chief of the Air Staff, 1940–5.

Ramsay, Admiral Sir Bertram (1883–1945). As Flag Officer, Dover, organised the Dunkirk evacuation, 1940. Deputy Naval Commander Expeditionary Force, TORCH landings, 1942. Commanded Eastern Task Force for the invasion of Sicily, 1943. Allied Naval Commander-in-Chief Expeditionary Force for the invasion of Normandy, 1944. Killed in a plane crash, 2 January 1945.

Rennie, Major-General Thomas (1900–45). Commanded 154th Infantry Brigade, 1942–3; 3rd Infantry Division, 1943–4; and 51st Infantry Division, 1944–5. Killed in action, 24 March 1945.

Richardson, General Sir Charles (1908–94). GSO1 (Plans), Eighth Army, 1942. BGS, Eighth Army, 1943. Deputy Chief of Staff, US Fifth Army, 1943. BGS (Plans), 21st Army Group, 1944–6.

Riddell-Webster, General Sir Thomas (1886–1974). Commanded Southern Command, India, 1941. Chief Administration Officer, Middle East, 1941–2. Quartermaster-General to the Forces, 1942–5.

Ritchie, General Sir Neil (1897–1985). Commanded Eighth Army, 1941–2; 52nd Infantry Division, 1942–3; and 12 Corps in North-West Europe, 1944–5.

Rommel, Field Marshal Erwin (1891–1944). Commanded the Afrika Korps and Panzer Armee Afrika, 1941–3. Commanded Army Group B in Italy, 1943. Inspector of the Atlantic Wall, and commander of Army Group B in North-West Europe, 1943–4. Wounded in an air raid in Normandy, 17 July 1944; committed suicide after being implicated in the July Plot to assassinate Hitler, 14 October 1944.

Simonds, Lieutenant-General Guy (1903–74). Chief of Staff, First Canadian Army, 1943. Commanded 1st and 2nd Canadian Infantry Divisions, 1943; 5th Canadian Armoured Division, 1943–4; and 2 Canadian Corps, 1944–5.

Simpson, General Sir Frank (1899–1986). Montgomery's Brigade-Major, 9th

Infantry Brigade, 1937–8, and his Chief of Staff, 5 Corps and 12 Corps, 1940–1. Deputy Director of Military Operations, War Office, 1942–3. Director of Military Operations, and Assistant Chief of the Imperial General Staff (Operations), 1943–6. Vice-Chief of the Imperial General Staff, 1946–8.

Smuts, Field Marshal Jan (1870–1950). Prime Minister of the Union of South Africa, 1919–24 and 1939–48. Created a Field Marshal in the British Army in 1941 and served in the Imperial War Cabinet.

Sosnkowski, Lieutenant-General Kazimierz (1885–1969). Commander-in-Chief, Polish Armed Forces, 1943–4.

Stuart, Lieutenant-General Kenneth (1891–1945). Canadian Chief of the General Staff, 1941–3; Acting GOC First Canadian Army, 1943–4. Chief of Staff Canadian Military Headquarters, UK, 1943–4.

Tedder, Marshal of the RAF Baron (1890–1967). Commanded RAF Middle East Command, 1941–3; and Mediterranean Air Command/Mediterranean Allied Air Forces, 1943–4. Deputy Supreme Commander Allied Expeditionary Force, 1944–5. Chief of the Air Staff, 1946–50.

Verney, Major-General Gerald (1900–57). Commanded 6th Guards Tank Brigade, UK and Normandy, 1942–4; 7th Armoured Division, Normandy, 1944; and 1st Guards Brigade, Italy and Austria, 1944–5.

Weeks, Lieutenant-General Baron (1890–1960). Director-General of Army Equipment, 1941–2. Deputy Chief of the Imperial General Staff, 1942–5.

Wilson, Field Marshal Baron (1881–1964). C-in-C, Persia-Iraq, 1942–3; and Middle East, 1943. Supreme Allied Commander, Mediterranean, 1944. Head of British Joint Staff Mission in Washington, 1944–7.

Notes

Notes to Introduction

1   BLM 49/36.

2   See Churchill, *The Second World War*, Vol. V, p. 376.

3   The letter to Brooke is reproduced in Hamilton, *Monty: Master of the Battlefield*, pp. 464–6.

4   See Documents 205 and 206.

5   See Robert Cowley (ed.), *What If? Military Historians Imagine What Might Have Been*, p. 347.

6   See Documents 36 and 44.

7   See the Hobart correspondence files in the Liddell Hart Papers in the Liddell Hart Centre for Military Archives.

8   See Document 207.

9   For those wishing further background on the historiography of the Normandy campaign, a good starting point is Carlo D'Este's influential critique of Montgomery's generalship, *Decision in Normandy*, published in 1983. Reference should also be made to Colin Baxter's *Field Marshal Bernard Law Montgomery, 1887–1976: A Selected Bibliography*, published in 1999, and Stephen Ashley Hart's *Montgomery and 'Colossal Cracks'*, published in 2000.

10   See Wilmot, *The Struggle for Europe*, pp. 369–70.

11   See, for example, Montgomery's 'Talk to Generals – 13 January 44' (Document 7), and in his letter to Lieutenant-General Crerar of 26 July (Document 134). Unfortunately Montgomery did not follow his own good advice that the best way to resolve problems was by face-to-face contact in his dealings with Eisenhower. The lengthy letters they exchanged in June and July 1944, reproduced in full in this volume, did not form the basis for a relationship of mutual understanding and trust. On the other hand Stephen Ambrose, in an essay entitled 'Eisenhower as Commander: Single Thrust versus Broad Front', argues that it was not at all certain 'that if Eisenhower and Montgomery had spent more time together they could have reconciled their differences or even understood each other … Given the difference in personality, national background, and position, it was inevitable that Eisenhower and Montgomery would disagree and that they would find it difficult to agree on what they were disagreeing about' (in Chandler (ed.), *The Papers of Dwight David Eisenhower: The War Years*, Vol. V, p. 40).

12   The quotation comes from a letter Field Marshal Lord Carver wrote to me on 3 June 1990. Lord Carver, who was the President of the Army

Records Society at the time, had just read the manuscript of *Montgomery and the Eighth Army* to assess its suitability for inclusion in the Society's publications programme. He concluded: 'My first feeling was that we had had almost all of it before in Nigel Hamilton's volumes; but, as I read through, I realised that we had much more, and that Monty was revealed, both as a person and as a professional soldier, in a way that no other method had done, and I congratulate you on it.'

Notes to Montgomery and his Papers

1   The letter is reproduced in full in Hamilton, *Monty: The Making of a General*, pp. 799–800.
2   See Chalfont, *Montgomery of Alamein*, p. 18.
3   The Dunkirk diary can be found at BLM 19 in the Montgomery Papers Part I.
4   Only one extract from the Log is included in this volume – see Document 13.
5   See Lamb, *Montgomery in Europe 1943–1945*, p. 12.

Notes to Documents 1–12, January 1944, pp. 15–40

1   The Prime Minister had sent a message to the Chiefs of Staff in London on 30 December 1943, requesting that they fly out to Marrakesh a digest of the outline invasion plans drawn up in 1943 by a planning team under Lieutenant-General Sir Frederick Morgan, the Chief of Staff to the Supreme Allied Commander (COSSAC). See Gilbert, *Road to Victory*, p. 631.
2   Document 2; Montgomery had selected documents typed up as Appendices 'A' to 'K' for this section of his personal diary, covering January, February and March 1944. Relevant documents were filed with succeeding instalments, but not copied and marked up as appendices.
3   Lord Moran refers in his diary to the encounter between Beaverbrook and Montgomery. Moran heard Beaverbrook tell Montgomery that he could have 'a great political future' after the war. See Moran, *Winston Churchill: The Struggle for Survival 1940–65*, p. 180.
4   For Montgomery and the planning for HUSKY, the invasion of Sicily, see Hamilton, *Monty: Master of the Battlefield*, pp. 241–68; and Brooks (ed.), *Montgomery and the Eighth Army*, pp. 217–44.
5   Montgomery flew to Algiers to confer with Eisenhower and Bedell Smith on 27 December 1943. In *Crusade in Europe*, p. 238, Eisenhower says that at the meeting he talked about a number of weaknesses in the COSSAC plan, of which he had seen a 'sketchy outline'. Later, in his memoirs, Montgomery recalled Eisenhower's telling him at Algiers that the COSSAC plan 'did not look too good' (Montgomery, *Memoirs*, p. 210). At the time, however, in a lengthy letter he wrote to Brooke on 28 December 1943, Montgomery refers to having discussed the command structure and the organisation of the various headquarters for OVERLORD, but makes no mention of the COSSAC plan. (See

Alanbrooke Papers for the original letter; it is reproduced in full in Hamilton, *Monty: Master of the Battlefield*, pp. 464–6, but with the date misprinted as 23 December.)

6   Admiral Ramsay had been appointed Allied Naval Commander-in-Chief Expeditionary Force (ANCXF) in October 1943.

7   Air Chief Marshal Leigh-Mallory, who had been confirmed as Commander-in-Chief Allied Expeditionary Air Forces in November 1943.

8   This document, the digest of OVERLORD flown out from London at the Prime Minister's request, is not extant in the Montgomery Papers.

9   This document illustrates that at this stage Montgomery's personal diary does not consist of a separate entry for each day. January is covered in entries headed '3 January', '12 January', '13 January', '14 January', '21 January' and '23 January'.

10 These conferences do not appear in detail in Montgomery's diary notes, but can be reconstructed from various documents in the Montgomery Papers and other contemporary sources. For example, Ramsay's diary, published in 1994 under the title *The Year of D-Day* (ed. Robert W. Love and John Major) gives more of a blow-by-blow account.

11 The codename for the proposed invasion of southern France, later changed to DRAGOON.

12 Eisenhower flew from the United States and arrived in London on 15 January.

13 Document 5.

14 Document 6.

15 On 7 January, see Document 4.

16 Ramsay's diary entry for this conference on 12 January sheds light on the problems he encountered in working with Montgomery: 'Meeting was much too big & was very badly staged as it was designed to imply that Monty was the supreme Comd^r & L.M. and myself subsidiary to him which was absurd as we are all on a level.' When Ramsay challenged him about this two days later, Montgomery apologised: 'Said he knew nothing about it' (Love and Major (eds), *The Year of D-Day*, pp. 6–8).

17 Montgomery learned of this when he flew to see Eisenhower at Algiers on 27 December 1943. As he wrote in his diary for 27 December, 'Eisenhower told me that I am to take complete charge of the land battle and that the American Armies will be placed under my command' (BLM 47/1).

18 Lieutenant-General Omar N. Bradley.

19 It is interesting to note this reference by Bradley to American public opinion as a factor in the military planning process. Compare (and contrast) Montgomery's comment in his diary notes for 26 May 1944: 'It is victories that win wars and not public opinion' (Document 52).

20 Lieutenant-General Sir Kenneth Anderson. Lieutenant-General Sir Miles Dempsey replaced him on 26 January 1944 when he returned from Italy.

21 Presumably Montgomery's Chief of Staff, Major-General de Guingand.

22 Document 5.

23 In letters to Lieutenant-General Bedell Smith on 13 January and General

Marshall on 17 January, Eisenhower refers to two 'not purely military' arguments for ANVIL. First, at the recent Teheran Conference a definite commitment to invade southern France had been made to the Russians. Secondly, the Allies had put a good deal of effort into preparing the French Army. ANVIL would allow it to play its part in the liberation of France. See Chandler (ed.), *The Papers of Dwight David Eisenhower: The War Years*, Vol. III, pp. 1655–6 and 1661–2.

24 Montgomery's notes for this address are the most substantial in his file of notes for talks given on his return to England. There are also briefer notes for his talks to the Staff College on 7 January (BLM 90/1) and to his own staff on 11 January (BLM 90/3). These are reproduced in full in Hamilton, *Monty: Master of the Battlefield*, pp. 490–3. Montgomery's script for this talk on 13 January can usefully be looked at in conjunction with a set of notes made by one of the audience, consisting of six closely typed pages. These are to be found amongst the official historians' papers at the National Archives (CAB106/1037). For example, the notes for points a–d of section 7 record Montgomery as saying: 'I would rather hit one good blow, go on with fresh troops to roll up the flanks, than make several small blows. When a good blow goes home, the battle becomes fluid and armor [*sic*] can be pushed through to form pivots for your attacks on enemy reserves. No thrust should be made by less than a division reinforced by about a regiment of armor or a brigade axis. You can ignore ground between for quite a time leaving it to be cleared up by reserves.' The note-taker is anonymous, but the spelling of 'armor' suggests North American origins.

25 Montgomery's intention in this address was to give everyone 'the "atmosphere" in which, from then onwards, we would all work, and later would fight' (Montgomery, *Memoirs*, p. 217). De Guingand later wrote that Montgomery's address 'was all of great value and it ensured that everyone was tuned into the same waveband' (*Operation Victory*, p. 353). It is interesting to compare Montgomery's speeches in early January 1944 with the transcript of the talk he gave on 13 August 1942 when he took command of the Eighth Army. See Brooks (ed.), *Montgomery and the Eighth Army*, pp. 25–8.

26 In his address on 13 August 1942 Montgomery said, 'By bellyaching I mean inventing poor reasons for <u>not</u> doing what one has been told to do'.

27 In the Field Maintenance Centre system supply dumps were established well forward under the control of a corps so the needs of individual units could be met as quickly as possible. See Ellis, *Victory in the West*, Vol. I, pp. 85–7.

28 This should be section 5, not 4, of the address.

29 For the reasons Montgomery chose the battle of Mareth (20–27 March 1943) as an example here, see his description of the battle in his diary notes in Brooks (ed.), *Montgomery and the Eighth Army*, pp. 184–7.

30 *Schwerpunkt* means the point of main effort; and *aufrollen* means to roll up, or turn the enemy's flank.

31 Tanks equipped with rotating chain flails, one variant of which was called the Scorpion, were used to clear paths through minefields.

32 Section 8 of the address was probably drafted for Montgomery by his Brigadier, Royal Armoured Corps, Brigadier G.W. Richards, whom he had brought back with him from the Eighth Army. According to Field Marshal Lord Carver, Richards 'greatly influenced Montgomery's views about tanks right up to the time he became CIGS after the war' (personal communication, 3 June 1990).

33 Montgomery inherited the train, called 'Rapier', from General Paget. It included four coaches containing offices, sleeping accommodation, messrooms and kitchens, and two wagons for carrying cars. De Guingand was sure that without the train Montgomery 'could never have carried out the immense programme he had set himself' (De Guingand, *Operation Victory*, p. 353).

34 As evidence of this, Montgomery included in his diary at this point a typescript copy of a General Order issued on 18 January by the US Third Armored Division. In it the commanding officer, Major-General Leroy H. Watson, said that all who saw and heard Montgomery 'were instilled with a feeling of great confidence in our leader' (LMD 54/1).

35 i.e. this was the brief Montgomery prepared for his presentation at the conference. In his diary Montgomery wrote briefly of the meeting: 'I put the case to the conference, explaining my dislike of the original plan and my suggested new plan of a five Divisional assault. My notes [this document] are attached at Appendix "C" [to the diary notes], and it will be seen that a strong case was put forward for adopting my plan. After discussion, my plan was agreed to' (LMD 54/1).

36 These appendices are not extant.

37 'What was loaded first had to be unloaded last. No mistakes could be made in this stowage. What use guns without ammunition? What use tanks without fuel? Everything had to be planned to the last little signpost and box of spares. Gradually a design was developed, and the broad outlines of tactical stowage were laid down' (Dalgleish, *We Planned the Second Front*, p. 43).

38 Not extant. During January Leese actually became very irritated at the way in which Montgomery was being allowed to 'skin' the Eighth Army of senior officers for OVERLORD. Leese was also aggrieved that it was only now that Montgomery had left Italy that the Canadian general, Harry Crerar, was sent out to gain experience, in place of Guy Simonds. On the same day that Montgomery wrote this friendly letter, 22 January, Leese wrote to his wife, 'as far as I am concerned, over all this O [Montgomery] has been 4 letters!' (Ryder, *Oliver Leese*, pp. 149–51).

39 Brooke, Cunningham and Portal.

40 Clement Attlee. According to Montgomery's 1944 pocket appointments diary (LMD 1/5), the meeting with Attlee took place at 2.30 p.m. on 14 January at 11 Downing Street; no further information is provided in Montgomery's papers.

41 Document 5.

42 See Document 9.

43 For the 'frightful troubles' over the planning for HUSKY, see Hamilton, *Monty: Master of the Battlefield*, pp. 241–68; and Brooks (ed.), *Montgomery and the Eighth Army*, pp. 217–44.

44 See Document 7.

45 See Document 8.

46 Major-General John Utterson-Kelso (1893–1972).

47 Brigadier, later General Sir, Harold Pyman (1908–71), wrote in his memoirs that the transfer to 30 Corps 'suited me admirably' (Pyman, *A Call to Arms*, p. 66).

48 In Italy the Anzio landings had taken place on 22 January, and were undone by the failure to follow these tactics.

49 The Prime Minister has written '<u>Secret & Private</u>' by hand at the top of this minute.

50 Not extant in Montgomery's papers.

51 The Prime Minister addressed a Personal Minute on the subject of waterproofing to Montgomery on 31 January (LMD 54/16); it is reproduced in Churchill, *The Second World War*, Vol. V, p. 520.

52 The number of vehicles taking part in the invasion greatly concerned the Prime Minister during the planning for OVERLORD. He returned to the subject with Montgomery after the 15 May Presentation of Plans at St Paul's School; see Documents 46 and 49.

Notes to Documents 13–25, February 1944, pp. 41–56

1 This is an extract from the 'diary' that Montgomery asked his Military Assistant, Kit Dawnay, to compile from D-Day onwards, with relevant documents typed up as appendices. It became known as 'the Log' (see p. 7). In the first section of the Log, written up by Dawnay after discussions with his commander-in-chief in the summer or autumn of 1944, Montgomery looked back at the planning phase in England. Montgomery makes no mention of the meeting with Sir James Grigg or the audience with the King in the diary notes he wrote in January/February 1944.

2 As usual it was Brooke who had to warn Montgomery that he was upsetting people. Brooke wrote in his diary for 24 January, 'After lunch Monty came to see me and I had to tell him off for falling foul of both the King and the S of S in a very short time. He took it well, as usual' (Danchev and Todman (eds), *Alanbrooke: War Diaries*, p. 516).

3 Montgomery's pocket appointments diary for 1944 (LMD 1/5) is quite full for the first half of the year, but has few entries once the Normandy campaign begins. Montgomery refers to his seeing Grigg on Tuesday, 25 January. They went for lunch with the newspaper magnate, Lord Kemsley, but presumably Montgomery found time to discuss with Grigg the problems that had arisen between them. Montgomery's pocket diary lists a meeting at 9.30 a.m. the same day with another newspaper owner, Lord Iliffe.

4   In his memoirs Montgomery says that it was reports that he had approved organisational changes in army divisions at his meeting on 13 January (Document 7) that upset Grigg. Montgomery continues: 'Brooke suggested that Grigg should ask me to lunch so that we could have a talk; I did not then know Grigg very well and welcomed the suggestion. At that lunch meeting I explained how much had to be done and how little time there was in which to do it. I apologised for going too fast and asked Grigg to trust my judgement on the operational necessity for what I had done; if I went too fast again I was quite prepared to be sent for by him and "ticked off"' (Montgomery, *Memoirs*, p. 218).

5   Montgomery's letter to Grigg of 1 June and Grigg's reply of 3 June are reproduced in full in Montgomery, *Memoirs*, pp. 245–6.

6   The audience with the King took place on 1 February. Montgomery broached the subject of the black beret whilst talking to Sir Alan Lascelles, the King's Principal Private Secretary, before the audience. Lascelles wrote in his diary for 1 February, 'Of his famous beret, he said, "My hat is worth three divisions. The men see it in the distance. They say, 'There's Monty' – and then they will fight anybody." I advised him to make this point to his Sovereign, who has been very critical of Monty's flagrant departures from the orthodox uniform of a general' (Hart-Davis (ed.), *King's Counsellor*, pp. 196–7).

7   Lieutenant-General Sir Ronald Weeks was a Territorial Army officer who had held a senior position with Pilkington Glass before the war. In March 1941 he became Director-General of Army Equipment, and in June 1942 he was appointed Deputy Chief of the Imperial General Staff, with responsibility for army equipment and organisation.

8   The schedule is too long to include here; see BLM 120/36.

9   Brigadier, later Lieutenant-General Sir, Edwin Otway Herbert (1901–84) had been one of the few 21st Army Group officers to survive Montgomery's 'purge' when he took over in January 1944. In his Lees-Knowles Lectures at Cambridge in 1948 Sir Ronald Weeks said that detailed planning of equipment requirements for OVERLORD had begun in the autumn of 1943 but became more concentrated when Montgomery arrived. 'I started a weekly meeting which General Herbert used to attend (he was then Brigadier Staff Duties for Field-Marshal Montgomery) on all "hot" items; I gather it was the bane of my G.S.O.1.'s, but it made things fall into place' (Weeks, *Organisation and Equipment for War*, p. 56).

10   The Secretary of State, Sir James Grigg.

11   For some undated notes in Montgomery's hand that appear to be a draft for part of this section, see LMD 58/1.

12   'H hour' was the time (as opposed to the day – D-Day) when the landings would begin.

13   AVREs were Armoured Vehicles Royal Engineers. The Ark (Armoured Ramp Carrier) was a turretless Churchill tank with ramps at either end for bridging purposes. Flails and ploughs were devices for clearing paths through minefields; likewise, Snakes consisted of lengths of pipe packed with

explosives, which would set off enemy mines when detonated, thus creating a clear path.

14   See Abbreviations pp. xiii–xvi. The different types of support landing craft are self- explanatory, except for the LCA(HR) – Landing Craft Assault (Hedgerow). It was fitted with four rows of six 'hedgehog' anti-submarine spigot mortars in the troop space. The salvo of 24 mortars would set off enemy mines above or below the water's edge. For a diagram entitled 'The Assault Technique', showing the layout of the different types of landing craft and armoured fighting vehicles in a brigade group approaching the Normandy beaches, see Montgomery, *Normandy to the Baltic*, diagram C.

15   Montgomery's exchange of letters with Eisenhower at this juncture (Documents 16, 18, 19 and 22) followed on from his decision on 18 February to agree to Eisenhower's proposal for a reduction in the number of LSTs and LCI(L)s available for OVERLORD to assist ANVIL, the invasion of southern France (see LMD 54/7). Admiral Ramsay reluctantly fell in behind Montgomery. That evening Montgomery dined with Brooke who was dismayed to learn that Montgomery and Ramsay had 'foolishly agreed to curtail the cross Channel operation to allow for a South of France operation' (Danchev and Todman (eds), *Alanbrooke: War Diaries*, p. 523). In Document 16 Montgomery starts trying – unsuccessfully – to undo the damage. On 21 February Admiral Ramsay had a meeting with the Prime Minister and wrote in his diary, 'I made it clear that I disliked the reduction & thought it was wrong. He said that Monty had been taken to task by C.I.G.S. for agreeing & that Monty had said that he had agreed gambling on the fact that Anvil would not take place & that we should get what we want. This is an iniquitous thing to do & has let me down badly' (Love and Major (eds), *The Year of D-Day*, p. 30).

16   General Sir Henry Maitland Wilson had succeeded Eisenhower as the Supreme Allied Commander in the Mediterranean.

17   For Montgomery's role in raising morale before D-Day, see Hamilton, *Monty: Master of the Battlefield*, pp. 486–96; and Brooks, 'Montgomery and the Preparations for Overlord' in *History Today* 34, June 1984, pp. 18–22. Not everyone could see the importance of what Montgomery was doing. Ramsay wrote in his diary for 17 February that it was wrong that Montgomery was away visiting troops when he should be taking part in 'high policy negotiations'. He concluded that Montgomery 'leaves everything to Freddy [de Guingand] & his staff with whom, in consequence, I have to negotiate. He does no work at all' (Love and Major (eds), *The Year of D-Day*, p. 28). Brooke noted in his diary for 28 February, 'Ramsay then came to dine and gave me some side lights as to how Monty was functioning. He is wandering around visiting troops and failing to get down to basic facts. Shall have to have him up again and kick his backside again!' (Danchev and Todman (eds), *Alanbrooke: War Diaries*, p. 527).

18   For the full text of Montgomery's speech at the Mansion House on 24 March, see Montgomery, *Memoirs*, pp. 226–31.

19 For Montgomery's handwritten draft of this letter, see BLM 108/2.

20 Documents 16 and 18.

21 The past week had been a difficult one for the Allies in Italy. The Germans mounted major attacks on the beachhead at Anzio, 16–20 February. At Cassino, the offensive by the New Zealand Corps that followed the bombing of the monastery on 15 February was called off on the 18th.

22 According to his pocket diary, Montgomery was reviewing commandos at Brighton that day.

23 General Rizzio was the GOC 7th Italian Army when Italy surrendered in September 1943. General Rizzio proposed that as Italy and Britain were now allies and he was the senior army general in southern Italy, the 8th Army should come under his command. Montgomery corrected Rizzio's error and thereafter found him a 'very decent chap' (Montgomery, *Memoirs*, pp. 197–8).

24 Document 19.

25 Harrison was Mountbatten's emissary. See Brooke's diary for 15 February 1944: 'After lunch Harrison, one of Mountbatten's staff officers, came to see me. We discussed Dickie's plans and his requirements for his offensive' (Danchev and Todman (eds), *Alanbrooke: War Diaries*, pp. 521–2).

26 HUSKY was the codename for the Allied invasion of Sicily in July 1943.

27 The Director of Military Training was Major-General Sir John Whitaker (1897–1957). Whilst serving in the Mediterranean Montgomery had written on a number of occasions complaining to Brooke and Nye that military doctrine and training were being laid down in the UK by people who did not have recent practical battle experience and failed to consult those, like himself, who did. (Montgomery believed that the basic points for fighting Germans that he had evolved with the Eighth Army were universally applicable, suitably adapted for different theatres.) For example, in December 1943 Montgomery wrote to Nye criticising a training pamphlet on the cooperation of tanks and infantry produced by 21st Army Group in the UK. It was Major-General Whitaker who wrote a long briefing memorandum for Nye, defending the pamphlet and the consultation process by which it was produced. One can deduce from points made by Whitaker that Montgomery's proposal in Document 24 would not have been particularly well received. See Brooks (ed.), *Montgomery and the Eighth Army*, pp. 342–7.

28 Almost certainly Lieutenant-General Sir Brian Horrocks. In June 1943 Horrocks had been badly wounded in a German air raid at Bizerta. He was still recuperating, but Montgomery held him in high regard and was anxious to place him in a suitable post. When Horrocks left hospital, Montgomery had him to stay the night at his flat near St Paul's School on 24 April. Horrocks later wrote, 'I did my best to impress him with my complete recovery but without much success. "You haven't recovered yet," he said. "Go away and get fit. Then we shall see"' (Horrocks, *A Full Life*, p. 179). Nevertheless, Montgomery must have thought that Horrocks was fit enough for a 'desk job'. At the end of April he wrote in his diary (Document 42) that Horrocks would be the best man to take charge of the Directorates dealing

with organisation and weapons at the War Office; and in a letter to Brooke on 19 May (Document 48) Montgomery suggested that Horrocks would be the man to carry out an enquiry into the value of Battle Schools in order to release manpower for 21st Army Group.

29 Of this section of the diary, Nigel Hamilton writes that Montgomery 'hated to admit defeat. In his diary he tried to put the best face upon it' (Hamilton, *Monty: Master of the Battlefield*, p. 530). As Ramsay wrote in his diary for 26 February, 'The decision as regards Anvil remains to be made' (Love and Major (eds), *The Year of D-Day*, p. 33).

30 i.e. at Anzio.

31 For example, Montgomery describes Alexander's failings as he saw them in his diary notes of 7 October and 27 October 1943. See Brooks (ed.), *Montgomery and the Eighth Army*, pp. 297–9 and 313–14.

Notes to Documents 26–33, March 1944, pp. 57–64

1 Document 20.

2 Document 21.

3 For Montgomery's demi-official (DO) letter to Eisenhower of 3 March 1944 (not included here), see LMD 54/22. Montgomery urged that a decision be taken on banning visitors from the coastal strip from Land's End to the Wash. The ban was imposed from 1 April.

4 Eisenhower was now sceptical about ANVIL taking place at the same time as OVERLORD. In a letter to General Marshall on 3 March he wrote, 'It becomes daily more apparent that a 2 Division ANVIL is out of the question' (Chandler (ed.), *The Papers of Dwight David Eisenhower: The War Years*, Vol. III, p. 1758). But the agreement that a final decision should be postponed until 20 March stood.

5 Montgomery's opinion of Leigh-Mallory varied over the next five months, ranging from describing him as a 'gutless bugger' (Document 69) to 'a very genuine chap' (Document 135).

6 General Kazimierz Sosnkowski (1885–1969) was Commander-in-Chief of the Polish Armed Forces from July 1943 to September 1944.

7 General Sosnkowski wrote on 7 March (BLM 97/7) to say that 'reasons of service of a most urgent nature' prevented him from receiving Montgomery when he visited Polish forces.

8 In Scotland on Monday, 13 March, as part of 'Tour No. 5'.

9 General Sosnkowski replied on 20 March (BLM 120/20) that Polish units would be brought up to strength 'as soon as we have access to the sources of Polish soldiers in France and Belgium'. Montgomery responded on 23 March (BLM 120/22) that if the Polish Armoured Division was not properly organised, with well-trained reserves, there would be no point in bringing it down to the Yorkshire training area as a prelude to its taking part in the Normandy campaign. A message from General Sosnkowski, then in Italy, was forwarded to Montgomery on 3 April (BLM 120/24), saying that he would do everything possible to comply with Montgomery's wishes. On 19 April Sosnkowski wrote (BLM 120/26) to confirm that the Armoured

Division would be completed 'at the expense of other Polish units in Scotland'.

10   The 1st Polish Armoured Division began to land in Normandy on 30 July 1944.

11   Montgomery learned that there were conditions attached to the use of the Polish Parachute Brigade (the Poles wished to protect the brigade for eventual use in the liberation of Poland) when Major-General de Guingand forwarded a letter from Major-General F.E.W. Simpson on the subject (not extant). Montgomery replied to Simpson on 20 March (BLM 120/21) saying that General Sosnkowski's conditions were 'unacceptable'. In his letter to Simpson, Montgomery wrote in the same vein as his comments to the Prime Minister that it was 'militarily unsound' and 'politically unwise' to allow nations such as Poland to make conditions about the use of their armed forces.

12   See Document 28.

13   Major-General Herbert Lumsden (1897–1945) was the Prime Minister's special representative with General MacArthur in the Pacific. He had just been visiting Britain for talks and had returned to the Far East on 12 March. Lumsden was killed when a Japanese kamikaze aircraft hit the bridge of USS *New Mexico* on 6 January 1945.

14   Diary notes for 3 March 1944, Document 26.

15   Montgomery's letter to Eisenhower of 3 March on the subject, incorporated as Appendix 'K' to his diary notes January to March 1944, see LMD 54/22.

16   Montgomery's handwritten notes for a similar talk to 2 Canadian Corps on 18 March can be found at BLM 90/6, and to his staff on 28 March 1944 at BLM 90/9.

17   These notes were distributed at a conference of army commanders on 20 March. According to the first paragraph of the minutes of the meeting: 'Notes by C-in-C dated 20 March 1944 were handed to Army Commanders and were discussed. C-in-C asked Army Commanders particularly to consider the allotment of a tank to bn comds in the assault, and stressed the very great importance of speedy penetration inland' (BLM 122/3).

18   Flails were tanks equipped with rotating chains to beat paths through minefields.

19   These notes were distributed together with Document 31 at a conference of army commanders on 20 March. According to the second paragraph of the minutes of the meeting: 'C-in-C referred to his Note dated 20 March 1944 on Air Requirements as viewed by the Army, and informed Army Commanders that this note had been agreed to by all concerned at the Supreme Commander's conference that morning' (BLM 122/3).

20   For paragraph 34, diary notes for 26 February, see Document 25; for paragraph 39, diary notes for 3 March, see Document 26.

21   However, the American Joint Chiefs of Staff, whilst accepting that an ANVIL simultaneous with OVERLORD was impossible, replied on 24 March that it should be postponed not abandoned. The argument between the British and Americans about the desirability of carrying out ANVIL, perhaps as early as 10 July, continued.

Notes to Documents 34–42, April 1944, pp. 65–96

1 Amesbury School was located at Hindhead in Surrey. Montgomery's son, David, had been educated there and the headmaster and his wife, Major and Mrs Reynolds, acted as his guardians. They provided Montgomery with a home and a place for quiet reflection.

2 Major-General Miles Graham.

3 Montgomery rounds off this section of his diary notes with a further four hundred words on the Italian campaign – 'a real good mess' – and particularly on Alexander's failings as a commander: 'He is a terribly nice chap and my very great friend; but he knows nothing about high command in the field' (LMD 54/1).

4 Weeks wrote to Montgomery on 23 March (letter not included here; see BLM 117/7) following a conversation they had had in the morning. The letter set out how the War Office consulted 'Commanders and Users' before issuing a General Staff (G.S.) Policy on Tanks; Weeks enclosed the latest General Staff Policy, dated 24 September 1943, which included long-term policy on Infantry Tanks and the 'Tortoise'. Design work began in 1944 on the heavily-armoured 'Tortoise', more a self-propelled gun than a tank, but the first six pilot models were not delivered until 1947, and it never went into production.

5 For Montgomery's letter to Nye of 28 August 1943 (BLM 117/2) and Nye's reply of 7 October, see Brooks (ed.), *Montgomery and the Eighth Army*, pp. 273–7 and 299–302.

6 Count Maurice Maeterlinck (1862–1949) was a Belgian dramatist, essayist and poet. It has not been possible to confirm this quotation or its author.

7 The cruiser tank was for wide-ranging mobile operations, so speed and manoeuvrability were the priority; the infantry tank was for close support of infantry operations and therefore protection (i.e. armour) was to the fore. As he says later in this letter, Montgomery believed that it was the third characteristic of a tank – firepower – that should always be the priority.

8 There are a number of typescript copies of these notes in Montgomery's papers. There is a copy in Eisenhower's papers. It has been re-typed, due, apparently, to wear and tear on the original. The typist has added by hand some amendments, with a note that 'General Montgomery's pencil alterations on the original have been reproduced in this copy.' These amendments are indicated in Document 36 here. It was Montgomery's normal practice to amend all copies of a document, but none of the copies in his own papers bears any alterations.

9 According to notes General Kennedy made at the time (*The Business of War*, p. 326) and Admiral Ramsay's diary (*The Year of D-Day*, p. 52), Montgomery's address lasted for an hour and a half.

10 Panzer Grenadier units were composed of mechanised infantry, equipped with half-track personnel carriers and attached to Panzer (armoured) divisions.

11 Rommel was given the job of inspecting the defences in the west in November 1943. He believed that Allied air power meant that the only

hope of stopping the invasion was to do so on the coast, and ordered the strengthening of the beach defences accordingly.

12 There are four diagrams, or maps, filed with Montgomery's THUNDER-CLAP address. They are labelled: A. Concentration and Marshalling Areas. B. Assault and Build up. C. Development of Land Battle. D. Administrative Layout. A and B show the order of battle as referred to here. There is a set of these diagrams with the THUNDERCLAP address in the Montgomery Papers Part II in LMD 56/2–5. Judging by the drawing-pin holes in the corners, they have been displayed at some point, but they are possibly not big enough (about 24 inches square) to be the maps used at Exercise THUNDERCLAP. Montgomery had the diagrams copied to go with the THUNDERCLAP address in his 'Notes on Planning the Campaign in North Western Europe' (the first section of 'the Log'). See BLM 74/4.

13 SS here means Special Service.

14 This must be diagram C referred to in note 12 above. On the diagram C in BLM 74 and LMD 56 the green, yellow and black 'phase lines' do not have target dates against them (as in the version in *Normandy to the Baltic*, Map 2), but Montgomery supplies the dates in his address. These 'phase lines' became part of the controversy at the time and subsequently over whether everything had gone 'according to plan'. The most thorough discussion of the evidence relating to the origins and significance of the phase lines is in Carlo D'Este, *Decision in Normandy*, pp. 90–9. Montgomery refers to the diagram and the phase lines in his diary notes for 4 August – Document 176.

15 I have not been able to find any other reference to BOOKREST as a codeword. It appears to refer here to the four rows of spigot mortars carried by the Landing Craft Assault (Hedgerow) which were intended to set off enemy beach mines.

16 I have not found a copy of this pamphlet, but of the many possible meanings of SSV, I think that Special Services Vessel is the most likely one here.

17 Waterproofing was done in three stages. After the second stage the vehicle could run for only a few miles before seizing up, and less than that once the final stage was completed.

18 For planning purposes 'Y-day' was code for 1 June 1944 – the date by which preparations for the landings were to be completed.

19 The 'hotel service' camps, established in the marshalling areas near the embarkation points, were designed to ensure that the troops set off 'in the pink of condition' (see Dalgleish, *We Planned the Second Front*, pp. 50–2).

20 'Air Defence of Great Britain', which replaced the term Fighter Command between November 1943 and October 1944.

21 CROSSBOW was the codename for operations to counter the German V1 and V2 threat.

22 Southwick House, just to the north of Portsmouth, had been taken over by the Royal Navy in 1941. In 1944 it became the headquarters of Admiral Ramsay and the Supreme Commander. Broomfield House was a smaller Georgian house, a little to the east, which Montgomery made his home in the lead up to D-Day. Fort Southwick was one of the Victorian forts on Portsdown

Hill, overlooking Portsmouth. A communications centre and combined headquarters were located in a complex of tunnels beneath the fort.

23 The cover plan and diversionary operations are described in Haswell, *The Intelligence and Deception of the D-Day Landings*, pp. 175–85.

24 Rear Maintenance Area.

25 For example, a joint British/US syndicate considered the 'implications of adverse weather on Operation OVERLORD'. For the papers relating to the exercise on 8 April and the different scenarios examined by the British, US and Joint Syndicates, see LMD 57.

26 Montgomery sent a copy of this memorandum to Brooke on 17 April: 'There is some slight tendency to "hang back", so I decided it was necessary to issue a firm directive' (Alanbrooke Papers 6/2/24). Brooke replied the same day, 'The directive should produce the required effect' (LMD 56/9). Montgomery also sent a copy to the Prime Minister, who replied on 30 April, 'For what my opinion is worth, it seems to be exactly the spirit in which the execution should proceed, and I only wish that a similar course had been attempted when the forces landed at Anzio' (BLM 93/4).

27 In his memoirs Bradley recalled being asked by Montgomery to explore the possibility of a 'tank knockabout' behind Omaha beach on D-Day. 'Although knowing there was scant chance of carrying it through, I nevertheless devised such a mission. As I anticipated, we never even tried it. In contrast to Monty, I had foreseen a hard enemy crust on the Normandy coast' (Bradley, *A Soldier's Story*, p. 241).

28 Lieutenant-General Sir Giffard Martel (1889–1958) had returned to England in February 1944 after being head of the British Military Mission in Moscow. He had then been injured in an air raid and lost an eye.

29 Martel's letter to Montgomery is not extant; Martel gives the gist of it in his memoirs, see Martel, *An Outspoken Soldier*, p. 277. Montgomery's message is also not extant; it may have been a verbal rather than a written one.

30 Montgomery had views on the design and use of tanks that were fundamentally different from Martel's. For example, Martel strongly disagreed with Montgomery's opinion that there should be a single Capital 'fighting' tank, rather than distinct Infantry and Cruiser types. Martel did as instructed here and did not send Montgomery his memorandum entitled 'Are we making the best use of our armoured forces?' He did send him a later memorandum on 'The experiences from the use of large armoured formations on the Russian front and their adaptation to present-day conditions.' Both are reproduced in Martel, *An Outspoken Soldier*, pp. 375–82. There may have been more to this snub than the fact that Montgomery did not wish to read Martel's memorandum. In the Martel Papers at the IWM there is a carbon copy of a letter from Martel to General Ismay, dated 17 March 1944. Martel says that a lieutenant-general should be appointed at the War Office to advise the CIGS on all matters connected with the design and use of armoured forces. Martel goes on, 'The success of the "Second Front" campaign – after the initial stages – will depend on the proper use of Armoured Forces. Who is going to advise as regards the direction and

co-ordination of all this vital work?' Ismay replied that it was too late to appoint anyone at the War Office, but perhaps there should be an adviser at SHAEF. We do not have the letter Montgomery received from Martel, but it may have canvassed the idea of appointing a permanent adviser on the use of armoured forces: hence Montgomery's rather abrupt response. See the Martel Papers 8/1a at the IWM.

31   Following his speech at the Mansion House on 24 March, Montgomery proposed a special service at St Paul's for 'The Public Hallowing of the Armed Forces of the Crown'. On 11 April he wrote to Grigg on the matter, enclosing a draft order of service drawn up by his head chaplain and a letter of support from the Archbishop of Canterbury (BLM 120/5). Montgomery suggested that the Coronation regalia should be used. Grigg informed the King's Private Secretary, Sir Alan Lascelles, who noted in his diary on 14 April – 'one could not help feeling that it was not far from being the Coronation of Monty' (Hart-Davis (ed.), *King's Counsellor*, p. 212). Grigg sent a copy of Montgomery's letter to the Prime Minister on 17 April. Earlier, on 22 February, the Prime Minister had minuted the Home Secretary that a national day of prayer for OVERLORD would be 'a great mistake' (Churchill, *The Second World War*, Volume V, p. 608), so Montgomery's idea had little chance of success. And indeed, on 18 April, the Prime Minister minuted Grigg that he would certainly 'never advise' the King to agree to the use of the Coronation regalia (Gilbert, *Road to Victory*, p. 744).

32   In the minute to Grigg of 18 April, referred to in note 31 above, the Prime Minister wrote, 'I am of the opinion that the Army Council should instruct General Montgomery to bring to an end his public tours and civic receptions. We are getting very near the great battle, and a bad effect will be produced if it is thought that the General immediately responsible is spending his time at demonstrations which are more appropriate after the victory than before ... There is a mass of intricate Staff work to be done, and the Army Council, yourself and the C.I.G.S. are directly responsible for seeing that this is not relegated to second place. If anything were to go seriously wrong and it were found that something had been neglected, the General would come in for heavy criticism' (Gilbert, *Road to Victory*, p. 744). Regarding his tours, Montgomery later wrote in his memoirs, 'I received an intimation that I should "lay off" these visits – to which I paid no attention, beyond replying that I had been asked to undertake them by certain Ministries in Whitehall' (Montgomery, *Memoirs*, p. 226).

33   Grigg stayed the night with Montgomery at Broomfield House on 2 May. Then on 3 May they visited army units in Hampshire and watched an invasion rehearsal at Southsea. There is a fascinating description of Montgomery 'in action' that day in the book by M.E. Clifton James, *I Was Monty's Double*, pp. 48–60. The actor was present at the same time as Grigg to study Montgomery's mannerisms before carrying out his impersonation as part of the OVERLORD deception plan.

34   The signature, probably of the civil servant responsible for organising Montgomery's tours of factories, is not legible.

35 Paragraphs 4 to 11 of Montgomery's diary notes are headed '14–28 April'. The first four paragraphs (not included here) give a brief outline of his tours and attendance at invasion exercises; then in these paragraphs Montgomery is in more reflective mood. The diary entry that *follows* paragraph 11 is headed '2 May'.

36 For the programme and other documents relating to Montgomery's visit to the fleet at Scapa Flow, 6–9 May 1944, see LMD 55/10–14.

37 For example, Montgomery's letter to Nye of 28 August 1943; see Brooks (ed.), *Montgomery and the Eighth Army*, pp. 273–7.

38 Demi-Official letter to Weeks of 3 April – Document 35.

39 For Montgomery's address on artillery on 30 April 1944, see BLM 90/13.

40 Montgomery was right. He himself turned to Horrocks as replacement for Bucknall to command 30 Corps in Normandy in August 1944.

Notes to Documents 43–53, May 1944, pp. 97–112

1 As well as his four Army commanders, Montgomery sent copies of this letter to Air Marshal Sir Arthur Coningham; Air Vice-Marshal Harry Broadhurst; Lieutenant-General Walter Bedell Smith and Air Chief Marshal Sir Charles Portal.

2 There are many contemporary first-hand accounts of the Presentation of Plans by speakers and observers – for example, in the published diaries of Brooke, Ramsay, Lascelles and Patton, who omitted any reference to Montgomery's address in his diary entry (Danchev and Todman (eds), *Alanbrooke: War Diaries*, pp. 546–7; Love and Major (eds), *The Year of D-Day*, p. 70; Hart-Davis, *King's Counsellor*, p. 219; Blumenson, *The Patton Papers 1940–45*, pp. 455–6). General Kennedy wrote a note after the meeting (*The Business of War*, p. 328).

3 Dawnay retained the original notes in Montgomery's handwriting after they had been typed up. They are to be found in the Dawnay Papers at the Imperial War Museum. There are only minor differences between holograph and typescript versions, for example, in the use of capital letters. There are also holograph versions of Documents 31, 35 and 38 in the Dawnay Papers.

4 Document 37.

5 Of the occasion Brooke wrote in his diary, 'Back to WO and finished up with Monty dining quietly with me. He was in very good form and bearing his responsibilities well' (Danchev and Todman (eds), *Alanbrooke: War Diaries*, p. 547).

6 Brooke's view of Alexander was very similar to Montgomery's. For example, see Brooke's diary entry for 11 April 1944: 'In the afternoon Alexander turned up to see me, back from Italy. Whenever I meet him again my first impression is one of marvelling at what a small calibre man he is!' (Danchev and Todman (eds), *Alanbrooke: War Diaries*, p. 539).

7 John Harding (1896–1989) was Alexander's Chief of Staff in 1943–4.

8 In paragraph 46 of the diary notes that Montgomery wrote at the beginning of June (see LMD 55/1), he expressed the view that Alexander 'might be compared to HINDENBERG in the Great War; he must have a LUDENDORF to do the business for him'.

9   General Mark Clark (1896–1984) commanded the US Fifth Army 1943–4, and 15th Army Group 1944–5.

10 The Allies' fourth and final battle to take Cassino lasted from 11 to 18 May 1944.

11 The lunch (at the Hyde Park Hotel) with Smuts and his son took place on 16 May. See Montgomery's pocket appointments' diary for 1944 (LMD 1/5).

12 The Presentation of Plans at St Paul's – see Documents 43 and 44.

13 In his memoirs Ismay says that the instruction to write this letter was the first one the Prime Minister gave him when they left the Presentation of Plans at St Paul's on 15 May (see Ismay, *The Memoirs of General The Lord Ismay*, p. 352).

14 Deputy Assistant Chief of Staff (Movement and Transportation).

15 Montgomery's reply to Brooke is Document 50; Montgomery's response to Stuart, following a meeting on 25 May, is Document 51, and Montgomery's diary notes on the subject are Document 52.

16 For the background to Montgomery's relations with the Canadians and Lieutenant-General Crerar in particular during 1944, see, inter alia, the section entitled 'The Responsibilities of the Canadian Army Commander' in Stacey, *The Victory Campaign*, pp. 41–6; and, more recently, Hart, *Montgomery and 'Colossal Cracks'*, pp. 155–78.

17 Eisenhower visited the 3rd Canadian Division (commanded by Major-General R.F.L. Keller) on 13 May. On the same day Crerar wrote to Stuart saying that the fact that he had not been informed indicated a tendency to forget his special position as Commander, First Canadian Army. Crerar continued: 'I do not propose to make an issue of this but it would be very desirable if the proper procedure in these matters could be clarified on the political level, and explained to SHAEF, while our Prime Minister is now here.' Hence this letter from Stuart to Brooke. See Stacey, *The Victory Campaign*, p. 44.

18 Brooke passed the letter to the VCIGS, General Nye, who wrote a two-page briefing note on the situation regarding battle schools on 21 May. Nye added by hand as a postscript, 'It seems to me to be an impertinence for a subordinate commander to suggest to you that you don't know how to get your staff going properly, and that an officer from outside – preferably one of his own nomination – should investigate and put things right!' The reference for the letter in Alanbrooke's papers is 6/2/24.

19 This letter, amongst other things, occasioned another 'Brookie-blast' at Montgomery. Brooke had dinner with Montgomery at Broomfield House on 25 May. He wrote in his diary: 'I had to tell him off and ask him to concentrate more on his own job and not to meddle himself in everybody else's affairs. Such as wanting to advise Alex on his battle, New Zealand PM on what to do with Freyberg, or WO how to obtain reinforcements! As usual he took it well' (Danchev and Todman (eds), *Alanbrooke: War Diaries*, p. 550).

20 This is one of many occasions when one wishes that Montgomery's contemporary diary notes had been a little more detailed. A fuller account

of the evening's events first appeared in Alan Moorehead's biography of Montgomery in 1946. Following on from Ismay's letter (Document 46), the Prime Minister arrived at Montgomery's headquarters. Montgomery ushered him into his study. He then said that he could not allow Churchill to discuss vehicle loadings with his staff. He explained that he was absolutely sure that the programme was correct, and that in any case it was too late to change things. If Churchill would not accept this, said Montgomery, 'that can only mean you have lost confidence in me'. Churchill gave way, and when he was introduced to Montgomery's staff, he said, 'I'm not allowed to talk to you, gentlemen'. Montgomery must have told the story to Alan Moorehead, who included it in his biography (*Montgomery*, pp. 194–6). Churchill took umbrage and later wrote that his interview with Montgomery had been 'misrepresented'. Montgomery had not threatened to resign – 'I should not have accepted such behaviour' (Churchill, *The Second World War*, Vol. V, pp. 543–4). Montgomery had the last word when he told the 'true story' in his memoirs, along virtually the same lines as had appeared twelve years earlier in Moorehead's biography (*Memoirs*, pp. 237–8). According to Nigel Hamilton, this encounter with Churchill would in later years become 'one of Monty's favourite stories' (*Monty: Master of the Battlefield*, p. 581).

21   The notes Montgomery used for these talks are not included here, as they are reproduced in full in his memoirs (see Montgomery, *Memoirs*, pp. 239–44).

22   Mackenzie King, the Prime Minister of Canada, was in England for a conference of Dominion heads. Montgomery's discussion with Mackenzie King took place over lunch at Broomfield House on 18 May. Montgomery wrote briefly in his diary notes: 'I like him immensely and we had a great talk about his Canadians' (LMD 55/1). However, a second-hand but revealing account of their talk over lunch can be found in Colonel Dick Malone's book, *Missing from the Record*, pp. 143–4. Malone had been Montgomery's Canadian liaison officer in Sicily and Italy, and had then returned to England before D-Day to take on the job of directing public relations for the Canadian Army. According to information obtained by Malone, Montgomery took the opportunity to cast doubt on Crerar's position. His starting point was that there would have to be British divisions serving in the Canadian Army. He continued, 'Obviously, if General Crerar proved inadequate in command he would have to be changed in fairness to the non-Canadian troops involved and regardless of Canadian feelings ... Would the Canadian Government back him up if he found it absolutely necessary to change General Crerar? The Prime Minister agreed on this point but said he hoped this course would never be necessary but if it was, he stressed the importance of trying if at all possible to find another Canadian Commander to replace him.'

23   'Crerar, when defending Canadian interests, resolutely stood his ground against the forceful Montgomery; whereas Stuart, in contrast, admitted that he found it impossible to do so' (Hart, *Montgomery and 'Colossal Cracks'*, p. 162).

NOTES TO JUNE DOCUMENTS

24 Stuart did not prolong the argument by replying to Montgomery. However, Crerar wrote to Stuart on 30 May saying that Stuart must assert the 'principle of Canadian autonomy', but that he, Crerar, had no intention of allowing it 'to endanger a military situation, or to cause bad personal and professional relations between Monty and myself' (Stacey, *The Victory Campaign*, p. 45). After further discussion with Crerar, Stuart wrote a lengthy letter to Brooke on 16 June. Stuart began by summarising Montgomery's views on Crerar's rights and responsibilities. Stuart said he regarded certain statements made by Montgomery concerning Crerar's 'operational responsibilities' as being 'out of line with the Visiting Forces' Act'. However, he felt that this was not the time for pressing 'constitutional points' when with a 'mutual spirit of understanding no practical difficulties should arise'. Brooke replied to Stuart on 17 June thanking him for his 'very practical outlook'. He told Stuart to let him know if 'at any time there was a danger of a misunderstanding'. (For both letters, see Alanbrooke Papers 6/2/25.)

25 This is the clearest statement from Montgomery before D-Day of his views on 'national feelings'.

26 The notes are included in full in Montgomery, *Memoirs*, pp. 239–44.

27 In his diary notes for 30 May (not included here – see LMD 55/1), Montgomery wrote: 'My talks to all senior officers are going well. It is a big job and I feel rather tired after giving one; you have to go absolutely all out, and get it across to the audiences of some 500 officers each; energy goes out of you and you are quite tired after each talk.' Montgomery was 56 years old.

Notes to Documents 54–99, June 1944, pp. 113–78

1 The Army Commanders were Dempsey, Bradley, Crerar and Patton. There is a more detailed account of the occasion in Patton's diary (see Blumenson, *The Patton Papers*, pp. 461–2). 'When the port was passed,' Patton wrote, 'General Montgomery toasted the four Army commanders. Nobody did anything about it, so I said, "As the oldest Army commander present, I would like to propose a toast to the health of General Montgomery and express our satisfaction in serving under him." The lightning did not strike me.'

2 The subject of the weather forecasting for D-Day and the succession of conferences at Southwick House is covered in detail in *Forecast for Overlord*, by the chief meteorological officer on Eisenhower's staff, Group Captain J.M. Stagg.

3 Montgomery's letter to Grigg of 1 June and Grigg's reply of 3 June are reproduced in full in Montgomery, *Memoirs*, pp. 245–6.

4 Montgomery rounds off this section of his diary notes up to 3 June 1944 with a further six paragraphs (numbered 46–51) giving his views on the 'chief actors' in the unfolding drama, including Churchill, Marshall, Eisenhower, Brooke, Grigg, Mountbatten, Wilson and Alexander. He concludes that 'we have a good team only in Western EUROPE' (LMD 55/1).

5 What Montgomery does not say here, but does say in his *Memoirs*, is that at the 0430 a.m. meeting, despite the weather forecast – 'I was for going'. He admits that had they persisted in 5 June, 'we might have had a disaster' (Montgomery, *Memoirs*, pp. 248–9).

6　The Naval Commander-in-Chief was Admiral Ramsay; Eisenhower's Chief of Staff was Lieutenant-General Walter Bedell Smith.

7　The references for Montgomery's Eighth Army diaries are BLM 27–48.

8　'J' was a network of battlefield reporting centres established to relay information gathered from wireless traffic direct to headquarters. Similarly 'Phantom' was a system for passing immediate battlefield information back to a commander. Montgomery discussed the two systems in a letter to Brooke of 14 October 1943, see Brooks (ed.), *Montgomery and the Eighth Army*, pp. 308–9.

9　Major-General Sir John Kennedy wrote in his diary for 6 June 1944, 'Monty said to me on the telephone that he intended to go over tonight. If things were not going well, he said, he would put them right; if they were going well, he would make them go better' (Kennedy, *The Business of War*, p. 330).

10　Rear-Admiral Sir Philip Vian (1894–1968) was commander of the Eastern Task Force.

11　Montgomery also met Eisenhower and Ramsay, who were off the beaches in HMS *Apollo* on 7 June. Ramsay wrote in his diary, 'Monty came on board & gave a quite cheerful description of the land battle but perhaps it was his intention to spread optimism in the face of an anxious situation. Anyhow he did it & I hope he'll be justified' (Love and Major (eds), *The Year of D-Day*, pp. 84–5). There is a photograph of Ramsay, Eisenhower and Montgomery on board HMS *Apollo* at the Imperial War Museum (reference A23929), with Montgomery wearing corduroy trousers, sheepskin-lined flying jacket and a reassuring smile.

12　Montgomery landed in Normandy at 0700 hours on 8 June.

13　M1, see Document 56; for M2, a sitrep to Eisenhower along the lines of M1, only shorter, because Montgomery had met Eisenhower during the day, see BLM 110/2.

14　Montgomery began to give his messages, letters and other documents an 'M' reference number. Montgomery and de Guingand communicated by letter or telegram until a cross-Channel telephone link was established on 13 June. De Guingand wrote to Montgomery on 13 June, 'It was good to hear your voice on the 'phone this morning; it is a great thing that we have got it through at last' (TNA WO205/5b).

15　Here and in following documents this is the time at which the message was sent. On 7 June Montgomery also sent a short sitrep to Eisenhower (M2) at 2000 hours (BLM 110/2).

16　SS here means Special Service i.e. Commando.

17　According to the annotations at the top of this letter Simpson circulated it at the War Office: it was seen by Brooke on 10 June; then by the DMI, Major-General Sinclair; by the ACIGS(O), General Kennedy; and by the VCIGS, Lieutenant-General Nye, on 11 June.

18　This means that the amphibious tanks were landed directly onto the beach from landing craft or ships, and not expected to 'swim' ashore.

19　Brigadier James Cunningham (1893–1982), 9th Infantry Brigade.

20　Brigadier Ronald Senior (1904–1988), 151st Infantry Brigade.

21 Lieutenant-Colonel H.O.S. Herdon, 2nd Battalion Royal Warwickshire
    Regiment – Montgomery's own regiment.
22 See Document 59.
23 This is the first of the 'M500' series, which Montgomery started for
    particularly important documents.
24 Montgomery has added '1200 hrs' beneath the date on this copy of the letter
    (LMD 59/3).
25 Summarising briefly the paragraphs in de Guingand's letter (carbon copy
    at TNA WO205/5b) referred to here: Paragraph 1. He enquires about the
    functioning of Tac HQ. 2. Hopes improved weather conditions will make
    bombing and build-up more effective. 3. He is flying to see Leigh-Mallory
    regarding air effort. 4. Fighter-bomber pilots want the bomb line to be
    moved nearer to forward troops. 5. For Bradley's build-up, fighting units
    to be given priority over units such as air construction. 6. Port-en-Bessin
    'petrol project is under way' (tankers moored off Port-en-Bessin discharged
    oil through pipelines to the shore). 7. Situation regarding 82 and 101
    Airborne Divisions still to be clarified. 8. Targets in the Pas de Calais to be
    bombed 'now and then' to aid deception plans. 9. First reports coming in of
    SOE activities. 10. Miles Graham will be visiting Normandy shortly.
26 Colonel E.T. 'Bill' Williams, Montgomery's head of intelligence.
27 This message had not reached Eisenhower by the following morning.
    According to Harry Butcher's diary, Eisenhower woke on 10 June in a bad
    temper because there was 'no information from Monty, who had agreed
    to radio every night his latest impression of the way the battle was going'
    (Butcher, *Three Years with Eisenhower*, p. 495). Montgomery sent nightly
    sitreps to Eisenhower on 7, 8, 9 and 10 June; there was then a gap before he
    sent the next one on 25 June (Document 88).
28 This message, sent by Montgomery at 1835 on 10 June, was delivered to
    Eisenhower in the early hours of 11 June: 'This morning at 4 a.m., Monty's
    signal arrived with a loud knocking on the door of Ike's caravan, waking the
    S[upreme] C[ommander] from a sleep into which he had just thankfully
    relapsed. The runner is supposed to come to my tent, and I read the signal,
    decide whether to hold or deliver. But this one went right to God' (Butcher,
    Three Years with Eisenhower, p. 496).
29 Ramsay toured the assault area in HMS *Kelvin* and visited the beaches on
    11 June. De Guingand replied to this letter later on 10 June: 'I received
    your signal regarding not being able to meet RAMSAY tomorrow. I quite
    expected that answer!' (see TNA WO205/5b).
30 The letter is M500 – Document 59; Johnnie is Captain J.R. Henderson,
    Montgomery's ADC.
31 1 Special Service (Commando) Brigade finally returned to England on
    7 September, to prepare for service in the Far East.
32 For the Personal Message of 10 June, see BLM 123/5 or the reproduction in
    Montgomery, *Forward to Victory*.
33 'B' here stands for 'Bullfinch', which was Montgomery's codename for the
    Prime Minister. In fact, Brooke had sent a message to Montgomery at 0120

hrs on 10 June (BLM 115/4) that he and the Prime Minister would visit Normandy on 12 June. Montgomery replied at 0930 hrs (BLM 115/5) that he would meet them and give them the full picture.

34 Dempsey and Bradley.

35 Major-General Cecil White (1897–1985) was Chief Signal Officer, 21st Army Group.

36 Sergeant Ship was Montgomery's mess sergeant who had returned from Italy with him at the turn of the year.

37 Dempsey wrote in his diary, 'Met C-in-C and Commander First Army at PORT-EN-BESSIN. We discussed future plans. So far as they affect my immediate operations, 5 American Corps will send one Division due SOUTH to CAUMONT on 12 or 13 June. This will tie up well with 7 Armd Div's intention to get VILLERS BOCAGE' (see TNA WO285/9). Montgomery's first *written* Directive (M502) to Dempsey and Bradley was not issued until 18 June – see Document 75.

38 With the Prime Minister, scheduled for 12 June.

39 This message regarding Leigh-Mallory is dated 12 June, but in his letter to de Guingand of 12 June (Document 69) Montgomery refers to having sent such a message 'last night' i.e. 11 June.

40 Leigh-Mallory (LM) rejected Montgomery's plans for an airborne drop in the Evrecy area, because he believed the risks for the airborne force, including being fired on as it passed over the Allied ships off the beaches, were too great (see Leigh-Mallory to Montgomery, 11 June 1944 in TNA WO205/5e). It proved impossible to create Montgomery's 'favourable conditions' – 1 Corps reaching Cagny and 30 Corps gaining the high ground above Evrecy – so there was no opportunity to use 1st Airborne Division. See Ellis, *Victory in the West*, Vol. I, p. 247.

41 Lieutenant-General Sir Frederick 'Boy' Browning (1896–1965) was commander of 1 British Airborne Corps. He had been staying in Normandy. On 9 June Dempsey had written an entry in his diary for 1300 hours: 'I discussed with Browning during the day the possibility of employing 1 Airborne Div SOUTH of CAEN on the evening of 11 June or later. He set in motion the machinery for planning and carrying it out' (TNA WO285/9). On his return to England, Browning did indeed go and see de Guingand, who wrote to Montgomery on 13 June, 'Boy Browning arrived back here this afternoon, and after a talk he left to see L.M. He is going to ring me tonight as to how things are proceeding. I have just spoken to DEMPSEY on the 'phone about a date for 1 Airborne Division, and he has given the 15th' (see TNA WO/205b). Frustratingly for Browning, none of the plans for the use of airborne forces came to fruition until Arnhem.

42 Possibly these notes, dated 12 June, were written by Montgomery for the briefing he gave to the Prime Minister and CIGS that day.

43 At OMAHA the American bombers had to bomb through low cloud and so delayed releasing their bombs for fear of hitting the leading invasion craft. This meant that thousands of bombs landed in the fields of Normandy well south of the beach defences.

44 For appendix, not included here for reasons of space, see LMD 59/5.

45 For the fighting round Villers Bocage 12–15 June, see Montgomery, *Normandy to the Baltic*, pp. 73–4, and Ellis, *Victory in the West*, Vol. I, pp. 253–6.

46 Director of Military Operations – Major-General F.E.W. Simpson.

47 Actually DUKW, although pronounced 'duck'.

48 MIKE was the sector of JUNO beach at Graye-sur-Mer.

49 Brooke wrote in his diary of this briefing: 'All as usual wonderfully clear and concise' (Danchev and Todman (eds), *Alanbrooke: War Diaries*, p. 557).

50 See Document 65 regarding Leigh-Mallory (LM).

51 Major-General Miles Graham, who was Montgomery's 'head A/Q' (head of administration and supply).

52 Montgomery has put a line in the margin against this and the following paragraph and marked them 'very secret' in red crayon. The King visited Montgomery on Friday, 16 June. See Document 72.

53 Lieutenant-General Dempsey.

54 See Document 67.

55 '"Do you *enjoy* fighting battles, Franklyn?" Brooke had broodingly asked the General commanding in Northern Ireland on a visit in July 1942; "I don't. I think Monty does"' (Fraser, *Alanbrooke*, p. 287).

56 General Bradley refers to the problem of the missing manifests in his memoirs. He wrote that the absence of manifests meant that supplies that were not required were unloaded, whilst much needed ammunition was left in ships. Despite repeated appeals to the Services of Supply, nothing happened until he complained directly to Eisenhower. 'The missing manifests came through without further apologies or explanations' (Bradley, *A Soldier's Story*, p. 305).

57 105mm ammunition.

58 The American artificial harbour – Mulberry Harbour 'A' – off Omaha Beach was wrecked in the storm that began on 19 June.

59 The words in italics here and in paragraph 34 below are additions in Montgomery's hand.

60 Major-General (later Lieutenant-General) Leonard Townsend Gerow (1888–1972).

61 Major-General Charles H. Corlett (1889–1971).

62 To accompany this lengthy typewritten letter, Montgomery wrote a short handwritten letter to Brooke that opened: 'I began enclosed letter to you yesterday morning – 13 June. I kept adding to it, and put in two more bits this morning. It may all seem a bit disjointed in consequence; but I hope will show you what I am doing' (Alanbrooke Papers 6/2/25).

63 See Document 71.

64 On 14 June Leigh-Mallory made a proposal to Montgomery for the use of heavy bombers to support a ground attack on Caen. 'When I made it,' Leigh-Mallory said in the diary notes he dictated to his personal assistant, 'he just swallowed it up, though even now I am not sure he will choose the right area' (see TNA AIR37/784). The operation was provisionally set for

17 June. However, Leigh-Mallory had not discussed the proposal with Tedder or Coningham. When Leigh-Mallory did speak to Coningham in the evening, Coningham telephoned Tedder to complain. The following day, 15 June, Tedder and Coningham flew to Normandy and broke up the planning meeting of RAF staff officers with Dempsey's staff at Second Army Headquarters. Montgomery was told that the plan for the use of the heavy bombers was off – see paragraph 40 of the diary notes in this document. Dempsey wrote in his diary, 'Both Tedder and Coningham are sure that it cannot be done effectively. For the present we will drop it' (see TNA WO285/9). Leigh-Mallory refrained from making any comment on the episode in his dictated diary notes until 10 July (see TNA AIR37/784).

65   Bradley later wrote that Montgomery had 'exercised his Allied authority with wisdom, forbearance and restraint … I could not have wanted a more tolerant or judicious commander. Not once did he confront us with an arbitrary directive and not once did he reject any plan that we had devised' (Bradley, *A Soldier's Story*, pp. 319–20).

66   According to Dempsey's diary he followed up this proposal at 2130 hours the same evening: 'Commander 8 Corps came to my headquarters and I discussed with him the possibility of employing his Corps to the EAST of the two rivers in order to envelop the RIGHT of the GERMAN line. He will study this tomorrow when I will discuss it with him again' (see TNA WO285/9).

67   Sir Alan Lascelles, who accompanied the King, wrote in his diary: 'The King then held a small investiture, elaborately staged by Monty, who made a speech about each investee (whose decorations, by the way, I had been carting about in a pouch ever since we had left London).' For Lascelles' diary entry for 16 June, see Hart-Davis (ed.), *King's Counsellor*, pp. 233–6. And see also Love and Major (eds), *The Year of D-Day*, p. 90, for a diary entry by Admiral Ramsay, who wrote: 'Thought that Monty was fine drawn & under considerable strain augmented by this visit.'

68   This letter crossed with a handwritten letter (also dated 18 June) from Montgomery, accompanying Directive M502, which arrived later in the day. In it Montgomery asked Eisenhower for his help in keeping visitors away. Eisenhower wrote 'already taken care of' alongside Montgomery's request (Eisenhower Papers, copy in Nigel Hamilton Research Papers at the IWM).

69   Montgomery had written to Grigg on 13 June (Grigg Papers 9/8/8) inviting him for a visit, which took place on 18 June.

70   Eisenhower had flown to Normandy for a conference with Montgomery on 15 June. There is a strong hint here that Eisenhower was already beginning to worry about the speed of operations. On 25 June Eisenhower wrote in similar vein to Bradley: 'I most earnestly hope that you get Cherbourg tomorrow. As quickly as you have done so we must rush the preparations for the attack to the southward with all speed. The enemy is building up and we must not allow him to seal us up in the northern half of the Peninsula' (Chandler (ed.), *The Papers of Dwight David Eisenhower: The War Years*, Vol. III, p. 1948).

71 Eisenhower was unable to do this on Tuesday, 20 June because of the storm that began the previous day. He spent 20 June at Bushy Park instead.

72 Not extant. Montgomery did not keep any of the letters written to him by Major and Mrs Reynolds during the war.

73 Captain Noel Chavasse was Montgomery's ADC.

74 The cartoon by Strube in the *Daily Express* of 12 June shows Montgomery in a jeep acknowledging a German general glaring down at him from a tank; the caption reads, 'Field Marshal Rommel, I presume'. In the cartoon by Strube of 16 June the portraits of the generals in full dress show Frederick the Great, Von Moltke, Napoleon and the Kaiser. Montgomery is driving past in a jeep and the caption reads 'The Man in the Sweater' (see LMD/5, one of a series of eight albums of press cuttings compiled by Major and Mrs Reynolds for Montgomery between 1942 and 1945).

75 A full distribution list for Montgomery's directives such as this is preserved in Montgomery's handwriting with M510 of 10 July (Document 111).

76 Details of SAS activities in France in June 1944 can be found in Strawson, *A History of the SAS Regiment*, chapter 11 and appendix.

77 Such was the success of FORTITUDE that the Germans continued to expect an attack in Pas de Calais until late July.

78 Major-General Joseph Lawton Collins (1896–1987).

79 Prior to D-Day Montgomery had received word that Grigg wished to be present in the invasion force on D-Day. Montgomery had written to Grigg on 14 May (BLM 114/1) saying that it was not advisable: 'your presence could not fail to be an embarrassment to some commander – however incognito you may wish to remain.' More easily put off than the Prime Minister, Grigg accepted this in a letter to Montgomery on 16 May (LMD 110/4). Montgomery sent a handwritten letter to Grigg on 13 June inviting him to visit on 18 June: 'the soldiers would know & hear about your visit, and would be pleased' (Grigg Papers 9/8/8).

80 M503 (not included in this selection) is a memorandum dated 18 June from Montgomery to the Military Secretary at the War Office, recommending the following to receive honours for their work in connection with OVERLORD: Lieutenant-General Dempsey, Major-General de Guingand, Major-General Graham, Brigadier Williams and Brigadier Belchem (see BLM 126/4).

81 The relationship between Montgomery and Dempsey and their respective roles in decision-making in Normandy is fully discussed in Hart, *Montgomery and 'Colossal Cracks'*, pp. 129–54. This episode is a particularly interesting one. To what extent did Montgomery's determination to 'grip' the battle mean that he acted as his own Army commander, consulting corps' commanders such as O'Connor and taking decisions with only token reference to Dempsey?
On 17 June O'Connor briefed Dempsey on the problems of a thrust by 8 Corps from the eastern end of the bridgehead: 'It is not an easy operation to stage owing to the lack of depth in the 1 Corps sector, the bottleneck of the bridges over R. ORNE, and the limited space available in the bridgehead

itself' (Dempsey's diary, TNA WO285/9). Sometime during the day on 18 June Montgomery went to see O'Connor and received a similar briefing (see Document 79). Then at 1830 hours Montgomery went to Dempsey's headquarters. It is instructive to compare Montgomery's diary notes here for this meeting with Dempsey's:

'Saw C-in-C at my Headquarters. I told him that I had come to the conclusion that an attack by 8 Corps from the bridgehead EAST of the two rivers is too risky. The bridgehead is too small to form up satisfactorily; there is no room to deploy artillery EAST of the rivers; the L of C would be dependent on the bridges, and there is always the risk that the enemy, who is very active in this sector, might upset our arrangements just before the start of the attack. The staff had been into the matter very carefully during the morning. I will therefore put 8 Corps in between 30 Corps and 1 Corps, attack in a South-Easterly direction, and secure the crossings over R ORNE NORTH of THURY HARCOURT' (TNA WO285/9).

What is very noticeable is that neither Dempsey nor Montgomery acknowledges any contribution to the discussion made by the other. Although it appears to be a case of military minds thinking alike, each man gives the impression that the initiative for changing the plan lay solely with him. However, looking at Dempsey's role as commander of Second Army, Stephen Ashley Hart concludes that, overall, the evidence suggests that this episode, 'where the Field Marshal and O'Connor seem to have marginalized Dempsey, constituted the exception rather than the rule' (Hart, *Montgomery and 'Colossal Cracks'*, p. 140).

82   Brigadier, later Lieutenant-General Sir, Maurice Chilton (1898–1956). Montgomery 'lent' Brigadier Charles Richardson, his BGS (Plans), to advise Dempsey. See Document 78.

83   See Montgomery's letter to O'Connor of 19 June, Document 79.

84   The queries in italics here are in Simpson's handwriting in the original document. He is presumably querying whether Montgomery means 31st Tank Brigade or 33rd Armoured Brigade (the former was not re-designated 31st Armoured Brigade until February 1945). See Joslen, *Orders of Battle*, Vol. I.

85   For the 'blitz' attack at El Hamma on 26 March 1943 see Brooks (ed.), *Montgomery and the Eighth Army*, pp. 181–95.

86   In his memoirs General Sir Charles Richardson wrote, 'I was sent by Monty to stay at that headquarters [of Second Army], and "sort it out". During the week I was there I found that all I had to do was to create the same system of consultation and generate the same mutual confidence that we had enjoyed with the RAF in North Africa' (Richardson, *Flashback: A Soldier's Story*, p. 181).

87   See note 81 above for the background to this letter.

88   Document 76.

89   Document 76; and see also Document 78 and note 86 above.

90   Montgomery actually delegated the task of writing to Sir Alan Lascelles, the King's Principal Private Secretary, to de Guingand. There is a carbon

copy of de Guingand's letter of 19 June, and Lascelles' reply of 21 June in TNA WO205/5c. Lascelles recorded in his diary on 21 June 1944 that the security breach was 'most unfortunate, but, as I pointed out to de Guingand, the SHAEF Censor had Wulff's stuff [Louis Wulff was the journalist who covered the King's activities] in his hands for at least an hour before it was released; and what is a censor for if not to cut out such palpable indiscretions on the part of Pressmen, who, quite naturally, try to put as much local colour into their stories as they can?' (Hart-Davis (ed.), *King's Counsellor*, p. 238).

91 Montgomery also wrote a short letter to Simpson on 20 June in which he said of the delays caused by the weather: 'It is all a very great nuisance' (IWM, Simpson Papers).

92 General Crerar crossed to Normandy with a small tactical headquarters on 18 June, but was told by Montgomery on 22 June that there was insufficient room in the bridgehead for First Canadian Army HQ to become operational. Simonds' 2 Canadian Corps became operational under Second Army on 11 July, and Crerar's Army HQ on 24 July.

93 Document 71.

94 Lieutenant-General Karl Wihelm von Schlieben (1894–1964) took command of the besieged Cherbourg fortress on 23 June. He surrendered on 26 June and resistance ceased the following day.

95 The proposed seizure of St Malo by airborne forces. See paragraph 6 of Montgomery's directive M504 of 19 June, Document 77.

96 See Brooke's diary for June 1944 for the lengthy discussions at this time over Mediterranean and Far East strategy.

97 The first German V1 flying bombs struck England in the early hours of 13 June. On 18 June a V1 struck the Guards Chapel at Wellington Barracks in London killing 119 people, including a close friend of Brooke's, Lieutenant-Colonel Ivan Cobbold.

98 On 12 June, when Brooke accompanied the Prime Minister to Montgomery's headquarters.

99 Montgomery wrote 'Top Secret and Personal' at the top of this letter. Leese had been annoyed with Montgomery in January 1944 over the recall of so many officers to England from Eighth Army to join 21st Army Group and other matters. However, on 8 May Leese had written to his wife, Margaret, 'I got a very friendly letter from O [Montgomery]! We now correspond again. It's a queer world' (see Ryder, *Oliver Leese*, p. 164). Montgomery's letters to Leese give no indication that he realised anything was amiss between them.

100 For Leese's five-page letter to Montgomery dated 11 June, see BLM 97/22.

101 Major-General George Walsh (1899–1972), Chief of Staff of the Eighth Army.

102 See BLM 122/4 for Montgomery's notes. The address is too long to include here, but there are substantial extracts in Hamilton, *Monty: Master of the Battlefield*, pp. 670–3.

103 Major-General, later General Sir, Lashmer Whistler (1898–1963). He took part in the North Russia Relief Force in 1919 and his stories of the Bolsheviks, or 'Bolos', led to his being given the nickname 'Bolo'.

104 Major-General Douglas Graham (1893–1971).

105 In fact, on 26 July Montgomery replaced Major-General Bullen-Smith by Major-General Rennie when he had recovered from his injuries.

106 Montgomery's Tac HQ was initially sited in the grounds of the Château de Creullet; on 23 June it moved to Blay, west of Bayeux. See Document 80 and note 90 above for Montgomery's complaint to Sir Alan Lascelles.

107 Major-General de Guingand ('Freddie') had suffered from gall-stones since 1942.

108 De Guingand had sent his letter, dated 24 June, by the Air Despatch Letter Service (operated by Hurricanes of 1697 Flight RAF, especially adapted for carrying mail). A carbon copy can be found in TNA WO205/5b. De Guingand had just received a brief note from Montgomery dated 23 June (also in WO205/5b) saying that there were reports by G1 (Liaison) officers that were 'highly suspect & must be carefully vetted'. In his letter of 24 June de Guingand says that reports were comparing British armour most unfavourably with German armour. He enclosed a report by a officer in 30 Corps named Bowring, which 'to my mind, is extremely dangerous', with a covering letter written by Chief of Staff of 30 Corps, Brigadier Pyman, which 'appears to be a thoroughly bad document'. De Guingand writes that if these sentiments reached the troops, they could 'have a very great effect upon their fighting'. Montgomery acted swiftly to nip this threat to morale in the bud – see Document 86.

109 The 6th Guards Tank Brigade had been a subject of dispute between Montgomery and the Prime Minister in April 1944, over a War Office proposal to abolish the Brigade in order to provide reinforcements for the Brigade of Guards. When Churchill rejected the proposal, Montgomery withdrew 6th Guards Tank Brigade into Army Group reserve. The Brigade did not land in Normandy until 18 July. See BLM 120/29–34.

110 For the background to the issuing of this order, see paragraph 6 of Montgomery's letter to Brooke of 27 June (Document 91) and note 108 above.

111 On the same day Eisenhower sent a memorandum to Tedder, saying, inter alia, that he hoped Tedder would make it his 'special province to keep in closest touch with General Montgomery or his representatives in 21st Army Group' (Chandler (ed.), *The Papers of Dwight David Eisenhower: The War Years*, Vol. III, p. 1952).

112 Regarding the start of the Second Army offensive – Operation EPSOM – Montgomery wrote briefly in his diary notes for 25 June: 'Second Army attack began. 49 Div. made good progress' (see Document 90 for diary notes for 26 June).

113 i.e. 20,000 Germans taken prisoner by the US Army.

114 This typescript letter is marked '<u>Top Secret. Personal</u>'. It has the reference '21 A. Gp/1093/C.-in-C.' rather than an 'M' number. The copy in the Alanbrooke Papers (6/2/25) is marked that it was seen by VCIGS and DCIGS (Nye and Weeks). It was delivered by hand by Dawnay. After writing this letter Montgomery sent message M32 to Brooke at 1900 hours

on 27 June (BLM 110/15) saying that Dawnay would fly over the following day and would bring the letter and explain the exact situation to Simpson.

115 Brooke had written on 23 June – Document 83.

116 Coningham was brought up in New Zealand, hence the nickname 'Maori', sometimes corrupted, as here, to 'Mary'.

117 See Documents 85 and 86.

118 I have been unable to find further details of this officer.

119 Armour-piercing discarding sabot shot, which was introduced for the 6-pounder anti-tank gun in 1944, had greatly increased velocity. The shot was held in a light casing (or sabot) that fell away when the round left the barrel of the gun.

120 Piat stood for Projector Infantry Anti-Tank.

121 The 'Firefly' was a Sherman tank with a 17-pounder instead of a 75mm or 76mm gun.

122 Document 86.

123 Brigadier John Currie (1898–1944) was killed by shellfire on 26 June.

124 Dempsey and Bradley. Dempsey's diary entry for this conference on 27 June reads: 'Flew to and from HQ 21 Army Group at BLAY. Bradley was there and we discussed present and future operations. First Army will be ready to strike Southwards on the axis LA HAYE DU PUITS–LESSAY–COUTANCES on 1 July' (see TNA WO285/9).

125 See Document 91.

126 See Document 92.

127 The Prime Minister had sent a message to Montgomery on 28 June, saying: 'All our thoughts are with you and your army under DEMPSEY. I send you my best wishes for the success in this formidable battle' (see LMD 59/14).

128 Document 91.

129 In his diary on 15 December 1942 Brooke refers to hearing 'rumours of Monty being sticky in his pursuit' after El Alamein. In his later notes Brooke says that he 'discovered that these rumours emanated from the two airmen, Coningham and Tedder, who were responsible for the air support'. This alerted Brooke to the fact that criticism of the army might stem from RAF officers such as Coningham. See Danchev and Todman (eds), *Alanbrooke: War Diaries*, pp. 348–9.

130 See Document 86.

131 The dispute with the Americans was over the proposed Allied landings in southern France – Operation ANVIL. Brooke had just learnt through ULTRA that Field Marshal Kesselring had been ordered by Hitler to make a stand south of the Pisa–Rimini line. Brooke thought this clinched the argument against ANVIL, but the Americans disagreed.

132 This is the only letter from Bradley to Montgomery during the Normandy campaign preserved in the Montgomery Papers.

133 i.e. 3 July, instead of 1 July as planned.

134 On the same day Bradley wrote to Eisenhower along similar lines, saying that he would attack as soon as possible: 'I am very anxious that when we hit the enemy this time we will hit him with such power that we can keep going and

cause him a major disaster.' Eisenhower replied on 1 July, 'I definitely agree with you that your attack must be strong when you start so you can keep going' (Chandler (ed.), *The Papers of Dwight David Eisenhower: The War Years*, Vol. III, p. 1968).

135 See Document 92.

136 There are no notes extant for this particular talk in the Montgomery Papers.

137 Document 98.

Notes to Documents 100–167, July 1944, pp. 179–260

1   In a message to the Combined Chiefs of Staff on 26 June, Eisenhower wrote: 'I attach such importance to the early launching of ANVIL that I am prepared to do my utmost to insure its success. Admiral Ramsay and General Montgomery share my conviction with regard to the importance of ANVIL.' For Eisenhower's message in full, see Chandler (ed.), *The Papers of Dwight David Eisenhower: The War Years*, Vol. III, pp. 1954–5.

2   Simpson gave Montgomery the background to this message in a letter dated 2 July (BLM 94/4): 'When your telegram M38 arrived last night, I at once telephoned to C.I.G.S. and his 56738 of 1 July was drafted and despatched by me in the light of what he said. I don't think what Ike said in his telegram [to the CCS] has really affected the final issue and C.I.G.S. therefore felt that it would only do more harm than good if you raised the matter with Ike and made him think that you were conducting a clandestine correspondence with the War Office.' In his five-page letter, headed '<u>TOP SECRET. PRIVATE AND PERSONAL</u>', Simpson gave Montgomery the background to the debate that had just taken place in London over ANVIL, but added: 'Please do not let anyone else ever know that I have told you how your alleged opinions have been bandied about.'

3   Document 100.

4   When Eisenhower visited Montgomery the following day, Eisenhower raised the subject of ANVIL and asked for Montgomery's views. See Document 102.

5   Not extant.

6   Montgomery does not make any reference to this meeting with Eisenhower in his diary notes for 2 July.

7   The sentence in italics is the addition in Montgomery's handwriting.

8   6th Battalion, The Duke of Wellington's Regiment.

9   The report by Lieutenant-Colonel A.J.D. Turner MC on the sorry state of the battalion he had just taken over can be found in full in a number of books, for example, Hastings, *Overlord*, pp. 148–9, and Lamb, *Montgomery in Europe*, pp. 109–12. The latter includes a discussion of why Montgomery sent the report to Grigg; 'I think you may like to see [it]' seems to leave a good deal unsaid. For background and another transcript of the report, see Delaforce, *The Polar Bears*, pp. 84–7.

10 Major-General Simpson spent the night of 6/7 July with Montgomery at Tac HQ.

11 Document 98.

12 For a summary of the opening phase of the American offensive in the bocage country that began on 3 July see Montgomery, *Normandy to the Baltic*, pp. 88–9; and for a detailed narrative, see Blumenson, *Breakout and Pursuit*, Chapter IV.

13 Second Army's offensive against Caen was codenamed Operation CHARNWOOD.

14 The relations of the air 'barons' with Montgomery and with each other during the Normandy campaign can be followed in Hamilton, *Monty: Master of the Battlefield*. As a contrast, the story presented from the perspective of Coningham and Tedder can be found in Terraine, *The Right of the Line*, pp. 607–58; and Orange, *Coningham*, pp. 194–210 and *Tedder: Quietly in Command*, pp. 262–73.

15 Tedder visited Montgomery in France on 29 June. Tedder's memoirs imply that he did not discuss Coningham with Montgomery: 'Immediately on my return I talked with Eisenhower, from whom I gathered that Montgomery had suggested that Coningham was being too critical and somewhat unco-operative' (Tedder, *With Prejudice*, p. 555). Montgomery does not mention either this meeting with Tedder, or the subsequent one with Coningham, in his diary notes.

16 Eisenhower saw Montgomery on 2 July, not 1 July.

17 By the time Brooke replied on 11 July (Document 113) the debate over ANVIL was past history, so he does not comment on Montgomery's views as expressed here.

18 This is Montgomery's first discussion of the system of command in North-West Europe that was to preoccupy him once the battle of Normandy had been won.

19 General Courtney Hicks Hodges (1887–1966).

20 Bradley, in fact, visited Tac HQ for lunch on the day this letter was written (7 July), accompanied by Patton. Patton wrote in his diary, 'After lunch, Montgomery, Bradley, and I went to the war tent. Here Montgomery went to great length explaining why the British had done nothing. Caen was their D day objective, and they have not taken it yet' (Blumenson, *The Patton Papers 1940–45*, p. 479). Montgomery does not mention the visit in his brief diary notes for 7 July – see LMD 59/1.

21 For Montgomery's 'Memorandum on British Armour' (M506), with a covering letter to the DCIGS (M507), both dated 6 July 1944, see BLM 117/14 and 117/16. The memorandum is too lengthy to include here. In brief, Montgomery sets out the views of 21st Army Group on which tanks needed improved engines, armour and armament. In particular, Montgomery desired as wide as possible an extension in the use of the 17-pounder, including to American armoured units, with improved capacity in high-explosive as well as armour-piercing ammunition. For Weeks' reply, dated 10 July, see BLM 117/17.

22 Montgomery had received adverse reports from Dempsey and Crocker regarding Major-General Keller's fitness to command 3 Canadian Division (BLM 119/7). Montgomery forwarded copies to Crerar on 8 July, saying

that he agreed but that he preferred the Canadians to take official action (BLM 119/8). See also Montgomery's diary notes for 8 July, Document 108.

23 Although Simonds was Montgomery's protégé, he proved capable of withstanding pressure from Dempsey and Montgomery to act against his own better judgement. Montgomery requested Dempsey to obtain a report from Simonds when 2 Canadian Corps HQ became operational regarding Keller's fitness to command a division in battle (BLM 119/12). Simonds replied to Dempsey on 27 July that he would not recommend Keller's removal from 3 Canadian Division as it would be 'regarded as a censure on the efforts of the division, in which the troops have fought hard and done creditably'. Dempsey forwarded this to Montgomery on 30 July with a covering note saying that he was ready to support Simonds because the 'morale of 3 Cdn Div is a most important matter' (BLM 119/13).

24 Captain Butcher wrote in his diary for 7 July: 'Ike has been smouldering and to-day burst out with a letter to Monty which, in effect, urges him to avoid having our forces sealed into the beachhead, take the offensive, and Ike would support him in every way, as if it were necessary to say this' (Butcher, *Three Years with Eisenhower*, p. 520).

25 Eisenhower had spent the period 1–5 July in Normandy.

26 G-2 was the Intelligence section of the staff.

27 Tedder had responded to Montgomery's criticisms of Coningham for not giving full support to the army by saying that he supported Coningham's opinion that 'the Army did not seem prepared to fight its own battles'. At a meeting between Eisenhower, Tedder and Bedell Smith on 6 July, it was agreed that Eisenhower 'should draft a letter which would tell Montgomery tactfully to get moving'. Hence this letter (Tedder, *With Prejudice*, p. 557).

28 According to *Normandy to the Baltic*, pp. 90 and 93, 16 GAF Division had been identified east of the Orne on 3 July and 276 Division near Tilly-sur-Seulles on 4 July; and 1 SS, 2 SS, Lehr and 21st Panzer Divisions were known to have been drawn wholly or partially into reserve.

29 Air Vice-Marshal Harry Broadhurst was in command of 83 Group RAF.

30 The orders for ANVIL to be carried out on 15 August had been issued on 2 July.

31 Eisenhower's Chief of Staff, Lieutenant-General Walter Bedell Smith, was known as 'Beedle' and 'Beetle'.

32 On Eisenhower's copy this was given the reference 'M508' by mistake, that number having already been used for Montgomery's letter to Brooke of 7 July; it was corrected to 'M509' on Montgomery's file copy.

33 Document 98.

34 For a summary of the Second Army offensive to take Caen, see Montgomery, *Normandy to the Baltic*, pp. 90–3; and for a fuller account, Ellis, *Victory in the West*, Vol. I, pp. 311–16.

35 There had also been a bombardment the previous evening by the heavy bombers of Bomber Command. In his brief diary notes for 7 July (LMD 60/1), Montgomery wrote: 'Bomber Command came over and did a most effective attack on the northern and N.W. outskirts of CAEN, as a

preliminary to the large scale attack to be launched by 1 Corps on 8 July. This bombing attack – 450 heavy Lancasters – is likely to have a decisive effect on the battle.'

36 Document 105.

37 Document 106.

38 See notes 22 and 23 above.

39 Eisenhower had sent a message from SHAEF to Montgomery timed out at 1130 that day saying, 'All of us are watching your present operations with enthusiastic interest' (LMD 60/6). Tedder was not so impressed by the scale of the offensive: 'Asked on 8 July what I thought of the present Army plans and attacks, I could only reply: "Company exercises"' (Tedder, *With Prejudice*, p. 559).

40 There are no notes for these talks in Montgomery's papers.

41 It is a minor point but the date of this conference is given as 10 July in all the secondary sources. The date 9 July is confirmed by the last sentence in message M46 (Document 109). In his brief diary notes for 10 July (not included in this selection) Montgomery simply refers to issuing Directive M510 and records the Allies' casualty statistics. The American breakout – Operation COBRA – and the British offensive – Operation GOODWOOD – developed out of this meeting on 9 July between Montgomery, Bradley and Dempsey. Carlo D'Este refers to it as 'one of their most important conferences of the campaign' (see D'Este, *Decision in Normandy*, pp. 332 ff.).

42 The holograph section is the distribution list (in italics) at the end of M510.

43 Document 98.

44 Despite this statement, Tedder felt that Montgomery still did not appreciate the need to speed up operations and that his objectives were too limited. 'I told Eisenhower on 11 July that in my view Montgomery's directive was most unsatisfactory. It seemed to be a repetition of the "Company exercises" to which I had objected a day or two before' (Tedder, *With Prejudice*, p. 561).

45 This and the following sentence are quoted back at Montgomery by Eisenhower in his letter of 21 July. See Document 137.

46 This circulation list is the only copy extant in Montgomery's papers showing how his directives such as this were distributed. Copy No 3 was initially for Patton, but Montgomery crossed out his name and put Crerar's.

47 The section in Eisenhower's handwriting is shown in italics.

48 Documents 106 and 109.

49 Of 7 July, Document 105.

50 Eisenhower met Alexander and his Chief of Staff, John Harding, at Bushy Park on 8 July.

51 Eisenhower met Churchill at Chequers on 9 July. Butcher wrote, 'Ike told me later that the PM gave him hell for insisting on the ANVIL operation' (Butcher, *Three Years with Eisenhower*, p. 525).

52 Montgomery's two most recent letters to Brooke were of 27 June and 7 July, Documents 91 and 104.

53 They had not met since Brooke's visit to the beachhead with the Prime Minister on 12 June.

54 Friday, 14 July.

55 The staff conference and dinner with Stimson on 14 July, are described by Brooke in his diary (Danchev and Todman (eds), *Alanbrooke: War Diaries*, p. 570).

56 Brooke no doubt wished to warn Montgomery in person that at a staff meeting on 6 July Churchill had been very critical of him, 'because operations were not going faster, and apparently Eisenhower had said that he was over cautious.' Brooke had accused the Prime Minister of abusing and belittling his generals, and a major row ensued (Danchev and Todman (eds), *Alanbrooke: War Diaries*, pp. 566–7). By the time Brooke did visit him on 19 July, Montgomery's position vis-à-vis the Prime Minister had become even more precarious because Churchill thought Montgomery's ban on visitors had been aimed at him.

57 See Document 104.

58 The commander of the Canadian Corps in Italy was Lieutenant-General E.L.M. Burns (1897–1985). He was removed from his post in November 1944.

59 In February 1917 Brooke was posted to be Chief of Staff to the commander of the Canadian Corps artillery.

60 General Andrew McNaughton (1887–1966) had taken command of the First Canadian Army in 1942. Under pressure from critics in Canada and amongst the British high command, and in declining health, he resigned in December 1943. He was succeeded by Lieutenant-General Crerar on 20 March 1944.

61 This is a significant sentence in terms of the relationship between Montgomery and Crerar. Although Montgomery attempts to influence Brooke against Crerar and in favour of Simonds in many documents in this volume, he knew that in the last resort Brooke would not permit Crerar's removal. Brooke seems to have enjoyed a good relationship with Crerar. He wrote in his diary on 29 March 1944: 'I have full confidence that Crerar will not let me down.'

62 General Sir Julian Byng commanded the Canadian Corps on the Western Front 1916–17, but his successor was a Canadian, General Sir Arthur Currie.

63 General Sir Thomas Riddell-Webster (1886–1974) was the Quartermaster-General.

64 For Montgomery's response see Document 123. He says he has not seen the actual letter but has the gist of it.

65 The Prime Minister had sent a message to Montgomery on 10 July congratulating him on the capture of Caen (LMD 60/9).

66 Deciphering messages such as this was apparently not the work of a moment. According to Harry Butcher's diary for 13 July, 'During the night, I had numerous phone calls, one of which informed me of an ultra-secret message in our private cipher from Monty. I arranged to have this brought at 7 o'clock this morning and spent an hour and a half with ATS Subaltern Cavaye while we boned out the message' (Butcher, *Three Years with Eisenhower*, p. 525).

67 Document 111.

68 Although Tedder had been unhappy with Montgomery's Directive 510, this message M49 – presumably the phrase 'far reaching results' in particular – led him to think that Montgomery had changed his mind and was going for a major all-out attempt at a breakout by Second Army. 'We gathered that Operation "Goodwood" would soon be launched, its purpose being to break into the area south-east of Caen' (Tedder, *With Prejudice*, p. 561). The reasons for SHAEF's high expectations and great disappointment regarding GOODWOOD are covered in many secondary sources; there is a good discussion of the subject in a lengthy footnote in Chandler (ed.), *The Papers of Dwight David Eisenhower: The War Years*, Vol. III, p. 2020.

69 This was the request that resulted in the Prime Minister's becoming incensed on 19 July that Montgomery was trying to prevent him from coming to Normandy.

70 This was the codename for the highest security classification for documents relating to D-Day and the battle of Normandy. Those cleared for access to such documents were known as 'bigots'.

71 Montgomery's Directive M510 of 10 July, confirmed by his message M49 of 12 July (Documents 111 and 115).

72 Document 116.

73 Dempsey does not refer to this meeting in his diary notes for 13 July.

74 Document 111.

75 Documents 115, 119 and 121.

76 The US breakout – Operation COBRA – was finally launched successfully on 25 July.

77 Document 118.

78 Document 117.

79 Documents 115, 117 and 119.

80 The major thrust of Operation GOODWOOD was to be an attack east of the Orne by Lieutenant-General O'Connor's 8 Corps – 7th Armoured, 11th Armoured and Guards Armoured Divisions.

81 Arthur Tedder – Document 121.

82 Montgomery had sent Eisenhower a message on 13 July saying that he was 'somewhat disturbed' at the time being taken to get the port of Cherbourg fit for use (BLM 108/10). See also paragraph 32 of Montgomery's letter to Brooke of 14 July (Document 123).

83 Document 113.

84 Lieutenant-General Simonds' 2 Canadian Corps (including 2nd and 3rd Canadian Infantry Divisions) took over 8000 yards of the front in the Caen sector on 11 July.

85 Montgomery is here referring to the comments he made about the Canadians in his letter to Brooke of 7 July – Document 104.

86 Brigadier Gerald Duke was Brigadier Q at 21st Army Group; Brigadier Mervyn Walters was in command of the British Mulberry Harbour B.

87 Major-General Donald McMullen was Director of Transportation at the War Office; 'Grove-White' may be a slip of the pen on Montgomery's part. Brigadier Bruce Gordon White was the Director of Ports and Inland Water

Transport and McMullen's deputy. Major-General Sir Maurice Grove-White does not appear to have been involved with the Mulberry Harbour project.

88   Montgomery sent this letter to the CIGS by hand of Dawnay. Dawnay also saw Simpson with instructions to give him further background information. In a letter to Montgomery on 20 July (BLM 94/5) Simpson wrote that Dawnay 'gave me certain verbal notes which he had made as a result of your talking to him'. One of the points related to the objectives of Operation GOODWOOD, and reinforced the 'nothing foolish' point Montgomery makes in para 24 of the letter. In an aide memoire Simpson wrote after their meeting, he recorded that Dawnay had told him Montgomery was aware that on the eastern flank was the 'only British army there is left in this part of the world ... Therefore, having broken out in country south-east of Caen, he has no intention of rushing madly eastwards, and getting Second Army on the eastern flank so extended that that flank might cease to be secure. All the activities on the eastern flank are designed to help the forces in the west while ensuring that a firm bastion is kept in the east' (quoted in Ellis, *Victory in the West*, Vol. 1, pp. 329–30).

89   Document 111.

90   Major-General Thomas Wilson (1896–1961). Erskine took over as Director of Infantry. The Military Secretary was General Sir Colville Wemyss. As senior military assistant to the Secretary of State for War, he was responsible for administering appointments.

91   Montgomery evidently felt it was necessary to put in writing the priorities for GOODWOOD to ensure that 'nothing foolish' happened at the eastern end of the Allied line in the forthcoming attack – see note 88 above.

92   There is a copy of this document, with this same addition in Montgomery's hand, in the Alanbrooke Papers 6/2/27.

93   Document 124. Dempsey's diary entry for 15 July is terse on the subject of this meeting: 'Met C-in-C at Headquarters 8 Corps and discussed next week's battle with him.'

94   See BLM 119/9; Montgomery's comments about 51st Division repeat those in his letter to Brooke – Document 123.

95   The Prime Minister sent Montgomery a message at 0045 on 17 July that read 'God with you' (LMD 60/2).

96   The Secretary of War was Henry Stimson.

97   However, Alanbrooke, in his post-war notes on his diary entry for 19 July, wrote apropos banning visitors: 'Monty then told me that Stimson had visited Bradley's HQ and had remained with him so long that orders for an attack could not be got out, and the attack had to be postponed for 24 hours' (Danchev and Todman (eds), *Alanbrooke: War Diaries*, p. 572).

98   The Prime Minister.

99   General Marshall sent a message to Eisenhower on 23 June, urging him to release the names of some of the American commanders of units serving under Bradley so that their exploits could be used for publicity purposes in the American press (see Chandler (ed.), *The Papers of Dwight David*

Eisenhower: The War Years, Vol. III, p. 1950). As Harry Butcher wrote in his diary for 22 July: 'The American people have keen interest and a right to know all we can tell them about the action of their boys in battle' (Butcher, *Three Years with Eisenhower*, p. 534).

100 i.e. enemy intelligence.

101 The Canadian part of the offensive was codenamed Operation ATLANTIC.

102 For narratives of British and Canadian operations 18–20 July 1944, see Montgomery, *Normandy to the Baltic*, pp. 100–4; Ellis, *Victory in the West*, Vol. I, pp. 327–50; and Stacey, *The Victory Campaign*, pp. 166–80.

103 The British Official History comments that Montgomery 'must have been misinformed about the true state of affairs' when he sent this message. 'This report was unfortunately inaccurate and misleading. The 11th Armoured Division had not reached either Tilly la Campagne or Bras; the few troops of the 7th Armoured who had passed by Démouville still had four miles to go before they could reach la Hogue, and the Guards were never within three miles of Vimont' (Ellis, *Victory in the West*, Vol. 1, pp. 344–5).

104 Eisenhower did as requested and visited Tac HQ on 20 June: see Montgomery's diary notes, Document 135. Presumably Montgomery did not want Tedder in particular to accompany Eisenhower.

105 According to Captain Butcher's diary for 19 July, 'this morning the PM called up, boiling mad, saying it would be a Cabinet issue, this business of Monty trying to tell the PM where he could and could not go. Ike took all the responsibility, and after explaining his desire not to bother Monty, the trip was laid on for tomorrow, with the Old Boy permitted to visit in the rear areas and not to see or bother Monty or other combat officers at all' (Butcher, *Three Years with Eisenhower*, p. 530). Brooke was due to visit Montgomery on 19 July. By what turned out to be a piece of good fortune, bad weather delayed his flight to Normandy that morning. He was therefore still in London at 9.30 a.m. when he was summoned to see the Prime Minister and found him in 'an unholy rage', accusing Montgomery of trying to stop him visiting Normandy. Brooke flew out to Tac HQ and took steps to defuse the row by getting Montgomery to send a letter (Document 134) inviting the Prime Minister to visit him whenever he wished. See Danchev and Todman (eds), *Alanbrooke: War Diaries*, pp. 571–3.

106 This is the letter that Brooke directed Montgomery to write to make peace with the Prime Minister. Brooke delivered it to Churchill and it 'worked like magic' (see Danchev and Todman (eds), *Alanbrooke: War Diaries*, pp. 571–3; and Document 135).

107 In his diary entry for 19 July Brooke concluded, 'What a storm in a china cup!' The episode is not even mentioned in Martin Gilbert's biography of Churchill. However, in the aftermath of the disappointed expectations over GOODWOOD, Montgomery was in an awkward position until COBRA was successfully launched on 25 July. Had Montgomery not had the opportunity to reassure the Prime Minister in the Map Caravan at Tac HQ, Tedder's campaign to get Eisenhower to take direct control and perhaps even replace Montgomery might have had more serious consequences.

108 Re Keller's possible removal, see Documents 104, 108 and 113.

109 Diary notes for 13 July, Document 120.

110 Document 115.

111 Document 134.

112 The message simply said, 'Thank you very much for your letter' (see LMD 60/26). However, in TNA Prem 3/339/11 there is a photocopy of Churchill's handwritten draft reply. There was a second sentence, reading, 'You may be sure I shall never be a burden but only a prop if ever needed'. Churchill crossed it out.

113 Documents 105 and 106.

114 It is interesting that Montgomery seems to have been unaware at this point how hard Tedder was working to have his hand removed from the tiller. Eisenhower had had a phone call from Tedder during the evening of 19 July, expressing disappointment over the lack of progress of GOODWOOD. According to Butcher, Tedder said that any recommendation Eisenhower cared to make regarding Montgomery would be favourably received by the British Chiefs of Staff. Tedder later wrote in his memoirs that this was misleading as it 'was quite beyond my powers to speak in the name of the British Chiefs of Staff'. However Tedder was clearly angling for Montgomery's demotion or removal. See Butcher, *Three Years with Eisenhower*, pp. 530–1; Tedder, *With Prejudice*, p. 563.

115 At his press conference Montgomery tried to persuade the assembled war correspondents that everything was going according to plan. De Guingand was present and later wrote, 'It was not a success, for I believe the war correspondents went away feeling that all was not well, and that possibly something was being held from them' (De Guingand, *Operation Victory*, p. 382).

116 Dempsey's diary gives the details: at 1630 hours, 'Saw C-in-C at my Headquarters. (a) Cdn Army will now take over the sector from incl the railway CAEN–MEZIDON to the sea. 1 Corps will come under command Cdn Army at 1200 hrs 22 Jul. (b) Second Army will take over from First Army the CAUMONT sector by 0600 hrs 24 July. This will require one division. (c) Second Army will secure the line BRETTEVILLE-SUR-LAIZE–POUSSY. (d) Second Army will prepare for the opportunity to be created by First Army. (e) Cdn Army will secure the line VIMONT–TROARN–CABOURG' (see TNA WO285/9).

117 Montgomery had invited Eisenhower – see Document 132.

118 In a letter to Simpson on 21 July Montgomery expanded on this: 'I had a long talk with Ike yesterday. It seems my name has been complete "mud" with the P.M. who considers I have been trying to prevent him personally from coming over here. I did not even know he proposed to come!! However I sent him a note by the C.I.G.S., and all now is well' (IWM, Simpson Papers).

119 The change in date that led to this amendment was conveyed to recipients of the Directive M512 in a memorandum sent out by Major-General Belchem on 22 July.

120　12th Army Group assumed control of US First Army and US Third Army on 1 August, when Patton's Third Army became operational. Patton's arrival in Normandy on 6 July had been kept secret as part of the FORTITUDE deception plan. On 14 July, Patton wrote in his diary: 'Brad says he will put me in as soon as he can. He could do it now with much benefit to himself, if he had any backbone. Of course, Monty does not want me as he fears I will steal the show, which I will' (Blumenson, *The Patton Papers 1940–45*, p. 481). 12th Army Group remained under 21st Army Group until 1 September.

121　Montgomery linked three documents and gave them an M500 series reference ('M513') as an indication of their importance: this letter of 21 July from Eisenhower, his message (M65) to Eisenhower on 22 July (Document 139) and Eisenhower's reply of 23 July (Document 143).

122　When Eisenhower visited Montgomery's HQ on 20 July he was aware that GOODWOOD had been halted and Tedder had spoken to him on the phone on the evening of 19 July hinting that he should ask for Montgomery to be relieved. On 21 July, the day after he visited Tac HQ, Eisenhower had a meeting with Tedder. Having heard the news of the assassination attempt on Hitler, Tedder said that Montgomery had lost an opportunity by his slowness. 'I asked him to act at once with Montgomery,' Tedder wrote in his memoirs. The result was this letter. Tedder saw a copy only after it had been despatched. He wrote that he commented to his personal staff that it was 'not strong enough. Montgomery can evade it. It contains no order' (Tedder, *With Prejudice*, pp. 565–7).

123　Document 106.

124　Document 111.

125　'Hit with everything' was no doubt what Eisenhower said to Montgomery at their meeting on 20 July. Montgomery had already responded before he received this letter by issuing Directive M512 on 21 July.

126　Confirmation that SHAEF was expecting a breakthrough – see note 68 above.

127　When they met on 20 July, see Document 135. 'We must preserve our organization' is presumably a reference to Montgomery's wish that Leigh-Mallory should continue in his post. On 22 July Eisenhower wrote to Portal saying that although he had initially had doubts about Leigh-Mallory's qualifications for the job, Leigh-Mallory's inexperience in support technique was 'rapidly being eliminated, and is, moreover, more than balanced by his fighting heart and desire to pull his weight in the team. I am extremely happy to have him' (Chandler (ed.), *The Papers of Dwight David Eisenhower: The War Years*, Vol. III, p. 2025).

128　Document 136.

129　See diary notes for 20 July, Document 135.

130　Churchill came to TAC on 21, 22 and 23 July. Captain Henderson, Montgomery's ADC, later recollected that it was 'common knowledge at Tac that Churchill had come to sack Monty' (Hamilton, *Monty: Master of the Battlefield*, p. 725). But Montgomery's briefing completely won over the Prime Minister. Churchill later wrote, 'The Commander-in-Chief was in the best of spirits on the eve of his largest operation, which he explained to me in all detail' (Churchill, *The Second World War*, Vol. VI, p. 24). According to Butcher, when Eisenhower spoke to Churchill on the phone on 25 July it was obvious that his visit to Montgomery had left him 'impressed with the strength of the military situation. The PM was supremely happy' (Butcher, *Three Years with Eisenhower*, pp. 535–6).

131 See note 121 above.

132 Document 136.

133 The Minister of Defence was, of course, the Prime Minister. Montgomery told Grigg in a letter on 24 July (Document 146) that this memorandum arose out of a request by the Prime Minister 'for some facts which he could "work into" his speech in the House on 2nd August'.

134 In his memoirs Grigg includes an extract from the Prime Minister's speech to the House of Commons in which this sentence features, preceded by some ironic humour on Churchill's part: 'In leaving this subject of equipment, I am going to do something that has never been done before, and I hope the House will not be shocked at the breach of precedents. I am going to make public a word of praise for the War Office. In all the forty years I have served in this House I have heard that Department steadily abused before, during and after various wars. And if my memory serves me aright, I have frequently taken part in the well-merited criticism which was their lot. But when I last saw General Montgomery in the field he used these words which he authorised me to repeat if I chose. He said: "I doubt if the War Office has ever sent an army overseas so well-equipped as the one fighting now in Normandy." That is what he said and I must say I think it is a well-justified statement' (Grigg, *Prejudice and Judgment*, p. 365).

135 Evacuation of casualties by air began on 13 June, a week earlier than planned. See Ellis, *Victory in the West*, Vol. I, p. 483.

136 Documents 137 and 139.

137 There is no indication in the Montgomery Papers when this photographic copy was made, or what happened to the original letter.

138 Commander C R 'Tommy' Thompson RN (1894–1966) was Churchill's personal assistant; Sir John Martin (1904–91) was his Principal Private Secretary.

139 Such a tour, including a visit to Caen, was arranged for Major-General Sir Hastings Ismay, Chief of Staff to the War Cabinet. Ismay wrote that he 'returned to London refreshed in mind and body' (Ismay, *The Memoirs of General Lord Ismay*, p. 361).

140 See note 121 above.

141 Document 139.

142 Document 137.

143 Document 136.

144 Tedder, having no faith in Montgomery's plan as expressed in Directive M512, was still trying to get Eisenhower to take action and form a Tactical Headquarters in France to take charge of the battle himself. In a letter to Eisenhower on 23 July he wrote, 'It is clear that in the recent operation to the

South of Caen, there was no intention to make that operation the decisive one which you so clearly indicated as necessary in your letters and signals to General Montgomery. An overwhelming air bombardment opened the door, but there was no immediate deep penetration while the door remained open' (Tedder, *With Prejudice*, pp. 568–70). If Eisenhower had read Tedder's letter when he wrote this message, he does not seem to have been influenced by it. Much later, in 1966, concerning Tedder's letter Eisenhower wrote: 'Tedder's impatience was understandable but his advice was often wide of the mark because of his exaggerated idea of what air could do for ground tactical operations' (Chandler (ed.), *The Papers of Dwight David Eisenhower: The War Years*, Vol. III, p. 2020).

145 The bomb plot against Hitler had taken place on 20 July; on 17 July Rommel had been seriously wounded in an RAF attack on his car.

146 Document 136.

147 HQ First Canadian Army under Lieutenant-General Crerar became operational at 1200 hours on 23 July. See Document 150.

148 The memoranda, all filed at LMD 60/30, set out the two sides of the dispute that had arisen between Crerar and the GOC 1 Corps, Lieutenant-General Crocker. In brief, the memoranda are: (i) Crerar's directive of 22 July for an operation by 1 Corps to relieve the Caen Canal and Ouistreham from close enemy observation and fire – as required in Montgomery's Directive M512. (ii) Crerar's memorandum of his conversation with Crocker on 24 July, in which the latter said that he had no troops fit or available to carry out such a limited operation that would achieve nothing at a cost of 500–600 casualties. (iii) Crocker's written statement of his objections. (iv) Crerar's comments on Crocker's statement.

149 Montgomery interviewed Crerar on 25 July and spoke to Crocker the following day.

150 According to Crerar's notes on the conversation, quoted in the Canadian official history, Montgomery rejected the idea of a switch because it would involve exchanging two corps staff at a difficult moment, and in any case Crocker's Corps would probably have to be put under First Canadian Army at some future point. The whole episode is discussed in Stacey, *The Victory Campaign*, pp. 196–8.

151 Crerar and Ritchie served at the War Office together in the mid-1920s; and Crerar was Commandant of the Royal Military College of Canada at Kingston, Ontario, in 1938–9.

152 In fact, after Montgomery's intervention, Crerar and Crocker had a less confrontational meeting and 1 Corps produced a plan for the operation proposed by Crerar, although changing circumstances meant that it was never carried out. Thereafter, according to Stacey, the relationship between Crerar and Crocker 'developed in a much more satisfactory manner than might have been expected'.

153 See Document 140 and note 134 above for the Prime Minister's use of Montgomery's memorandum.

154 Grigg thanked Montgomery in a long and discursive handwritten letter,

dated 25 July. Grigg wrote of the Prime Minister that 'as a result of your ministrations both oral & written he is now in an extremely good temper with us & intends, I think, to blow our own trumpet as well as yours in his next public pronouncement' (see LMD 110/6).

155 The attack down the Caen–Falaise road by Lieutenant-General Simonds' 2 Canadian Corps was codenamed Operation SPRING. It achieved its objective of keeping the Germans' attention fixed on the Caen sector, but the Canadians suffered 1500 casualties and the offensive was not continued on 26 June. In describing operations on 25 June the Canadian Official History says that 'excepting Dieppe, it was the Canadian Army's costliest day of operations in the Second World War' (see Stacey, *The Victory Campaign*, pp. 183–96; and Ellis, *Victory in the West*, Vol. I, pp. 377–9).

156 For a narrative of the American breakout – Operation COBRA – see Blumenson, *Breakout and Pursuit*, Chapters XI–XIV.

157 Lieutenant-General Lesley James McNair (1883–1944) had been Commanding General of the Army Ground Forces in the United States since 1942. In July 1944 he had just taken over from Patton as commander of the fictitious First US Army Group in south-eastern England, a key element in Operation FORTITUDE, when he made the fatal decision to observe the opening of Operation COBRA. See Hesketh, *FORTITUDE: The D-Day Deception Campaign*, pp. 248–50 and 269–71.

158 Document 144.

159 The holograph addition is shown in italics.

160 In addition to his directive on the operation in the Caen canal area, referred to in note 148 above, Crerar had also sent Crocker a number of copies of a general Tactical Directive on the need to confound German expectations by employing both surprise and firepower when mounting an attack, together with extracts from a lecture he had given. These two items ran to six typed foolscap pages (see LMD 60/30). Crocker no doubt considered that Crerar was guilty of trying to teach his grandmother to suck eggs.

161 Document 148.

162 Lieutenant-General Sir Archibald Nye, the VCIGS, visited Montgomery on 26 July.

163 After lunch the Prime Minister sent for Brooke, who wrote in his diary: 'Eisenhower had been lunching with him and had again run down Montgomery and described his stickiness and the reaction in the American papers! The old story again: "He was sparing British forces at the expense of the Americans, who were having all the casualties."' Brooke was asked to dine the following evening with Eisenhower and Bedell Smith (Danchev and Todman (eds), *Alanbrooke: War Diaries*, pp. 574–5).

164 Montgomery does not refer to a visit by Leigh-Mallory in his diary notes for 26 July (Document 153). In the diary notes he dictated for 26 July, Leigh-Mallory recorded that Montgomery 'had a Russian Admiral and four Generals dining with him. After dinner, we got down to business and the results of our planning will, I hope, appear in due course' (see TNA AIR37/784).

165 Probably prompted by Eisenhower, Tedder went to see Montgomery on 1 August to arrange a conference to examine the technique of air bombing in the light of the four times heavy bombers had been used in the land battle. Montgomery sent a telephone message to Leigh-Mallory at 1600 hrs that day to say that no date had been fixed for the conference because he felt there should be a careful staff study of the problem first. Montgomery's file note recording the substance of the telephone message to Leigh-Mallory continues, 'Tedder has expressed his view to me today that when things have not been 100% good the probable reason is that the soldier has not expressed clearly to the airman exactly what he wanted done. I have told Tedder that I disagree strongly with that view, and that to the best of my knowledge the Army Comd. and his Air Group Comd. have always been quite clear as to what each wanted of the other' (see LMD 60/42).

166 This is the document Montgomery labelled 'A' and refers to in his diary notes for 27 July (Document 159).

167 The purpose of the visit was a briefing session and lunch. Nye was accompanied by his Military Assistant, Major Peter Earle, whose diary is preserved at the Imperial War Museum. On arrival at Tac HQ, Earle wrote in his diary that they received a military briefing: 'In his caravan Monty was at his best. Clear, simple, understanding, of single mind and purpose. Without the caravan at lunch he was terrible. Raucous, loud acting, public house jokes …' Despite this, Earle became one of Montgomery's Liaison Officers in April 1945.

168 This is the document Montgomery labelled 'B' and refers to in his diary notes for 27 July (Document 159).

169 Montgomery explains in Documents 155 and 159 that this must refer to the fact that the Canadians were unable to secure May-sur-Orne and Tilly on 25 July. It was not a 'serious setback', but unfortunately it had apparently been put out to the press in that way. Sir Alexander Cadogan, PUS at the Foreign Office, wrote in his diary for 27 July: 'Press v. gloomy about Normandy but found out later this had been put out by a junior American numbskull in SHAEF – probably anti-Monty' (Dilks (ed.), *The Diaries of Sir Alexander Cadogan*, p. 651).

170 This is the document Montgomery labelled 'C' and refers to in his diary notes for 27 July (Document 159).

171 M515 of 27 July, Document 157.

172 Quite such a pessimistic headline does not appear in Montgomery's two newspaper cuttings albums covering July 1944 (LMD 5 and 10). Perhaps they were simply omitted from the selection. The most downbeat headline, in the *Daily Sketch* for 25 July, refers to a 'lull' in the fighting.

173 See Stacey, *The Victory Campaign*, pp. 190–2 for the 2nd Canadian Infantry Division in Operation SPRING.

174 The original is Document 149.

175 Document 136.

176 The re-grouping was carried out at speed, so that the new operation in the Caumont sector – Operation BLUECOAT – was launched on 30 July.

177 Document 136.

178 Royal Warwickshire Regiment.

179 Para 75 refers to diary notes for 26 July – Document 153.

180 Document 154.

181 Document 156.

182 Document 158.

183 Document 157.

184 Chandler (*The Papers of Dwight David Eisenhower: The War Years*, Vol. IV, p. 2041) notes that M68 was Montgomery's response to Eisenhower's message – Document 163 – pressing him to speed up the attack. However, Montgomery has annotated his copy of Eisenhower's message 'Received 2200 hrs on 28–7–44. B.L.M.', by which time M68 had already been sent out (1730 hrs).

185 Montgomery stuck the original letter in his letter album (BLM 1) in the 1960s. There is also a transcript of the letter, possibly made in July 1944 so that a typescript copy could go as an appendix to Montgomery's diary notes (see Document 164). In 2006 the only copy of the transcript in Montgomery's papers was found in an envelope that was labelled in Montgomery's hand, 'Brooke's letter re Ike's complaint that the British were not doing their share of the fighting in Normandy July 1944' (LMD 112/1). Montgomery may not have had it copied until later, when he wanted to give a copy to Arthur Bryant, who quotes it in *Triumph in the West 1943–1946*, pp. 243–5.

186 By this Brooke presumably means the question of whether the British and Canadians were doing their share of the fighting in Normandy.

187 As usual Brooke gives a candid account of the dinner in his diary entry for 27 July; see Danchev and Todman (eds), *Alanbrooke: War Diaries*, p. 575.

188 Eisenhower wrote to Brooke on 4 August saying that he had called on Montgomery twice 'on the spur of the moment' and was intending to stay in France from Monday, 7 August. Brooke replied on 5 August: 'I am delighted that matters settled themselves without your needing to call on me to accompany you on your visit to Monty' (Eisenhower Papers, copy in the Nigel Hamilton Research Papers at the IWM).

189 Document 157.

190 Document 157.

191 Orders had been issued to General Maitland Wilson in the Mediterranean on 2 July 1944 to carry out the landings in the south of France on 15 August.

192 Operation FORTITUDE kept German forces in Pas de Calais until late July.

193 Dempsey's diary entry reads: '1400 Flew to Headquarters 21 Army Group and saw C-in-C. Drove with him to Headquarters First Army and saw General Bradley. My attack with the RIGHT wing of Second Army will start on Sunday 30 July in order to take advantage of the favourable situation which is arising. Fire support will be sketchy, but it is most desirable to take advantage of the situation as soon as possible' (TNA WO285/9).

194 Document 161.

195 Message M68, Document 160.

196 The Polish Armoured Division began to land in Normandy on 30 July.

197 Eisenhower was able to fly to Normandy that day after he had written this letter: see Montgomery's diary notes for 29 July – Document 167.

198 Document 163.

199 Document 160.

200 For this meeting, see diary notes for 28 July, Document 164.

201 Montgomery repeats this criticism of Eisenhower for always talking 'at the top of his voice' in a letter to Brooke on 14 August (Document 197).

202 Operation BLUECOAT. For summaries of the fighting 30 July–4 August, see Montgomery, *Normandy to the Baltic*, pp. 112–14; and Wilmot, *The Struggle for Europe*, pp. 438–42.

Notes to Documents 168–211, August 1944, pp. 261–310

1 Grigg headed this letter 'PRIVATE AND PERSONAL'.

2 One of these was via Brooke – see Montgomery's letter of 27 July, Document 156. There appears to be no direct communication with Grigg on the subject of the press at this point.

3 The reports that Second Army had suffered 'quite a serious set-back'; see the Prime Minister's letter to Montgomery of 27 July, Document 154.

4 Presumably when they dined together on the evening of 27 July.

5 Brigadier Alfred Geoffrey Neville, who was in charge of public relations for 21st Army Group.

6 Roosevelt was elected for a fourth term as President on 7 November 1944.

7 There is no apparent reason why Grigg spells Coningham's name incorrectly here. General Patton uses the same spelling in his diary.

8 Badnam (or badname) means to speak in a disparaging manner about someone.

9 Richard Lamb describes the manner in which Grigg stirs up Montgomery against Eisenhower and others in this letter as 'inexcusable' (Lamb, *Montgomery in Europe 1943–1945*, p. 155).

10 The head of the SHAEF Public Relations Division in August 1944 was Brigadier General Thomas J. Davis. On 12 August Butcher visited Davis in hospital: 'T.J. has worn himself down as Public Relations chief,' he wrote in his diary (*Three Years with Eisenhower*, p. 549).

11 Sir Archibald Sinclair was the Secretary of State for Air 1940–5. It has not been possible to identify the 'bogus airman'.

12 Montgomery headed this letter 'Private. Personal and Top Secret'. He usually addressed Grigg as 'Secretary of State' rather than 'P.J.'

13 Simpson has annotated this letter 'Written about 8pm' under the date.

14 Rennes was occupied by the Americans on 4 August after the Germans evacuated it; the citadel at St Malo held out until 17 August and the Ile de Cézembre off St Malo until 2 September. Montgomery's information is frequently over-optimistic at this time.

15 Even with his old friend Simpson, Montgomery would not drop his guard

by appearing to concede that his operations had not gone 'according to plan'.

16   Major-General Erskine had been GOC 7th Armoured Division since January 1943. 'Adverse reports' on Erskine by Dempsey and Montgomery, dated 3 August, can be found at BLM 119/15. Erskine was replaced by Major-General Verney on 4 August. See also Document 171.

17   Montgomery had brought Lieutenant-General Gerard Bucknall back from the Mediterranean to command 30 Corps. 'Adverse reports' on Bucknall by Dempsey and Montgomery, dated 2 August, can be found at BLM 119/14. Bucknall was replaced by Lieutenant-General Horrocks on 4 August. See also Document 171.

18   This message is stamped 'ULTRA TOP SECRET' at the top and then in typescript it is marked 'Special Unnumbered Signal. Personal, private and confidential'.

19   The progress of the message is charted by annotations indicating that it was sent at 0745, received at 1105 and delivered at 1411 hours. Montgomery has written on it, 'Received 3 Aug 44 at 1500 hrs. <u>BLM</u>'.

20   The Prime Minister visited Montgomery on 7 August. See Document 181.

21   Montgomery has annotated the draft '<u>ULTRA TOPSEC</u>' and 'Sent 1230 hrs on 4 August 1944'. There is a copy of the message as circulated at the War Office at LMD 118/29. For some reason it was transmitted in two parts. The first part, ending 'that will be enough', was sent at 1237 hours, the second part at 1240 hours. The version circulated at the War Office omits paragraph 6.

22   US 8 Corps, commanded by Lieutenant-General Troy H. Middleton. The whole of Third Army originally had the job of clearing the Brittany peninsula and capturing ports through which American supplies were going to come. On 3 August Bradley issued a Letter of Instruction to the effect that now that the German disorganisation seemed so thorough, Patton was to use only 'a minimum of forces' for Brittany. The remainder were to be ready to attack eastwards. For the importance of this change of plan, see Ellis, *Victory in the West*, Vol. I, pp. 403–4; and Blumenson, *Breakout and Pursuit*, pp. 430–2.

23   The Prime Minister replied on 4 August saying he wished to visit Montgomery on 5 August, accompanied by the First Sea Lord, to discuss naval activity to help clear up the Brest peninsula and the question of switching the ANVIL/DRAGOON landings to Brittany. See LMD 60/44.

24   This letter is a good example of Brooke's involvement in senior appointments and anticipating possible changes. Why Montgomery had formed this view of O'Connor is not explained in Montgomery's papers.

25   Lieutenant-General Sir Sidney Kirkman had taken command of 13 Corps in Italy in February 1944.

26   Lieutenant-General Sir Richard McCreery had been in command of 10 Corps in Italy since August 1943, having been Alexander's Chief of Staff 1942–3.

27   Horrocks took command of 30 Corps on 4 August.

28   Brigadier Harry Ripley Mackeson (1905–64) took command of 22nd Armoured Brigade on 10 August 1944.

29 Major-General F.E.W. Simpson, Director of Military Operations.

30 Montgomery's nightly sitreps to Brooke in response to this request begin on
    5 August (BLM 110/31) and continue until 7 May 1945 (BLM 113/40).

31 i.e. air portable.

32 Document 175.

33 This refers to the map showing 'Development of Land Battle' used by
    Montgomery for his address at Exercise THUNDERCLAP on 7 April – see
    LMD 56/5. The map was the origin of the controversy over the significance
    of the 'phase lines' (see Document 36 and note 14 for April's documents) set
    out at the Exercise.

34 Document 175.

35 M517: Document 177.

36 No copy extant in the Montgomery Papers.

37 There is a carbon copy of Bucknall's two-page letter of 3 August, concerning
    the speed at which 30 Corps should have been expected to carry its objective
    on 30 July, in the Bucknall Papers 80/33/1, folder 12, at the IWM.

38 Major-General Douglas Wimberley (1896–1983). Wimberley moved from
    the Staff College to be Director of Infantry at the War Office in 1944.
    Erskine became Head of the SHAEF Mission to Belgium.

39 On 4 August Brooke had sent Montgomery a copy of a letter dated 31 July
    from Sir Alexander Cadogan, PUS for Foreign Affairs, saying that the
    Foreign Secretary had 'heard from certain private sources that there have
    been some rather bad cases of looting by some of our units in Normandy'.
    Brooke replied asking for 'more definite evidence', but none seems to have
    been forthcoming (see LMD 123/3, 4 and 6). Those under suspicion may
    have included Montgomery and his staff at Tac HQ. Colonel the Hon Leo
    Russell had been appointed as chief staff officer at Tac HQ at the instigation
    of de Guingand. Russell was shocked to find in July 1944 that the young
    officers on Montgomery's staff were augmenting the rations at Tac HQ with
    livestock (particularly a pig) found in the Normandy countryside. Russell
    regarded this as looting, but after failing to convince Montgomery and then
    de Guingand that this was a serious matter, his employment at Tac HQ
    ceased and he returned to England on 18 July. Russell's written report (see
    LMD 123/2), dated 4 August 1944, was read by the VCIGS but shelved.
    However, Russell was the son of Baron Ampthill, and it is possible that if he
    spoke out about the behaviour of Tac HQ officers this might have reached
    influential ears by the end of July. When he came to write his memoirs,
    Montgomery certainly thought that it was rumours being spread in London
    'by a colonel that I had removed from my Tac Headquarters' that had led
    to the Foreign Office complaint (Montgomery, *Memoirs*, p. 264). As an
    example of comments made by Leo Russell, John Colville, Churchill's
    private secretary, wrote in his diary on 3 October 1944: 'Dined with Lady
    Ampthill. Guy, Leo and Phyllis Russell were there. Leo told me he had
    resigned from Monty's staff in France (a) because of the bombing of French
    towns, much of which he had reason to think unnecessary from the military
    standpoint, (b) because Monty allowed his own staff to loot and rejected

Leo's protests, (c) because Monty was at heart "a fascist"' (Colville, *The Fringes of Power*, pp. 153–4).

40　Montgomery wrote to François Coulet (1906–84), the Commissioner of the Republic for the region of Normandy, on 7 August asking for any evidence of looting (LMD 123/7). Interestingly, amongst M. Coulet's family papers there is Montgomery's letter, and the handwritten draft of a reply: 'I am sorry to say that, in fact, many cases of looting have been reported to me … I know one must make allowances for fighting men in the front line but all the same the thing is worrying because of the effect it is beginning to have on the relations between the troops and the population. If you think you can stop it I would be very grateful' (copy provided to me by Lady Liddell Hart in 1984). However, M. Coulet must have changed his mind about sending this letter to Montgomery, who records in his memoirs: 'I took the matter up at once with M. Coulet, General de Gaulle's representative in the lodgement area, and was informed that he had received no complaint and that I could rest assured that the allegations were without foundation' (Montgomery, *Memoirs*, p. 264). However, on 10 August Montgomery did send a letter to Bradley, Dempsey and Crerar saying that he had received 'well-substantiated reports' of looting and that if any were proved, 'the offender must be taken to task' (see TNA WO205/5d).

41　The Prime Minister's message (LMD 60/44), dated 4 August, said that he wished to discuss naval activity to help clear up the Brest peninsula and the question of switching ANVIL/DRAGOON to Brittany.

42　For the background to the Prime Minister's short-lived campaign to have the south of France landings moved to Brittany, see Gilbert, *Road to Victory*, pp. 874–81.

43　According to Martin Gilbert, Churchill's aircraft 'arrived over the Cherbourg peninsula, but was then recalled, as fog on the landing strip at which Churchill was expected had caused a preceding plane to crash, and all of its occupants had been killed' (Gilbert, *Road to Victory*, p. 877.) Churchill flew to France on 7 August and visited Montgomery for an hour – see Document 184.

44　His name had been taken in vain by Eisenhower in early July – see Documents 100, 101, 102, 103, and 106. In his memoirs Montgomery somewhat confuses the two occasions when he was involved in discussions over ANVIL after D-Day. He says it was in early August that Eisenhower sought to enlist his support for mounting ANVIL in the face of pressure from the Prime Minister to abandon it. 'I wish now – as I have often wished – that I hadn't half-heartedly concurred that early August day' (*Memoirs*, p. 221). In fact, this fits better with his meeting with Eisenhower on 2 July. In early August it was Churchill who tried – unsuccessfully – to win Montgomery over to the idea of switching the landings from the south of France to Brittany. In his memoirs Montgomery expresses the view that ANVIL was 'one of the great strategic mistakes of the war' (ibid.).

45　Montgomery also sent a short sitrep (M80) to Brooke at 2215 hours that evening (see BLM 110/32).

46   On Hitler's orders the German army launched a counter-attack westwards
– Operation LÜTTICH – in an attempt to reach the sea at Avranches and
cut off the American divisions to the south. For narratives of the defeat of
the Mortain offensive, see Blumenson, *Breakout and Pursuit*, pp. 456–75
and Ellis, *Victory in the West*, Vol. I, pp. 412–16. The Allies were warned
during the evening of 6 August of the impending German attack by ULTRA
– 'a secret source', as Patton refers to it in his diary for 7 August. There
is nothing in Montgomery's papers that gives credence to Group Captain
F.W. Winterbotham's assertion, published in 1974, that ULTRA had given
warning as early as 2 August – a claim now discounted by historians (see
Winterbotham, *The Ultra Secret*, pp. 148–52, and Bennett, *Ultra in the West*,
pp. 115–19).

47   The German garrison of Lorient did not surrender until 9 May 1945.

48   Liaison Officer. For the system of Liaison Officers, see Montgomery,
Memoirs, p. 531.

49   See Document 178 and note 42 above.

50   The Canadian attack towards Falaise, codenamed Operation TOTALIZE.

51   For the decision to direct the Americans north towards Alencon to 'close the
ring' behind the German forces in the Mortain Pocket, see note 55 below.

52   For a narrative with maps of the Canadian Operation TOTALIZE 7–10
August, see Stacey, *The Victory Campaign*, pp. 216–31.

53   Major-General Keller was replaced in command of 3rd Canadian Infantry
Division by Major-General D.C. Spry.

54   US XV Corps took Le Mans on 8 August.

55   This key decision, the origins of the Falaise–Argentan gap/pocket, followed a
telephone conversation between Bradley and Montgomery. Eisenhower wrote
a personal diary entry on 8 August that the Canadian attack from Caen was
not making much progress. 'It therefore appears to me that the American right
wing on this front should swing in closer in an effort to destroy the enemy
by attacking him in the rear. On a visit to Bradley today I found that he had
already acted on this idea and had secured Montgomery's agreement to a
sharp change in direction towards the northeast instead of continuing directly
towards the east, as envisaged in M-517' (Ferrell (ed.), *The Eisenhower Diaries*,
p. 125; see also Blumenson, *Breakout and Pursuit*, p. 492).

56   Paragraph 8 is the first paragraph of the diary notes for 7 August, Document
181.

57   The holograph additions are shown in italics.

58   German tanks and other vehicles set on fire by air attack. In a message to
his COs on 18 August Crerar enumerated the results of Allied air attacks on
German tanks under the headings 'flamers', 'smokers' and 'damaged' (see
Stacey, *The Victory Campaign*, p. 258).

59   For a description of the 'short' bombing, see Stacey, *The Victory Campaign*,
pp. 223–4.

60   Lieutenant-General Sir Humfrey Gale (1890–1971) was Deputy Chief
of Staff and Chief Administrative Officer at SHAEF; the Quartermaster-
General (QMG) at the War Office was General Sir Thomas Riddell-Webster.

61 Lieutenant-General Sir Frederick Morgan (1894–1967) was Deputy Chief of Staff at SHAEF.

62 Mountbatten had lunch with Eisenhower in Normandy on 17 August, so it is likely that this was the day he also saw Montgomery, although it is not referred to in the latter's diary notes. In a letter to Oliver Leese on 21 August, Montgomery wrote: 'Dickie Mountbatten came to see me the other day. He is a most delightful person but I fear his knowledge of how to make war is not very great!! You ought to go out there as his Army C-in-C, and keep him on the rails!' (IWM, Leese Papers).

63 General Marshall sent Eisenhower a message on 8 August regarding the possibility of getting American divisions into Europe more quickly by sending them through Brest. Eisenhower replied on 9 August that he was 'not willing to detach from the main army at this juncture additional forces merely in order to save a week or so in the time of capturing the Brest peninsula ports' (Chandler (ed.), *The Papers of Dwight David Eisenhower: The War Years*, Vol. IV, pp. 2062–3).

64 Document 177.

65 Document 177.

66 Document 185.

67 Nantes was occupied by the Americans on 12 August. The citadel at St Malo held out until 17 August.

68 Diary notes for 7 August, Document 181.

69 Diary notes for 8 August, Document 183.

70 Document 187.

71 Document 177.

72 Document 187.

73 Document 189.

74 Document 177.

75 Brigadier (later General Sir) Horatius Murray (1903–89) was commanding 153rd Infantry Brigade in Normandy. He took over as GOC 6th Armoured Division in Italy on 21 August.

76 Document 188.

77 Document 177.

78 Document 189.

79 For Personal Message of 11 August, see BLM 123/19 or the reproduction in Montgomery, *Forward to Victory*.

80 Document 190.

81 A vast number of words have been written about Bradley's decision on the evening of 12 August to order Patton to halt south of Argentan, at the agreed boundary between 12 and 21 Army Groups, when Patton wanted to go on to Falaise and close the 'gap'. Patton blamed Montgomery, but Bradley later wrote that he alone made the decision, for good military reasons, without consulting Montgomery about a possible change in the boundary line. He goes on to criticise severely Montgomery's conduct of operations on the northern side of the gap. Eisenhower was having dinner at 12 Army Group HQ on the evening of 12 August and supported Bradley's decision (see

Bradley, *A Soldier's Story*, pp. 375–8 and Eisenhower, *Crusade in Europe*, p. 305; and discussion of the decision in Blumenson, *Breakout and Pursuit*, pp. 506–9). When Montgomery came to write his memoirs, he must have been aware that there had been a good deal of post-war criticism over his conduct of operations in mid-August (including by his own chief of staff; see de Guingand, *Operation Victory*, pp. 406–10). However, it was not a matter over which he felt the need to defend himself. In fact, he does not discuss events from the end of July to 20 August at all in his memoirs, except to say that Patton's remark on the evening of 12 August that he could 'drive the British back into the sea for another Dunkirk' was the kind of thing that exacerbated the 'feelings' between British and American forces after the battle of Normandy. See Montgomery, *Memoirs*, p. 262.

82 Document 192.

83 Of 9 August – Document 184.

84 On 8 and 9 August – see Danchev and Todman (eds), *Alanbrooke: War Diaries*, pp. 578–9.

85 Brooke was in Italy 19–24 August.

86 Argentan itself was not occupied by the Americans until 20 August.

87 The Canadian attack on 14 August was codenamed Operation TRACTABLE.

88 Major-General T.G. Rennie had succeeded Major-General Bullen-Smith as GOC 51st Highland Division on 26 July 1944.

89 There is some additional detail regarding this conference in Dempsey's diary for 13 August: 'Flew to 21 Army Group and there met C-in-C and General Bradley. We discussed future operations – particularly as regards Army Group and Army boundaries; and the bringing up by Third Army of another Corps directed on LAIGLE. So long as the Northward move of Third Army meets little opposition, the two leading Corps will disregard inter-Army boundaries. The whole aim is to establish forces across the enemy's lines of communication so as to impede – if not to prevent entirely – his withdrawal' (TNA, WO285/9).

90 Document 195.

91 There is a version of this in Montgomery's diary under 13 August. See Document 196.

92 Prince Bernhard of the Netherlands (1911–2004) became Commander-in-Chief of the Dutch armed forces in September 1944.

93 Eisenhower had established his Advance Command Post near Tournières in Normandy on 7 August.

94 Montgomery could be confident that such comments would be received sympathetically by Brooke in the light of Brooke's own comments about Eisenhower in his letter to Montgomery of 28 July (Document 161).

95 For M92 of 14 August, see BLM 115/15.

96 For the Canadian attack – Operation TRACTABLE – launched on 14 August and leading to the capture of Falaise on 16 August, see Stacey, *The Victory Campaign*, pp. 238–51.

97 Document 198.

98 See Document 200.

99 Document 202.

100 It was somewhat premature to say that the eastern end of the Falaise Pocket had been closed on 17 August. The First Canadian Army and the First US Army linked up at Chambois on 19 August, but it was not until 21 August that the gap was 'at last closed in strength' (Ellis, *Victory in the West*, Vol. I, p. 447).

101 But Bradley did not agree entirely. Was this a case of Montgomery hearing what he wanted to hear? Or was Bradley guilty of being too reticent in order to avoid a confrontation with Montgomery in full flow? Montgomery was sure enough of the position to write to Brooke on 18 August that Bradley agreed entirely with his plan (Document 206). And when, at a meeting on 23 August, Montgomery found that Bradley did not support him, he concluded that he had 'changed his mind'. Montgomery recorded in his diary that Bradley 'now considers that 12 Army Group should go off eastwards and invade the SAAR. This was a new one on me and clearly IKE has been persuading him – or Bedel Smith' (see LMD 61/1). Montgomery included this version of events in his memoirs. Bradley took the opportunity to rebut it in *A General's Life*, the autobiography published after his death. He accused Montgomery of writing not only 'incorrectly' but also 'deceitfully'. The contemporary record in Montgomery's diary notes seems to show that the charge of deceit is unjustified, although he may have been guilty of self-deception (see Montgomery, *Memoirs*, pp. 266–8; Bradley and Blair, *A General's Life*, pp. 313–14).

But was Montgomery ever guilty of deliberate misrepresentation in a situation like this? There is a clear hint that Kit Dawnay thought he was in his essay in *Monty at Close Quarters*. One evening Montgomery asked Dawnay to remain in the room while he urged Eisenhower to agree to a single-thrust advance into Germany. 'In the end,' writes Dawnay, 'Monty's relentless arguments reduced Ike to a condition of speechlessness and he said he was ready for bed. I got him a whisky and soda, escorted him to his room and then came downstairs again. Monty immediately said "Get this message sent to the C.I.G.S." I wrote it down at his dictation and was astonished to discover that he was claiming that Ike had agreed in general with the single-thrust strategy. I read the message back and asked if it was correct. He assented. I said: "May I say something, sir?" "Yes, certainly." "Ike does *not* agree, sir." His only comment was "Send that message, Kit." And so I did. But Ike had not agreed' (Howarth (ed.), *Monty at Close Quarters*, p. 16). So was this deceit, or did Montgomery simply believe that speechlessness meant consent?

102 Document 206. In his message replying to Montgomery on 18 August, Brooke simply said that he entirely agreed with 'your plan contained in M99' (LMD 117/17).

103 Document 204.

104 In his memoirs Kennedy includes an account of this visit written at the time (Kennedy, *The Business of War*, pp. 341–9).

105 Although Montgomery says he had not previously discussed the matter with Eisenhower, Butcher writes in his diary entry for 14 August that Montgomery had proposed to Eisenhower that he should be given all the

maintenance available to Allied forces, and then 'his 21st Army Group could rush right on into Berlin' (Butcher, *Three Years with Eisenhower*, p. 551). Bradley confirms that it was on 13 August, 'that busy, vexing Sunday' as he puts it, that Montgomery had unveiled to him his plan for a massive single thrust to Berlin, with all the Allies' resources under his command (see Bradley and Blair, *A General's Life*, p. 310).

106 The V2 rocket campaign against England began on 8 September.

107 See note 101 above.

108 Brooke replied the same day saying that he entirely agreed with 'your plan contained in M99' (LMD 117/17). Montgomery discussed the matter with Eisenhower at Tac HQ on 23 August, having found earlier in the day that Bradley had 'changed his mind' about 12th Army Group and 21st Army Group operating together (see diary notes for 23 August: LMD 61/1).

109 See BLM 110/45.

110 The 51st Highland Division (1 Corps) complained on 19 August that the previous day there had been 40 incidents of attack on them by Allied aircraft, resulting in 51 casualties. For this and other examples, see Stacey, *The Victory Campaign*, p. 257.

111 See BLM 110/47.

112 This incident arose from a story filed with the Associated Press by American journalist, Wes Gallagher. Eisenhower announced on 14 August that Bradley would command US 12th Army Group. The following day Gallagher reported that Montgomery and Bradley were now on the same level, apparently based on information he had been given at Patton's Third Army HQ. According to Harry Butcher, this was passed by Ministry of Information censors, by-passing SHAEF. The report was put out by the BBC on the 9 p.m. news on 15 August, causing angry comment in the British press about Montgomery's 'demotion'. The story was corrected by SHAEF. However, SHAEF's correction did not explain that it was only a matter of timing and that, come 1 September, Montgomery and Bradley would indeed be on an equal footing under Eisenhower. So there were now grumblings in the American press about 'British dominance'. As a result, Eisenhower sent a long message to General Marshall on 19 July, explaining how the confusion had arisen and the true position regarding the command structure. See Butcher, *Three Years with Eisenhower*, p. 556; Chandler (ed.), *The Papers of Dwight David Eisenhower: The War Years*, Vol. IV, pp. 2074–7; and Lamb, *Montgomery in Europe*, p. 181.

113 The leading article condemns SHAEF's handling of war news as 'amateurish, inconsistent and confusing'. Zec's cartoon picks up on this by showing Montgomery and Eisenhower looking over their shoulders and then rapidly turning their heads to look forwards. Looking back the headlines are 'Pessimism', 'There's still a long way to go', 'Monty's demoted' and 'Nazi resistance stiffening'; and looking forwards they read 'Optimism', 'Terrific advances – anything may happen', 'Monty is <u>not</u> demoted' and 'It's in the bag'. The caption to the cartoon reads 'That's S.H.A.E.F. – That was!' See Montgomery's newspaper cuttings album, LMD 5.

114 See BLM 126/20.

115 Message to the Prime Minister M101 of 18 August, a brief sitrep, see BLM 110/46.

116 See BLM 110/48.

117 In return, according to Eden's memoirs, Montgomery 'expounded to me his own plan for future operations, then under discussion between him and the Supreme Commander. Montgomery was already looking keenly and far into the future, beyond any present argument.' Later in the week, Eden noted in his diary on 25 August that in meetings with Nye and Ismay, both had talked 'about Ike's proposal to take over direction of operations himself. His plan and Monty's are not the same, latter implying greater concentration of force towards Pas de Calais and Flanders' (Avon, *The Eden Memoirs: The Reckoning*, pp. 468–9).

118 In his thank-you letter, dated 22 August, Eden wrote to Montgomery, 'All that you told me was of the utmost value to me, and I need hardly tell you how glad I was to have this opportunity to hear from you at first hand about the battle, and about your plans for the future. I was deeply impressed by all that I saw in Normandy, and not least by the fact that all the troops I saw were so obviously fit and confident. They have the mien of victors about them' (LMD 113/1).

Notes to Appendix, pp. 311–13

1 However, in October 1944 O'Connor offered his resignation over Montgomery's removal of one of O'Connor's subordinates (Major-General Silvester of the US 7th Armoured Division) without consulting him. Dempsey persuaded O'Connor to withdraw his resignation, but in November Montgomery agreed to O'Connor's posting to be GOC-in-C Eastern Army, India (see Baynes, *The Forgotten Victor*, pp. 240–6).

2 In 1940, when Brooke was in command of 2 Corps and Montgomery of the 3rd Infantry Division.

3 Possibly prompted by Brooke's letter, Montgomery commended this passage from Kipling's *If* to all the men of 21st Army Group in his Personal Message of 23 October 1944 (see BLM 123/24, reproduced in *Forward to Victory*). Another fan of the poem was General Patton. He wrote to his son on 21 August 1944 that he had 'used one principle in these operations':

> Fill the unforgiving minute
> With sixty seconds worth of distance run.

That is the whole art of war, and when you get to be a general, remember it! (Blumenson, *The Patton Papers*, p. 52)

4 For a further score or more of letters congratulating Montgomery on his promotion, see BLM 97.

5 Alexander was promoted to Field Marshal in December 1944, backdated to the capture of Rome on 4 June.

Bibliography

I Manuscript material

A Imperial War Museum

This volume draws on the following collections at the IWM:

The Montgomery Papers

Part I

    Section A: Letter Album 1914–46, includes letters to Montgomery from Brooke and Grigg during the Normandy campaign.

    Section E: Papers January 1944–May 1946.

Part II

    Section A: Montgomery personalia, includes betting book, autograph album and pocket diary for 1944.

    Section B: Press cuttings albums.

    Section E: Papers January 1944–May 1946.

The papers of

    Major-General David Belchem.

    Major Tom Bigland.

    Lieutenant-General Gerard Bucknall.

    Lieutenant-Colonel Christopher Dawnay.

    Major Peter Earle.

    Lieutenant-General Sir Oliver Leese.

    Lieutenant-General Sir Giffard Martel.

    Major and Mrs Reynolds.

    General Sir Frank Simpson.

The Nigel Hamilton Research Papers contain photocopies of Montgomery material from archives in North America, including the Eisenhower Library at Abilene.

B Other archive repositories

Churchill Archives Centre, Churchill College, Cambridge: Grigg Papers.

Liddell Hart Centre for Military Archives, King's College London: Alanbrooke Papers; O'Connor Papers.

The National Archives, Kew:

    AIR37/784 Diary of Air Chief Marshal Sir Trafford Leigh-Mallory.

    CAB106/1037 Notes for Staff Conference, 21st Army Group, 13 January 1944.

CAB106/1064 Extracts from General Crerar's diary.
Prem3/339/11 PM's visits to Overlord June 1944 – March 1945.
WO205 21st Army Group: Military Headquarters Papers.
WO285 Papers of Lieutenant-General Sir Miles Dempsey, including his diary 6 June–13 September 1944, 'The First 100 Days. Operation Overlord – from the beaches to the Dutch frontier' (WO285/9).
Southampton University: Mountbatten Papers

II Published works

A Books by and about Montgomery

Barnett, Correlli, *The Desert Generals* (Kimber, 1960).
Baxter, Colin F., *Field Marshal Bernard Law Montgomery, 1887–1976: A Selected Bibliography* (Greenwood Press, 1999).
Brett-James, Antony, *Conversations with Montgomery* (Kimber, 1984).
Brooks, Stephen (ed.), *Montgomery and the Eighth Army* (The Bodley Head/ Army Records Society, 1991).
Chalfont, Lord, *Montgomery of Alamein* (Weidenfeld and Nicolson, 1976)
Clifton James, M.E., *I Was Monty's Double* (Rider and Co, 1954).
Hamilton, Nigel, *Monty*: Vol. 1 *The Making of a General 1887–1942* (Hamish Hamilton, 1981).
—— *Monty*: Vol. 2 *Master of the Battlefield 1942–1944* (Hamish Hamilton, 1983).
—— *Monty*: Vol. 3 *The Field Marshal 1944–1976* (Hamish Hamilton, 1986).
—— *Monty: The Man behind the Legend* (Lennard Publishing, 1987).
—— *The Full Monty: Montgomery of Alamein 1887–1942* (Allen Lane, 2001).
—— *Montgomery: D-Day Commander* (Potomac Books, 2006).
Hart, Stephen Ashley, *Montgomery and 'Colossal Cracks'* (Praeger, 2000).
Henderson, Johnny and Jamie Douglas-Home, *Watching Monty* (Allan Sutton, 2005).
Horne, Alistair and David Montgomery, *The Lonely Leader: Monty 1944–1945* (Macmillan, 1994).
Howarth, T.E.B. (ed.), *Monty at Close Quarters* (Leo Cooper, 1985).
Kirby, Norman, *1100 Miles with Monty* (Sutton, 1989).
Lamb, Richard, *Montgomery in Europe 1943–1945* (Buchan and Enright, 1983).
Lewin, Ronald, *Montgomery as Military Commander* (Batsford, 1971).
Montgomery, Field Marshal B.L., *Ten Chapters, 1942 to 1945* (Hutchinson, 1945).
—— *Forward to Victory* (Hutchinson, 1946).
—— *Normandy to the Baltic* (Hutchinson, 1947).
—— *El Alamein to the River Sangro* (Hutchinson, 1948).
—— *The Memoirs* (Collins, 1958).
—— *An Approach to Sanity* (Collins, 1959).
—— *The Path to Leadership* (Collins, 1962).
—— *Three Continents* (Collins, 1962).
—— *A History of Warfare* (Rainbird, 1968).

Montgomery, Brian, *A Field Marshal in the Family* (Constable, 1973).

Moorehead, Alan, *Montgomery* (Hamish Hamilton, 1946).

Thompson, R.W., *The Montgomery Legend* (Allen and Unwin, 1967).

—— *Montgomery the Field Marshal* (Allen and Unwin, 1969)

B Memoirs, edited diaries and papers and biographies

Avon, Lord, *The Eden Memoirs: The Reckoning* (Cassell, 1971).

Baynes, John, *The Forgotten Victor: General Sir Richard O'Connor* (Brassey's, 1989).

Belchem, Major-General David, *All in the Day's March* (Collins, 1978).

Blumenson, Martin, *The Patton Papers 1940–45* (Houghton Mifflin, 1974).

Bradley, General Omar N., *A Soldier's Story* (Eyre and Spottiswoode, 1951).

—— and Clay Blair, *A General's Life* (Sidgwick and Jackson, 1983).

Bryant, Sir Arthur, *Triumph in the West 1943–46* (Collins, 1959).

Butcher, Captain Harry C., *Three Years with Eisenhower* (Heinemann, 1946).

Chalmers, Rear-Admiral W.S., *Full Cycle: The Biography of Admiral Sir Bertram Home Ramsay* (Hodder and Stoughton, 1959).

Chandler, Alfred D., Jr. (ed.), *The Papers of Dwight David Eisenhower, The War Years*, Vols III–V (Johns Hopkins University Press, 1970).

Churchill, Winston S., *The Second World War*, Vols V and VI (Cassell, 1952 and 1954).

Colville, John, *The Fringes of Power: Downing Street Diaries*: Vol. II, *1941–April 1952* (Sceptre, 1987).

Dalgleish, Major John, *We Planned the Second Front* (Victor Gollancz, 1945).

Danchev, Alex and Daniel Todman (eds), *Field Marshal Lord Alanbrooke: War Diaries 1939–1945* (Weidenfeld and Nicolson, 2001).

De Guingand, Major-General Sir Francis, *Operation Victory* (Hodder and Stoughton, 1947).

—— *Generals at War* (Hodder and Stoughton, 1964).

—— *From Brass Hat to Bowler Hat* (Hamish Hamilton, 1979).

Dilks, Professor David (ed.), *The Diaries of Sir Alexander Cadogan 1938–1945* (Cassell, 1965).

Eisenhower, Dwight D., *Crusade in Europe* (Heinemann, 1948).

Ferrell, Robert H. (ed.), *The Eisenhower Diaries* (W.W. Norton, 1981).

Fraser, General Sir David, *Alanbrooke* (Collins, 1982).

Gilbert, Martin, *Road to Victory: Winston S. Churchill 1941–1945* (Heinemann, 1986).

Grigg, Sir James, *Prejudice and Judgement* (Cape, 1948).

Hart-Davis, Duff (ed.), *King's Counsellor* (Weidenfeld and Nicolson, 2006).

Horrocks, Lieutenant-General Sir Brian, *A Full Life* (Collins, 1960).

—— and Eversley Belfield, *Corps Commander* (Sidgwick and Jackson, 1977).

Ismay, General Lord, *The Memoirs of General Lord Ismay* (Heinemann, 1960).

Kennedy, Major-General Sir John, *The Business of War* (Hutchinson, 1957).

Liddell Hart, Basil (ed.), *The Rommel Papers* (Collins, 1953).

Love, Robert W., Jr, and John Major, *The Year of D-Day: The 1944 Diary of Admiral Sir Bertram Ramsay* (University of Hull Press, 1994).

Malone, Dick, *Missing from the Record* (Collins, 1946).

Martel, Lieutenant-General Sir Giffard, *An Outspoken Soldier* (Sifton, Praed, 1949).

Moran, Lord, *Winston Churchill: The Struggle for Survival, 1940–1965* (Sphere, 1968).

Morgan, Lieutenant-General Sir Frederick, *Overture to Overlord* (Hodder and Stoughton, 1950).

—— *Peace and War* (Hodder and Stoughton, 1961)

Orange, Dr Vincent, *Coningham* (Methuen, 1990).

—— *Tedder: Quietly in Command* (Frank Cass, 2004).

Pocock, Tom, *Alan Moorehead* (The Bodley Head, 1990).

Pyman, General Sir Harold, *A Call to Arms* (Leo Cooper, 1971).

Richardson, General Sir Charles, *Flashback: A Soldier's Story* (Kimber, 1985).

—— *Send for Freddie* (Kimber, 1987).

Roberts, Major-General G.P.B., *From the Desert to the Baltic* (Kimber, 1987).

Ruge, Friedrich, *Rommel in Normandy* (Macdonald and Jane's, 1979).

Ryder, Rowland, *Oliver Leese* (Hamish Hamilton, 1987).

Smyth, Sir John, *Bolo Whistler* (Frederick Muller, 1967).

Tedder, Lord, *With Prejudice* (Cassell, 1966).

Weeks, Lieutenant-General Sir Ronald M., *Organisation and Equipment for War* (Cambridge University Press, 1950).

C General works

Belfield, Eversley and H. Essame, *The Battle for Normandy* (Batsford, 1965).

Belchem, Major-General David, *Victory in Normandy* (Chatto and Windus, 1981).

Bennett, Ralph, *Ultra in the West* (Hutchinson, 1979).

Blumenson, Martin, *United States Army in World War II, The European Theater of Operations, Breakout and Pursuit* (Center of Military History, Washington DC, 1961).

Cowley, Robert (ed.), *What If? Military Historians Imagine What Might Have Been* (Macmillan, 1999)

Delaforce, Patrick, *The Polar Bears: Monty's Left Flank: From Normandy to the Relief of Holland with the 49th Division* (Sutton, 1995).

D'Este, Carlo, *Decision in Normandy* (Collins, 1983).

Ellis, Major L.F., *Victory in the West*: Vol. I, *The Battle of Normandy* (HMSO, 1962).

Florentin, Eddy, *Battle of the Falaise Gap* (Elek Books, 1965).

Fraser, General Sir David, *And We Shall Shock Them* (Hodder and Stoughton, 1983).

Gelb, Norman, *Ike and Monty: Generals at War* (Constable, 1994).

Harrison, Gordon A., *United States Army in World War II, The European Theater of Operations, Cross Channel Attack* (Center of Military History, Washington DC, 1951).

Hastings, Max, *Overlord: D–Day and the Battle for Normandy 1944* (Michael Joseph, 1984).

Haswell, Jock, *The Intelligence and Deception of the D-Day Landings* (Batsford, 1979).

Hesketh, Roger, *FORTITUDE: The D-Day Deception Campaign* (St Ermin Press, 1999).

Ingersoll, Ralph, *Top Secret* (Partridge Publications, 1946).

Joslen, Lieutenant-Colonel H.F., *Orders of Battle*, Vols 1 and 2 (HMSO, 1960).

Keegan, John, *Six Armies in Normandy* (Jonathan Cape, 1982).

Lewin, Ronald, *Ultra Goes to War* (Hutchinson, 1978).

Moorehead, Alan, *Eclipse* (Hamish Hamilton, 1945).

Neillands, Robin, *The Battle of Normandy 1944* (Cassell, 2002).

—— and Roderick de Normann, *D-Day, 1944: Voices from Normandy* (Weidenfeld and Nicolson, 1993).

Pogue, Forest C., *United States Army in World War II, The European Theater of Operations, The Supreme Command* (Center of Military History, Washington DC, 1954).

Reynolds, David, *In Command of History: Churchill Fighting and Writing the Second World War* (Allen Lane, 2004).

Stacey, Colonel C.P., *Official History of the Canadian Army in the Second World War*: Vol. III, *The Victory Campaign* (The Queen's Printer, Ottawa, 1960).

Stagg, J.M., *Forecast for Overlord* (Ian Allan, 1971).

Strawson, John, *A History of the SAS. Regiment* (Secker and Warburg, 1984).

Terraine, John, *The Right of the Line* (Hodder and Stoughton, 1985).

Tute, Warren, *D-Day* (Sidgwick and Jackson, 1974).

Wilmot, Chester, *The Struggle for Europe* (Collins, 1952).

Winterbotham, F.W., *The Ultra Secret* (Weidenfeld and Nicolson, 1974).

Index

Officers are shown with the rank they finally attained. As Montgomery is involved in every page of the book, the entry under his name is quite brief, highlighting a few aspects that may be of interest.